RHOME
A Pioneer History

By Catherine Troxell Gonzalez

Originally Published in 1979
Copyright © Catherine Troxell Gonzalez

Paprback Version Published in 2013
ISBN 978-1-940130-06-4

Published by Eakin Press
An Imprint of Wild Horse Media Group
PO Box 331779 • Fort Worth, TX 76163
www.WildHorseMedia.com

PREFACE

One summer not long ago, I drove down to the Gulf Coast to visit friends and to look at the water. It was then that my good friend, Gracie Aiken Sawyer, suggested that I attend the Genealogical Institute at Samford University in Birmingham, Alabama, that summer. This visit to Alabama resulted in my beginning interest in the Morris family genealogy. The interest deepened as I gathered information about the family and their move to Rhome, Texas. Before long, I was completely involved in this history of Rhome.

Members of my family, Virgie Bobo Renshaw, and Comer Dossey, provided me with information about Rhome. From Comer I received Colonel Benjamin Morris's safety deposit box with his correspondence about the building of the present day town of Rhome. From Virgie I received much information about the Morris family and also the original map that had been drawn up by the townsite agent. My cousins on the Troxell side of the family, Christine Barker Donald, Katherine Wilson Hudnall, and Gladys Troxell Merritt, provided me with a ready-made history of the Troxell family.

Rosalie Gregg, with her deep interest in and concern for the Wise County Historical Association, provided microfilm of the early day newspapers. The microfilms have been the best source of information that I have found for the history of the town. My deepest appreciation goes to Roy Eaton, editor of the *Wise County Messenger,* for permission to copy "any and everything" from the old issues of the *Messenger.* The *Decatur News,* which is now defunct, provided much information about the period.

I searched the United States Census records of 1860, 1870, 1880 and 1900, for information about the inhabitants of Prairie Point and Rhome. The State Archives in Austin provided information about the businesses in Rhome and Aurora.

Finally, the interest of my friends and acquaintances has been a source of inspiration for me. Their contributions of family histories and old pictures from family albums have helped me to recreate this picture of Rhome as it was in the old days. During the final years of her life, Mrs. Kate Shaw, my father's baby sister, helped me tremendously with her pictures and her memories of the past. Her interest and encouragement have been of great value to me. Mrs. Ann Bobo High, my cousin, has been my sounding board for this project. Many times she has listened to my reading of parts of the book and to my questions about people who lived here.

It was my decision to stop the story about the end of World War II. Rhome seemed to have changed about that time. Many of our

MRS. KATE TROXELL SHAW

young people moved away, never to return; many new people moved into Rhome. I shall leave it to some future writer to tell the remainder of the story. Rhome is growing, and perhaps there will be much to add to this first volume.

While I am certain that I have not included all of the history of Rhome, I have spent many long hours collecting and sorting the information that I have included. It is my hope that this information will not offend anyone too much, but will help to recreate the past days of Rhome for the reader.

It is with much love and appreciation that I dedicate this book to the memory of Mrs. Kate Troxell Shaw, my aunt, and to Colonel Benjamin and Roxana Morris, my great grandparents. Without these dear ones it would not have been possible to complete this work.

C. T. G.

COLONEL BENJAMIN MORRIS and Roxana Blair Morris.

ABOUT THE AUTHOR

Catherine Troxell Gonzalez, a native of Rhome, Texas, is the great granddaughter of Colonel Benjamin Morris, who owned the land that became the original townsite of Rhome. She is the daughter of James Robert Troxell and Rena Morris Troxell. Her grandfather, William Wade Morris, was the eldest son of Colonel B. Morris.

Mrs. Gonzalez is a graduate of Texas Technological College and North Texas State University. She is a retired school teacher, having taught English, history, and government in Texas schools for thirty-five years, including the public school systems of Rhome, Bowie, Bridgeport, Lubbock, Denton, Aldine, and Northwest. She has one son, James David Hastings, by her first husband, Jack Hastings. Later she was married to David Gonzalez. Today she is divorced and living in Rhome, where she has her home located on original Morris land.

Mrs. Gonzalez has done free-lance writing, publishing gardening articles in *Flower and Garden, Horticulture,* and the *Workbasket.* She enjoys traveling and hopes to make several freighter trips in the near future. She has been to Europe twice and South America once. Oil painting and genealogy are other hobbies that she pursues.

TABLE OF CONTENTS

PREFACE iii

PART I.
    Chapter 1—Prairie Point, 1854 to 1870 1
    Chapter 2—Rhome Prior to the
        Coming of the Railroad 9
    Chapter 3—The Railroad Story 16
    Chapter 4—The Early Years, 1880 to 1900 25
    Chapter 5—Growth of the Town, 1900 to 1920 . . . 78
    Chapter 6—Boom and Depression Years—
        1920 to 1945 157

PART II.
    Family Biographies (arranged alphabetically according to the surname of the father and then the surname of the mother 235

PART III.
    Memories of Rhome, Circa 1925 355

FOOTNOTES 361

INDEX 375

Prairie Point Town Plat

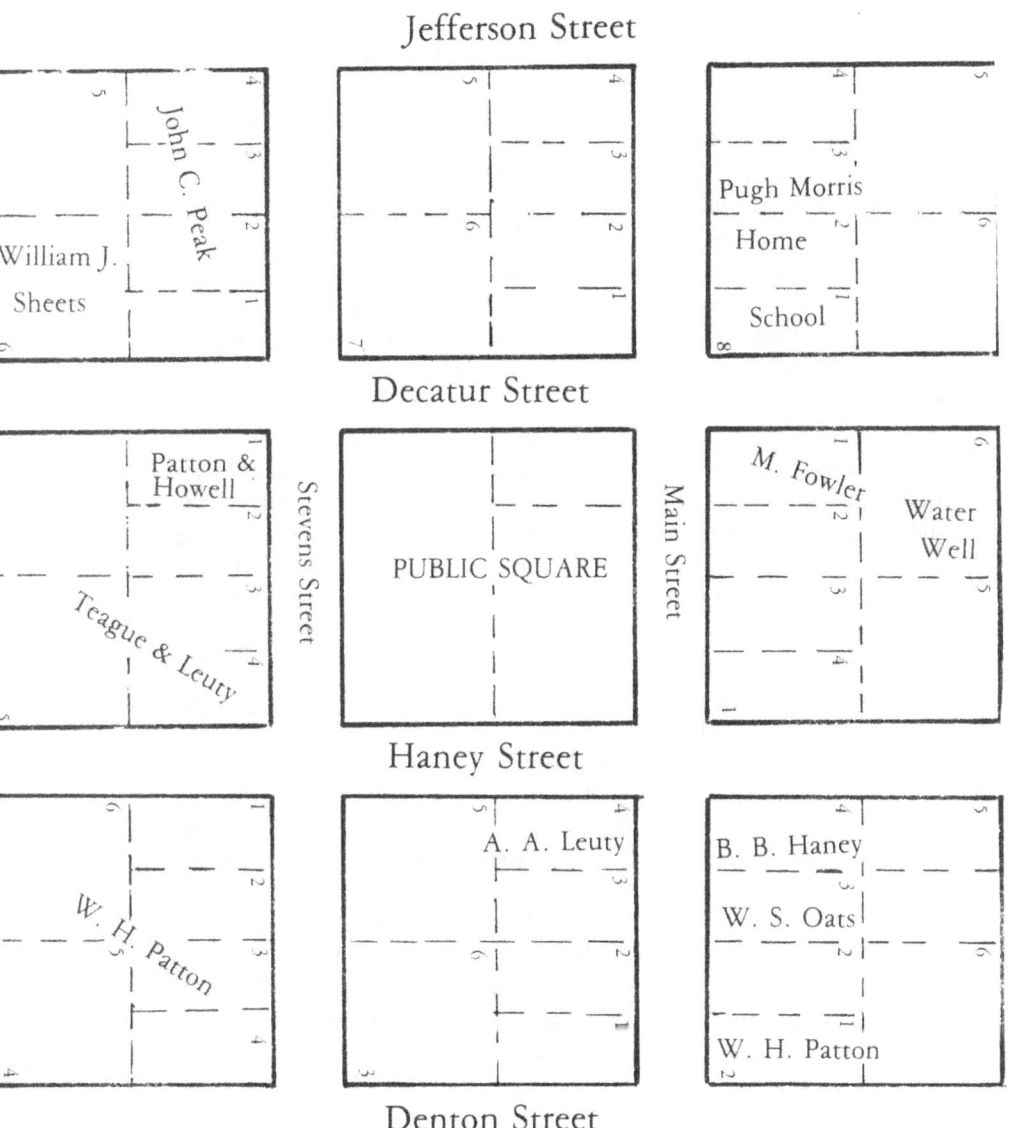

½" = 33'

Chapter 1

PRAIRIE POINT

Although the stories about the origin of Prairie Point are numerous and varied, probably the settlement, the early counterpoint of Rhome, came into existence simply because it happened to be at a crossroad point of two stagecoach lines. The road from Denton to Jacksboro crossed that of Fort Worth northward to Taylorsville. Decatur, as it is known today, originated about the same time as Prairie Point, and for some years afterward the two villages were the largest in Wise county after it was formed in 1854. The 1860 United States Census records Decatur and Prairie Point; so they were in existence at that time. The 1850 census does not record Wise county. The *Decatur News* of November 21, 1902, states that the first settlement was made near the place where the town of Rhome now stands about 1855. At that time Wise county was regarded as the 'wild and woolly west', and the government held out inducements to settlers in the shape of 160 acres of land as a homestead at 50ᶜ per acre. A few hardy pioneers, among them the Stewarts, Pattons, Oats, Leonards, Woodys, Pruntys, and others took advantage of this offer . . . These early settlers found the area well supplied with water and an abundance of convenient timber.

It is quite possible that one of the first buildings in the vicinity of Prairie Point was the log cabin that was built about 1855, probably before Sam Sheets bought the land. The small building was known locally as "The Crossroads Tavern," where travelers often rested overnight.

The earliest recorded purchase of land by Sam Sheets was April 25, 1859. The original land patent had been made to Nelson W. Ellis, later sold to Edward J. Tadlock, who then sold it to Samuel Sheets in 1859. From that time on Samuel Sheets made numerous purchases of land from Alonzo Young, Dr. Alfred McCarty, W. H. Cundiff, and others. One of the purchases of land from Isaac Newton came from the W. C. Holmark survey.

Samuel Sheets occupied the building formerly called the "Crossroads Tavern" as his homestead. Mr. Sheets drew up a town plat of Prairie Point, and began selling town lots in the area. Purchases and recording of lots in the town of Prairie Point began in 1859, according to county records; the town plat was not recorded and is not available, but from the old deeds and records, the author has suggested a possible town plat. Since travel was difficult, it is quite possible that the actual recording of purchases was often delayed for months at a time. The town of Prairie Point eventually contained at least seven or eight streets, a public square, numerous businesses, a hotel, and a school building. It probably had several saloons, but the ownership of these businesses was not located among the recorded deeds.

Pictures exist today that are called the Prairie Point schoolhouse; however, it is more likely that they are the pictures of a later building which was constructed for the town of Rhome on the site of the earlier school. Without doubt the wooden structures which housed the businesses of Prairie Point were moved or destroyed during the ten or fifteen years between the existence of Prairie Point and the beginning of the town of Rhome. Very few people remained to mark what had once been the second largest village in Wise county.

Surmising from the old deeds and the location of the schoolhouse, which remained known while the other structures disappeared, the principal street of the village must have had the name of Main street. It is the street that today runs east toward the Van Meter property. Meredith Fowler purchased a lot across the Main street from the northwest corner of the Public Square. Further east along Main street in Block 2 were lots occupied by B. B. Haney, W. S. Oats, and W. H. Patton. The two streets north and south along the Public Square were probably Decatur street on the west and Haney street on the east side of the Public Square.

Since Meredith Fowler's lots 1, 2, and 6, ran along Decatur street and cornered on Water street, it must be assumed that the street directly parallel and north of Main street was Water street. Along with this assumption must certainly go the further idea that Meredith Fowler had drilled a well and had a windmill to provide water for the town, since Prairie Point had very little other reason to use the title "Water" street.

A. A. Leuty owned lot 4, block 3 on Haney street. The street south of the Public Square paralleling Main street was probably Stevens street. The author was unable to locate the exact lot where H. E. Stevens lived or worked; however, it was the custom to name the street after one of its prominent residents. Occasionally, the blocks were referred to by letters instead of numbers in the old deeds. Thus block 5 would also have been called block E. Since lot 1 also seemed to belong to a firm named Patton and Howell, perhaps Leuty sold the lot to the mercantile firm from Decatur. Teague and Leuty owned the lots on the other end of that block on Stevens street. Denton street paralleled Decatur and Haney streets on the east side of town. This street probably connected Prairie Point to the later Fairview settlement, thence eastward toward Denton.

Another puzzle was the existence of Jefferson street which ran north and south along land owned by John C. Peak in block 6. Today it is generally conceded that the schoolhouse stood slightly east of the spot where Pugh Morris built the house that remains in Rhome today. The writer suggests that the schoolhouse was probably located on lot 4 of block 8 of Prairie Point. This would have it on the corner northwest of the Public Square. Oatie Oates recalls the name "West Point" for the old school which he attended there.

Since our Wise county courthouse has burned three times, and records have been recopied often, human error being almost inevitable, the plat suggested might have resembled the town of Prairie Point. It is to be hoped that someone will someday discover the true plat.

Since Sam Woody, one of the very first inhabitants of Wise county, arrived here in 1853, the first positive census is the one in 1860 which lists Prairie Point as the precinct for the entire southern part of Wise county. This makes almost impossible problems for a historian since the area included in this precinct also names the settlers in the communities which later became Boyd, Aurora, Newark, Fairview, Prairie Point, and others.

The 1870 census would be ideal for our purpose since Aurora was just beginning to become a community, but unfortunately that census record is incomplete. The very reason that it is incomplete perhaps suggests part of what happened to Prairie Point. The South was just beginning to recover from the wounds suffered through the Civil War, and because of the absence or loss of its manpower, census enumerators themselves were at the mercy of ravaging Indians from the Oklahoma territory and from merciless renegades who roamed the countryside, taking whatever they wanted from the helpless settlers. During the war only a brigade of men over sixty and young boys under sixteen were left to protect the settlers. Most of the people had moved to larger, better protected areas, and except for a few hardly souls who had built their homes for protection, there was virtually no one left in Prairie Point after 1863. To make matters worse, the younger boys often turned renegade and raided their own neighbors.

Petitions were located in the Texas State Archives which revealed the pitiful condition of the inhabitants of the county. The petitioners were asking the State Legislature for protection along the frontier. They spoke of raids by the Kickapoo Indians, as well as others, and attacks by renegade whites, who stole their horses and killed the residents. The following quote is from Memorial Number 255 from the Texas State Archives:

> Petition asking for frontier protection   1866
> To the Honorable, the house of Representatives at the City of Austin Assembled
>
> Your petitioners, Citizens of the County of Wise and State of Texas would respectfully represent to your honorable body through our representation, that we are Citizens . . . Consequently exposed to many privations and dangers incident to a frontier life, and that since the late war has ended, we have been entirely left unprotected until recently when a few soldiers belonging to the United States Army have been stationed at Jacksboro and Fort Belknap, which force is entirely inadequate for our protection. Bands of hostile Indians and reckless white men and negroes are constantly committing crimes and depredations in our country unequalled in any portion of the history of this country. It appears from late events that the frontier Counties have been selected as a field of operations for thieves of all kinds and color. The good citizens of this County have protected themselves for a long time as best they could, but our citizens are now leaving their homes and seeking places where they will not be disturbed by Indians and those cooperating with them and if we do not get protection soon the frontier counties will be abandoned which will be against our interest. Thousands of cattle have been driven from here, Northward and by whom it is difficult to say, either by Indians or white thieves and probably both. Our horses are driven off day and night often in the presence of their owners and last but not least our citizens are continually being murdered and scalped, their mangled bodies left often for days, food for birds and beasts. Many have been captured and carried off and very probably put to the severest torture that Indian ingenuity can invent and if now living are lingering out a miserable existence far from homes, friends, Parents, brother, and sisters and in an uncivilized country amidst savages. Two little boys 8 and 10 years, sons of Moses and James Ball, were captured by Indians about eight months ago, and have not been heard from . . . Many instances of the same kind could be given but we deem it unnecessary. Now we appeal to you as representatives of the people to legislate in our behalf as you think best and the emergency requires . . . This we ask and if granted will ever may . . . July 27, 1866.
>
> Since writing the above the Indians have come within one mile of Decatur and stole and drove off 211 horses.

The above excerpt was signed by many names which may be recognized as residents of Decatur, plus some from the Prairie Point area, such as Brawley H. Oats, M. D. Tully, A. E. Allen, and B. B. Haney.

Among the citizens of Prairie Point were two teamsters, one butcher, a school teacher, two stock raisers, about thirty farmers, one brick layer, one broom maker, four blacksmiths, one wagon maker, one or two carpenters, two physicians, one hotel owner, five merchants, one painter, one cooper, one miller, two day laborers, one engineer, and two widow ladies. One of the more amusing items to be found in the 1860 census was the listing of a family consisting of "Lady" and "Gentleman" for occupations.

W. C. P. Brock was the owner of the hotel which housed his wife Martha and five children, Mary C., James, John, Joanah, and Margarite, as well as W. H. Patton, a merchant; R. C. Collins, a merchant; Horace Patton, a merchant; William West, a painter; Henry A. and Thomas Stephens, merchants.

Other residents of Prairie Point were Solomon W. Adam, a broommaker; Amos Bailey, a farmer; Davidson Bourland, a cooper; Perry G. Brock, a farmer; Benjamin and Ira Burdick, farmers; Joseph C. Chance, a farmer; John Conn, a farmer and lawyer; Greenberry Duncan, a farmer; Jeremiah Fleming, a farmer; Thomas J. Fleming, teamster; Meredith Fowler, carpenter; John Fritz; George and George W. Fritz, blacksmiths; B. B. Haney; Addison Holmes, engineer for mill; James Isbell, farmer; Amos Kinder, farmer; Joshua G. King, stock raiser; Josiah Lawley, farmer; William Lewis, day laborer; Frank Lovell, carpenter; Abraham A. Leuty, blacksmith; Henry R. Maple, a miller; Jacob Moffat, a farmer who was reported to have been killed by the Indians; J. S. Morris, teacher; Dr. Alfred McCarty, physician; Wm. B. McGalughir, bricklayer; S. G. S. McGarrah, farmer, Jim McKinn, farmer; J. J. Hudson, stock raiser.

Still others residing in Prairie Point were Jacob Nash, farmer; Elizabeth Oats; William S. Oats, Jr., farmer; Henry J. Pamplin, school teacher; John C. Peak; G. B. Pennington, stock raiser; E. D. Perkins, school teacher; Henry L. Phillips, farmer; Martin Rude; Samuel Sheets, farmer; W. H. Simpson, wagon maker; H. E. Stevens; Nathan Sweet, farmer; Jane E. Tadlock; James W. Tarkenton, farmer; E. A. Teague, blacksmith; John Teague, farmer; Mark A. Tully, teamster; Marshall D. Tully, butcher; Stacy Tully; A. J. Warren, farmer; William West, painter; John Yaller, Christian clergyman; A. T. Young; Hugh Young, farmer. These are only a few of the names of the 1860 census, but they are the names that were found listed closest to those people who were known to be actual residents of the town. Since many of these names are later found in Aurora and in Newark, it is likely that when the people began moving back into the area, they settled nearer the Trinity river because of the availability of wood and water. Thus many of these names are found in the 1880 Aurora precinct census.

However, the Indians and renegades were not the only menace which hindered the continued growth of Prairie Point. A very unfortunate incident probably caused much unhappiness in the community. The hatred which flamed to a much greater extent in Cooke county also touched Prairie Point and its citizens. Many of these settlers had migrated to this part of the country from northern states, without slaves and with a dislike for a war which was not really their own cause.

Some of the leaders of Texas had remained neutral to the cause of slavery; some others, equally strong Unionists, remained loyal to the South because of their love for the State of Texas. One leader, however, could never compromise his position or remain neutral.

> Sam Houston gave "lip service" to the Confederacy but never conceded that secession was either right or legal, and his influence was felt throughout Texas. He refused to take the oath of allegiance to the Confederacy . . . He gave aid and comfort to the enemy by opposing martial law and conscription, and by casting reflections upon Jefferson Davis.[1]

It is quite possible that the thinking of these leaders of Texas influenced the thinking of some residents of these northern counties of Cooke, Denton, and Wise. The hot, dry summer of 1862 in Texas was the setting for a dangerous plot, known as the "Peace Party" conspiracy. The most violent action occurred in Gainesville, Cooke county, Texas. Nevertheless, the tiny hamlet of Prairie Point was also affected by the upheaval.

> The organization was secret, with signs, grips, and passwords. The members were first sworn to secrecy, and those who were found worthy were entrusted with three degrees. The first degree bound the member to secrecy and obligated him to avenge an attack on a fellow member. The second degree supposedly tested the candidate on robbery and jayhawking, while the third obligated him to support a movement to re-establish the old Union.[2]

One of the leading members of the Peace Party movement was a Dr. Alfred McCarty, an early resident of Prairie Point. According to old deeds, Dr. McCarty once owned and lived on land patented to Timothy Carpenter, although he was a physician for the entire community of Prairie Point. On November 26, 1861, Samuel Sheets bought property from A. M. McCarty and wife, which was probably within the Prairie Point township. McCarty had obtained this land through a patent from the State of Texas on July 21, 1860. Since McCarty was a leader in the Peace Part movement, it was probably the cause of his selling out his property and subsequently moving to Gainesville, where the movement was much larger and stronger.

The other men involved in the affair were also prominent in the affairs of Prairie Point. For example, John Conn at one time was appointed to serve as attorney for W. C. Cundiff. According to Clif Cates' *Pioneer History of Wise County*, the five men who were tried and convicted in Decatur were John Conn, Ira Burdick, Jim McKinn, Parson Maples, and ____ Ward. It was ironic that John Conn had been a member of the Confederate guard sent from Wise county to Gainesville to remain during the trials of forty men there. The acreage of Ira Burdick was sold to James R. Wheeler in a warranty deed dated September 10, 1862. This was apparently shortly before the death of Burdick.

The plot was uncovered by a Confederate soldier from Wise county who was visiting in Gainesville. Newton Chance was approached by a drunken officer of the Peace Party organization, who asked Chance to become a member of the secret order. Chance immediately reported this conversation to General William J. Hudson, who ordered the arrest and trial of those Gainesville citizens who were involved in the conspiracy. At the same time General Hudson ordered Captain John Hale of Wise county to arrest the peace party members of this county. Because of McCarty's recent move from Prairie Point to Gainesville, it was natural that other Prairie Point citizens were suspect.

> A trial commission of fifty, presided over by Reverend William Bellamy, a Methodist preacher, was formed. Five men were convicted and hanged. Others were sentenced to serve the Confederacy.[3]

According to Cates' *Pioneer History of Wise County*, the convicted men were hauled, sitting on their coffins, to the Swan pasture at the western edge of Decatur and hanged by the neck until dead.

With this most recent horror on their minds, it is no wonder that many of the settlers found it to their advantage to move from the area of Prairie Point. Most writers of the story point out that many of the members of the plot were loyal, respectable citizens who had been lured into conspiracy in the hope of ending the conscription of their sons and other relatives into the Confederate army. Although the movement quietened down in the northern part of the state, it became bitterly rampant in other parts, where it was known as the

Union League. However, no more reports were found of the movement in Wise county. Perhaps all were sickened by the bloodshed of the hangings of almost a hundred men in the northern part of the state.

For approximately ten more years, this area was simply a crossroad, as it had been in the past with perhaps a tavern and the old schoolhouse remaining to mark the spot that once had been the second largest town in Wise county.

Chapter 2

RHOME AREA PRIOR TO THE COMING OF THE RAILROAD

After languishing for approximately ten to fifteen years, old Prairie Point began filling with new settlers to mingle with those hardy characters who had remained or at least had retained their land in the area. Among those who were here to greet the new comers were the Mark Oates family and the Samuel Sheets family. Settlers surged into this part of Texas during the post-war depression that prevailed throughout the United States. The Aurora and Fairview communities were beginning to settle here. Aurora was established as the precinct for the United States census for 1870. On April 10, 1871, Samuel Sheets sold 455 acres in his Prairie Point holdings to Whit W. Fain, as shown by deed recorded May 9, 1871, Book K, p. 36, Wise County Courthouse, Decatur, Texas.

Before the railroad was built through the area, life for those who lived in the vicinity of the future town of Rhome must have been most difficult. Aurora served as the postoffice and trading center for the area. There were only a few business houses in Aurora, according the *Texas Business Directory of 1878-1879*. There were no banks available for the residents except one in Denton and two in Fort Worth. Although Aurora provided three druggists, the only available physicians at this time were found in Fort Worth: Drs. Crawford and Wheeler, Dr. T. P. Day, and Dr. A. D. Wheeler. If the people traveled as far away as Dallas, they might be treated by either Dr. R. C. Campbell or Dr. Carl Murray. The three drugstores in Aurora were John Baylor and Company, Mullins and Ward, and A. Goldman.

Since the nearest blacksmith was located in Decatur, a farmer had to know how to do his own work as a smithy. Also, there were no boot and shoe dealers; however Aurora did list one boot and shoe manufacturer, J. M. Hixon. If one wanted to purchase a wagon, it had to come from Dallas, as did work by civil engineers or surveyors. Undertakers, caskets, and coffins, as well as a trained dentist, were to be found only in Dallas.

If the farmer could manage to raise a crop of cotton, it had to be hauled to the one cotton gin in Fort Worth, the Fort Worth Compress Company.

Aurora did have three dry goods stores: those of J. K. Ezell, Killough and Company, and T. B. Stephens and Company. The furniture store closest to Rhome was located in Decatur under the name of William Spears. For a flour and grist mill, one must have traveled to the mill at Decatur which belonged to Chas. More. There were also two general merchandise stores at Aurora: those of S. L. Choate and of J. W. Grant.

The five grocers listed for Aurora, the trading center for all the settlers around 1878, were John Baylor and Company, J. K. Ezell, J. W. Grant, Killough and Brothers, Venelleter and McCracken. If a man could not manage his own harness-making, he had to travel to Decatur over a very lengthy route since no direct road had been established between old Prairie Point and the county seat at Decatur.

There were no hotels listed for Aurora or for Decatur, although one could stay in Fort Worth's establishments with a choice of five different hotels. Though it is difficult for today's generation to imagine, there were no ice manufacturers nearer than Fort Worth. By the time one tried to haul ice from Fort Worth, it had very likely melted to small chunks.

There were no lawyers listed for Wise county. If cases were to be tried in Decatur, the lawyers must have traveled from Fort Worth or Dallas. Aurora, however, did have a justice of the peace, Col. C. C. Leonard. Also, there was one, and only one, liquor dealer, a gentleman by the name of P. M. Malone.

Aurora had no milliners, lumber dealers, meat markets, or marble works. Tombstones, if they were to be had, were hauled by wagon from Dallas. Denton or Fort Worth provided paint for the houses built in the Aurora area.

Northeast of the old Prairie Point community was the beginning of another community which became almost as much a part of Rhome as Rhome itself. The citizens of Fairview traded, at times attended church and school, visited, and made themselves a part of the life of Rhome. By the middle of the 1870's many of these hardy pioneers had migrated to Texas from Illinois, Ohio, Tennessee, and other northern states. "In 1872 a group of people from the state of Illinois hitched to their covered wagons and came to the state of Texas. The covered wagons were loaded with personal belongings and each one of the wagons had the old familiar black wash pot hanging on the side."[1]

Among the earliest to arrive in Fairview were the families of Caleb Jackson Van Meter, Joshua Mount, William T. Thurmond and his son John Favor Thurmond, John Troxell and his son Henry Troxell in 1875. The Jacob Young Carpenters arrived about 1880, and John Will Layfield and his brother Jefferson Davis Layfield settled here about

THE FARM HOME at Fairview of John and Mary Troxell.

1895. Others who located near Fairview around the 1880's were the Henry Taylors, W. A. Taylors, Eli Bentons, John Rowans, James H. Rowans, Dan C. Caldwells, Jasper Fords, Benjamin Fords, John A. Askeys, and Robert R. Bryans. Many of these names were taken from the 1880 U. S. Census records, as well as a list of reminiscences of H. H. H. Hambright as published in the *Wise County Messenger*.

> When the new settlers had found their future home sites and camps were made, work began. After some time, a main path was formed from one camp to the next. This path, or road, ran straight east and west. The road eventually received the name of Illinois Lane in remembrance of the people's home state.[2]

No one today really knows how the name Fairview came about, but there are several possibilities. One story from the Troxell family history tells of how the settlers viewed the area around Fairview.

> Henry Troxell's family tells that they were heading for West Texas and had stopped at Deep Creek to camp for the night. Deep Creek at that time was thriving, the oldest building in Wise County being a residence built there by Uncle Sam Woody. Upon learning of their planned destination, Uncle Sam urged them to delay their trip just one day so that he could show them prairie country to the east of Deep Creek. The next day when

they viewed the Fairview community, they were so much impressed that they decided to stay.³

The Troxell families had come from a small town in the state of Kansas that bore the name of "Fairview." As Joe Max Wilson states in his history of Fairview, it was beautiful country. ". . . the view from the Thurmond hill looking to the prairie land of this area was a *fair view.*"⁴

The settlers of Fairview found they could use the land for cultivation or for grazing purposes. The first fences in this area consisted of planting bois-d-arc hedges along their farm boundaries. Many of these first hedges can still be found. They ran the complete length of Illinois Lane, but were torn down when the new paved road was built in 1954. The Thurmonds planted many walnut trees along their boundaries, and some of these trees are still in existence. "The story goes that all the people in the settlement had to get their water at Oliver Creek until they dug their water wells. While the Thurmond family was at the creek, the girls gathered walnut seeds and upon returning home, they got their hoes and planted the seeds all over the farm".⁵

John Favor Thurmond was one of the leading citizens of the Fairview community. In fact, he was responsible for donating land for the Thurmond Fairview cemetery, the Fairview Baptist church, and the Fairview schoolhouse. "In 1878, John F. Thurmond provided land near his home to build a school which was called Fairview. It remained there for three years at which time a new school was built on the southwest corner of his farm, 1881. The school house still remains in the same location."⁶

The Fairview Baptist Church was chartered in 1895 with Mrs. J. F. Thurmond and Mrs. J. Will Layfield as charter members. Prior to that time, they felt the need of religious services; so they met in their homes and had prayer meetings. Later they were able to get an occasional minister to come and preach for them. These meetings were held in the school house, a custom which was followed in almost all the early settlements, including Prairie Point. Services were held in the school house until 1913, at which time the present church building was erected. John Rowan was the pastor at that time.

The Thurmond Fairview cemetery came into being because of a death in the Thurmond family.

> When the daughter of John F. Thurmond died in July, 1883, a site was needed to bury her. John Thurmond told some of his neighbors to look for a plot of land to bury the child. They did. They decided on a piece of land on the southwest corner of the farm near the school and campground. This was the start of a

cemetery. Then again, another death took place in the Thurmond family. John Thurmond's father died in August and was the second person buried in the cemetery. Following this, John F. Thurmond donated two acres of land to be used for this community as a cemetery . . . Later J. F. Thurmond donated another acre and a half.⁷

The cemetery association for the Thurmond-Fairview cemetery was formed in 1906. Memorial services are held on the first Sunday in May each year. At this time the business of the association is transacted.

During the twenty some odd years in which Prairie Point was beginning and ending, the man who was to be responsible for the establishment of the present-day town of Rhome was living in Clayton and then in Eufaula, Alabama. Colonel Benjamin Morris had been born in Martinsville, Henry County, Virginia, in 1829. As a buyer of tobacco and cotton, he had traveled the beautiful Chattahoochie river, where he met and married Roxana Blair in Clayton, Alabama. Together with his father-in-law, William Blair, he had operated a general merchandise store in Eufaula, Alabama. When the depression of the late 1870's became severe, the two men sold out their holdings in land and merchandise. In August, 1879, William Blair retired and Benjamin Morris, then a Colonel from his service for the Confederate States of America, packed up his large family and transported them to Texas, where it was rumored that living could be more prosperous than in Alabama.

The *Eufaula Times and News* of August 14, 1879, reported the departure of the Morris family as follows: "Colonel Ben Morris and family, also of this city, will soon follow in the wake of Mr. W. A. Hancock and Mr. Edgar McKinzie, and will settle in Weatherford." At least, the departure was accurate, but the destination given shows how little was really known then about Texas. Harry Philpott Owens, in his *History of Eufaula, Alabama, 1832-1882*, states that the cause of the general plight of inhabitants of the South at this time was an economic one: "Over production of cotton and other economic conditions which created the panic of the 1880's caused many small farmers to lose their lands. Almost daily, some small farm was being sold '. . . under the hammer . . .' in Eugaula."

With courage and hope in their hearts, the Morris family set out for Texas. Their tickets were purchased for Fort Worth, Texas. Along with the other family furniture and household goods was packed a Steinway Grand piano which Roxana Morris had requested as a wedding gift from her father, William Blair. The piano graced the Morris living room during early years, and later was given to Mary and Edward Morris for their young girls. Ann High, a grand-daughter of Benjamin Morris, tells the story of its having been dismantled and placed on the back porch because it was in the way of dancers in the parlor. There it remained in disgrace until it rotted away.

Family legend tells that Roxana Blair Morris had the money for the family's new home sewed into a money belt around her waist. Her father, William Blair, had provided the funds to purchase much of the new land, fifteen hundred acres including the old Prairie Point area. In addition to Benjamin and Roxana, the family included William Wade, age 22; Edward Mitchell, age 20; Benjamin Logan, age 18; Robert Sidney, age 14; Elizabeth Tabitha, age 12; Richard Briggs, Mattie Roxana, Mary Early, James Pugh, age 4; and sparkling, brown-eyed Maggie Mae, age one year and nine months. Accompanying the family were several faithful former slaves who considered themselves a part of the family. Thus quite an entourage embarked on the long journey to the unknown area, Texas.

Somewhere along the line they were side-tracked in their desire to go to Weatherford. Soon after their arrival in Fort Worth, William Wade Morris, the eldest son rode horseback north from the village on the Trinity river. Again depending upon family legend, young Morris was favorably impressed with an area east of the Trinity river, high upon a hillside where the land was rich and black. However, he rode on north to the residence of an old time settler, Sam Woody. It was not difficult for Woody to persuade Morris that his first choice was best, and the young man returned to the area that is now Rhome, Texas.

Deeds found in the county clerk's office in Wise county, Texas, show that on March 9, 1880, Benjamin and Roxana Blair Morris purchased the land from Whit W. Fain of Wise county and Fain's daughter and son-in-law, A. J. Day and F. M. S. Day of the county of Lipscomb, at a cost of $4500.00. Since there were approximately 1500 acres in the plot of land, this cost figures about $3.00 per acre. The same deed, recorded in Book T, pp. 379-382, on June 3, 1880, shows that the purchase consisted of 50 acres of the J. C. Tatum survey, 160 acres of the N. W. Ellis survey, 95 acres of the W. W. Fain survey, 160 acres of the Ben Lewellen survey, 130 acres of the W. S. Oates survey, 240 acres of the W. C. Holmark survey, and 547 acres of the M. E. P. P. R.R. Co. survey. The later recorded plat of the city of Rhome is located in the heart of this area.

The Morris family settled into a house which Mr. Fain had occupied with his family after purchasing it from Samuel Sheets. The Morris family expanded the house to serve their large family. This

THE HOME OF Col. Benjamin and Roxana Blair Morris. This house was the site of the original log cabin that served as the Crossroads Tavern for Prairie Point. The house is gone, but a grandson still lives at the location.

house, pictured in the *Fort Worth Star Telegram,* June 21, 1937, was the original cabin that had been the old Cross Roads tavern at Prairie Point. When Benjamin Morris moved his family into their new home, he settled down for the remainder of his life. At this time, the area was still known as Prairie Point, although the old town was gone, except for a school house which Oatie Oates remembers calling at a later date, "West Point." The tax receipt for Benjamin and Roxana Morris's land for 1883 shows that it was paid at the Aurora Station; so Rhome was still not recognized as a town at that time.

Chapter 3

THE RAILROAD STORY

Through the efforts of a Fort Worth banker and financier, Major K. M. VanZandt, the Texas Legislature on May 26, 1873, issued a charter for the building of a railroad through Wise county to connect Fort Worth with Denver City, Colorado. However, owing to the panic of the late 1870's, eight years passed before the work of construction began. General Granville Dodge, a man fully experienced in the building of western railways, was persuaded to invest in the project. On April 27, 1881, General Dodge contracted to build the Fort Worth and Denver City railway northwestward from Fort Worth. The charter was drawn up authorizing the issuance of $25,000.00 per mile in first mortgage bonds. They estimated the cost at $20,000.00 per mile, but General Dodge suggested that the bonds be sold at twenty-five thousand dollars per mile so that the treasury of the company would have a surplus to account for future needs of the company.

The first grading for the railway was begun at Hodge, a station on the Missouri Pacific railway, five miles north of Fort Worth. With the building of the railroad also came the construction of townsites along the track. This brought the first townsite agent to Colonel Benjamin Morris's land to contract for the future town of Rhome. In a deposition made years later, Colonel Morris stated that he had originally made an agreement with a man named Washburn, Chief Engineer of the Fort Worth and Denver City railroad company. At the time of the conveyance of the land, Washburn had died; so the conveyance was made to another man named R. E. Montgomery. One of the little ironies of the story is that although Colonel Morris tried for years to learn the connection between R. E. Montgomery and General Dodge, he died still not knowing that Montgomery was actually a son-in-law of General Dodge. The following quote is from a deposition made by Colonel Morris concerning the conveyance of land to R. E. Montgomery, as a trustee for the Pacific Railroad Improvement Company, which in reality was the Texas and Colorado Improvement Company, a company which belonged to General Dodge: "We did so convey lands to him [Montgomery] as trustee for the Pacific Railroad Improvement Company. The land so conveyed was 100 acres to be laid off in town lots, out of the Tadlock and J. C. Tatum survey and the Memphis and El Paso survey." To a question concerning the money paid for the land, the answer was as follows: "There was no money paid." When Colonel Morris was asked about other considerations to be made for the land, he answered that he was giving the right of way about two miles across the land that was in his wife's name. ". . . they were to lay out a town there. The agreement was that they were to give us cheap freights there on heavy goods to build up the town, to assist us in building up the town . . ."

This was the beginning of a struggle that was to lead to bitter and lengthy lawsuits over a period of almost twenty years. The quarrel with Montgomery was finally ended around 1899, with the court's refusing to retain the suit because the statute of limitations had run out on Montgomery's case. This situation was typical of many of the struggles between land owners and townsite agents, who sought to gain control of the town.

The original agreement between Montgomery and Colonel Morris had been executed on April 8, 1882. Under the terms of this instrument, Montgomery was to draw up the town plat, and lots were to be sold to individual buyers. At the end of one year's time every alternate, unsold lot was to be returned to the original owner, Colonel Morris. It was agreed that two blocks, numbers eleven and fourteen, of the township should be retained, undivided, for the occupancy of the Morris family. These blocks were not conveyed to Montgomery. They worked quite hard to assure that no business houses would be placed close to these lots. The plat of original Rhome is recorded in the Wise county courthouse records in Book 5, on page 640.

The *Daily Democrat-Advance* of Fort Worth, Texas, records on April 20, 1882, the following notice: "Excursion to Decatur. On Monday, May 3rd, the Fort Worth and Denver City railway will run an excursion train to Decatur for the convenience of those who will want to attend the sale of town lots on that day and the grand ball in the evening. The train will leave the Texas and Pacific depot at 7 o'clock a.m. Fare for the round trip will be two ($2.) dollars." The next week on April 27, 1882, there was a note from the Rhome correspondent to the *Wise County Messenger:* "Invitations are out for the grand ball to be given by the citizens of Decatur, May 3, 1882, in honor of the completion of the F. W. & D. C. railway to that city. There will no doubt be a large attendance from this city." Thus it is certain that this kind of entertainment was not to be passed up. Certainly, Rhome citizens must have attended in full force.

There were to be two trains daily between Fort Worth and Decatur, carrying passengers and freight. The trains were to start from the Texas and Pacific depot where tickets were also sold. A further announcement from the railway company gave added zest to the excitement. There was to be a telegraph line ready for the transaction of commercial business at its office at the Pacific Railway Improvement Company's office on Houston street. This company title printed in the Fort Worth newspaper lends credence to the belief of Colonel Morris that the townsite improvement company was a bogus company, as he often and loudly asserted.

The question of a name for the town was discussed at length by Montgomery and Colonel Morris. Family stories have it that the Colonel wanted to name the town after his wife, Roxana, but that she refused to have it named for her. Montgomery argued for the names of Aurora, Calif, or Wyse; however, Colonel Morris was adamant about not accepting Montgomery's suggestions. A compromise was made, and the town was named for one of the outstanding citizens of the town, Colonel B. C. Rhome, a gentleman and land owner who was a close personal friend of Colonel Morris. Colonel Rhome was prominent, not only in local affairs but also in State business. At one time the *Fort Worth Daily Gazette* named him as a possible candidate for governor of the State. Also, Colonel Rhome had been responsible for the building of the first stone building in the town of Rhome.

There is no actual date for the naming of Rhome, but possibly the first published reference to the name was made in the *Wise County Messenger* about 1885. The argument continued in letters between Montgomery and Colonel Morris, with the townsite agent very reluctant to give in to a choice other than his own. The second annual report of the Board of Directors to the stockholders of the Fort Worth and Denver City Railway Company mentioned Aurora as being between Hodge and Decatur. It was not until the third annual report in October, 1884, that the company referred to the town by its name of Rhome. The third annual report also mentions a Calif as being the next station after Wichita Falls; thus R. E. Montgomery finally managed to use one of his choices as a townsite name.

The dates of the construction of the first depot and the first section house for the Fort Worth and Denver City railway company are not known, but probably the first depot agent and telegraph operator was B. W. Stephens. The *Messenger* notes on October 8, 1887, that Mr. Stephens was being transferred to Vernon, Texas, and that a Mr. O. L. Thomas was to succeed him. By December 29, 1893, Mr. Thomas had been succeeded by Mr. H. Y. Wymer.

The depot and pump house received a new coat of paint, as reported by the *Messenger* on August 22, 1894. Thus we know that the depot must have been built at least several years earlier, thus accounting for the need for new paint. By November 5, 1895, Mr.

VIEW OF RHOME, Texas, circa 1900. The reader will note from the location of the depot at the head of First Street that this is the first depot built in Rhome. The second depot was north of this location.

Wymer had been replaced by the "genial and accommodating depot agent," Mr. W. E. Gallaspy, who married Miss Mattie Keith of Fort Worth on June 18, 1896. During Mr. Gallaspy's honeymoon, Mr. Joe Mulholland acted as agent. The following year a Mr. J. Cole succeeded Gallaspy for a short period, and then by the middle of the next summer, Mr. Gallaspy returned to Rhome. In 1906 Mr. Walter Bellah succeeded Mr. Gallaspy, only to be transferred to Decatur and succeeded by Mr. Daugherty of Memphis, Texas. On July 13, 1906, J. D. Dotterer, then the depot agent, jumped from a moving train and damaged his foot badly.

Rhome went through agents quite fast, for by June 16, 1908, W. N. Thompson had resigned as agent for the Denver and was relieved by a Mr. Wisdom of Dundee. On January 21, 1916, the *Decatur News* reported that Mr. Willis, operator at the depot, who had been working in the place of H. O. Wilson, had returned to Wichita Falls, Texas. On March 10, 1916, H. O. Wilson and family left for Miles, Texas. Mr. B. Casey relieved Mr. H. O. Wilson for a short period of time. On November 21, 1916, Mr. and Mrs. B. Casey left for Toyah where Mr. Casey had accepted a position with the Texas and Pacific railroad.

The *Decatur News* reported on May 9, 1917, that the Fort Worth and Denver railroad was building a new depot at Rhome, which would be located north of the old depot. This must mean that the first depot was located (in the center) of First street. 1917 was also the year that J. H. McGlothlin became Rhome's depot agent, a position which he held until the depot was closed in April, 1959.

RHOME'S SECOND DEPOT.

The *Wise County Messenger* reported on February 9, 1899, that the Fort Worth and Denver City railroad company was repainting the depot, section house, pump house, and tank, thus indicating that the section house must have been built at least several years before, probably at the same time that the first depot was built. In 1906 the Rhome newspaper called the *Light* reported that the Denver had put in drain boxes around the depot, making it much better for the traveling public.

One note of beauty that the old timers in Rhome might remember was the railroad park. On August 27, 1894, Tom Hogan was reported as setting out bermuda grass in the park. In June and July of 1895 the *Decatur News* reported that Mr. Hogan had been running the lawn mower in the park and that it was then "a thing of beauty, the flowers and trees are looking so well." It occupied the intersection of First and Front streets, approximately northeast of Harvey's grocery store today. Occasionally, the park was burned off in the spring so that the green grass would be pleasing to all passersby.

As many generations of Rhome youngsters will remember, one play site was the "old railroad dumps." Thus, paraphrasing Mrs. Ella Pegues' title for the history of Aurora, it is appropriate here to mention "The railroad that almost was." A report in the *Wise County Messenger* for February 21, 1885, states that the leading businessmen of Aurora had a railroad meeting and appointed a committee to confer with other committees at Fort Worth and Gainesville as to the feasibility of Aurora's being made a point on the proposed extension of the Gulf, Colorado, and Santa Fe railroad. On June 27, 1885, the *Messenger* reported that a prospector for the Dallas and Northwestern railroad, Captain W. H. Lemons of Dallas, met with the citizens of Aurora. At that time a committee composed of C. C. Leonard, J. A. Elder, and John Ellars were appointed to consider the proposal.

With the interest arising in Aurora for a railroad, the Fort Worth and Denver City railroad began to consider a branch line to Aurora from Rhome, possibly to go on toward Bridgeport. The writer, apparently hoping to persuade the Aurora citizens to accept a branch line, predicted that the line would make Aurora a trade center of the county.

The people along the route were very much interested in a road, as evidenced by the following item from the newspaper at Aurora, the *Chronicle*, dated November 14, 1885: "From Dallas to Boonville near the western boundary of Wise County, it is about 76 miles, and the grade of the D. P. and S. E. railroad is finished except about two miles through the lands of Colonel B. Morris and Eb Day. All this cost somewhere in the neighborhood of $250,000. Now the question is often asked, are these parties who planted this grand sum of money going to allow this project to peter out, and besides all this, will Dallas with her millions of dollars and untold wealth that will pour into her coffers from the magnificent country it taps allow it to fail? We think not."

However, it quite likely that they were mistaken in their information about the grading, since the following excerpt came out in the *Messenger* as late as February 5, 1889, from the Rhome reporter: "A contractor for the Dallas and Pacific railway came in on the Denver from Fort Worth this morning. He is looking around for a storage room for a commissary for the construction department of the new road and says teams, scrapers, etc. will be unloaded here Thursday next, preparatory to commencing work on the above named road at once. He came to look into the conveniences, etc., for unloading a construction outfit."

A Rhome newspaper called the *Gazette* of March 9, 1889, is quoted as saying that the town was filled to overflowing with railroad men and their outfits. "It seems as though a road is going to be built somewhere through this country. If Dallas is at her old game of bluffing, she is playing a heavy game. Five carloads of stock and scrapers came in on the Texas and Pacific yesterday evening on the way to Rhome to work on the Dallas road."

A quote from the Rhome reporter to the *Wise County Messenger* on March 17, 1889, continues the story: "Two cars containing construction outfits were sidetracked here yesterday for the purpose of commencing work on the Dallas, Southeastern and Pacific railway. Carpenters have been busy all day putting in shelving, etc., in a house here to be used as a commissary."

There must have been some difficulty still about the route of the new road, since Simpson Bobo of Aurora was quoted as thinking that the D. S. & P. would not cross the Denver road at Rhome, but some miles further south near the head of Indian creek. Nevertheless, by May 1, 1889, the people of Grapevine and Roanoke were bending all their energies toward securing the Dallas railroad. The surveying corps was supposed to be in Rhome that week, and the matter was to be settled by May 13, 1889.

However, on the 3rd of July, the Rhome reporter to the *Messenger* was not so optimistic as he had been in the past: "The Dallas, Southeastern, and Pacific railway people are still running lines in and around this place. They say they want to come here if practicable. We would like also to have their road, but the amount of bonds they want is entirely too high for so small a town as ours." Although the citizens of Aurora continued to push for the railroad, this seemed to be the final blow to the success of the road. As late as January 30, 1890, commissioners were appointed to condemn the right of way for the Dallas, Pacific, and Southwestern across Colonel B. Morris's land.

Later a telegram from Decatur stated that the commissioners were assessing the railroad $2500.00 for between sixteen and seventeen acres of land. The *Messenger* announced that Mr. R. W. Pringle, the contractor, would continue to push the work, and that the grading would soom be completed and ready for tracklaying.

An excerpt from the *Messenger* on April 15, 1890, announced that a gentleman from Throckmorton had reported to the *Dallas News* about the condition of the railroad as follows: ". . . the Dallas and Pacific was about the liveliest corpse of the kind yet recognized in the northwest. All roads lead to Rhome." By April 29, 1890, the citizens of Aurora were beginning to get anxious about the condition of the road. "They have not lost hope by any means, but need it in their business and must have it in time to carry off the crop this fall." Finally, on May 14, 1891, the newspaper reported that a receiver was supposed to be appointed for the Denver, Pacific, and Santa Fe Railroad Company. This was evidently the end of the railroad story for Aurora, and the children of Rhome were left with the small mounds of dirt for their future play.

During most of his quarrel with R. E. Montgomery, Colonel Benjamin Morris used two Fort Worth lawyers, Orrick and Hogsett. At one point he felt it necessary to explain to them his complete confidence in their work. In doing so, he told the following story about himself:

> I will close by saying that we feel that confidence in you that I once saw exhibited . . . I had occasion to go down the St. Lawrence river from Montreal to Quebec, Canada. This was when I was quite a young man in 1848 on a boat called *La Belle*. We came to a falls . . . whose waters boiled and ran like a mill race. To me it looked as though no boat could live in it a moment. The bells rang. I saw from the Canadian side a man in a small canoe shoot out from the bank, making directly to our boat. He hitched his canoe to the boat and sprang up the gang ladder, his eye fixed on the pilot wheel. The bell tinkled. The boat backed. She shot the rapids like an arrow. She would go on probably a hundred yards. The bells would tinkle. She would come to a short stop and back again and shoot another rapid. This to me seemed a life time. I have been in many battles during our unpleasantry with our Northern brethern, but I never suffered one millioneth part of the fear that I did on that boat. But now to the confidence exhibited by others on this boat, (which we have in you as our attorneys). They laughed and made merry, did not even stop playing cards. One old sympathetic gentleman came up to me and said, "My young friend, you seem to be alarmed!" My tongue almost refused to utter a word. I was terror-stricken, appalled. I had noticed the nonchalance of the others with pain. The old gentleman continued, "That Indian at the pilot wheel has been carrying boats through these falls for thirty years and has never yet met with an accident or a mishap. That was the reason for the other passengers' great confidence in his ability to move us safely into placid waters." This confidence myself and wife, I will say again, we have in you as our attorneys.[1]

The Fort Worth and Denver City Railroad Company made many innovations in its operations that improved the quality of its service to Rhome patrons. For example, on March 5, 1887, the *Messenger* reported the purchase of four new standard eight-wheel locomotives to meet the demands of its increased trade along the line. Also, on January 19, 1889, a new stock pen was reported at Rhome. "The Fort Worth and Denver City has put us up a splendid stock pen in the last few days, a thing which should have been done several years ago, for they have lost several car shipments of stock, owing to the absence of it." Then on July 13, 1889, a really new invention was put into use on the railroad. "The Fort Worth and Denver railroad has put on double-deck cars for the shipping of calves, sheep, hogs, etc., which is of interest to those who are engaged in shipping stock of this kind. This will reduce the rate on car lots to nearly one-half of the former cost."

The company had its share of troubles. On December 15, 1889, a northbound freight set fire to the pastures of C. J. Svenson and Colonel B. Morris, which burned off quite a number of acres of grass. "Later in the evening, about good dark, a fire broke out in the hay barn of McKittrell, Wilkerson, and Company, commission merchants of St. Louis, whose pasture and hay farm is just south of the Svenson pasture. The barn with its content, about fifteen hundred bales of hay, was entirely consumed. It is not known positively how this fire originated. Some think, however, that it was caused from sparks from the railroad engines." This was a common occurrence along the railroad, in addition to the killing of cattle and horses. On several occasions in the early days of the railroad before extensive fencing was done, accidents, as well as fires, were common happenings along the railroad. One of the more unusual stories on November 12, 1887, brought out the fact that women's liberation is not exactly new.

> As a northbound extra freight train was nearing the station last night about eleven o'clock, five cars of the train left the track and tumbled over a slight embankment, completely smashing them up. It is supposed the accident was caused by the switch spreading, causing some of the cars to take the switch track and the others to run on the main line. One of the cars was loaded with sacked corn, which was uninjured. The other four cars contained railroad material, ties, rails, etc. No one received any injuries, although two women presumably of the demi-monde class, who were beating their way, were in one of the derailed cars, but fortunately came out of the wreck, intact and were seen this morning wending their way toward Aurora, apparently none the worse for the wreck.

Chapter 4

THE EARLY YEARS — 1880-1900

Merchants and Business Houses

Although Rhome was not included in the *Texas State Gazeteer and Business Directory* until 1890-1891, it was already a thriving little city long before that time. By 1883, Rhome had a school and a windmill, and Colonel B. C. Rhome was beginning the construction of the stone building that became Rhome's first permanent business structure of its size. The venture was reported by the *Wise County Messenger*:

> B. C. Rhome has commenced on a magnificent stone room which is to be occupied by W. J. Rogers, and rumor has it that he has purchased one block of building lots and will soon commence to build nice stone business houses on the same.[1]

On the same date the *Messenger* also reported the completion of the first windmill for the town of Rhome. This new structure was expected to supply an abundance of water for the new town. "The knowing ones used to say that was all she needed to make her as good a town as there is on the line, as we are backed up by one of the best farming vicinities in the State."[2] It is likely that this windmill was the one constructed on the back of lot 16, block 10 of the original survey of Rhome, according to the county records. Deeds Book 23, Page 515, records the sale of lots 15-16, block 10 from B. C. Rhome to W. E. Ward. ". . . except 20 feet off the rear end of lot 16, upon which a well and windmill is situated in the town of Rhome."[3]

Before 1890 some of the first merchants in Rhome were C. P. Harrison, Morris and Brothers, B. C. Rhome, J. P. Perkins, Stanley and Lum, F. M. Hatler, J. H. Mount, Alexander Wilmouth, J. M. Stephens. Undoubtedly, there were others, but these names have been collected from the newspaper files of those dates.

In 1890 the *Texas State Gazeteer and Business Directory, Volume III*, records the emergence of the new town.

> RHOME. A new post office in the Ft. W. & D. C. Ry. in Wise county, 15 miles southeast of Decatur, the county seat, and

STREET SCENE IN Rhome, circa 1925, showing the old stone building which was built by Col. B. C. Rhome.

nearest banking point. It contains Baptist and Methodist churches and a public school. Stage, twice daily to Aurora; fare 50 cents round trip. Population 200 Tel., W. U. Exp., Pacific. L. L. Ward, postmaster.
Davis, J. H., hotel
Hatler, F. M., farm implts.
Harrison, C. P., livery and farm implts.
Hawkins, W. H., railroad and exp. tel. agent
Keele, Miss Mattie, milliner
McLain, S., blacksmith
Perkins, J. P., grocer
Rhome & Ward, Dry Goods and Notions
Stephens, B. W. & J. M., grain and hay
Watson & Nelson, saloon
Wilmurth, A., hardware and groceries[4]

Rhome businesses grew during the 1880's; however, there were some setbacks. The *Wise County Messenger* reports that on February 7, 1885, the dry goods store belonging to Morris and Brothers was burned. "Mark Oats was in the city (Decatur) on Thursday, from whom we learned that Morris and Brothers dry goods store at the town of Rhome was burned on Wednesday night. Loss about $4500. Insured to about half that amount."[5]

Rhome's first significant business failure was perhaps that of the

Carpenter-Rhome Company. A report from the *Alvord Messenger*, carrying a Rhome dateline, was the first news of the collapse: "The Carpenter-Rhome Company was closed today at 1 o'clock by an attachment made by Baits, Reede and Cooley of New York. Papers were served by a deputy sheriff. Their claim is $7000."[6] Apparently, the Rhome branch was managed by F. M. Hatley, who made an assignment in favor of C. J. VanMeter, one of his creditors. "By order of the Carpenter-Rhome Company, the sheriff today employed men to make an inventory of the stock at this place (Rhome)."[7] The Carpenter-Rhome firm was quite large with the main store in Decatur and branch houses at Henrietta, Jacksboro, and Rhome. "It is the heaviest failure that has ever occurred in this part of the State. It is said that claims aggregating near $40,000.00 are already filed. The goods are now being invoiced."[8]

Other Carpenter-Rhome stores which were closed were the S. J. Kelsey store in Sunset, and the T. F. Chedester store in Paradise. Indications are clear, however, that Colonel Rhome did not intend to lose his investments in these stores. On January 31, 1886, the *Wise County Messenger* reported that Colonel Rhome had left on a trip to New York City. On February 20, 1886, the *Messenger* reported that the sale of the Carpenter-Rhome goods was again postponed until the next Tuesday. There was talk at this time about a compromise settlement that would be made. The next week's edition of the *Messenger* had the following cheerful report from the Rhome reporter:

> The firm of B. C. Rhome & Company have bought the goods of the Carpenter-Rhome Company at this place and commenced their sales yesterday. The community is much rejoiced that the business is so pleasantly arranged.[9]

By the middle of the next month there was a report that Carpenter and Rhome were moving their stock of hardware from Decatur to Rhome.

On July 17, 1886, the *Wise County Messenger* carried a report of the destruction by tornado of the Stanley and Lum hay warehouse at Rhome. Businesses changed hands frequently in those days. There was a report of a new partnership in business in Rhome on March 27, 1886, that of Dawson and Harrison, who were grocery merchants, but the following year their stock of goods was sold to a Mr. Mount, who was probably J. H. Mount. On January 8, 1889, it was reported that Mr. B. W. Stephens' brother, J. M. Stephens, had bought the grain business that belonged to Alexander Wilmouth, and that Mr. Stephens would continue to operate the business in the same location.

On April 27, 1890, the Rhome reporter gave a very optimistic report on the progress of the town of Rhome. "This town and community is certainly on a boom, judging from the large number of wagons in town every Saturday. Our merchants seem to be selling lots of goods."[10] During April of the same year a setback to business occurred with the destruction of the iron bridge on the West Fork of the Trinity river. This bridge had been constructed southwest of Rhome at a place later called the VanMeter crossing. The county was not defeated by this loss because a new bridge was built there which is probably the old iron bridge that remains to this day.

On February 8, 1891, the *Messenger* reported that Roe Helms had purchased property at Rhome and had moved to it from Springtown. The location of the Rhome property is unknown to the writer, but a later letter from the railroad townsite agent connects Roe Helms with a business property which he operated in Rhome. The letter was dated May 4, 1898, from Fort Worth, Texas. "Dear Sir: Please write me at Fort Worth by what right or authority you are occupying the right of way of the railway at Rhome with your saloon."[11] Since at this time the railway company owned only fifty feet on each side of the railroad, the saloon must have been placed perilously close to the roaring of the engines, perhaps a bit too close for the enjoyment of its patrons. At least, Rhome was the typical frontier town of the times, with saloons that must have been the bane of existence for Rhome's good church folks. There were other saloons along the area which gained the name of "Smokey Row" instead of its legal name, Front Street.

The *Wise County Messenger* of February 25, 1891, reported the sale of J. H. Mount's hardware department to W. M. Helm and C. P. Harrison. Mr. Mount continued his grocery business and in addition, he added a line of dry goods. Thus William Monroe Helms operated the saloon only as a side-line to his hardware business.

While all the merchants were stocking up on goods to appeal to their customers, one clever young lady, Miss Mattie Keele, planned to appeal to the women in the family. The *Messenger* reported on April 4, 1891, that Miss Keele had just filled her millinery shop with nice spring goods. In this day of hatless ladies, it is interesting to note that straw and silk frames were decorated with feather, bows, flowers, and other decorations for the ladies' benefit. Many a young Rhome matron must have spent hours there in Miss Keele's shop planning just the right combination to catch some young gentleman's eye.

On June 20, 1891, the *Messenger* reported the advent of a druggist. "Z. B. Bobo, formerly in the drug business in Aurora, commenced today the erection of a large business house in our town for the purpose of opening up a drug and furniture trade."[12] This building was erected where Rhome's drugstore stood for decades. The building of 1891 was removed in 1910 and a new brick building took its place.

The first mention of a lumberyard was made on September 14,

1891. "Will Morris, our lumberman, is stocking up with a fine assortment of lumber."[13] This addition came just in time to profit from the mass exodus of Aurora's inhabitants to Rhome about 1891. The lumberyard was built west of the railroad right-of-way in the northeast section of town, where it remained until it was torn down to make way for new developments. On this same date a general report of the progress of the town appeared in the *Messenger*:

> It has been so long since we have seen anything in your paper from these parts, we conclude perhaps that your readers may forget that there is such a place as modern Rhome, hence we write.
>
> Our town is on the improve. Mr. Everidge, our blacksmith, is thoroughly refitting his dwelling. Will Logan is building himself a neat and commodious residence, which, when finished, will be a credit to himself and our town. J. P. Perkins has bought property and will build a fine residence on it in the next few weeks. Zack Bobo has built a fine business house, and is stocking it with fresh drugs and furniture.
>
> Our merchants are all now stocking up with new goods for the fall and winter trade, and all seem to be doing well and appear happy. W. J. Rogers has sold a carload of buggies this summer and a carload of wagons in the last month, so one can plainly see that our big wheat crop, together with the promise of a full yield of cotton has stimulated the people all over the county. Every house in Rhome is occupied and tenant houses are in great demand. A brand new beef shop is our latest addition in business.
>
> Our town has two cotton buyers: Mr. Mount and Mr. Ward, and they are both active in the business and from the number of bales being bought here it would seem that the people consider this is a good market. More anon. X2Y2[14]

The identity of the reporter X2Y2 is not known, but among those old timers who remember him, most think that the reports from Rhome were written by H. H. H. Hambright. It is quite possible that he used this signature simply for its honor, since everyone knew that he was writing the reports anyway.

On September 20, 1891, the *Messenger* reported that a general merchant named A. L. Keeter, who had been doing business at Keeter, had rented a store house from Colonel B. C. Rhome and would move his business to Rhome. At this same time it was reported that "parties interested" would commence the erection of a large ware and storage house the following week. The building was to be of corrugated iron, and the dimensions were to be 40 by 140 feet. This size would make it one of the largest buildings in town.

At this point in the story of Rhome, there appeared an item with the dateline of "West Fork."

> Rhome has the (spotted) fever to build and new houses mark the "spots" and rival towns may get scared.
>
> Buggies are almost as thick as grasshoppers, and some of the Rhome merchants even wanted to sell us one, but we'd take the bighead. A sled is the safest for us yet.[15]

The old windmill built in 1883 finally wore out and Rhome bought a new windmill. On October 29, 1891, it was reported that men were at work taking out the old pump and tearing down the old windmill. "This old mill and pump have been 'hors de combat' for about two years."[16]

In 1892 Morris Brothers stocked a new item, the pump organ. On March 5, 1892, the *Messenger* reported that W. W. Morris was canvassing the county selling the celebrated Estey organ. Those wishing the best organ in the market were advised to await a call from him.

Cameron and Company of Fort Worth decided in May, 1892, to erect a grain elevator in Rhome.

> Parties interested were up from Fort Worth yesterday selecting site, etc. An elevator of adequate proportions will be a paying institution from the start, because the crops surrounding here are as fine as ever raised, and the receipts last year, according to the books of the railroad and our flour mill were over 100,000 bushels, and with an elevator the receipts would nearly double that amount. The locality of the elevator will be somewhere near the artesian well of the Union Pacific railway. As a shipping point of the earth's products on the Denver road, an examination of the company's books will show our town to compare favorably with any of the towns on their line—none excepted.[17]

On May 31, 1892, the *Messenger* reported that the Union Pacific was loading their machinery for the purpose of going to Wyoming to repair one of the company's wells in that country.

> Why they should abandon this well so suddenly before completion, and when it would have only required a short while to complete it, cannot be learned. The manager of the well outfit that secured such a large flow in one of the wells at Denton . . . said after examining the different dirts taken from the well here, that the drilling was stopped about 90 feet above flowing water.[18]

ANOTHER VIEW OF the thresher rig. The water tower in the rear is the one used by the Fort Worth and Denver City Railroad.

However, the work on the Cameron elevator was proceeding as had been expected. On July 9, 1892, the company was unloading machinery for the elevator, which was nearly ready to receive the immense wheat crop that was almost ready to be threshed. The reporter to the *Messenger* suggested that since Rhome was a cotton shipping point, the next thing needed would be a large cotton warehouse.

By July 12, 1892, work on the artesian well at Rhome was under way again. The reporter stated that the drilling was down 900 feet and that two cars of casing had been received for the well. Again work was temporarily suspended. On August 2, 1892, the *Messenger* reported that an artesian well outfit had again begun work on the Denver's well; however, it was not destined to be completed that year.

The *Decatur News* reported in 1893 that the capacity of the railroad well had been tested and found to have an abundant supply of water, which was said to be thoroughly impregnated with sulphur. However, a month later there was a further report that the railroad people were filling up the well so as to make it the depth of about 350 feet, cutting off the lower strata of water, as it contained properties which would render it unfit for use in boilers. On the 6th day of June, 1893, the huge tank of the Fort Worth and Denver City railroad was reported to be completed, containing 1000 barrels of water and ready for use.

In January, 1893, the *Decatur News* had a forward-looking report for the town of Rhome. "Our town is still improving. Mr. W. J. Rogers is making some additions to his dwelling, which when completed will make it the most elegant and substantial residence in town."[19] The newspaper also reported that some of the business fronts had been decorated with beautiful and artistic signs.

Mr. W. E. Ward, of the firm of Rhome and Ward, had purchased Mr. Rhome's interest in the firm, and would continue business in his own name. "Billy has a host of friends who wish him the fullest measure of success."[20] A new businessman appeared in Rhome news reports about February 7, 1893. Mr. W. J. Rogers had sold his stock of wagons and wire to Mr. J. E. Neel.

Rhome had its share of traveling salesmen, or drummers as they were called then. The Cottage Hotel, owned by H. H. H. Hambright, was the first hostelry to cater to people passing through Rhome. There was a large sign on the side of the hotel facing the railroad so that potential customers would see it as soon as they got off the train. The exact date of its construction is unknown, but the *Messenger* carried an advertisement for customers as early as 1893, stating that when one went to Rhome, he should stop at the Cottage Hotel. In 1896, there was a report that Mr. John Colville had just completed a bay window to the Cottage Hotel on the east side facing the railroad. The second hotel was built about 1901. "Rumor says that there is to be another fine residence erected in the very near future that will exceed anything yet in our city. The supposition is that it is to be another hotel."[21] This writer best remembers this hotel as belonging to her great grandmother, Mrs. M. F. Davis. However, an earlier report names a Mr. Worley as the hotel man. "Mr. Worley, the hotel man, has bought out I. T. Sandifer's grocery store and is selling goods right along."[22] Many references were made to different salesmen who visited the town on a regular basis. On May 2, 1893, Mr. Carter of Carter Bros. and Company of Louisville, Kentucky, spent a few days at the Cottage Hotel. Another favorite was the salesman for Platter Grocery Company in Fort Worth. He became such a great friend of W. W. Morris that later one of the Morris grandsons was named Brooks Morris in honor of the salesman friend.

The Rhome reporter to the *Decatur News* on August 19, 1894, lamented the fact that Rhome did not have a first class dry goods store. Also, he thought that Rhome needed a good doctor. On November

THE COTTAGE HOTEL at Rhome in its later years.

15, 1894, it was reported that a good many land buyers were coming to Rhome with a view to buying some of the fine prairie land. Also, several parties were searching for a business location. "We hope in the near future to see Rhome a hustling, business town."[23] In preparation for the coming of cold weather, the town had unloaded four carloads of coal for the town and neighborhood.

On June 26, 1895, Timothy S. Mount of Fort Worth began preparations to move his large stock of hardware to Rhome. The next month it was reported that the Mounts' hardware store was in full blast and was quite an acquisition for the town. This same fall season W. W. Morris moved his hardware store from the south side of First Street to the north side, occupying the eastern unit of the old stone building. The *Decatur News* referred to a "town square," which obviously did not exist. Perhaps because of the early planning of an extremely generous width of First Street, it seemed almost like a town square. In December, 1894, the Rhome reporter was still referring to the splendid opening for a drygoods store. A full year later, the reporter was touting Rhome as the liveliest little town in northwest Texas, but in the spring of 1896, he was still lamenting the fact that Rhome did not have a good drygoods store.

The *Texas Gazeteer and Business Directory of 1896-1897* gave the population figure for Rhome. Since 1890, the population had almost doubled.

> RHOME. Population, 350. On the F. W. and D. C. Ry., in Wise county, 16 miles southeast of Decatur, the county seat and banking point. It contains 3 churches, a flour mill, a public school and hotel. Stage to Aurora; fare 50 cents round trip. Tel., W. U., Exp., Pacific. L. L. Ward, postmaster.

Bobo, Z. B., drugs
Centre, L. E., livery
Dossey, W. J., physician
Edwards, Rev. S. M., (Baptist)
Fagan Bros., blacksmiths
Gallaspy, W. E., railroad and tel. agt.
Hambright, H. H., hotel and notary
Keele, Miss Mattie, milliner
May, Rev. R. S., (Methodist)
Morris, W. W., General store
Mount Bros., general store
Mount, T. S., hardware and impts.
Perkins, J. P., groceries
Roe & Helm, corn mill and gin
Rogers, W. J., real estate
Stanfield, Rev. R. W., (Presbyterian)
Ward, John L., Subscription and laundry agent
Woodward, Mrs. L., music teacher

Miss Mattie Keele reported that she had just received her immense stock of fall millinery goods on November 5, 1895, and was ready for the people to come to get their new hats for the winter. However, from the reports of the next April in 1896, Miss Keele must have had a friendly rival in the millinery business since the paper stated that Miss Mattie Keele and Mrs. B. Casey had just returned from Dallas where they selected their millinery goods. During the same week Mrs. B. Casey gave her spring millinery opening on Friday and Friday night. By 1900 the millinery business had changed hands again, for the paper reported that Mrs. Tennie Yoakley had sold her millinery shop at Rhome to Mrs. Davis. Since Mrs. B. Casey moved away from Rhome, it must have been her shop that was sold at that time.

In February of 1896, both the Mount Brothers and W. W. Morris had received carloads of wire and farming implements, indicating that there would be a great deal of plowing for this particular year.

During the week of April 16, 1896, Rhome suffered through a severe wind storm which blew the tin roofing from Colonel B. C. Rhome's stone building. Two of the rooms were occupied by Mount Brothers Hardware Company, and everything in their building, as well as the room occupied by W. W. Morris, got very wet and was greatly damaged. The next month the Mount Brothers bought half of the stone building on the west side of the building. They restored the roof, painted the building and moved their stock of dry goods into the new store.

Not long after W. W. Morris restored his part of the old stone building and continued in business, he suffered another set back. There may have been other burglaries in the town, but this occasion was the first recorded in the newspaper of the area. The *Decatur News* gave the following report: "Will Morris' store was broken into last Sunday night and two shot guns, a target rifle, two or three pistols, and some razors were found missing Monday morning. As yet no clue."[24]

With all the sales of wheat and cotton in Rhome, it stands to reason that there had to be scales erected in the town. The *Wise County Messenger* notes on April 24, 1896, that a public weigher had been elected in Rhome. Mr. E. Senter received 156 votes for the position. On July 6, 1896, the *Decatur News* reported that Mr. Timothy Mount had erected a new pair of scales south of his store.

In 1897 the farmers and businessmen were predicting a mammoth wheat crop. As a result, the businessmen were stocking their stores and the farmers were equipping themselves to handle the deluge of wheat. On April 27, 1897, Mount Brothers received a carload of binders and binding twine. *The Wise County Messenger* reported the new hope instilled in the hearts of the elevator owners:

> In 1891, which was the great wheat year in Northwest Texas, wheat elevators were built at nearly every station along the line of the Fort Worth and Denver railroad from Rhome to Clarendon. Since that year continuous failures have prevented these elevators from being run at a profit; consequently, they stood, like spectres of former greatness, telling of the "has been"; they are now being remodeled, refitted, and repainted, ready for the mighty crops that will bulge their sides with fatness and cause their busy machinery to hum.[25]

In June of that year it was reported that the harvesting machine men had sold thirty-two machines at Rhome and the farmers were still buying. The wheat was rank and heavy, and the old binders could not handle the tremendous crop. The wheat crop must have fulfilled their expectations because a report in October stated that W. W. Morris had received a carload of new wagons.

To return to the grocery business, in February of 1897, the papers reported that Logan Brothers had put in dry goods and grocery stores at Rhome. C. P. Harrison had sold his property to Z. B. Bobo and moved away from Rhome, but others were ready to come into the town. In November of 1898 there was a report that Henry W. Smith of Waxahachie had been in Rhome all week looking out for a location for a day goods establishment. The *Wise County Messenger* reported in February of 1899 that Gill and Smith of Aurora had bought lumber and would commence the next week to erect an elegant dry goods store near the depot. In June, 1900, Gill and Smith moved their large stock of dry goods and clothing to Rhome.

This was the year of great growth for Rhome. On February 22, 1898, the *Decatur News* reported that the new school house had been completed. Also, came the report that Dr. Burch had built a neat office at Rhome. Mr. Z. B. Bobo had extended his business establishment forty feet at the back, and Dr. Dossey had built a new residence on Morris Street. The following September the Rhome reporter to the *Wise County Messenger* indicated his surprise at the growth of Rhome in a three-months' period that he had been away from the town.

> ... When I arrived at Rhome, I was astonished to note the improvements that had been made since I left (three months before this). Rhome has got a double shuffle on her now sure enough. There has been sixteen new buildings erected during the last three months. There is now a perfect deluge of wheat and cotton on the streets.[26]

Also, on February 3, 1899, T. W. Weems had rented the J. P. Perkins' stand and would move his hardware store there that week. On March 8, 1899, the papers reported that Logan Brothers were doing some handsome work on their stone structure.

For a short period of time in 1899, Rhome supported a newspaper. In February, 1899, a gentleman named J. M. Burer of Dallas spent the week in Rhome, investigating the possibility of establishing a newspaper here. A paper was started and was named the *Rhome Gazette*. The paper did not flourish, and a report by the Newark correspondent to the *Wise County Messenger* made rather clear the reason why it did not succeed.

> The *Rhome Gazette* is on our stool with a few locals and a liberal amount of advertising, but reads rather foreign, so largely

cut off from its office at Dallas. How would a paper, *The Newark Review* do for our progressive little city?[27]

About the turn of the century, S. H. Green completed a new windmill and reservoir and got ready to supply the town of Rhome with water. With the increase in population, the need for water caused the drilling of many water wells from this time forward.

At the turn of the century Rhome was tremendously proud of its growth. Business was booming, the population was growing, and the citizens felt that they had something to brag about. In fact, they were considering the possibility of incorporating, although incorporation did not come until decades later.

> ... That Rhome upholds expansion is daily demonstrated. Fourteen of Aurora's most prominent citizens have purchased lots here and will proceed to erect houses on each lot. Hurrah for the hedge city, the gem of Wise County! The citizens are putting forth every effort to enlarge the population so we can incorporate in 1899.[28]

Manufacturing Interests

Early Rhome was not noted for development of heavy industry, but the few instances of manufacturing that have been attempted have been either notable successes or notorious flops.

There had been a grist mill in old Prairie Point, but at the time the plat of Rhome was drawn up, there was no milling being done in the area. However, Colonel Benjamin Morris wanted the town to grow, and flour was one of the essentials for a town to develop a good economy. Thus Block B in the town plat was set aside for the purpose of a flouring mill. From an interrogation of Colonel B. Morris in 1899, the colonel tells that the block was given to Bradford Stephenson for the purpose of putting up a fifty barrel flouring mill, as it was expressed in the deed that was given to Stephenson.

The first mention of a flouring mill in the newspapers came from the *Wise County Messenger* on September 5, 1885. "Several more Illinoisans are seeking homes near Rhome. The citizens of that place are praying for a flouring mill."[1] A second reference to a mill was made in January of 1889, when the Rhome reporter stated that the finest opening in this portion of the state for a flour mill was right here in Rhome. "We ship more grain than any other station on the road, and have no mill to make our flour."[2]

The problem of the mill was settled the next year. By April of 1890 the *Messenger* carried a description of the building of the new mill.

> The foundation for our new roller flouring mill has been commenced and work on the mill will be pushed ahead as fast as possible. The mill house will be three stories high. The machinery

will come brand new from the factory, and of the latest designs and improvements. We have felt the necessity of a good roller mill here for sometime and are surprised why one has not been built here before this, for there is more grain raised in this portion of Wise county than any other portion of twice this size, and Rhome stands at the head of the grain shipping stations on the Denver road. We make a good average crop every year, and a flour mill run jam up, and on good business principles here, will, every time, show up the profits on the right side of the ledger.[3]

Things went slowly on the construction of the mill. Before the month was over there was a report that the work was at a standstill. However, this stoppage was caused by an excess of rain and a delay in getting the lumber to continue the work. When the trouble was over, work went along at a good pace. In July, 1890, came the report of the machinery being installed. "The machinery for the Rhome roller mill company has arrived, and is being put in place. It is of the latest improved pattern, and looks as pretty as parlor furniture."[4] By March of 1891 Rhome's reporter stated that the roller mill was doing a good business and was turning out a quality of flour equal to that of Fort Worth. "The new wheat crop is still rolling in, and our roller mill is humping itself, turning out new flour, which is being taken as fast as it is made."[5]

In Decatur, the agent for the Rhome Milling Company was H. H. Fields, who owned and operated a feed store. Also, there was a report from West Fork about the Rhome mill. "When one's corn is ground at the Rhome mills, it makes him think they forgot to toll it, besides the good meal he gets. Hurrah for the Rhome mills."[6]

The summer of 1892 was a very busy one for the Rhome roller mill. The reporter again said that the mill was running night and day on the new wheat crop. Cameron Lumber Company of Fort Worth was building a new elevator in Rhome at that time which was reported to have a capacity of twenty thousand bushels. In 1893 it was necessary to remodel the mill according to a notice in the newspaper from the manager of the mill, Mr. A. E. Hargrave.

> For the benefit of our customers and others, I wish to say that we have remodeled the Rhome roller mill and are now running and will continue to run until about May 15th, and solicit the patronage of all who have wheat they wish to exchange for flour. We do a general custom business and guarantee our flour to be as good as any made in the State.[7]

On December 29, 1893, came the report that W. J. Rogers had purchased the Rhome roller mill, and that the property would be transferred in a few days' time. The elevator was reported as receiving a good deal of wheat in 1894, but some of the largest raisers of wheat were holding their wheat for a better price. At this time the miller was a man named R. L. Myers. In November, 1894, came the report from both county papers that the mill had a new owner.

> The Rhome Flouring Mill is the only flouring mill located in Wise county. It is now owned and operated by Mr. A. D. Goodenough, who has recently purchased the plant and will refit it with all the modern improvements. Being the only mill in the county, it should have the substantial support of both the farmers and merchants of the entire county. Mr. Goodenough is paying the highest price for wheat out of which he makes a most excellent quality of flour. This flour he furnishes to merchants and consumers at figures that successfully meet all competition. His High Patent brand cannot be excelled by any flour in the market. Let our merchants once introduce this flour to their customers and their business will increase and the success of the Rhome Mills will be assured.[8]

The *Messenger* advertised in December of 1894 that the best brands of flour were High Patent and Golden Crown, both made by the Rhome Flouring Mills. About this same time Mr. Goodenough installed a large pair of scales for the mill and made general improvements for the entire mill.

Then came a surprise for the residents of Rhome. Suddenly, without any prior notice, word came that the mill was to be sold. Decatur was very anxious to obtain the mill and its trade, as shown by the following quote from the *Messenger:*

> Decatur would be very unwise if she failed to secure the mill now offered her. Mr. Goodenough is the right man for this place. Let Decatur meet him in a progressive, wide-awake manner and the roller-mill will be secured. It would be better for Decatur than a mill elsewhere as it will bring Rhome trade up here. Let everybody wake up.[9]

The question of the roller mill began to gain momentum. For added zest, Greenwood entered the scene with her own bid for the mill. The *Wise County Messenger* carried the following quote from the *Greenwood Enterprise:*

> The roller mill question is getting interesting and there is no doubt that more of the citizens of our county would be benefited by the building of a good mill at Decatur than any other point in

Wise county. But the mill we must have, and if the people of Decatur do not want it, Greenwood will begin to look after the matter. We have fine water and plenty of fuel. When will we meet to organize the milling company? Some man suggest the time and place and we will let the people know.[10]

The following commentary was added to the *Greenwood Enterprise* quote: "Everybody, hold your breath a little while and just see what Decatur's going to do."[11] This report shows the temper of the area over the matter of the mill.

In the meantime, what were the people of Rhome doing about the threatened loss of their mill? In this case the county newspapers were silent. In fact, for a couple of years there was virtually no comment from Rhome about the mill or any other matter. Either the reporter from Rhome failed to send in any reports, or the Decatur newspapers failed to print the reports. Since there was no news stories, we must return to original sources for information. In the interrogatory that was filed in one of the trials over the townsite lots, Colonel Benjamin Morris told of having threatened to enjoin A. D. Goodenough from moving the mill, probably on the basis of ownership of the land. Also, he related the fact that the townsite agent, R. E. Montgomery, had given another deed to the lot to A. D. Goodenough at the same time that Morris was preparing the papers to enjoin Goodenough from moving the mill.

On April 26, 1895, a lengthy letter was published from a gentleman at Paradise concerning the mill:

> I see that Decatur is considering plans for securing the mill. This is not exactly what Decatur should do; but she should get the mill at once and take time to consider personal gains afterward. It is not a matter that personal interest of small jealousies ought to control, but it is a matter of vital interest to Decatur, to every town, and to every citizen in the county. Decatur needs the mill to win back her lost prestige among North Texas towns. It would open for Decatur new channels of trade which in twelve months time will add to her business thirty per cent.
>
> Other things being equal the county towns would far prefer to buy flour from the capitol of the county. The farmers are compelled to change their industries, but debt and stringent money render it necessary for them to have help to make the change. Decatur is able to help; so let her build the mill and the farmer can then give up the cheap mule, pony and cotton, and find a market at his door for his grain and a mill to crush his corn into food for the profitable cow and pig. Wise county is one of the richest counties in the State, and not a first class mill in it.
>
> No wonder the farmers complain of hard times and of not

> having a market . . . She (Decatur) must use her influence, and lend a helping hand in getting good roads to every town and community in the county. To illustrate, there is not a road from Decatur to Rhome, or to the Illinois settlement. This ought not to be. The southeastern part of the county needs a road to the county town, so that her citizens will not be compelled to travel twenty miles to get ten miles from home . . .[12]

On November 6, 1896, a train wreck occurred about three miles north of Rhome on the Denver road, but in relating the story, a Decatur reporter placed the wreck as being about ten miles south of Decatur. The tempers must really have flamed in this area over the matter of losing the mill. Finally, as a last straw, Newark entered the race for the mill with the following published plea:

> Several are calling for a flouring mill here and we think a plant with a fifty barrel daily capacity could do well. The location is good, with water in abundance and on one of the best roads in Texas.[13]

Again the reporter from the *Messenger* added his own postscript to the letter from Phoenix, the Newark reporter: "Decatur is going to have that mill, so Newark need not try for it!"[14]

In the mean time, however, the *Decatur News* carried its own report of the situation. Apparently, the Rhome reporter was not so irate with the *News* as with the *Messenger*. At least he sent in a report of the mill situation.

> A. D. Goodenough went to Fort Worth this morning; he has his mill torn up and has sent the rollers off to have them worked over; the mill will be stopped about one month for general repairs and cleaning up the machinery.[15]

Within a month the *Decatur News* was reporting the fact that they were tearing down the old mill at Rhome and loading it on cars for Decatur. "We have inquiries from parties about putting up a new mill at this place."[16] The truth of the matter was that Goodenough loaded his machinery on box cars of the Fort Worth and Denver Railway and shipped it to Decatur. This circumvented the suit for enjoinment with which he was threatened. By the time Rhome citizens learned the truth, the mill was already in Decatur. In July, 1897, Decatur was advertising their new roller mill as the finest of its kind in the state. The reporter also stated that their mill was crowded with orders.

Rhome was not to go long without a mill. They did not intend to be out-done by Decatur. As early as April 6, 1900, the new owners had started on construction of the new mill to be built for Rhome.

> Mount Brothers are fast having the rock quarried to build a new mill at the old site at Rhome to grind the big crops expected in the future, and now, if the people would only build that talked-of factory to manufacture our cotton, we'll still feel the more "in it", and we hope they may.[17]

The story of the Mount Brothers roller mill will be continued in the next chapter of this book.

During all the time that the struggle for the roller mill was brewing, the Cameron Elevator was continuing to serve the wheat growers of the Rhome area. There was a period of bad times in July, 1895, when the elevator was closed because of so much damaged wheat. By August of the same year there was a continued lament about the poor conditions. There was no market for wheat. The mill was torn up at this point and presumably being shipped to Fort Worth. The farmers were greatly discouraged by these facts, as well as the fact that the continued dry weather gave a poor outlook for future wheat crops. In spite of the complaints of dry weather, there was a report at the end of August that the elevator was again closed because of the wheat being damaged by so much rain.

On May 19, 1896, tragedy struck the elevator again. "Rhome was blessed by a good rain last Friday. It came down in torrents for one hour and a half. Lightning struck the Cameron Elevator and tore a hole in the top of the roof about ten or twelve feet."[18]

A better time came for the farmers in the year of 1897. The wheat yield was about twenty-three bushels to the acre. The wheat buyers, Mount Brothers and Skeen, were busy buying and shipping the excess of wheat. Mount Brothers were buying for M. P. Bewley and Logan Brothers, and Skeen bought for the Cameron Mill and Elevator Company of Fort Worth. By July 26th they had bought and shipped out forty car loads, counting six hundred bushels to the car load. However, there was again a depressing fact for the farmers to face. Wheat was selling at approximately sixty-eight cents, and many of the farmers were refusing to sell at that price.

There was a report in December of 1899 that a local milling company had bought ten thousand bushels of wheat from farmers around Rhome. There had been about twenty thousand bushels shipped out of Rhome, and it was estimated that fully one third of the last crop was still in the hands of the farmers. This wheat bought by a local company was probably that bought by Mount Brothers in anticipation of the function of their future roller mill operations.

STEAM THRESHER RIG being operated near Rhome, Texas.

While wheat seemed to be king in Rhome, there is some question that perhaps it was closely rivaled by the real king of the South, cotton. Perhaps the first gins built here in Rhome were those built by Roe Helm. On January 31, 1895, it was announced that Roe Helm was building a new gin in Rhome. The business certainly must have been profitable because by the beginning of the summer Mr. Helm had increased the capacity of his first gin stand. "Roe Helm will soon have three gin stands in position for the two thousand acres of cotton planted around Rhome."[19] By July Mr. Helm was busily getting his gin ready for the coming deluge of cotton. "Roe Helm has gone to Fort Worth after the large boiler for his gin. He is fixing up generally for business."[20] By August, the work was really in progress. The farmers were working hard to get their cotton crop to the market place. "Roe Helm's gins are running day and night. Cotton picking is the order of the day. Most all of the boys of the town are in the cotton patch."[21]

There was no further comment on the cotton situation until the fall of 1900 when the reporter was aglow with news that cotton farmers were really reaping good prices for their product. "Cotton is pouring in lively and the farmers are all wearing smiles on account of the advance price of that staple."[22]

Farmers and Their Farms

While industry was important in the economy of Rhome, none of it would have been possible without the farmer. This was primarily a farming community, and it was the farmers' work that supported all the other activities in the area. Farming had been carried on since the days of old Prairie Point, although the crops probably changed in size and type. The first mention of farming in the newspapers came from the *Wise County Messenger* of July 17, 1885, a report probably written by H. H. H. Hambright, one of the most prolific writers in the county.

> Rhome, July 14. The shrill whistle of the threshing engine is heard all around us "from early morning till dewy eve," as our little town is situated in one of the best grain raising sections in Northwest Texas. Notwithstanding the apparent sufficiency of threshers, the farmers, or a great many of them, say that a third more custom threshers could do profitable work this season.
>
> Wheat and oats are beginning to come into the market very lively, and the farmers are shipping in their surplus last year's corn, for which they are getting fifty-four cents shelled.
>
> Mr. Simpson Bobo, one of our largest cotton raisers, was here this morning and says that he never saw such a great and

rapid improvement of cotton as there has been in the last five days, and that if weather is favorable from now on, we will make more than can be gathered.[1]

On the 25th of July, 1885, it was reported that Mark Oates had four acres of oats that yielded a hundred bushels per acre.[2] This, of course, does not sound like the crops which are harvested today, but one must consider the farming methods and machinery that the farmer of that day had to use. It must have been an outstanding yield at that time.

On October 3, 1885, the *Wise County Messenger* carried a front page story on the Farmers' Alliance of Rhome. This alliance had begun in Texas about 1875, but after it was reorganized about 1879, it expanded into a national organization. It was born out of the desperation of the farmer at the low prices he had to take for his produce. They were particularly interested in the sale of school lands only to those people who intended to settle the land and farm it. Also, they felt that the railroads should be assessed at full value for taxation purposes. In this case, the farmer felt at a disadvantage in dealing with the railroads, who often set rates that favored one group over another. The members of the Farmers' Alliance felt that the capitalists and strong corporations had shamefully abused the farmer. Projects proposed by the Farmers' Alliance were the establishment of joint-stock stores and cooperatives.

At least one gentleman from Rhome was not in favor of these proposals. On October 24, 1885, the *Messenger* carried a story from L. L. Ward of Rhome:

> L. L. Ward, Esq., of the village of Rhome, was here on Thursday. Mr. Ward is not a member of the Farmers' Alliance, but he insists the farmers have a perfect right to store cotton in their own yards and require buyers to go there to buy it and very truthfully observes that a town which undertakes to baffle farmers in their efforts to secure unity of action in their dealings will drive them, their cotton, and their custom trade to more generous towns.[3]

The deeds were not recorded until March 20, 1889, but records show that on October 9, 1885, Colonel Benjamin Morris had deeded to the trustees of the Farmers' Alliance Joint Stock Company, Block 11, 80 feet east of the northwest corner, thence south 118 feet, thence east 55 feet, thence north 118 feet, thence west 55 feet to the place of beginning. This deed is recorded in Deeds Book 14, p. 451, in Wise County, Texas. A second deed was also recorded on the same date by which the president, L. E. Caffew, and the secretary, W. E. Burrows, deeded the land back to B. Morris. Apparently, the Rhome Farmers'

Alliance was organized in 1885 and disbanded sometime after 1892.

A story carried in the *Wise County Messenger* stated that the *Messenger* was the official paper for the Farmers' Alliance. From that date forward almost every edition carried one or two stories about the Alliance. In a meeting held that same week, Colonel B. Morris was appointed as one of three men who were to fix uniform rates of yardage for the Alvord, Decatur, and Rhome Alliances.

The Alliance decided to build its own granary at Rhome to store the grain that belonged to its members. "The Farmers' Alliance is erecting here a splendid granary and will soon be prepared to receive all the cereals that our rich prairies produce."[4] The Alliance began as an organization primarily to help the farmers in their plight, but in its efforts to halt the growth of the railroads and other large corporations, it soon became involved in politics.

It was during these years that James B. Hogg became governor of Texas. Governor Hogg fought against the railroads and the large corporations. He wanted regulation of the railroads so that the farmer would have a better chance to profit from his own labor. Also, Governor Hogg wanted the State of Texas to be able to control the corporations within its boundaries. The Texas Railroad Commission was formed, and after long and bitter struggles, Governor Hogg was able to separate the railroad monoplies already established in Texas. The following excerpt was taken from a personal letter from Governor Hogg to Colonel B. Morris:

> You may rely upon it, my friend, lying reports to the contrary notwithstanding, that the hope and ambition of my life has been, is now, and I expect it to continue to be, that the Railway Commission and the Stock and Bond Law will be the protection and the salvation of the producing classes of this State from corporate rapacity and oppression; and that at no time have I relinquished, in the slightest degree, my friendship for and support of those measures throughout.[5]

The Alliance was still in existence during the summer of 1891. In July it was reported that there would be a big picnic on July 5th to celebrate Independence Day under the supervision of the Rhome Alliance. Distinguished speakers were expected to attend.

Sometime between the time the granary was built and 1892, the aims of the Alliance became more radical than most of the Rhome farmers could countenance. The Alliance demanded that the State confiscate the railroads. This smacked of socialism, and certainly the strong Democrats of the county could not accept this stand taken by the Alliance.

In 1888, Rhome suffered one of the worst winters in memory of the people of that time. "Black, threatening clouds hang above us, indicative of snow tonight, while under foot is one solid sheet of ice. It has not been so cattle could graze since last Friday."[6] By the end of the month conditions were still depressing for the farmers. "A cold, blinding sleet has been falling nearly all day and the ground is white as if we had had a snow. Such weather is telling on the cattle, and is drawing them considerably . . . ."[7] Thus the cattle situation was quite desperate, but on the other hand the weather was good for the wheat crop. It had been two years of drought, and the farmers were depending upon the wheat crop to pull them out of the bad situation.

> While money is scarce in our county, the consequences of two crop failures, yet all of our farmers seem to be sufficiently equipped to make another crop, and are delving into Mother Earth with more vigor and determination than we have seen before. They are all cognizant of the disasters that will follow another drought, and are determined to let no shortcomings of theirs cause a failure in crops.[8]

In March the bad reports were still coming. The reporter made his statement succinct: "Bad weather, snow still continuing. Cattle suffering."[9]

Rhome survived the winter of 1888. There was not much news about the farming community for the next year, but by 1891, they were back in shape and in March of that year they were busy planting their new crops. "Our farmers have all been very busy lately planting the crops, most of which are in the ground in splendid condition . . . ."[10] That same month their concern over their stock was proven by the purchase which a group of farmers made. "A club of prosperous farmers living on the prairie in the neighborhood of Rhome have recently purchased at a cost of $1000.00, a fine stallion."[11] The farmers were well along with their work and were very confident that that year would bring a bountiful yield, as a report in May indicated:

> Acreage of wheat 10 per cent less than last year. Prospective yield good, lowest estimate being 15 bushels per acre, some claiming over 20. Full acreage of corn, all looking well. Small acreage in oats, but looking well. Increased acreage in cotton, it is about 10 days late, a good stand. Farmers up with work.[12]

During the middle of June it was reported that Ben Morris had threshed out 2650 bushels of wheat for his crop that year.

Farming prospects were rather dull for 1893-1894, and most of

BEN MORRIS, A son of Col. B. Morris.

the news was rather depressing. One note stated that Jim Day had sold a car load of mules in August and had gone to San Augustine to deliver them. Mr. Sam Harris received a car load of sheep from south Texas about that same time, and Colonel B. C. Rhome had begun to sell off a good many small tracts of land for farmers in his large pasture east of Rhome. The reporter thought that when the pastures east of Rhome were cut up into small tracts, the merchants of Rhome would see more prosperity. In September, 1894, the farmers were again discouraged by the low price of wheat. Many of them were planning to plant cotton to replace the wheat. In September there was a report of a car load of hogs from east Texas being unloaded in Rhome to be fed on wheat. At the same time the cotton buyers were very active. Mount Brothers were buying in large quantities. "Receipts at the depot yesterday amounted to eleven hundred dollars."[13] The Rhome reporter suggested that this would be a splendid opening for a steam gin and outfit.

By June, 1895, the town was reported to be full of men and boys looking for work in the wheat harvest. Roe Helm was getting ready to start his two fully-equipped threshing machines ready to go to work as soon as the farmers got ready for him. Prospects for that year and the following year must have been exceptionally good because the farmers were making additions to their farms and equipment. "John Thur-

FRONT STREET, RHOME, Texas, circa 1902. Thresher rig being unloaded at railroad station. The gentleman with the little boy is Judge H. H. H. Hambright. The small boy is Hiram M. Helm.

mond has under construction a fine 100 barrel tank at his residence three miles northeast of Rhome."[14] Colonel Morris was breaking two hundred acres of stubble and getting it ready for wheat again in 1895. Several months later Roe Helm, Charles Harrison, and Major Reeves were preparing to put in three hundred acres of cotton for Colonel Morris's farm. "There will be no place for the birds to build their nests on that place this year."[15]

Nevertheless, their efforts were doomed to failure. The following report came from Rhome in 1896:

> Rhome—While the increase in acreage in cotton in this vicinity was over 200 per cent, yet the number of bales will not be larger than the last crop. I am an old cotton raiser, and I never saw as many worm flies or millers as there are and have been for ten days. In fact, some eggs have hatched and the worms are at work. It is only a question of a few days until the crop will be destroyed.[16]

> Rhome—All the first crop of cotton gathered; heavy top crop, but fear it will not mature. There has been 500 bales of cotton shipped from Rhome this fall. A great deal of cotton in the year not sold. Wheat coming into the elevator today lively; price 85 cents a bushel.[17]

Finally, after years of disappointment, the farmers got a good year for wheat. 1897 must have been a perfect year since they had to call in threshers from other communities in order to gather the big harvest. "A thresher from Cedar Hill, Dallas county, came in on Monday on the 9 o'clock local to help thresh the immense wheat crop raised in this vicinity."[18] In fact, there must have been several good years for the wheat farmers. On December 15, 1899, the reporter stated that the wheat was looking good and also that Rhome had shipped twenty-six car loads of wheat that year. The Rhome mill had bought 100,000 bushels of wheat. There was a complaint that winter that Rhome was running low on coal because there had been no extra box cars to carry coal. "Nearly everybody is out of coal; the reason is because they cannot get cars to haul it."[19]

The year of 1900 also brought the farmer a good harvest, despite the fact that weather conditions made life miserable for the worker.

> The excessive hot weather for the past few days has caused several prostrations in the harvest fields. Last Thursday was so intensely hot that five horses which were being worked to binders fell dead in the fields. The farmers are cutting at night now instead of day time. The wheat in this locality is the best ever seen beyond any doubt. The crop is just about half harvested.[20]

Natural Resources

When one thinks of Rhome and its natural resources, it is quite likely that would seem to be a real shortage. Water is the first of God's gifts that comes to mind, and that has been fairly abundant for the citizens, but there are some other stories about natural resources that may surprise the reader. Since water is covered in the drilling of the different wells in town, it is not necessary at this point to repeat those stories.

Early in the twentieth century there is a story about the discovery of oil in a water well drilled for the Fort Worth and Denver City railroad, but the really exciting story for the citizens of Rhome in 1885 was the rumor that gold might be uncovered by some enterprising miners.

> Mark Oats and others are becoming intensely excited over an imaginary unearthing of hidden gold in the south part of the county. They have dug 20 feet or more into the bowels of the early, have a steam engine to pump out the water, and Aladdin's wonderful lamp never lighted a hotter trail to riches than they imagine they are on.[21]

The gold was never found, but at least it did create some wild excitement for a few days.

Another venture in which Mr. Oats and Colonel Morris engaged was much more successful. However, this time the discovery was not made in Rhome, but at least it was for the good of the Rhome residents.

> Colonel Morris and Mark Oats of Rhome . . . are prospecting for coal in Pleasant Valley, near Bridgeport. It is hoped they will meet with good success and succeed in finding plenty of coal. They have leased over 500 acres of land in the valley and seem determined to find out whether or not the coal is there.[22]

Apparently they were successful because in November of the same year a report came from Bridgeport that there was plenty of coal there.

> Bridgeport coal mines in this county are now in active operation. Large quantities of coal are now being hauled into Decatur, a great portion of which is being shipped to other points.[23]

Transportation and Communication

Rhome was perhaps more fortunate than many other frontier towns. Because of the Fort Worth and Denver City railroad, Rhome had good transportation and communication almost from its very beginning. Of course, good roads were of prime importance, and they were built in course of time, but until that period, the people had the railroad to bring in products and to take out the produce they needed to sell in the city.

The first discussion of a highway came about the time of the mill problem. The importance of a highway to Decatur was the subject of one news item:

> It is very important that a road be opened from Decatur to Rhome. In order to get to Decatur, some of the people in the Illinois settlement at present have to travel nearly twice the distance that they would if a direct road to Rhome was opened. This puts time, practically, almost as near Fort Worth or Denton as to Decatur. That trade properly belongs here and no pains should be spared to bring it here. Besides the people of that section are entitled to a direct road to the county seat.[1]

To the citizens of Rhome this must have seemed a very devious move. After all, it occurred at the time Decatur was making an intensive effort to acquire the mill from Rhome.

When the citizens of Fairview wanted to visit relatives near the Deep Creek community, they usually drove across the large ranches that surrounded the communities. Mrs. Kate Shaw tells the story of her sisters who made the drive across the ranches to the west of Fairview. That evening on their return to their home they were frightened by cowboys from one of the ranches who chased them part of the way. They almost ran the horses to death trying to escape.

On April 30, 1897, came news of a new road law for Wise county. The law read that beginning at that time, the county commissioners would be the road commissioners, each for his own precinct. "The trouble with our road work heretofore has been that it has had no efficient head. The wisdom of this new arrangement is clearly seen by what Commissioner Hart has accomplished in the last two months."[2] The Newark reporter for the *Wise County Messenger* stated that the bridges on the Rhome and Decatur road were said to be impaired enough to endanger life and property and should be repaired at once. There must have been some kind of road from Rhome to Decatur at that time; however, it was after the turn of the century that the Meridian highway was finally built to connect Rhome and Decatur.

Besides the telegraph, Rhome had a post office from the very early days. Samuel C. Snead was the first postmaster, appointed on February 9, 1883. Sam Snead's bond was signed before the notary, Justice of the Peace L. L. Ward, and signed by witnesses, R. R. Bryan and William Finlayson for a fee of $1.00. Colonel Benjamin Morris was very interested in Rhome's obtaining a postoffice from the beginning of the town, and he had used his influence with an old friend from Alabama, Senator James L. Pugh, to have the post office opened in Rhome. The following is an excerpt from a letter which Senator Pugh wrote to Colonel Morris:

> United States Senate
> Washington, D.C.
> December 20, 1882.

Dear Ben,

    I rec'd your letter yesterday and this morning I interviewed Maxey who has been chairman of the committee on Post offices . . . and is now a member of that committee which gives him the ear of the chief of the P. O. Department. Maxey informs me that he had received a letter from you on the same subject mentioned in your letter to me. I told Maxey that you were the smartest man in Texas, and that he could make out of you a most valuable friend by serving you in the matter of your Post Office. He told me that he would do all he could for you . . .

>   Truly your friend,
>   James L. Pugh[3]

On February 4, 1884, George W. Whittington became postmaster of Rhome. He served until November 4, 1885, when Lawrence L. Ward was appointed postmaster. Mr. Ward served for five years, and then on May 13, 1890, Francis M. Hatler was given the office of postmaster. Mr. Hatler was in that post until November 7, 1893, when Lawrence L. Ward returned to Rhome as postmaster. On April 4, 1895, Lucy A. Ward was the official postmaster of Rhome, but the *Decatur News* carried a story on April 24, 1895, about the postmaster whom they called "Johnny Ward." "Johnny Ward, our postmaster, has been making considerable improvements the last week on the post office building, and moved the large safe of Ward Brothers in it, which will be of great convenience to him."[4] Mrs. Sallie Bobo Christian remembers that Johnny Ward was married to Lucy A. Ward and that his full name was Judge John L. Ward. In the *Texas State Gazeteer and Business Directory, 1896-1897*, John L. Ward was named as the subscription and laundry agent for Rhome. According to this information, it is assumed that Mr. Ward was probably the assistant postmaster, serving under his wife, since he was operating other businesses besides his postoffice position.

W. W. Whitesides succeeded Mrs. Ward as postmaster on September 22, 1897.[5] From 1897 to 1914, Mr. Whitesides served as postmaster and had his post office in a small room on the side of the barber shop. "This location can be recalled as being the same barber shop that was later operated by Mr. Joe Brown."[6] Apparently, Mr. Whitesides found it necessary to change the combination of the large safe that was used in the post office. According to a letter found in Mrs. Kate Shaw's files, Whitesides wrote to the company who made the safe, The Cincinnati Safe and Lock Company, to ask how to change the combination. They informed him that the safe was originally shipped to Baker, Smith, and Matthews of Granbury, Texas, on February 4, 1889. This must have been the company from whom Ward Brothers bought the safe prior to the time that John Ward moved it into the postoffice building. The company described the safe lock, and advised Mr. Whitesides that there was a "key" inside the safe which he could use with their instructions to change the combination.[7]

Rhome's Churches

Rhome has always been a church-going town. During the many years of its existence, the people have supported five different churches, and four of those are still in existence. With the exception of the school, Rhome's churches were the first organizations in the town. Four out of the five churches first organized their congregations and met for several years in the school building before they were able to move into their own structures. Prior to that time it is certain that they attended church with the people of Aurora. The churches of Rhome often shared their own buildings with others, as well as sharing their meeting dates. Often the Baptists would have church on two Sundays of the month; then on the two alternate Sundays, the Methodists would hold services. Sharing was a way of life in those times.

The earliest date of a pastor assigned to any church in Rhome is the assignment of F. V. Evans, as shown by the original church register of the present-day United Methodist Church, originally the Methodist Episcopal Church of Rhome. Evans was appointed on November 17, 1884, and was removed on November 23, 1887. During his appointment to Rhome the first members were registered as transferring by certificate on January 1, 1886. These members were Green W. Baker, W. E. Williams, J. F. Crockett, William B. Crockett, M. F. Cates, Roxana Morris, Acia A. Terrell, and S. A. Baker. It is assumed that Pastor Evans also served Aurora, Anneville, and possibly Newark during this period. Nannie M. Perkins transferred into the church by certificate on March 16, 1886. The first person registered as coming into the church by vows was Ben L. Morris, a son of Roxana and Colonel B. Morris, on September 19, 1886. Others who came into the church during Pastor Evans' appointment were Mattie R. Morris, M. E. Crockett, Walter R. Walker, and J. T. Lilley.

The next Methodist minister to be assigned to Rhome was J. A. Smith, who came on November 28, 1887, and was removed on November 13, 1888. During this time C. M. Johnson joined the church by certificate. The third pastor was S. L. Ball, who came to Rhome on November 24, 1890, and was removed on November 11, 1891. According to the records, there seems to have been very little growth during this period. There were only three new members, who came in by vows: Lou Morris, Mary Early Morris, and Lizzie Crockett.

On November 16, 1892, Colonel Benjamin Morris and his wife Roxana deeded a lot to the church for the purpose of building a church house. This lot, number 8, in block 7, was deeded to the church trustees, S. D. Stanley, G. W. Watkins, John W. Prunty, W. L. Wilson, J. F. Roberts, and their successors in office in trust. Since the name of John W. Prunty appears on the church register as transferring from Aurora on January 16, 1902, it must be assumed that these trustees were appointed for an Aurora-Rhome circuit. The close association might have stemmed from the fact that the parsonage was at Rhome although there was no church building here. The parsonage was built during March, 1891. "Rhome is on a boom. The M. E. Church for the Aurora district have located their parsonage here and the building is now in the course of construction, to be completed in a short time. It was located here on account of this being a healthy place."[1] On April 7, 1891, the *Wise County Messenger* reported that the pastor, Reverend Ball had moved into the new parsonage at Rhome. The church records possession of a parsonage and one vacant lot at Rhome valued at $600.00.

From the Quarterly Conference records on May 23, 1895, there comes a notation that permission had been given for a church to be built at Rhome. The Methodist were unhappy at the fact that they did not have a building. "The Methodists are holding a protracted meeting under an arbor on College Hill. Everyone seems to be greatly interested."[2] On September 5, 1896, the pastor, J. S. May, reported to the Quarterly Conference that the church was hampered by the fact that it did not have a home of its own, and that the Methodist children were forced to attend schools not under Methodist care. This was soon remedied because the Quarterly Conference records of July 8, 1900, note the following progress: "N. G. Holt, W. S. Alderson, C. B. Floyd, and F. E. Shank were elected a committee to build a church house at Rhome."[3]

In the period from 1892 to 1895, the Methodist Church grew much faster than it had in the first five years of its existence. Entering the church rolls during this period were Emma Schroder, William A. Helm, Nancy A. Parsons, M. F. Davis, Allice Cates, John P. Perkins, James P. Cates, Annie L. Crockett, James Pugh Morris, Robert E. Cates, Minnie Alderson, Charley Alderson, Willie E. Crockett, Maggie Mae Morris, Sallie Helm, Ruth Helm, Col. Benjamin Morris, William Wade Morris, W. S. Alderson, J. E. Alderson, Thomas M. Poteet, Cora S. Poteet, Louisa May, John P. Gill, Eliza Lockridge, Nancy E. Whitaker, Noah Reeves, Ollie Reeves, Julia Reeves, Lizzie Reeves.

It was on May 9, 1896, that August Thorell became one of the first transfers from Aurora. Others who joined the church during the period of 1896 to 1900 were Rudy A. Alderson, John E. Reeves, Nannie Reeves, Nannie Sims, E. J. Fairchild, Mattie Roberts (Smitherman), Alma Anderson, Lola M. Sherwood, Bettie A. Sherwood, C. B. Floyd, Lula Floyd, Mary A. West, F. E. Shanks, Josie Shanks, Grace Shanks, Ruth Shanks, Ida Shanks, and John Scott.

The second church to be organized in Rhome was the First Baptist Church. It was organized on the third Sunday of August, 1890. The church was first called "The Baptist Church of Christ at Rhome, Texas." Later it was renamed "The Rhome Missionary Baptist Church." It was not until 1944 that the name was finally changed to "The First Baptist Church at Rhome, Texas."[4]

Prior to that time the Baptists in Rhome were active although they did not have a formal church organization. The *Wise County Messenger* reports on a Baptist meeting in Rhome during 1886.

> Rhome, May 31—The district meeting of the West Fork Baptist Association was held in this place on Friday night. A large number of delegates were in attendance. A mass meeting for the Sunday school was held here on Sunday morning, appropriate speeches being made by the children. The association closed on Sunday night . . .[5]

Apparently they were not hampered by the lack of a building in which to meet, and it is probable that they met as the other churches did, in the school building.

The organizational meeting was conducted by the Reverend T. W. Sturges of Springtown, Texas, and Reverend J. F. Young of Decatur, Texas, who acted as the presbytery, and the following persons were received as charter members: F. M. Hatler (deacon), Jane Hatler, William Keele, Elizabeth Keele, Mattie Keele, C. P. Harrison, Zeddie Harrison, L. L. Ward (deacon), Lucy A. Ward, Mattie Hawkins, Isabel Wilmuth, Ella Rogers, Gussie Greene, Lillie Greene, W. T. Green (church clerk), Mary T. Greene, Mattie McCarty, Alley Phillips, M. E. Truax, N. S. Reece, M. E. Seely, Bunnie Day, Ollie Truex. That Sunday night the following members were received: Mrs. Bettie Bobo, Mrs. Sarah Keele, Miss Katie Gardner, and William Keele, Jr.[6]

At the first meeting the Reverend T. W. Sturges was called as pastor, and W. T. Greene was elected church clerk. The church began by setting its regular meeting date on the third Sunday of each month, with a service on the Saturday night preceding. The Reverend E. D. Landers was called as pastor the next year. J. L. Ward was elected church clerk, and William Keele became church treasurer.

The first Sunday school was organized on the first Sunday of April, 1891, with J. H. Mount as superintendent. The church minutes of 1892 give the plans that were made to build a house of worship:

Saturday night before the third Sunday in August, 1892, the Missionary Baptist Church of Christ at Rhome, Texas, met and after divine worship by Bro. Swinford, was called in conference. Visiting brethern were invited to seats with us, an opportunity was then given for the reception of members. The question of building a church house came up, and on motion of J. L. Ward, F. M. Hatler, and William Keele, Sr. were appointed as a committee, and J. H. Mount treasurer for the same.[7]

The above mentioned men were named as trustees for the purpose of building the church house. In September, 1892, the trustees reported that they had succeeded in getting a lot for a house of worship. The lot which they secured was acquired from Colonel B. Morris and Roxana Morris for the sum of one dollar. The deed is recorded in the Wise County deeds book, Volume 5, Page 640, and was a warranty deed made to the trustees appointed by the church. The same three men were then appointed as a building committee for the church. In May, 1893, the church minutes show that $482.00 had been collected on the building fund.

The first church building to be erected in Rhome was completed in 1893. It was a one-room frame structure with a belfry and a bell. The fact that it was completed before August, 1893, is made certain by an item published in the *Wise County Messenger:*

> The meeting at the Baptist church closed Friday night with very satisfactory results. The church building was then tendered to the Methodists for their use during their protracted meeting, which was gratefully accepted by Rev. H. P. Shrader, who began a meeting last Saturday night. We like to see such a Christian spirit. When we see hatred, envy, and prejudice exhibited by the different religionists, we think as the poet expressed it: "Alas for rarity, Of Christian charity, Under the sun."[8]

From this time on, the Methodists and Baptists shared Sunday services, with each church meeting on two alternate Sundays.

The Baptist Herald was quoted in the *Messenger* on January 5, 1894, as follows: "The new Baptist pastor at Rhome, S. M. Edwards, is moving in a good way. The church has recently enjoyed a good revival. They will paint their new house soon."[9] Another interesting item taken from the church minutes of July, 1895, tells about the janitor, or sexton, as he was then called. The church had voted to pay William Keele thirty cents per year for each family in the church.

Z. B. Bobo was elected church clerk in August, 1895. That same year the Reverend S. M. Edwards was pastor, and the church voted to pay him $100.00 per year for one-fourth time each year. During these and succeeding years, the church was very strict in disciplining its members. The membership in 1895 was 51. The church was seated with benches which were built by a committee of church members.

The third church organized in Rhome was the Church of Christ. "September 14, 1891, sixteen brethern of the Church of Christ met and organized into a congregation. Charter members were Mr. and Mrs. G. W. Knight, Mr. and Mrs. D. R. Becker, M. P. Benton, J. W. Watson, Eli Benton, Janie Ovver, Ellen Benton, M. R. Watson, O. P. Benton, Mertie Prunty, A. S. Knight, Lettie Hall, E. Strunk. The minister was D. R. Hall."[10]

As with the other churches, the Church of Christ met in the school building for a number of years until they provided a house for their church in 1905. Mrs. Juanita Chambers remembers attending church services in the old school located on the hill where it had been in Prairie Point days. An item from the *Messenger* in 1900 reported on a meeting that the church held. "A protracted meeting is in progress at the Christian church at Rhome."[11] The building for the Church of Christ was constructed on a lot which was deeded to the church by Colonel Benjamin Morris and his wife Roxana Blair Morris. It was recorded in the Wise County Record of Deeds, Book 56, Page 341. Since the deed was filed for records on the 5th day of November, 1904, it is quite probable that the building for the church was constructed in the next year, 1905. A. L. Benton of Rhome was the person who had the deed recorded.

The Cumberland Presbyterian Church of Rhome was first organized at Aurora. During the very early days Rhome members attended services in Aurora; however, as early as 1894 there was talk of moving the church to Rhome. ". . . and I also understand that the arrangements have been made to move the Cumberland Presbyterian Church at Aurora to Rhome."[12]

Several years passed before the arrangements were completed. Nevertheless, the Presbyterians in Rhome were taking positive steps toward a church. A report from the Fairview correspondent gave the following account as early as 1886. "The Presbyterians are having quite an interesting meeting at Rhome. They have had 26 conversions, four joined the church by letter, and several have been reclaimed."[13] Certainly, without a building, they too must have met in the school house on the hill.

The actual organization of the church at Rhome came at the end of 1899 through the efforts of Reverend W. C. Rutledge.

Reverend Rutledge of Valley View is here in the interest of organizing a Cumberland Presbyterian church and moving the church edifice from Aurora to this place. As some of the members of that place have moved away, it is deemed expedient to move the structure to Rhome.[14]

The next week the *Decatur News* carried the story of the organization of the church. It is possible that the first minister was a Reverend Wood, since the following item was reported the next year from Aurora: "Reverend R. W. Stanfield of Rhome will fill the place at the Presbyterian church recently vacated by Rev. Wood."[15] From the minutes of the Presbytery of Guthrie, Spring Meeting 1900 came the following information: ". . . A new church to be known as Rhome was taken under the care of Presbytery, and J. W. Beard, its representative, was admitted to a seat. Rev. W. C. Rutledge, who was appointed at the last meeting of Presbytery to visit Rhome and organize a church, reported that he had discharged that duty."[16]

According to Mrs. Kate Shaw's records, the following persons were members of the Cumberland Presbyterian Church at Rhome: Mrs. Emma Stevenson, Mrs. Rachel Logan, Mrs. Mary Bowers, Mrs. B. P. Jones, Mrs. Kate Beard Smith, Miss Jennie Hambright, Miss Addie Hambright, Miss Jonny Beard, Miss Georgia Beard, Mrs. M. E. Stanfield, Ben Hambright, Hiram Hambright, H. H. H. Hambright, Miss Fannie Long, Miss Lulu Jones, Mrs. F. E. Foster, Mrs. Tennie Yokley, Mrs. H. H. H. Hambright, Mr. and Mrs. John Beard. It is not certain that these were charter members of the church, but certainly they were very early members.

Education

The first mention of a school for Rhome was found in Civil Docket of the Justice of the Peace, Precinct 5, Wise County, Texas. There was a listing of the donation of a lot for a public school house in the town of Rhome, Texas, on March 12, 1883. The names of the grantors were Benjamin and Roxana Morris, and the grantee was G. B. Pickett and his successors in office at Decatur, Wise County, Texas. G. B. Pickett was probably the county school superintendant at that time. This lot was in the same location as the Prairie Point school house. Later a lot designated as a cemetery was given to the school, but in these early days the school was on the hill above Rhome.

The first school teacher was a Miss Jennie Morrow. "The public school here is progressing finely. There are 56 scholars enrolled and several more who have not entered. Miss Jennie Morrow, the teacher, is meeting with perfect success."[1]

By 1885 the school was succeeding well enough to add a music department. "Miss Ada Hockett of San Antonio will take charge of the music department of Rhome High School, commencing her work next Monday morning. She is one of the most thorough teachers in the state."² The school must have certainly encouraged the fine arts since the same month brought the announcement of a literary society for Rhome. By December of 1885 came the news of still another teacher for the school. "The town of Rhome is but two years old and has several fine store buildings and pretty residences. Professor Williams, late of Mississippi, is teaching a successful school at Rhome."³ Possibly at this time it had become a two-teacher school.

The school building was the center of social and religious life for the town, as it was in most small communities. Since it served such as important position in the town, it was necessary to see that it was maintained in good condition. Hence the following story from the *Messenger*:

> During the past week our town has been alive with holiday festivities. Among the entertainments given, none deserves the commendation of the citizens more than the festival given for the benefit of the school building. By the faithful efforts of the ladies, money enough was received to put the building in comfortable condition.
>
> At its last meeting the Rhome Literary Society elected Charles Harrison as president and Miss Lula Cates as secretary for the ensuing term.
>
> The school was an acknowledged success. We now have one of the best schools in the county.⁴

In September of 1886 Professor Williams opened his school at Rhome. At the end of that month came the report of what was probably the first teachers' association for this part of the county.

> A teachers' association for the southern portion of the county was organized yesterday at Aurora. Mr. D. R. Becker of Rhome was elected president, and Dr. J. D. Burch of Aurora, vice-president. The leading objectives of the association will be the adopting of a uniform series of textbooks for the schools of the county. Monthly institutes will be held. This is an important work. The teachers of Tarrant are invited to cooperate with the teachers of Wise.⁵

It may seem strange that this group was called a teachers' association since the officers were not teachers, but just influential members of the community, perhaps school board members. However, it was a beginning that has continued to the present time. Uniform textbooks are now selected by state law, and teachers today still have in-service training. The plan for uniform textbooks was put into effect in Wise county because on November 6, 1886, the teachers met in Decatur and adopted the following uniform series of textbooks:

> Spellers, Swinton's; Readers, Barnes'; Geographies, Swinton's two-book series; Physical Geography, Maury's revised; Histories, Barnes' revised; Algebras, Wentworth's; Geometries, Wentworth's; Grammars, E. Reed and Kellogg's two book series; Composition and Rhetoric, Hart's; Physics, Steele's revised; Physiologists, Tracy's; and Penmanship, Spencerian System.[6]

The complete list was given because it might be of interest to know what subjects were considered important at that time.

In December of 1886, C. J. VanMeter and W. E. Williams of Rhome served on a committee to petition the state legislatures to give each county in the State a superintendent. This committee was appointed by the Wise County Teachers' Convention. Despite its success and progress, the teachers were not the best paid workers in the county. In January of 1887 came a note from the *Messenger* that the county still did not have money in the county treasury for the school teachers. Although they were not well paid, there were still requirements made of them that must have taxed the weaker teachers:

> The board of school examiners are not extremely rigid, but hold themselves strictly bound by a code of rules they have laid down for their government. They propose 20 questions upon each branch of study, and will not grant a certificate to an applicant who falls below 50 per cent in any branch, nor if the applicant falls below 75 per cent on general average of the branches required to be passed in the grade of certificate sought.[7]

In 1887 D. R. Becker was the teacher for the Rhome school. In January of 1888 the honor roll was given, listing the following names: Mamie Marshall, Lizzie Crockett, Minnie Fulton, and May Knight. At that same time came good financial news for the teachers. "The county treasurer requests us to inform the teachers that he now has school money to pay out the first and second months' vouchers for the current school year."[8] Sometimes the school year ended because of a lack of funds, and then a subscription school was held, as happened in March 1891. The regular school year closed on March 24, 1891, and the subscription school opened two weeks later. In between semesters, the students were given the opportunity to take penmanship. "Prof.

A. A. Lawson has just closed a ten lesson session in penmanship, and gave the people entire satisfaction, so much so that they proffered to give him another class later on in the summer."9

At the end of the same month came exciting news for Rhome citizens. The idea probably gave rise to the name that was given to North Second Street, running toward the western edge of the town. Many references were made to people buying lots on College Street, and those lots were located on North Second. So the dream of a college for Rhome must have taken root as early as 1891.

> A gentleman from the eastern portion of the state was here a few days ago, and proposed to build and equip a splendid college building for a fine school, if our citizens would promise to give him support commensurate with our ability. The citizens are heartily in favor of it, and we don't think there will be any trouble in meeting his proposition, which is from all we can learn very liberal.10

Apparently, things did not work out, but the progressive attitude of the citizens is evident in the fact that they considered such an undertaking for a community as small as Rhome was at that time.

The public school opened in October, 1891, under favorable prospects. Prof. McGhee of Dallas county was the principal, and the reporter felt that the community would be assured of an A-1 school for that year. Honor rolls were published for 1892 and 1893. The first list contained the following names: Miss Lena Gardner, Miss Mamie Becker, Miss Annie Becker, Miss Katie Gardner, Miss Maggie Morris, Miss Ruth Helm, Miss Maggie Oates with Miss Ivie Helm as the teacher. The next year the following were on the honor roll under the same teacher: Mr. Bill Dewees, Master Virgil Helm, Misses Mamie Becker, Annie Becker, Willie Carpenter, Alice Huff, and Maggie Morris.

In August of 1893, Mrs. Ella Watkins of Decatur had been employed to teach school at Rhome. The next year a new teacher, Mrs. Gladney Short, had taken over the school. By 1895 there was talk of building a new school house for Rhome. "The ladies are getting up an old maid's sale to come off Wednesday, February 20, at the school house. Proceeds to go for the benefit of a new school house. Everyone invited, and all are expecting a big time."11 The ladies were really working toward the fund for the new school. On February 25, 1895, came the report that the old maid's sale was a success. ". . . all the old maids were sold, and everyone had a splendid time."12 The same issue of the paper reported that an elocutionist from St. Paul, Minnesota, had performed in Rhome, giving half of the proceeds to the school house fund. In June of that summer an ice cream supper was reported for the 4th of July, with the proceeds to go toward the school house funds.

The writing school for the summer of 1895 was to be taught by a Mr. J. H. Whitlock of Osage, commencing about July 5th and ending July 15th. The school must have been an attractive place to teach because of the paper reported numerous applicants for the position at Rhome, among them Ben Short of Aurora, G. C. Timmins of Springtown, and Miss Lelia Woodward of Decatur. The school election for trustees was held on the 6th of June, and D. R. Becker, A. A. VanMeter, and H. H. H. Hambright were elected for the following year. Miss Woodward was elected to teach for that year.

The literary society was continuing with success. The Rhome reporter had some fine compliments for the leading members of the group. "John Ward, Elmer Senter, and Ben Hambright are the Clay, Calhoun, and Patrick Henry of the literary society."[13] Rhome apparently could not quite abandon the idea of a college, since the reporter still referred to it in January of 1896. "We had quite a nice Christmas tree at the college on Christmas eve."[14]

In 1896, Miss Annie Bedecarrax from Springtown was the teacher at Rhome school. Finally, in 1897 came the long awaited news of a new building for the Rhome school. "We expect the school house at our place to be completed by the 24th in time for the Xmas tree Christmas Eve. The school will give an entertainment for the benefit of the new school house in the near future."[15] With the growth of the new school came a boom in enrollment for the school. "The public school has commenced, and the number of scholars already matriculated is 75. The enormous cotton crop which has been raised in the vicinity will prevent a good many students from entering until December."[16] In 1899 Rhome again had a new teacher, Mr. H. C. Hazen, and 79 pupils were enrolled in November. On December 25, 1900, the Christmas tree for the community was again held at the school house.

Medicine: Doctors and Druggists

Perhaps it is due to the fact that Rhome is situated on a high, windy hill, but at least we have never had the problem with plagues that our neighbors have endured. In 1886, Fort Worth and Dallas both reported smallpox epidemics. An item from the *Fort Worth Gazette* was quoted in the *Wise County Messenger* of February 27, 1886: "Decatur is sensible. If she quarantines at all, she will quarantine against Dallas and all other towns afflicted with smallpox."[1] Apparently, the epidemic in Fort Worth was not so severe as that in Dallas. "Our grain merchant spent last night in Fort Worth. He says there is no more danger from small pox in Fort Worth than in Rhome."²

On March 27, 1886, the Rhome correspondent filed a story on the healthy condition of the town: "This is certainly a healthy community. In seven months there has not been a single death or serious attack of sickness in the place."³

For several years there were no further reports of illness. Then suddenly there burst on the scene a plague of proportions unreckoned with in the area. The first report in the county came in a report to the *Wise County Messenger* with an Aurora dateline.

> A report of "several deaths and others expected to die," published in the *Dallas News* of the 10th, is calculated to injure this town (Aurora) and the material interests of the people. There has been a death, but no others are "expected to die," and there are no new cases. In a few days, when the excitable portion of our community take a good breath after their run and a calm thought after their excitement, we will have them back here declaring "It was the other fellow" who got scared.⁴

A Rhome reporter sent in the following story on February 20, 1890: "Great excitement reigned in the town of Aurora on Sunday the 9th inst. caused by an alarm of spotted fever. Many people were on the point of moving out."⁵ Doctors from Fort Worth were called in to help attend the ailing citizens of Aurora. On February 26th a report from Fort Worth, quoted in the Wise County Messenger tended to minimize the effects of the epidemic.

> Dr. Broiles received a letter this morning from a physician at Aurora stating that matters are improving. Only one new case is reported, but the physician thinks that three of the patients will die. If so, the total number of deaths will amount to eleven out of sixteen cases. In former reports mention was omitted of cases a mile or so from Aurora. It is said by an Aurora gentleman who was in the city today that the five cases which recovered are in a pitiable condition, some of them disfigured for life. It is said today that the physicians who went to Aurora are not agreed that the malady was cerebro-spinal meningitis.⁶

By March 1st, the doctors of Fort Worth had agreed that the disease was actually cerebro-spinal meningitis.

> The doctors of Fort Worth, who have been in attendance at Aurora, declare the disease at Aurora to be cerebro-spinal men-

ingitis, or spotted fever, as some call it. They say it is an acute infectious disease, sometimes epidemic, but non-contagious.

The outbreak of cerebro-spinal meningitis at Aurora has been checked. Only four deaths reported. The citizens of Decatur and Fort Worth deserve much praise for prompt action in sending nurses and physicians to the suffering village.[7]

From an Aurora reporter came the following report to the next edition of the *Wise County Messenger:*

Our afflicted town is rapidly assuming its usual appearance. Instead of 40 deaths, as read by an acquaintance coming from St. Louis, there have been four among those living here. A fifth death in the town—that of a young man who came here from the Territory. He left here for his home in Tarrant county, but was sent back here because he had a chill when he got to where he lived. There are no new cases and the few sick are convalescent.[8]

As probably will be noted, there was only one report from Rhome. However, in the county it seemed to be the great sport to bait another town if possible. Hence the following story from the Paradise reporter:

"A little malice now and then
Is relished by the best of men."

At least it seems so in the villages of Aurora and Rhome. A Rhome correspondent wrote sometime since that Dr. Beall of Fort Worth had cleaned up the filth and dirt of Aurora; they positively deny the assertion that charged that Aurora compared with Rhome smelt like a cologne bottle to a rotten oyster. The affinity of twin sisters should be united with tenderer cords than these.[9]

The writer was unable to find the story to which the Paradise correspondent refers. The baiting must have worked because on March 26, 1890, the following story was reported from Aurora:

The spotted fever which raged so violently in this little village a few weeks ago, but which has now entirely abated here, has recently broken out in the vicinity of Rhome, and the citizens of that city are greatly alarmed. At the recent illness of Mr. Hambright's son Edgar, not a soul from Rhome would go near him for fear of catching the fever. One of Aurora's citizens went and nursed the suffering young man until he died, which was about twenty-four hours after he was taken sick, then other citizens from Aurora went to the assistance of the afflicted family. This is the first time Aurora has been called on to bury one of Rhome's citizens.[10]

The ire with which the preceding quote was written shows the bitterness which prevailed between the frightened citizens of both towns. Unfortunate as it may seem, the Rhome correspondent filed the following story on April 4, 1890: "Second, would have your readers know that we of Rhome are having very good health, all the rain we need, and a goodly portion of sunshine, which taken together makes us happy and causes all nature to smile around us."[11] Actually, the citizens of Aurora called to Rhome to attend the ill boy were probably the doctors, but tempers flamed over the situation, which was not all caused by the epidemic and its effects. The bitterness engendered by the location of the railroads probably had its share in the general feeling of enmity between the two towns. In addition, the publicity given to the situation added fuel to the fire.

The spotted fever epidemic flared again in the area according to reports from Rhome printed in February of 1891. "Several families who reside at Springtown, about 18 miles from here, and who have relatives in and around our town have come here in order to avoid the spotted fever or spinal meningitis. They report several deaths, and say the people are very much excited over the matter."[12]

Rhome did not have a physician for several years after its beginning. They depended upon the doctors from Aurora to tend their illnesses. For example, the *Texas State Gazeteer and Business Directory of 1890-1891* did not list a doctor for Rhome, but in the 1896-1897 edition, W. J. Dossey was listed as the only physician for Rhome. According to a report in the *Decatur News,* Dr. Dossey of Kentucky had located in Rhome for the practice of medicine.[13] "Dr. W. J. Dossey seems perfectly satisfied with this location; he is getting a good practice here and the people are already thoroughly satisfied; he is well up in his profession."[14] By January of the following year, Dr. Dossey was preparing to build himself an office east of Mr. J. P. Perkin's store. "Dr. Dossey has completed his office and is now ready for business."[15]

Before Dr. Dossey moved to Rhome, Dr. J. D. Burch of Aurora took care of the Rhome citizens during their illnesses. In the years from 1882 to 1896, Dr. Burch cared for so many of the Rhome citizens that they felt he was really one of their own. Many Rhome children were named for him. However, in 1896, Dr. Burch sold his property at Aurora, and moved his family to La Porte, Texas.[16]

As has been mentioned before, the first and only druggist in

Rhome was Mr. Z. B. Bobo, who erected the first drugstore here in June, 1891. Through his kindly interest and assistance, many young men were influenced in their choice of profession. One of the first young men to accept a position in the drug store was Charles Alderson, who came to work about March 22, 1897.

Social Life, Amusements, and Recreation

Before 1900 life in Rhome was not boring, but it was certainly different from that which we expect today. The biggest celebrations seemed to have been the weddings; nevertheless, they managed to find other sources of entertainment, also. One of the first notes in the newspapers to indicate the activities of the citizens was the reference to a performance of a magician: "The legerdemain and sciopticon performance of Prof. Green on last night afforded much amusement for the children."[1] This entertainment was probably given at the school house, since that was the location of most of the activities of the community.

Games were played, from checkers to baseball. Rhome has always been noted for its checker players; however, in these early days, the champion checker player seemed to have been a Decatur player, according to the Rhome reporter. "B. P. Patterson of Decatur, and Wise County's noted checker player, was a visitor in our town yesterday."[2]

One of the activities that our ancestors enjoyed is not available to us in Texas today. At that time horse racing was one of the major sports that occupied one's spare time. Rhome had a race track for some time just east of the Fort Worth and Denver railroad tracks and the depot. The *Wise County Messenger* in 1889 described race tracks in both Decatur and Alvord. In fact, the results of the races in Alvord were quoted by the *Messenger* each week. From the *Messenger* of October, 1889, comes the fact that Decatur had horse races two miles south of town on a race track built there for that purpose.

In the 1890's entertainment became a little more sophisticated. "Hoyt's opera troop has been in town a day or two and showed at the local school house Saturday night."[3] However, physical activities still out-ranked the theater. On February 4, 1895, the Rhome reporter told of exciting activities: "Rhome is still on the move, big snow, and all the people are taking sleigh rides. About fifteen sleighs were in town Tuesday."[4] Fishing and plover hunting were always favorite sports. Bicycling was enjoyed by the younger set. In February and March of 1895 there were stories about new bicycles in town. "Will Gallaspy, Hiram Hambright, and Tom Flynn have been taking in the town on Mr. Gallaspy's new bicycle."[5] "Issac Keele and Tim Mount have been

PHOTO MADE IN front of Dr. J. D. Burch's house in Aurora. Dr. Burch is standing by son Charlie on tricycle. Another son, McAfee Burch is in the wagon. Flora McAfee Burch is standing on the porch. Grandmother Maria Drummond Burch is sitting in the rocker. Uncle Wayland is sitting on the far side of porch.

taking in the country on their new bicycles."⁶

During the summer of 1896, baseball bacame a leading sport for the citizens. It might come as a surprise, but at this time Fort Worth sent its team to play the Rhome nine. "The 4th of July was duly celebrated by the people of Rhome. The firing of anvils, a big picnic, and a baseball game between Fort Worth and Rhome took up the day. The score resulting in 20 to 24 in favor of Fort Worth."⁷ The next week the Rhome club went to Decatur, where they fared even worse. "On Monday the Rhome club came up to Decatur, but the game was rotten. The Rhome boys are nice folks, but they can't play ball a little bit. The score stood 50 to 5 in favor of Decatur."⁸ This loss did not dampen Rhome spirits. Baseball continued to be one of the favorite sports in the community. However, in 1899 a new sport momentarily took the eyes of the Rhome boys, if not the girls.

> The weather is simply beautiful. There was a badger fight pulled off at the Richard and Alderson livery stable Sunday morning. The badger was a large fine one. Mr. Ed Stark, the line repairer for the F. W. & D. C. R.R. Co. pulled the monster from its hiding place, and the dogs nabbed him with the courage of a lioness. Mr. Starks is a native of Iowa, and has only been in Texas for a few days. He said it was the first badger fight he had ever experienced. After the fight, Mr. Sparks went to his room and brought out a box of fine cigars, which were relished by all who participated in the fun.⁹

The community also enjoyed social events with a great relish. Often a wedding party occupied the attention of all the town. One of the very first mentioned in the county papers was that of a Miss Bost. "The young people of our town were highly entertained by Mrs. Perkins, one of our best ladies, on last Wednesday night. She gave an elegant entertainment in honor of Miss Bost, one of our visiting ladies."¹⁰ By the first week in April of that same year, Miss Bost was wed to a Mr. Wilmouth.

> On yesterday 12 o'clock a party of citizens accompanied Mr. Bost, who lives a few miles from town. At half past 3 o'clock, Mr. Wilmouth and Miss Lizzie Bost were united in the bonds of wedlock, Rev. Mr. Evans officiating. The party returned to town where an elegant repast was served at the residence of the groom's father.¹¹

The next wedding which was noted in the newspapers was that of B. C. Rhome, Jr., who married Miss Minnie Rider of Weatherford during the week of September 17, 1892.¹² In 1894 a double wedding ceremony excited the towns people, when two of the Helm girls married. "Mr. Charlie Whitesides and Miss Ruth Helm, Mr. Jess Plumbly and Miss Sallie Helm were married Thursday, August 9, 1894, at 2 o'clock at the residence of Mr. Roe Helm. Quite a number of their friends and relatives witnessed the ceremony, and all join in wishing them much happiness on life's tumultous sea."[13] Shortly after that time in 1894, Mr. Seymour Mount married Miss Kate Browning. "Mr. Seymour Mount, our popular dry goods merchant, and Miss Kate Browning, an accomplished young lady of Copperas Cove, were married at that place November 4, 1894. Their many friends wish them much joy and happiness through life."[14]

Birthdays and parties occupied much of the attention of the young and old. A report from Decatur in 1894 told of the birthday of one of Rhome's octagenerians:

> Mr. William Logan of Rhome celebrated his 80th birthday on Monday, the 8th inst. There was a family reunion, a large number of his children and grand children being present, also Mr. J. T. Day and family. Mr. Logan has resided in that vicinity for 40 years and is a Texas pioneer known throughout West Texas.[15]

Certainly many other birthdays, weddings, and entertainments occupied our ancestors, but these were a matter of newspaper record and as such were chosen for examples of the social life enjoyed in Rhome before 1900. For example, one such party given before the turn of the century was that of the Misses Henderson:

> Miss Willie Carpenter of Fort Worth is visiting the Misses Hambright. Mrs. Hambright presented her daughters with a beautiful piano this week. On Tuesday evening last the Misses Henderson entertained their many friends on Bois'D-Arc Avenue. Those in attendance were Misses Carpenter, Hambright, Morris, Alderson, Shaw, Fairchild, and Wilkerson; Messrs. Hambright, Shaw, Prunty, Hunt, Castle, Leonard, Morris, and Whitesides.[16]

Besides the activities which occupied them in the city of Rhome, they found other sources of entertainment. Fairview was one of the nearby spots where they found enjoyment. "Quite a crowd of young folks went to Fairview last Saturday night to attend a basket supper. They report an exceedingly nice time; the net proceeds amounted to $58.75."[17] On another occasion a group attended a flower carnival in Fort Worth. "Mrs. Fairchild, Miss Laura Davis, Mrs. D. P. Shaw and family, Henderson Reeves, and Hiram Hambright took in the flower carnival in Fort Worth."[18]

Rhome and Politics

Having survived the nationwide economic depression of the early 1870's, the American farmer looked forward to a period of economic recovery. He expected the railroads to help provide a tremendous boost to the economy for the farmers; therefore he supported, even bought stock in, the railroad companies. However, the future was not to be as rosy as it had been predicted to be. As the number of farmers increased, the tremendous production from the farms swamped the markets, and prices that produce could demand fell down and down. By 1893, the grumbling roared louder and louder from the farm sections. From the following report, Rhome was included in the uproar:

> It may be true, but it seems somewhat paradoxical that the demonitization of silver will enhance the prices, and that to cut off one-half the volume of our circulation will cause the remaining half to spread out and make money cheaper than it is now. What our farmers are grumbling about is that it takes too much wheat and too much cotton to buy a dollar, see?"[1]

Texas had been a member of the Solid South since the Civil War, but as has been stated earlier, many of the residents of Texas, particularly the North Texas area were from the North, and their support of the war could have been only half-hearted at best. Thus the word *solid* does not particularly fit. Almost all Texans were Democrats, but some of these Democrats were very conservative in their political thinking. On June 25, 1886, there was a mass meeting of Democrats at Garvin. "B. Morris was chairman of a mass meeting of Democrats held at Pleasant Grove school house on Friday, June 25, 1886. They urged all laboring men to join the Democratic Party."[2] A convention was called by the chairman of the Democratic Executive Committee for July 17th at the courthouse in Decatur.

On July 24, 1886, the convention was called to order by John A. Gordon. B. Morris was elected chairman; and John W. Moore, secretary. In August, the *Wise County Messenger* printed an excerpt from a Fort Worth paper. "B. Morris, Esq., from Wise county, delegate to the Galveston State Convention was in Fort Worth yesterday on his way south. Mr. Morris is a fair specimen of the excellent material that the convention will be made up of."[3]

During October of 1886, commissions were issued to the presiding officers of the general election for that year. Ben Ford was the officer commissioned to hold the election in Rhome. After the election the report of the voting for the Rhome precinct was as follows: Grover Cleveland, 43; Streeter, 6; Benjamin Harrison, 4; and Jim Fisk, 8. Cleveland did not win that election, but there was no doubt about his popularity in the Rhome area. It was a bitter defeat for the farmers of this community.

The next presidential election brought more interest in the governor, apparently, than in the president. James Stephen Hogg was running against George Clark of Waco on the Democratic ticket. The popularity of Hogg in Rhome is shown by the following statement from the *Wise County Messenger:* "A joint discussion was had here last night between Mr. Clay Mack, a Clarkite, and Mr. Tom McMurray of Decatur, a Hoggite. It was very evident to Mr. Mack before the close of the debate that he had struck a regular *Hoggwallow* town."[4]

On June 25, 1892, the *Messenger* carried a quote from the *Dallas News* of June 12, 1892.

> Simpson Bobo, a wealthy farmer residing near Aurora, was here yesterday. He is as angry a man as Texas contains on account of what he terms snap judgment taken by Governor Hogg's friends in calling off the county primaries. Mr. Bobo says that there are any number of Democrats in Wise county who knew nothing about the primaries until the Hoggites had held their caucuses and instructed for their favorite, thus accomplishing an underhanded and unprincipled piece of chicanery which the good people of Wise do not endorse."[5]

The fight must have really become bitter in the area. The *Messenger* warned candidates on October 16, 1892, that they were beginning to print the tickets that week and that if the candidates' names were left off, it would be the candidate's own fault. The next week found another comment from Fort Worth about Simpson Bobo's support of Clark: "Mr. Simpson Bobo of Aurora, Wise county, was in the city today. He says a resolution against Hogg is going on in his section. At the primaries Clark had but six supporters, while now there is a club there of over 100 of his enthusiastic supporters. Governor Throckmorton's speech made many converts among the people, who have the greatest confidence in his leadership."[6] Despite the strong show of support before the election, the results show that lack of support for Clark had not really changed. On November 8, 1892, it was reported that Clark had 5 votes; Hogg, 149, and Nugent, 46.

In 1893 there was not much interest in politics. In fact, in Rhome there seemed to be a general attitude of disillusion.

> There is very little interest among our people in political matters as they are not expecting offices. "Reform is necessary in the civil service." Will the people who did the voting demand that this plank of the democratic platform be rigidly enforced, or was it merely a "catch" to ensnare voters? How is it about one hundred dollars a month which the M.C.'s vote themselves to employ secretaries to assist them in their arduous labors, which consist principally in distributing garden seed, keeping up their fences, and drawing their salaries. We hope the people will speak out and elect the last one of them to stay at home.[7]

The farmers still grumbled about the fact that it took too much wheat and too much cotton to buy a dollar.[8] The Rhome reporter was against some of the actions of other parts of the country in hanging President Cleveland in effigy. His suggestions made much more sense, and were certainly more practical.

> The daily newspapers report from quite a number of places, the hanging in effigy of President Cleveland. This is all wrong. If the people desire to be heard in the present exigency of the county, let them sent monster petitions to Washington demanding free coinage. Let the petitions go forth from every city, village, and hamlet, and if possible send delegations who shall present them, and Congress will certainly be moved by such an overwhelming popular demonstration and even a stoical executive would not be indifferent to their demands.[8]

By August the farmers were still discouraged about their situation and the possibility that the government might not act to help them.

> The news from Washington is quite discouraging. We fear silver is doomed. Our only hope is that United States senate. We hope it may stand like a rock against the demands of the Eastern oligarchy. And then if we only had a president who had the will, the nerve, and the strength to wield the battle axe, with which Jackson clove the helmet of money power.[9]

In November, 1894, came the report that the election was over and that the "pops" had carried Rhome. It was a very quiet election. The reporter said that everything went off nicely.

In 1895 a new interest occupied the county. The silver question was not forgotten, but matters closer at home took their attention. The courthouse at Decatur had burned, and the question arose about moving it to some other location.

> Mr. Burchard and Mashow, from the Dan neighborhood, were here on the 9th inst., talking something like they wanted the Courthouse moved to Alvord. I think the Rhome people, or a majority of them, are for Decatur, provided the Decatur people want it, but they can't find out whether Decatur will donate anything to build it or not. Most of them have the idea that those other competing towns will build the courthouse without cost to them.[10]

Representatives from all the competing towns visited Rhome during the weeks before the election. The reporter stated that the town was full of men from Bridgeport, Alvord, Paradise, and Decatur. Excitement was at a fever pitch in the struggle for the courthouse. When the election results were reported, Rhome had voted with the successful town. The vote ran as follows in the town of Rhome: Decatur, 40; Bridgeport, 11; Alvord, 8, Paradise, 9.

Then it was back to the same old question of the farm prices and free coinage of silver. "Almost everyone in this part of the country are for Bryan and free silver. Politics is the leading topic of conversation."[11] In September of 1899 Ben Morris and W. J. Logan were appointed delegates to the State Industrial Convention in Dallas, to be held on October 20-21 of 1899.

Another question which called for the attention of the Rhome citizens was that of prohibition. With the number of saloons established in Rhome, it was inevitable that the problem would become of intense interest in the town. There may have been earlier movements toward prohibition of the sale of alcoholic beverages in Rhome, but the first mention in the newspapers came in 1887. "D. R. Becker, who lives south of Rhome, came in to see us on Monday, and says his neighborhood is almost solid for prohibition."[12] Within a few days the report of a prohibition election came in the newspapers. Rhome overwhelmingly voted to retain prohibition under the local option law.

> Today the citizens of Wise county voted for and against prohibition. The vote at this voting box (Rhome) is: For prohibition, 38; against, 16. We have had local option for nearly two years, and it is to be decided for the next twelve months. Aurora is 105 for prohibition and 56 against.[13]

By April, the citizens for prohibition really began to work in earnest. "The Prohibition Club organized here on the 19th inst., has another meeting next Tuesday night. Able and logical speakers are booked to be here. The Aurora Club will join to aid, and give interest and enthusiasm."[14] On July 19th, the organization was still functioning. They heard two speakers on prohibition that night in Rhome.

Military Organizations

With the Civil War not far behind them and with world conditions in an unsettled state, it is natural that the young men of Rhome should be concerned with military problems. Mexico and Spain both threatened the peace that had settled over our country. Thus came word of an organization of young men in the area. Since it was certainly a thing that was being done all over the country, Rhome's interest was not unusual. "There is an expression to form a military company between the towns of Aurora and Rhome."[1] Immediately after this report of interest came the actual formation of the company.

> The young men of Rhome and Aurora met last night for the purpose of organizing a military company. Mr. E. W. Williams was called to the chair and Mr. Derryberry was made secretary. The company is to be called the "Wise County Rifles." It was organized with 20 members. As soon as the requisite number is secured and other matters arranged, a petition will be made to the Governor for guns, etc. W. W. Mottis was elected captain; W. E. Williams, 1st lieutenant; J. L. Harper, 2nd lieutenant; J. D. Burch, sergeant; and the Rev. R. Stanfield, chaplain.[2]

Their concern was well-founded because during the next month came a report about armaments being shipped to the Texas border. "Ten gun-carriages have been shipped from New York to San Antonio in the last few days. It begins to look like there will be war with our neighbors over the Rio Grande."[3] A week later came the report that Mexico would back down and that there would be no war with that Republic. This signaled the end of the military interest at the time. The Decatur Rifles died out in February, 1890, and it is likely that the interest in Rhome and Aurora also waned about the same time.

Ten years later, however, their interest in war was not so enthusiastic perhaps, but this time they were called upon to serve in the Spanish-American War. The following report was published about one young man forced to serve in that conflict.

> Mr. Fred Rhode, a very prominent young man of Rhome, returned Tuesday from Santiago, where he has been fighting with Uncle Sam for the cause of justice and humanity. Mr. Rhodes was tendered an informal reception at the residence of Mr. and Mrs. R. I. Stevenson immediately upon his arrival. He is thoroughly disgusted in regard to Cuba. He was in the Santiago

fight, but came out unscratched. When asked to be interviewed by the Messenger correspondent, he declined owing to the fact that he was worn out and needed rest.[4]

Law and Order in Rhome

Crime has never played a major part in the history of Rhome. In face of the crimes that have been committed in Rhome, the people of the town were generally victims rather that perpetrators. Before any fingers are pointed, however, let it be said that at one time or another, almost every family in Rhome, with the possible exception of the ministers and their families, had at least one family member who encountered problems with the law. It was an accepted fact of the times, particularly since the charges were more often than not, disturbing the peace, disturbing public worship, racing a horse on a public road, loud talking, or selling beer on Sunday, actions which do not necessarily call for a court trial today.

The very first mention of crime in connection with Rhome was the night that a Deputy U. S. Marshal spent the night at the hotel in Rhome, accompanied by a mail robber whom he was taking to Graham for trial.[1] The first mention of an actual crime committed in Rhome occurred in 1892.

> Burglars entered the store of Rhome and Ward, and J. E. Neel last night. In J. E. Neel's they got a 6 shooter, two gold watches, one silver watch, several pocket knives, $1.40 in change from the money drawer, and several other articles. Rhome and Ward missed nothing but a little change from the money drawer.[2]

The next crime was more amusing than serious, since it involved only a hat:

> A week or more ago a young man appeared here. He understood something about telegraphy, and being sociable, was becoming quite a favorite. On Friday night be bought a $5.00 hat from Mount Bros. He did not know whether it became him or not. He stepped down to the depot to let the boys say how it became him and "if it suited him" he would return and pay for it. It evidently did not suit, for he has not returned.[3]

More money was involved in the next mention of crime in or near Rhome. Mr. G. G. Ellars was accosted by robbers and relieved of his money and watch.

> On last night about 10 o'clock as Mr. G. G. Ellars was on his way from Aurora to Rhome, he was held up by two highwaymen and relieved of $105—5 $20 bills and one $5 note. They also relieved him of his good watch. He was riding along slowly on his horse when suddenly two men raised up near the roadside with drawn pistols and commanded him to halt and dismount. After dismounting him, they marched him about a quarter of a mile into a pasture from the roadside and went through him. This done, they ordered him to make track toward home and never look back.[4]

On March 27, 1893, a young man was arrested for being drunk in a public place and running his horse through public streets in the town of Rhome. However, there were other people arrested for such things as leaving the carcass of a dead cow in a public highway in Wise county, unlawfully killing domestic birds, failing and refusing to work public roads, and stealing agricultural products, a case which involved the theft of five or six watermelons of a value of $1.00 and was dismissed for want of prosecution.

Another brush with the law concerned the road situation. At that time the nearest road from Rhome to Aurora was through Stephens' pasture. It was a constant concern to farmers that some careless drivers would leave a gate open and allow the cattle to get out. Roads were through pastures and ranch lands rather than being the public highways that we enjoy today. State maintenance was also not one of those pleasures enjoyed during those days. Hence the following story from the *Messenger*:

> The near way through Stephens' pasture to Rhome has again been closed through some care-for-nothing parties leaving the middle gate open and the stock mixed from each pasture; but we've petitioned them to reopen it until our petition to open the nearer cut along the B. W. Stephens' school land line bordering the M. E. & P. R.R. and J. W. Greer's and Foster's homesteads can be acted upon by the honorable Commissioners' court, which we with many others, as the urgency of the case demands. Also several check roads through this community, by the present inconvenienced neighbors, should be studied and will be opened to stay; for this way of traveling eight miles for one, continually soon amounts to more than it's profitable to stand. Just think about it, friends.[5]

Chapter 5

GROWTH OF THE TOWN ——1900 to 1920

For Rhome, the new century dawned bright and prosperous. The little town, having about 125 families, had a population of about 250 persons. In 1902 the *Decatus News* published a short history of the town:

> In the days of old it was said that "all roads lead to Rome" as the political metropolis of the East. So it is today that all roads lead to Rhome, Wise county, Texas, when the homeseeker starts out to find a productive and reliable country in which to make a permanent residence. Particularly has this proven a Mecca to men from the grain raising sections of the north who have found here a vast area of deep, rich prairie soil, which cannot be excelled for wheat, oats, corn, cane, barley, etc. The prairie country continguous to the town in generally a magnificent semi-black waxy soil, covered with a luxuriant growth of the finest and most nutritious grasses until cultivated, when its true worth is known.[1]

Although many of these families have already been mentioned, it seems appropriate to list those who were here at the turn of the century. The following names have been taken from the 1900 United States Census rolls with the addition of a few who perhaps came here shortly after the census was taken:

W. S. Alderson	Ellen Benton	Arthur Blankenship
Thomas W. Anderson	Fred Bowers	Robert Blankenship
Boyd Barker	James Hodges	E. E. Shankles
William Barrett	Silvester Hoffman	F. E. Shanks
John W. Beard	Jeff Huddleston	Drury Shaw
Zachariah B. Bobo	Albert James	Claude Shaw
William W. Bowers	Clay James	George Short
Will Bowman	John W. James	Ben Short
William J. Boydston	Acey Jennings	Martin E. Simpson
Aftie Blankenship	Jim Johnson	Phil M. Smitherman
Tom Brown	William Keele	Robert Stanfield
Will L. Brown	Issac Keele	Charlie Sullivan
Whitt Brown	William Larrson	George W. Sullivan

Charles W. Bryant	Jeff D. Layfield	William A. Taylor
George P. Bryant	Thomas Lee	August Thorell
M. M. Bryant	Tom Leonard	F. H. Thurmond
Jess Bunnell	William Lockridge	John Thurmond
Edgar W. Byers	B. W. Logan	Emily Tilley
D. C. Caldwell	William J. Logan	Henry Troxell
Thomas E. Callahan	Charley Lynch	John Troxell
D. Carpenter	M. McDonald	Joe Troxell
Ed Carpenter	George W. Martin	Abishi Vanmeter
Bud Casey	Charlie Merritt	Caleb J. Vanmeter
G. P. Cherry	Pete Monson	Jacob Vanmeter
Robert Dacus	Benjamin Morris	S. D. Vaughn
James C. Davis	W. W. Morris	George Walker
James Day	Kizzie Mounts	James Ward
Martin Dobbs	Seymour Mounts	H. I. Watkins
William Dossey	Timothy Mounts	John Webb
James Fagan	Jonas Newby	Jeff Weems
Enoch Farrell	Ben F. Oats	Eliza D. West
Henry C. Felts	Marcus T. Oats	John West
William J. Finlayson	James Payne	John White
Jasper Ford	J. R. Purdue	H. Whitesides
William D. Fulton	Noah Reeves	Tom Wilkerson
R. L. Garrett	Elijah Richards	James Williams
Colonel Gilmore	Fred Ritter	Alexander Wilmouth
H. H. H. Hambright	John E. Rives	Sam Wilson
Charley Hamilton	Gus Rodin	William Winters
James H. Hampton	W. J. Rogers	William Wiseman
Albert Harris	Jeff Rogers	Abner Witt
Wiley Harris	William A. Rogers	E. Wright
Corley Hatler	James H. Rowan	William H. Wright
Francis Hatler	Elmer Senter	Jess Yoakum

Merchants and Businesses

The new century found the business people with almost the same problems that they had had in earlier days, but these new decades were to be a period of real growth for the town. Prices of some of the groceries sold in town might be of interest to the reader. In 1899, a pound of tacks brought .05 cents a pound. A can of beans cost .05 cents; 15 pounds of bacon sold for $1.28. Apples were .10 cents a dozen, and a ten-pound roast cost .70 cents. These items were billed to Colonel B. Morris by the W. W. Morris grocery store. Prices did not change much; at the end of this period, porterhouse steak sold at .09 cents a pound.

In August, 1901, W. S. Alderson bought the livery stable which had belonged to Richards and Watkins. In October of the same year,

MR. A. FAIRCHILD, pioneer Rhome blacksmith. The two story building is the Masonic Lodge. The building beside it is the Lyric Theater.

Mr. Alderson took a partner in his business. "W. S. Alderson has sold one-half interest in his livery stable to a Mr. O'Neal. We wish a new firm an abundant success."[2] In July, 1908, Sid Alderson opened a new livery barn. Another livery stable owner was Edward E. Shankles, who operated his business for years before selling out to J. J. Eagan. In 1915 E. E. Shankles moved his real estate business to Fort Worth.[3]

Along with the livery stable business necessarily must come the blacksmith.

No town or community can get along without a blacksmith. Some are good and some are bad. Rhome is fortunate in having a smith who understands his business and has built up a fine patronage by his superior workmanship, as well as his courteous treatment to all. This gentleman is Mr. Neel McEachin. Whatever he does, he does well . . . He strives to give satisfaction.[4]

Rhome had a number of grocery stores during this period. For example, on November 8, 1901, a firm named Morton and Byers were putting in a new stock of groceries in the store building that had recently been vacated by Louis Tilley. Mr. T. J. Weems also owned a grocery store in 1902.

Among the mercantile establishments the New representative visited in Rhome was that of Mr. T. J. Weems who is no novice when it comes to selling goods. He has been at it a number of years—long enough to learn that good goods, low prices, and courteous treatment is the only road to success. Mr. Weems is known by almost every man, woman and child in the south half of Wise county. He moved to Aurora some twenty years ago and has seen his section develop step by step. Mr. Weems has demonstrated his ability to keep up with the procession and is today conducting one of the most extensive establishments in Rhome.[5]

About this time John Dison sold out his interest in the Richards and Dison grocery store to W. S. Alderson, who had been in the livery stable business. C. C. Leonard was also one of Rhome's successful grocery store owners.

The leading grocery store of Rhome is that of Leonard and Co. under the management of that well-known and popular citizen, Mr. Tom Leonard, who has been a citizen of this immediate section for many years. In this store can be found everything that is fresh and nice in the way of staple and fancy groceries. There is no big expense in running the establishment and a little money spent here goes much further than at some other places. The people of this section have found Mr. Leonard to be a man of his word and in every transaction will deal fairly. He holds out no baits, but asks only a living profit . . . The reputation of Rhome as a trading point has been built up and sustained by the pluck and enterprise of her businessmen and this firm has been one of those in the front ranks.[6]

In 1904 it was reported that C. C. Leonard was building a new store

DALLAS LOGAN, a brother of Bud Logan.

building. This building is probably the building which serves as the firehall today. "Mr. C. C. Leonard will commence the construction of a stone building here soon."[7] Mr. Leonard kept his grocery store for about four years. Then in 1908 there was a report of a salvage sale for Mr. T. W. Leonard. "Messrs. Nance and Rector of Decatur have been conducting a salvage sale for T. W. Leonard this past week. Both gentlemen are well experienced in conducting these sales and we understand that the sale at this place has resulted in heavy trade at Leonard's store."[8] It was in 1910 that Mr. E. L. Smitherman opened his grocery store in the same building. "E. L. Smitherman has opened a new grocery store on West Main."[9]

By 1915 Mr. Bill Harmon was putting in groceries and getting ready to open a cafe in the Morris building on South Main.[10] Perhaps

W. W. MORRIS Mercantile and General Merchandise store. Left to Right: Reedy Williams, John Dyson, unknown, Jim Troxell, Ed Smitherman, Claude Shaw, unknown, W. W. Morris, unknown, unknown.

it might be wise to explain the seeming inconsistency in the street names. This writer has come to understand that when one speaks of the town square, they mean the exceptionally wide street that was First Street according to the original town plat. In the first block west of Front Street, stores were referred to as being North Main and South Main, according to which side of the street they were on. Stores in the second block west were referred to as being on West Main Street.

About this time, oil as a fuel, as well as for other purposes came into general use in Rhome. The following use would not be recommended today, but in those hot, dusty days, it served its purpose. "Mr. J. T. Weems had his store floor treated to a good coat of oil which makes it a great improvement."[11] In fact, the writer can recall that in the old red brick school building, the floors were oiled.

Another type of business which was especially successful in Rhome was the general merchandise or mercantile store. Logan Brothers operated one of the most successful stores in the community. Mr. H. I. Watkins and Alvey Rogers were clerks for Logan Brothers.

From 1904 to 1905 the Mount families were in the process of selling out their businesses in Rhome and moving away from the area. In February, 1904, Mr. Seymour H. Mount moved to Hereford, Texas. In April came the following report from Rhome: "Messrs. Emmett Mount and Jim Gill are in the Territory opening a stock of goods for Mount Brothers."[12] Then in 1905 the last of the Mount Brothers left Rhome for the Territory. "Mr. Timothy Mount will move his stock of goods to the Indian territory. G. P. Cherry will occupy the building vacated by him."[13]

In March, 1905, a newcomer from Union Grove arrived in Rhome to engage in the mercantile business. "Grant Ellers, having rented his farm and sold his effects, left for Rhome this morning with the intention of engaging in some kind of mercantile business."[14]

Mr. G. P. Cherry, who had bought the Mount merchandise building, sold out his stock in 1906. "G. P. Cherry has sold his stock of merchandise to a company in Vernon, and they are now moving it to that place."[15] Morris Brothers General Merchandise Company still occupied the old stone building that had been built by B. C. Rhome.

> The wide-awake little city of Rhome is to be complimented upon having such a wide-awake and progressive business man as Mr. Morris. His establishment is one that would be a credit to a much more pretentious city. The house he occupies is substantially built of stone and is about forty by one hundred feet in size and is filled full of heavy and shelf hardware, cutlery, guns, ammunition, tinware, china, and glassware, fine line of heating and cooking stoves, and so neatly arranged that it is a pleasure to look

upon it. In addition, there is a splendidly assorted line of staple and fancy groceries which are fresh and for sale at common sense prices. A line of justly celebrated Mcline wagons are to be found here for the accomodation of the farmers, together with binders, mowers, and all kinds of farm implements. Mr. W. W. Morris, the genial proprietor, is entitled to be called almost a native of Wise county, having lived here about twenty-two years. He has been engaged in the mercantile business for seven years. He is also manager of the lumber yard of A. J. Rowe at this place.[16]

In 1906 there was a report of a change in bookkeepers for the Morris establishment. "G. S. Blackman has resigned his position as bookkeeper for W. W. Morris. H. C. Hazen now occupies his place."[17] The next bookkeeper for the Morris Brothers was James R. Troxell, who worked there until he resigned to become a rural mail carrier in 1914.

In 1915 Miss Nora McCurdy accepted a position with Logan Brothers Mercantile Company; however, by 1917 Logan Brothers was selling out its stock of goods to a Mr. Bogy of Bridgeport. At that time the Citizens Mercantile Company put in a new stock of goods and groceries in the building recently occupied by Logan Brothers. "Miss Nona George has accepted a position with the Mercantile Company."[18]

One of the essential businesses for a community was the meat market. In 1902 the market business was carried on by Marco Hill. "Here is where you can get the kind of meat you call for, it it's in the shop, and the proprietor makes every effort to keep the market supplied with good wholesome meats at all times; and one can depend upon its being fresh."[19] By 1905 two men who had operated meat markets moved to Decatur. "Turner and Scott, our former meat market men, moved last Friday to Decatur, where they have gone into the market business."[20] Richard and Hill had supplied them with ice. Then in 1906, John Frank White built a new ice house for Rhome. Later White sold meats as well as ice. By 1908, the Rhome reporter listed Tom Brown as the owner and proprietor of a meat market. In 1913, the paper stated that Frank White had sold his meat market to Palmer Brothers and would likely move to Fort Worth. An advertisement in the *Decatur News* in 1915 had the Palmer Brothers offering meats, bread, and groceries, as well as barber work, cleaning and pressing, and fitting of new suits.

At different times during these two decades, many other businessmen operated in the community. For example, in 1901 it was reported that E. W. Byars had bought a washing machine business, and that a Bink Sherwood was also here in the washing machine business. There was one unusual item that this author was unable to interpret, although it does sound interesting: "Some crows only build nests for themselves and mates, but the Boyd Crow has recently completed a nest in Rhome for John Kennedy, and Mr. Kennedy has opened up a stock of goods."[21]

A report in 1901 brought news of construction under way in Rhome. "The prospects for a wheat crop are much better than anticipated. Rhome is steadily on the improve. Rumor says that there is to be another fine residence erected in the very near future that will exceed anything yet in our city. The supposition is that it is to be another hotel."[22] This hotel is probably the one which was directly across the street north from the Cottage Hotel, owned by the Hambrights. In later years this second hotel was known as the Davis Hotel, operated by Mary Frances Cates Davis, wife of the Constable, John Davis. It was probably built by a Mr. Worley, since he was referred to as "the hotel man" in a 1909 quote in the *Decatur News*. "Mr. Worley, the hotel man, has bought out I. T. Sandifer's grocery store and is selling goods right along."[23]

A good description of the Cottage Hotel was given in the *Decatur News* in 1902:

> While visiting Rhome recently, the News representative had the plesure of stopping at the hotel kept by that well-known and excellent lady, Mrs. H. H. Hambright, and we recall the visit with a fond memory. The house has been maintained about ten years, and by reason of the excellent service, splendid table fare, and cordiality of the hostess, has become one of the most popular hostelries on the Denver road. Nothing is too good for the tired and hungry guest who stops beneath the hospitable roof of Mrs. Hambright, and all the comforts of home are to be found here. Old-time hospitality, coupled with all modern accomodations, are found here, and the traveler finds real pleasure in stopping here. We can recommend the house to everyone.[24]

Among the businesses which catered to personal grooming and improvement of looks was the barber shop. One of the first barbershops was operated by a Mr. Charles Alexander in 1908. In 1902 there had been a barber who established his shop in what was then called the postoffice building. This building was probably the building that was used on the south side of Main Street. In 1915 there were advertisements for George O. Palmer and Joe H. Brown, a barber who remained in Rhome until his untimely death in the 1930's. An advertisement from the 1915 issue of the *Decatur News* described the establishment of Mr. Brown as follows: "The Palace of Comfort, Good cigars, Fancy candies, Fountain drinks, Hot or cold baths, Hair cuts and Shaves. We work to please you. J. H. Brown and Co., Rhome, Texas."[25] This writer remembers with special pleasure the cool

RHOME'S FIRST HOTEL, which was owned by Judge H. H. H. Hambright. It occupied the location where the Harvey Grocery stands today.

darkness of the ice cream parlor, the wrought iron chairs, and the delicious Eskimo pies with chocolate that did not taste waxy as it does today! "Tom Sparks is now employed as soda fountain dispenser at the Palace of Sweets."[26] Another barber came into Rhome in 1916. "Mr. Louderdale and family from Floydada, Texas, have moved to Rhome. Mr. Louderdale is to barber with Mr. Palmer on the south side of the Meridian Highway."[27]

Another phase of personal grooming was the millinery business. Many different ladies engaged in this profitable service. After the earlier mentioned milliner, Miss Keele, there was Mrs. M. F. Cates Davis in 1905. A notice in a Rhome newspaper, the *Light,* reported that Mrs. Davis had just returned from Dallas, where she had been in the interest of her millinery business at Rhome. In 1908 there was an advertisement in the *Wise County Messenger* that more fully described Mrs. Davis' establishment:

> . . . I will also open a new and complete line of millinery at Rhome, Texas, September 1st. I will have many great bargains to show the trade and hope you will not fail to avail yourselves of them . . . I have an experienced trimmer who will give you courteous attention.[28]

The writer was unable to obtain the name of this trimmer. In 1909, Mr. and Mrs. John Davis moved their establishment to Alvord. Rhome was not to be without a milliner for long, however. "Mmes. Dickson and Oates of Wichita Falls have put in an up-to-date stock of millinery goods in the Hambright building on East Main Street."[29]

At times it seems as though the reporter for Rhome wrote stories about prospective businesses for the town simply because he hoped the suggestion might bring in new growth. "There is talk of a big furniture establishment being put in Rhome. Let 'er come. We need it and we are in for it, too. This is a good place for one—no better could be found."[30] A short time later we find the reporter dreaming again. "A large drug firm in Fort Worth is figuring on putting in a large drug business in Rhome."[31]

On the 25th of August, 1916, there was a report of a new event for Rhome that is the basis for an old family story among the Morris family. "Over a hundred men are working on the pipeline running from Electra to Fort Worth, which makes Rhome a lucky place."[32] Colonel Benjamin Morris was so determined that Rhome needed natural gas that he spent quite some time sitting in his pasture west of town with his shotgun, insisting that the pipeline had to connect to the city of Rhome if the company intended to put it through his land.

Rhome did, indeed, receive gas from the line, making the city an even nicer place to live than before. "The Lone Star Gas Pipe Line people have moved their pipe from Rhome and have distributed it on the right-of-way three-quarters of a mile west of town. Rhome is to be supplied with natural gas soon."[33]

Manufacturing Interests

The new roller mill for Rhome was fast taking shape early in 1900. "Mount Brothers are fast having the rock quarried to build a new mill at the old site at Rhome to grind the big crops expected in the future and now, if the people would only build the talked-of factory to manufacture our cotton, we'll still feel the more 'in it', and we hope they may."[1] By June the *Decatur News* reported that part of the machinery for the new flour mill had been received and was being put in. Things progressed swiftly after that, for by October came the report that the mill was functioning properly. "The roller mill is running day and night and turning out a good grade of flour."[2] Things must have really gone well for the new operators because in April there came from the Newark reporter the fact that the Mounts were enlarging the capacity of their mill to meet their orders. There was a retraction of this statement about a month later, however. "Rhome is still improving and quite a painting has taken place at Rhome recently. If you dwell at Rhome now, you have to do as it does. I'm sorry I was led to write that Mount Brothers had enlarged their mill capacity, when Seymour informs me that they only added some more machinery. They, as we, are not inclined for a water boom; so we correct it."[3] It was during this time that Mount Brothers were getting ready to convert to oil for fuel at their mill instead of wood or coal. The *Decatur News* carried on account of the roller mill in 1902.

> Rhome can boast one of the best flouring mills in the state and its reputation is spreading abroad every day. It has been running two years, and is owned by Mount Bros., men who have been identified with this section for many years. They were for a long while engaged in the mercantile business, but realizing the demand for a first class mill in this excellent wheat region, they built the Rhome Mill and elevator two years ago. The proprietors never contemplated anything but a first class establishment, so installed in the new plant the best machinery that money could buy. It is equipped with the best Plansifter system and all modern appliances that go toward getting a good sample of flour. Solely because of the superior quality of its product this mill has invaded the territory of competitors and has a constant demand

for flour. The capacity is 150 barrels per day and has plenty of storage capacity for grain, consequently is enabled to run all the year around. The News is pleased to state that this is one of the most important institutions of the Prairie City.[4]

During the winter of 1903, the mill changed hands again. This time it was bought from the Mounts by L. W. Renshaw, Mrs. L. W. (Virgie Bobo) Renshaw said that the family still lived in Boyd at that time. They had two shifts running at the mill, and because they were busy day and night, Mr. Renshaw often slept on a bag of wheat in the mill during the hard work. Mr. Renshaw had partners in the mill, or at least there were others who owned stock in the mill. Among them were a Mr. Malone, Steve Lillard, and others. The next spring, work started on a new grain elevator for the mill. "Excavation for the new grain elevator has begun; it is to be constructed principally of steel, and will have a storage capacity of about 85,000 bushels. This will be another valuable addition to our city."[5] By May of the same year, it was reported that the mill had again increased its capacity. "Everything at Rhome is lively now. Two wheat elevators are going up, giving employment to a large force of men . . . The Rhome Milling Company are increasing the capacity of their plant at this place from 150 to 200 bushels per day, and with elevator capacity of 100,000 bushels, they expect to be able to supply a greater part of Texas with a splendid quality of high patent flour."[6] These steel elevators are probably the elevators which are still standing at the old mill today. Except for installation of a new boiler in June of 1906, there was little news of the mill until 1912. The company was certainly growing. "The Rhome Mill Company contemplates purchasing a 5-ton motor truck. The company's elevator at Newark necessitates so much hauling between here and Newark a motor will be a great advantage to them."[7] Rhome had many different millers as well as salesmen, among whom were Jim Malone, W. T. Leonard, F. E. Shanks, Mr. Stone, and S. F. Larson. The Rhome Mill grew and prospered exceedingly during these years. "The Rhome Milling Company leads when it comes to market. There is no place in the whole country that will pay you so well for what you have, let it be anything—hogs, cotton, cottonseed, wheat, oats, corn, etc. They lead the list."[8]

The milling business was not the only manufacturing concern that was growing. The gin owners were getting their share of the profits, also. The Byers Compress, which probably belonged to Edgar Byers, had brought an innovation in cotton ginning. They were testing the new round bale press in July, 1901.

> The Byers Round Bale Company made their final test last week. They put up three very neat bales of cotton, and they are very proud of their success. They think that they have made a perfect success. The bales weigh from 250 to 300 pounds and are a perfectly solid mass of cotton, there being no core at all. They claim this a very important feature in their favor, as other round bale presses have a core of iron which must be taken out of each bale. The press being automatic, it does not require anyone to work or adjust any part while running. These bales range from 17 to 19 inches in diameter by 36 inches in length. "I forgot to state above, that our genial young townsman, Mr. Edgar Byers, is the sole inventor of the round bale press."[9]

Somehow, this invention must not have been a complete success, since there was a notice in the *Messenger* in September that Mr. Byers had bought another business: "Mr. E. W. Byers has bought a washing machine business. We hope he will have a splendid success."[10]

Roe Helm's gins were having other competition, also. By 1902 W. M. Stephens had built a new gin in Rhome.

> W. M. Stephens' gin is now in full blast and its facilities enable it to "keep up with the procession" and patrons do not have to wait long for their turn. The gin is provided with every convenience and with good machinery operated by experienced hands a splendid sample is the result. You drive up under the suction pipes and the machinery does the rest while you drive a few steps to get your seed, then a few feet more and your bale is dumped into your wagon. The gin has a capacity of forty bales a day, and if our readers patronize Mr. Stephens, they can rest assured that they will be kindly treated and will get a No. 1 turnout. Mr. Stephens is a reliable gentleman, and the News can guarantee satisfaction to all who take their cotton to him to be baled up.[11]

In 1905 there was a report about a cooperative ginning enterprise developing in Rhome. "The citizens of Rhome are taking active measures in erecting a company gin at this place."[12] This competition continued with the report that L. W. Renshaw was building a cotton gin in addition to his milling business.

> Mr. L. W. Renshaw this week purchased the Baptist parsonage property adjoining his commodious flouring mill, which he will use for the building of a new gin house. The erection will begin at an early date, and all machinery and everything to complete the large and up-to-date gin will be in readiness before the next ginning season.[13]

In April, 1906, there was another report about the new gin for the Rhome Milling Company: "Rhome's New Gin—Rock is being hauled for the new gin house and the erection will begin as soon as sufficient rock is put on the ground. The house will be a stone building and the best in this part, and equal to the one at Bridgeport."[14] Unless a later gin was rebuilt on the old site, the plans for a rock gin did not develop fully. The old building which was there was a metal building. However, a report in May, 1906, stated that the rock walls for the gin house were about three feet high and that the work was being pushed rapidly. In October, 1908, the *Messenger* stated that the gin in Rhome had put up 100 bales of cotton and was running two full crews day and night. There were no further reports about the gins until 1916 when it was noted that a Mr. Will Hardin from Oklahoma had taken a position as ginner for the Rhome Milling Company.

Whereas, the Rhome gins and flouring mill were roaring successes, the Rhome creamery project was a dismal flop. For several years prior to the building of the Rhome creamery, which was a cooperative venture of the farmers and businessmen in the community, the county newspapers carried running commentary through excerpts from agricultural magazines about how great the need was for creameries in Texas. There were meetings and discussion groups urging the building of creameries. For example, the following is an excerpt from *The Decatur News*:

> Invitations to address an assembly of farmers next Saturday on details and essentials of the dairy business today were mailed to prominent creamery men of the State, and if same are accepted, this new phase of farming will get its first general impetus at that time in this community. Should no success be attained in getting a speaker for next Saturday, the effort will be renewed, according to the promoters of the idea, until the susceptible and waiting minds of the farmers are supplied with the information.[15]

In the fall of the same year there appeared a discussion on creameries which could not fail to interest the farmers who owned cattle. It rather subtly suggests to the man that Rhome could support a herd of two to three hundred cows.

> A creamery completely equipped for the manufacture of butter will cost from $2000 to $3000 and the expense of operating will amount to about $1500 per year. In order to keep up the equipment and to maintain itself a creamery should have the cream from at least 250 cows every day in the year. It is also well

> to have this number of cows distributed among as great a number of farmers as possible, and if they can be interested in the business, they will increase their herds every year . . .[16]

The preceding excerpt was taken from the *Agricultural Bulletin*. From the excessive amount of space over a period of two years that was devoted to promoting the idea of creameries, it must be suspected that someone had something to gain besides the farmers and businessmen who were to provide the money for the experiment.

On March 10, 1911, there was an article urging the Decatur people to subscribe a sum of $1000. The promoter suggested that this was merely to secure home endorsement and patronage of a Decatur creamery. "He has already established a market for his products, is a splendid businessman and hustler, and is skilled in the business and it would be a seemly thing for this community to take hold at once and land this enterprise."[17] To the writer one word in the last quote seems to describe the entire situation. The man was a hustler, and he must have had a little bit of the silver-tongued orator in him, for he certainly sold his idea to Rhome. Apparently, he missed the chance to set up a creamery in Decatur, but the farmers of Rhome were certainly taken by the idea of this form of investment.

> Mr. J. J. Miller of Kansas City, has sold, for a Chicago firm, machinery for a creamery in Rhome. The people have subscribed $3,900 worth of stock and the contract has been signed up, the ground bought and deeded to the company, and the buildings are under construction. This will be a great addition to the town of Rhome. The stockmen and farmers are given credit for this valuable addition to the city, as they are the people who subscribed most of the stock.[18]

Mrs. Ina Thurmond of the Fairview community was the first to call the attention of this writer to the fraud that was perpetrated on the citizens of the area. She said that the farmers all around the country bought cows and prepared to enjoy the profits of their investment. Only one batch of butter was made. It did not sell, and the entire scheme fell through. Possibly where the investors had made their mistake was in failing to realize the possibility of having to store the butter. Without facilities to keep the butter fresh, they lost money.

The youngsters of Rhome will remember playing in the empty building around the huge vats that were used to make the butter. The foundations remained in place for many years, a bittersweet memory of the grand mistake.

Agricultural Interests

Rhome has always been a farming community, and in the early 1900's, it was a truly booming farm town. The farmers and ranchers raised many different breeds of cattle. "Mr. B. C. Rhome carried about thirty head of fine Hereford cattle to the fat stock show at Fort Worth. After the show is over, the herd will be divided and part will be brought back to the ranch while the others will be taken to El Paso, where they will be shown during the state cattlemen's association. Mr. J. T. Day also carried a bunch of short horn Durhams."[1] In 1904, J. T. Day, D. C. Caldwell, and William Wright all drove or shipped their cattle to Fort Worth in March. That same month a load of hogs was shipped to Fort Worth. "Ike Richardson shipped a car load of fine hogs to Fort Worth packing house today."[2]

In 1906, there was a report of a fine stallion for sale in Rhome. "A big, black, sleek Percheron stallion has been on exhibition on our streets for the past four or five days. The price asked is $3,600, but no buyer has yet been found."[3] The author was unable to determine whether or not the horse was sold in Rhome, but certainly there were other valuable horses belonging to Rhome's ranchers, according to an unfortunate happening. "A valuable horse belonging to Tom Stevens broke its neck several days ago by falling into an uncovered well."[4] During that same year J. M. Scott and Logan Brothers shipped two or three car loads of fine yearlings to Fort Worth.

In 1909 cattle were shipped to the northern part of the country. "Thirteen carloads of cattle were shipped from here to Kansas City Tuesday, and were accompanied by Archie Van Meter, Sam Renshaw, Joe Helm, and Bob Hudson."[5] In 1917 it was reported that ranchers from Rhome were buying cattle in South Texas to ship to their ranches here. "Dr. Henry Trigg and Joe Day are home from South Texas where they bought several hundred head of cattle and sheep and will have them shipped to their ranch near Rhome."[6] L. W. Renshaw shipped a car load of hogs to Fort Worth in 1916.

Despite the thriving business in livestock, there were setbacks. "Messrs. W. J. Logan and Bob Hudson lost about twenty-five head of horses on their ranch near Newark last week. The horses licked the boxes which had contained a preparation for making a dip for stock and died immediately."[7] Another jeopardy for cattle was the Fort Worth and Denver City railway. Reports that cattle or hogs had been killed on the tracks were frequent. "Mr. C. H. Hiett, claim agent for the Fort Worth and Denver Railway is here this week on business. Mr. Hiett says he has twenty claims for adjustment on livestock to this one place. The F. W. and D. C. has been killing lots of stock of late. Last week they killed one fine cow for Mr. Horton and several hogs for Mr. Morris."[8]

Another hazard to stock raising became so persistent over all of Wise county that in 1904, the *Messenger* devoted several columns to a discussion of the problem.

> The most tormenting condition that the farmers of Wise county are compelled to endure in these days of gentle civilization is the ravages of that heinous animal—the wolf. In certain communities the depredations upon roving flocks of turkeys, the fowls of the barnyard, and the young pigs have reached such an alarming condition that the citizens have been moved to supplicate the county government for protection from the harrowing and destroying pest. Every section of the county outside the town lots and streets is at all times exposed and menaced, and it is only by resorting to troublesome and expensive devices that the ravages do not increase a hundred-fold. In a year's time the expense of feeding a pack of hounds, whose sole duty is to sleep in day time and bark the wolves away at night, amounts to considerable drain upon the resources of any small farmer renters, who are hardly able to feed their families, much less a pack of hungry and yelping hounds.
>
> Again it is touching the very pinnacle of discouragement for a family to leave home for church or a day's neighborly visit to return and find they had entertained a wolf unawares during their absence and provided for his gustatory entertainment the choicest specimens of their flocks or pigs of the pen . . . The county government should find its excuse for action in this matter![9]

What action, if any, the county took is unknown, but the problem did not go away because in 1915 there were still reports of wolves preying on cattle, just as there are today. "Tol Caldwell, A. C. Alexander, I. T. Green, O. H. Barker, and several others on a big wolf hunt last Tuesday night were successful in getting one of the loaf wolves which has been in Newark country for some years."[10]

Wheat was still the big source of income for the Rhome farmers. Corn and cotton were not so extensively grown in Rhome as was wheat. There was mention in 1904 of the sowing of millet since the wheat had been cut. C. J. VanMeter brought in an unusual product in December, 1915. "C. J. VanMeter brought in from his farm Tuesday, three miles northeast of town, several bushels of fine, large Irish potatoes and sold them to our merchants for a good price. These potatoes are from vines that came up voluntarily since last August."[11]

With wheat the big crop for Rhome, it was not unusual for the farmers to import threshers from other communities when the big crops were ready for harvest. "There was a thresher and engine from Mansfield unloaded here the first of the week to help thresh the big wheat fields around Rhome . . . The pretty favorable weather of the past week is ample reason to believe that much wheat has been knocked out of the hulls. Today, in looking over the prairie farms in the northwest round to the south, we counted the smokes from eight or ten thresher engines, not over one to six miles away."[12] The next jubilant report from Rhome came in April of 1910 when it was reported that the farmers were all elated with the prospects of the coming crop. "One steel separator has already been unloaded at this place and four cars of coal ordered for threshing the wheat. The outlook is good for plenty to eat in Rhome country this year."[13] Another boom year for Rhome's wheat farmers was 1915. It was estimated that there were 150,000 bushels of wheat stored away in the granaries where they were being held for better prices. That was also the year when the first mention was made of gasoline tractors being sold in Rhome.

On July 13, 1906, the *Light* reported that there were three gasoline engines in full operation daily at Rhome, not over fifty feet apart. One was at the elevator, elevating wheat, and two others were just across the railroad attached to the drill machinery, drilling the Denver road's new deep well.

> A carload of new gas tractor engines were unloaded here this week and sold to farmers of this community to be used in furnishing power for plowing wheat stubble land.
>
> Quite a revolution in farm tractors has taken place in this section in recent years. Nearly all farm implements and machinery, including self-binders, mowers, plows, etc., being drawn or propelled by gas motors; horses and mules being almost eliminated by the larger farms.[14]

By June of 1916 there was a distributing agent right here in Rhome for Ford tractors. "M. T. Oates and Co. of Rhome are distributing agents for the Ford Tractor in Wise and Denton counties and will demonstrate the tractor in Decatur in a few days. A cordial invitation is extended to everybody to come and see this famous tractor in action."[15] In 1918, with war conditions on the mind of every one, there was a long article about a meeting of the Wise county threshermen, urging them to handle their machinery well and to save every grain of wheat possible by cutting at the right time and storing it properly.[16]

During this period there were several reports of cotton farming in the community, but the earlier expectations of the farmers for cotton were not fulfilled. Wheat had displaced cotton to a great extent. In October of 1907 it was reported that the ginners expected to gin between 1000 and 1500 bales of cotton. Most reports showed that the hot dry weather and rain at the wrong time had hurt the cotton crop. "Reports from different sections of the Rhome country indicate that the three-inch rain Sunday and Sunday night did great damage to the cotton crop. Farmers report that all their open cotton is lost and many stalks are lying flat on the ground. The rain was beneficial to the wheat and oats."[17]

Natural Resources

Rhome has never been especially noted for its natural resources. Water has been a commodity without which the town could not exist. By 1908 Rhome citizens were concerned about the water supply; hence the following report:

> W. W. Morris has leased one of the old abandoned wells from the Fort Worth and Denver, and is erecting a large tank. He will install a gasoline engine and will arrange to supply the town with good, pure, wholesome mineral water. The probabilities are that a large pavilion will be erected soon and Rhome will become one of the greatest health resorts in the nation. The water has been analyzed and found to contain very valuable mineral properties.[1]

Apparently these dreams of the reporter and the developer of the well did not come true, since Rhome did not become a resort area. In fact, at the end of that particular month there was a report of a water famine. "The past week has been one of extreme heat with little wind to temper the vertical rays of the sun. This condition in conjunction with a water famine has hampered the populace considerably. The wind is blowing today and the windmills are running full time, thus insuring an abundance of water."[2] One year later another well with a gasoline engine was planned for the business district. "Mr. Frank Griner is digging a well on his lot back of his store building. With the aid of a gasoline engine he will furnish the business part of town with water."[3]

In August of 1908 another water well brought new excitement to Rhome. On the strength of earlier reports about the well, a stock company was organized at Rhome for the purpose of boring for oil.

> It has been learned through Lube Nichols of Fort Worth, who is fostering the scheme, that a five year lease has been obtained on several acres of land lying almost in the heart of Rhome and upon which there are unquestionable evidences of oil. In 1890 the Fort Worth and Denver Railway company bored a well near the above mentioned land and struck a flow of oil at a depth of 1,300 feet. They were digging for artesian water, but when the oil was struck, the well was filled up and nothing more done with it. When the strike was first made, oil flowed freely for miles, eventually finding its way to Elizabeth Creek, four to five miles southeast of Rhome. The people who once saw crude oil flowing directly through the center of town have often wondered why this field has not long ago been developed. Mr. Nichols declares that he will have a well drilling outfit at work in the field in a very few days, or just as soon as the company is organized and arrangements thoroughly perfected.[4]

On July 6, 1906, Contractor J. M. Scott had been drilling another new well for the Denver road. A report in the Rhome newspaper, the *Light,* reported that the new well had been sabotaged. "Contractor J. M. Scott for the Denver's deep well has now drilled about 96 feet. He had up to last week drilled about 160 feet in another well, the drill failed to work and it was found that a large piece of iron had been dropped in the well by an unknown person and a new well had to be started."[5] Apparently the second well succeeded without further ado. The sabotuer was never discovered, and today it is left for one to wonder why anyone objected to having an oil well in Rhome. There was no further news about the stock company; thus the writer must suppose that the plan failed.

Further interest in oil for Rhome continued, however. In 1915 there was another report in the *Messenger:*

> It has been supposed for years that oil could be had at Rhome. If they would go after it, a number of geologists have investigated this matter and now believe we are within about 2000 feet of it. To have this oil reached and brought to the surface for absolute proof, about 12,000 acres of land was leased at a sacrifice by the owner. $20,000 will be spent in the next few days in sinking two wells 2000 feet each.[6]

There was a further report on the company early in 1916. "The prospects for oil business in this county are not any better than they ever have been to the public, but the company who has been working in this behalf for some time, surely see something, or else they are wild catting on a mighty big scale. When any company or individual sees fit to invest several thousand dollars, there is usually something at the other end of the line."⁷

Transportation and Communication

The new century brought about many changes in the life of Rhome's citizens. The railroad and the telegraph system continued in growth, but there were other new developments in the form of the telephone and the automobile, for which the highways were developed.

In 1902 there was great interest in the new railroad planned for Rhome. The reporter who called himself "Scribbler" had trouble in getting information, but the gossip about the new line continued. In 1906 an article from the Rhome newspaper called the *Light* answered some of the questions.

> Surveyors were in Rhome last Saturday who surveyed a plot beyond the switches of the Denver road in the south part of town on the old Dallas grade. We could get no inside information, while it is supposed by some that the survey is for the Denver road; that two more large wells for an extra pump station, which the Denver has been figuring on for some time, may be sunk; others believe that the Dallas branch will soon be built through Rhome. Rumor has it that all material for the building of this branch has been purchased. We cannot vouch for the truthfulness of these rumors, but something is going to be done in the near future.¹

In February of this same year Walter Bellah, who had been depot agent for Rhome, accepted a position at Decatur and his position in Rhome was filled by a Mr. Daugherty of Memphis, Texas.

This writer has been unable to locate the exact date for the building of the section house at Rhome, but the first mention of it came in a notice about a case of smallpox in 1901. Then again in 1906, it was reported in the *Light* that the section crew from Rhome was called upon to work on a wrecked freight train near Fort Worth on the Denver Road. In February, 1906, there was an announcement in the *Light* that the Denver had put in drain boxes around the depot, an act which made traveling much easier on the passengers arriving or leaving Rhome. In March of the same year the section crew began work on the railroad proper. "The railroad crew, consisting of a large number of workmen, who are repairing all the bad places on the Denver road, were here the first of this week. They pulled up nearly all of the old steel rails and ties on the switches and replaced them with new ones."²

During the summer of 1906 the Fort Worth and Denver railroad began to make plans for a new well for the railroad. In fact, they were beginning extensive improvements at Rhome. "Contractor Williams is here with his teams for the purpose of lengthening the side tracks at this place and grading for the 'Y'. They will make their passing track long enough to hold fifty more cars! They expect to be here about three weeks."[3]

In May Contractor John Scott had his well machinery on the ground ready to begin drilling the new well. Then came trouble for the driller. "Contractor John Scott for the Denver's deep well . . . found that a large piece of iron had been dropped into the well by some unknown person, and a new well had to be started."[4]

The work on the Y switch was progressing well. "The Denver road has purchased four acres of land from Colonel B. Morris near the Rhome Mill, paying $700 for the whole. The land will be used for the Y switch."[5] Two men from Fort Worth, S. N. Mayfield and R. V. Griffin, were surveying for the switch that was to be built.

On July 13th the *Light* gave a report of unusual activity around Rhome. "There are three gasoline engines in full operation daily in Rhome, not over fifty feet apart. One at the elevator, elevating wheat, and two just across the railroad attached to the drill machinery, drilling the Denver road's deep well."[6] In August of 1906 the company was tearing away the old cotton platform and building a new one. This was just another improvement in their service for the town of Rhome.

February, 1908, brought the announcement of reconstruction of the Fort Worth and Denver City railway.

> Today was pay day with the employees of the Fort Worth and Denver City railway at Rhome. Something like 200 men were at the station early this morning to receive their monthly stipend. The men who were paid off are engaged in the entire reconstruction of the Denver road. The work is advancing very fast and the reconstruction gang is now within three and one-half miles of Rhome. The entire dump has been widened and ballast rock is being laid from six to twelve inches deep. New ties are being used throughout.[7]

Many accidents happened along the Fort Worth and Denver, but one of the most terrifying involved two prominent young Rhome ladies.

> Sunday evening at 1:30 Miss Lizzie Caldwell and Miss Lizzie Reeves while going to the latter's home, three miles north of this place in a single buggy were struck by a light engine on the Fort

Worth and Denver railroad, and both were thrown from their buggy and seriously injured. Miss Caldwell is probably fatally hurt. She has been unconscious since the accident. The point at which the dirt road intersects the railroad is a very dangerous place, being in a deep cut, thus rendering it impossible to see a train until one is on the tracks. The light engine was the second of No. 20 and was following the first section very closely. After the first section passed, the young ladies drove onto the track and their attention being drawn by the reason of the train just passed, they did not think of looking out for another train. The engine was running about fifteen miles an hour at the time it struck the buggy. The buggy was demolished and the horse was thrown over a fence, but was not hurt very much. Dr. Bacon Saunders of Fort Worth was telegraphed for and came on the first train. It is thought that Miss Caldwell will not recover.[8]

Miss Caldwell did recover from the accident and lived with her family on the Caldwell place near where the accident occurred until her marriage to Mr. Tom Leonard.

A second accident occurred at Rhome in 1919, again involving two trains.

Six passengers were hurt, one seriously, when the engine of one train on the F. W. & D. crashed into another train in the yards at Rhome during the fog Thursday morning . . . A Pullman car was wrecked in the Rhome collision. Passengers were thrown from their berths into the aisle. This train was standing still when the second section of it rammed it from the side coming in on a switch . . . The F. W. & D. had surgeons and ambulances at the passenger station in Fort Worth to meet the wounded.[9]

The railroad was not the only means of transit for the citizens of Rhome. With the advent of the automobile at the beginning of this period, the demand for improved roads grew.

We would like to second the motion of the other scribes in favor of better roads. Let us keep up the agitation until our commissioners court submits the special tax question to a vote. Then, if we are not wonderfully mistaken, we will have better roads. There is no good reason for the question to be under discussion so long if our citizens would only act. And then if our commissioners still refuse to submit the matter, we will come pretty near knowing when to cast our votes for when another election comes around.

> Another feature in the working of the roads that should be seriously considered in justice to all concerned: that is, a disposition on the part of some commissioners in the not so very remote past worked a few roads leading from the county seat to their own immediate vicinity, and in some instances to their own immediate vicinity, and in some instances to their own door. But if we worked the roads by taxation we would be pretty apt to have road supervisors that would give justice to all concerned.
>
> We believe that Dallas' good roads convention is a good thing if the delegates who have been appointed will attend. But we have already heard the Rhome delegate to say that he would not attend. So if those who are entrusted with the business fail to act, what can we hope for?[10]

Numerous such complaints on the road situation were made including a letter from "Uncle John" to "Uncle Ned" published in the *Messenger* on January 15, 1906, in which Uncle John voiced just such complaints as the aforementioned.

However, complaints were not the only step that was made. Without any doubt, the Uncle John just mentioned was J. F. Thurmond, who took it upon himself to do something constructive about the road situation.

> J. F. Thurmond is the first to lead the procession. He came in from his farm Monday morning in an old-style fashion—driving four large mules and riding the off wheel one, dragging a sure enough split log drag over the public road. Though the road was cloddy, dry, and crusty, it did fair work. Mr. Thurmond tried the drag on our streets to show how it would work.[11]

This same work was continued by the Fairview citizens during that month:

> In the Troxell and Thurmond neighborhoods the farmers are taking quite an interest in the welfare of the public roads. Since the last rains and nearly all the first of this week they have been dragging the roads as far this way as M. T. Oates' farm. Since J. F. Thurmond made some experiments with the split log drag two weeks ago, it has proven beneficial and these energetic farmers have gone at it in dead earnest.[12]

This work must have brought about some conflict in the vote for the roads tax in 1907. Although the tax won in the county, Rhome voted 42 votes against and no votes for the tax. However, by 1907, there was an effort to do something about roads for Rhome. "The county road grading outfit is doing some very substantial work on the roads in this part of the county. They have also graded the streets of Rhome which adds very much to the appearance of the town. This is the first work the county has ever done on the roads in this community since the creation of the world."[13]

The buggy gained a rival about this time, which made it imperative that Rhome have good roads. "Rhome's first auto made its appearance Saturday. It was purchased by C. E. Martin."[14] Mr. Martin was the cashier of the First National Bank. Within a short time, many of Rhome's substantial citizens purchased their own "touring cars."

The automobile brought new business to Rhome, and new businessmen followed. The garage was an inevitable establishment. Shortly after C. E. Martin bought his first car, Ellis C. Troxell put in the first garage in Rhome about 1912. The 1913 issue of the Wise County Messenger carried a picture of the Hupmobile, which was one of the leading cars sold at this time. In December, 1915, there was a report that Mr. Troxell was selling his garage and moving to Miles, Texas:

> Our old friend Ellis Troxell is to leave Rhome this week for Miles, Texas. He is a home product that is appreciated. Born and reared in our midst, when he had grown to manhood, he established a garage at Rhome, being the first garage ever located here. He has made himself an almost master mechanic and has established a reputation few men ever reach. We are sorry to lose a citizen like Mr. Troxell, but as our town did not grow to satisfy his wants, he is looking for a larger place. He has sold his establishment to Marvin Holt, who receives our good wishes, also.[15]

Soon after his purchase of the Troxell Garage, Mr. Holt took in an assistant, a Mr. Brammer. "The new garage men, Brammer and Holt, seem to be very busy keeping the autos in repair."[16]

With the coming of the automobile came the demand from Rhome citizens for help in maintaining the Meridian Highway and other public roads. An appeal was published in the *Wise County Messenger* in the form of a petition from the citizens of Rhome.

> CITIZENS OF RHOME WANT GOOD ROADS. Messenger Readers in the Wheat Belt Ask Assistance of Commissioner. To the Wise County Messenger, Decatur, Texas: The undersigned citizens of the Rhome community have read with great interest all of the recent communications published in your columns in reference to our public roads, and especially the Meredian Highway.

STREET SCENE IN Rhome. 1910. Beginning of an auto race, to Decatur.

> This community is most vitally interested in this particular road, as it is of great value to our town and community. We esteem it as of as much value as the railroad, and owing to its neglected condition, we greatly fear we will lose this road and the benefits it affords us. While our community is not too thickly settled as other parts of the county, and does not furnish as many voters, our lands are among the most valuable in the county and carry the highest taxes, and hence we pay a larger part of the taxes than other parts of the precinct and county. Yet strange to say, the roads of our part of the precinct seem to be totally neglected. Practically nothing has been spent by the commissioners court on the improvements of our roads . . . And in this connection we suggest that a mass meeting of the citizens of the county interested in public roads be called to meet in the near future in Decatur to formulate plans for a more efficient and economical management of our highways.——

D. C. Caldwell	W. A. George	A. B. VanMeter
W. L. Russell	M. Holt	Clyde McCurdy
J. H. Brown	B. L. Morris	W. W. Brown
Chas. Hudnall	Z. B. Bobo	J. P. Mullinax
W. W. Morris	A. E. Butler	B. W. Logan
E. L. Smitherman	W. T. Leonard	Ans. Thorell
J. H. Rowan	J. T. Day	John Askey
J. Judge	Joe Day	W. J. Logan
I. M. Judge	Joe Robinson	J. J. Eagan
R. L. Bryan	Quint Woody	R. J. Anderson
E. G. Bryan	L. B. Barker	L. W. Renshaw
W. J. Finlayson	J. A. Martin	G. D. Culp
Oake Martin	Luther Martin	J. F. Thurmond
W. T. McCurdy	Sam T. Lillard	L. B. Douglas
A. C. Alexander	Earl VanMeter	

Many owners of new cars were mentioned in the news of 1917. The Ford seemed to be the most popular among the citizenry. "D. H. Perry and B. W. Logan bought new Ford cars this week, from the Decatur Motor Company."[18] Later on that same year it was reported that Mr. and Mrs. W. W. Morris had gone to New Mexico in their car and would be back in about two weeks. Cart Wright and M. E. Simms had also bought new automobiles that same week. Tom McCurdy had purchased a new five-passenger car during the last month of 1916.

On October 19, 1917, there was an answer to the petition from the Rhome citizens, as well as from other petitioners from the county.

> Answering the petition of the voters living along the Meridian Highway through Wise county, the commissioners' court

has ordered the election for November 17. Elections will be held at Rhome, Decatur, Alvord, Aurora, and Nickelville. All qualified voters living within the prescribed zone are entitled to participate in the election that means so much to the progress of the district. If the bonds are voted the government will contribute a like amount of money, and forty miles of the best character of public road will be constructed . . .[19]

In November of 1917 it was reported that the vote was a landslide in favor of the new road. "Work on the highway will start in a short time. The road will have a number of 'kinks' taken out and the distance reduced by several miles. One hundred and sixty thousand dollars will be expended and the annual auto tax of this county will maintain the road in first-class order."[20] It was planned that the Denver Railroad would be paralleled almost the entire route and that a number of railroad crossings would be eliminated, especially the crossing just south of the nine-mile tank.

Just before Christmas week in 1917, it was announced that Rhome would have auto service to Fort Worth for the Christmas shoppers. "The Rhome Jitney will make two trips a day to Fort Worth until the holidays are over. Leaving hours are 7:30 a.m. and 1:00 p.m.; returning 11:30 a.m. and 6:00 p.m."[21] This must have been an exciting prospect for the shopper who was able to make the trip without the inconvenience of having to board the train to Fort Worth and then taking a taxi to the stores. The jitney undoubtedly delivered its customers much closer to the shopping center of town. Such were the early beginnings of later bus service to the small community of Rhome. Nevertheless, everything was not rosy in the automotive picture. There were those who did not relish the prospect of having automobiles making noise about their homes and businesses. In December, 1917, it was reported that anti-auto societies were being formed in Wise county be people who were disturbed by the noise and danger of the vehicle. Also, there were accidents. "Judge H. H. Hambright, who was run over by an automobile and hurt pretty badly, is recovering slowly, and we hope to see him up and about soon."[22] Furthermore, there were laws governing the use of the automobile. "It is against State law now for a boy or a girl under eighteen years of age to drive an automobile. Remember this! It is also against the State law to have a headlight that throws rays of light more than four feet high on the roadway in front of your car."[23]

By the spring of 1919 the actual work on the Meridian highway was beginning. "Contractor J. F. Hamer moved his gang into the county the first of this week and is now located on the lower end of the road near the Tarrant county line . . . The Meridian road will have a fifty-foot right-of-way; from bar-pit to bar-pit the distance will be 32 feet and the crown will be 24 feet wide. Clean crushed gravel will be laid on this crown to a width of sixteen feet and at a depth of 8 inches. When it is completed, this will be one of the very best roads in the State."[24] The road was estimated to cost $160,000, with the state assuming half of the cost; the county, the other half.

Exciting as this new mode of transportation must have been to the citizens of Rhome and the rest of Wise county, in 1915 came an event which was even more thrilling. "The first exhibition ever given at a Wise county entertainment by an aviator will be staged at the fair park during the big entertainment next week. Reports from all communities in this section are to the effect that the people are coming to witness the first flight of this daring birdman. First flight, Tuesday, the opening day."[25]

Communication also made great strides during these first decades of the new century. Once again in 1904 came the announcement that Rhome was to have a newspaper. "Another enterprise, which we were about to overlook, is that we are to have a newspaper, the first issue to come out this coming Thursday, and will be known as the *Rhome Courier*; 'just watch Rhome grow'."[26] The name *Courier* was possibly a mistake, since about two years later Rhome's newspaper was called the *Light*, a venture which lasted about two years. The final report of the *Light*, Rhome's longest surviving newspaper venture came in August of 1906. "We expect to give the readers our final announcement or farewell write up in our next issue or possibly this *Light* is the last one. Such small interest, enterprise, and appreciation taken of the paper in advertising doesn't justify us to remain with you longer."[27] Thus the *Light* faded out for Rhome in a rather sour manner.

The next connection Rhome made with an attempt at the news media came through a page published in the *Decatur News*. In 1915 R. E. Leonard advertised for local, personal, or social news for the page. " . . . I want the Rhome page to reflect Rhome and all its interests. Items from surrounding country will be appreciated. Orders for job printing and advertising will be appreciated and promptly cared for."[28]

First mention of a telephone exchange for Rhome was a brief item on July 19, 1901. "Rhome has a telephone exchange!" From a Chronological History of the Rhome Telephone Exchange there is a note that in 1900 an exchange was built and owned by a Mr. Bason and operated by Mr. Wood Russell. There was no further mention of the telephone service until September of 1905 in a clipping from the *Light*. "There are four telephone gentlemen in Rhome this week looking after and improving the long distance lines through this place."[29]

This first telephone exchange was probably located in a small building just behind the Bobo Drug Store. On October 20, 1905, it was reported that Dr. D. A. Carpenter had bought the office which the telephone exchange had occupied to use as his doctor's office. The next week came a report that the telephone exchange management was building a new office. "The Telephone Exchange management is having a new office built on Main Street between James' tin shop and W. W. Morris' warehouse, and will move this week to its new quarters."[30]

In November of 1905 there was a statement that the exchange had been sold. Mr. Sam A. Brammer was the gentleman who had purchased the office. "Mr. Brammer is a clever young gentleman and we are glad to have him in our little city."[31] During the middle of the next month it was reported that Mr. Brammer was moving his family from Aurora to Rhome.

Connections to the Rhome line were quickly made. During the month that Mr. Brammer moved to Rhome, it was reported that an extra independent phone line and an extension of the Boyd line was being subscribed to and all possibilities were that it would be extended to Rhome via Aurora. In 1906 there was a story which showed the extent of the need for telephone communications in the farming areas around Rhome. "A telephone connection has been completed from the telephone exchange office to C. C. Leonard's farm. The line is made mostly of barbed wire, used for field and pasture purposes. The line is just as good as if it had been made of telephone wire."[32]

It was also in 1906 that a change in the ownership of the exchange was again made.

> Tom Stephens of Aurora has bought the telephone exchange system from S. A. Brammer. Mr. Stephens will remodel the system by putting in a new up-to-date switchboard, rebuilding the central office to provide it with more room, putting in a new lead cable, etc. J. Wood Russell is at present manipulating the system, and Rhome will soon have one of the best in the county.[33]

Three years later it was announced by the *Wise County Messenger* that the Decatur Independent Telephone Association would soon be building a thru line to Rhome.

> Manager Newcomb of the Decatur Independent Telephone Association is now building a thru line to Rhome, which will soon be completed. Decatur business men put up the money which made the line possible. When this line is finished, Decatur In-

dependent Exchange will be connected with direct lines to Rhome, Boyd, Bridgeport, Chico, Alvord, Greenwood, and Slidell . . . Subscribers may talk free to any of these places or through their exchanges, while outsiders are only charged a toll of 15 cents.

From the above it is readily seen what a great convenience the Independent telephone system is coming to be in Wise county. It connects the whole county, as one exchange and presents a convenience that is indeed great at a very small cost.[34]

This accomplishment brought the entire county together through the instant communications system that it provided for the county's citizens. Rhome finally had an outlet to the outside world that was more satisfactory than that which the older telegraph system had provided. The citizens of the Fairview community pooled their resources and built a line from there to Rhome in order to call for help in time of emergencies.

In 1910 it was reported that the new telephone exchange would probably be ready for operation by November 1st. This location was probably the same that the telephone exchange has occupied to the present date. By 1915 the telephone connections were made from coast to coast. "The first telephone conversation between the Atlantic and Pacific coasts was held yesterday. . ."[35] During November of that year Thurmond Hudnall was listed as one of the general managers of the independent exchange. One of his jobs was to repair phone lines and boxes and to put in new batteries.

During World War I, the federal government took control of the American telephone and telegraph system. "The Government is preparing to relinquish control next month of American cable lines and to restore the telegraph and telephone systems to private ownership immediately after enactment by Congress of laws necessary to safeguard the properties."[36]

One final note about the telephone system came in 1920 from the *Messenger*. " 'Miss Glennice Looney is our new "'Hello girl,'" Miss Lena Brammer having resigned her position as operator for the telephone company to enter business college."[37]

From 1897 to 1914, W. W. Whitesides continued as postmaster with his office located in the small room on the side of the Brown barber shop. During the 1901 there was mention of the carrying of the mail from Aurora to Rhome. "Mr. R. B. Tanner was the lucky bidder on the contract for carrying the mail from Aurora to Rhome, and will enter the work on December 10th."[38] This was a contract job and not the rural free delivery service which was still to come. It was in 1903

MAC BURCH, EARLY citizen of Rhome.

that the Rhome reporter first mentioned rural free delivery for Rhome.

> I see in many instances that the government is establishing the rural mail delivery service for the accomodation of the public. We believe this is to be a first-rate idea, and Scribbler is of the opinion that Rhome should have about five rural delivery routes. We believe that this would increase business in nearly every respect. We would like to hear what other Rhomans think about it.[39]

On May 14, 1904, the rural letter carriers of Wise county met in Decatur and formed an organization for rural carriers. Rhome was not represented here because it was not until 1906 that the first rural route was established in Rhome. "The first rural carrier was M. W. (Mack) Burch who served a 21 mile route with horse drawn 2-wheel cart. This original Route No. 1 was established in 1906, and primarily, gave service to rural patrons in and around the community of Aurora."[40] The year before this first route was established, we find that a woman had taken over the duties of carrying mail from Aurora.

> Miss Ruth Daniel, the pleasant and popular granddaughter of B. R. Tanner, who had been carrying the Aurora mail from this place for the past three weeks during Mr. Tanner's protracted illness, reports her grandfather fast improving. Miss Ruth certainly deserved a great deal of credit for driving the buggy during those muddy and rainy days, coming and returning with the mail.[41]

In February of 1906 Mr. Tanner was again given the contract for carrying the mail from Rhome to Aurora. However, this contract was discontinued when the United States Postal Department established the first rural free delivery route later that same year. Seven years later the mail carrier, Mack Burch, passed the State Bar examination and moved to Decatur to practice law. In March, 1913, his vacancy was filled by James R. Troxell, who continued to serve this route west of Rhome for many years. Three months later in June, 1913, Route No. 2 was established and patrons of the Fairview and Blewett communities received their first rural delivery service. John R. Whitehead began a long career in the postal service with his appointment to this job.

> C. E. Shaw was the next postmaster and served from two different locations from 1914 to 1922. His first location was in "Squire" Hambright's law office, across the street from the Old Stone Building, and on approximately the same site now occupied by P. L. Harvey. He later occupied a small space in the old

MR. J. R. TROXELL, carrier for Route 1, and Mr. Joe Taylor, postmaster, standing by Mr. Troxell's mail hack that was pulled by "Old Dan". The Benton Grocery is in the background. The Lyric Theater is the connecting building.

JOHN WHITEHEAD AND his mail hack. Mr. Whitehead carried the mail on Route 2 for many years.

CLAUDE SHAW, POSTMASTER of Rhome, Texas.

> Perkins Grocery Store, a big red painted frame building on the northwest corner of the same block, the corner presently occupied by the Fina Service Station.[42]

The newspaper reported Mr. Shaw's appointment. "Claude Shaw has recently been appointed postmaster at this place and will take charge of the office Wednesday."[43]

One amusing story was related by the *Decatur News* concerning an eclipse of the sun. "The Rhome postmaster was greatly alarmed over the eclipse of the sun last week. He had gotten hold of some poisonous literature on the subject which threw him a wild fever of excitement. He believed there would be a total darkness and made an effort to force the mail carriers to take lanterns with them, and he was well equipped with material in the post office for light. A great disappointment prevailed when he realized that the eclipse was going off and only a small portion of the sun had been covered."[44] Actually, the carrying of lanterns was not a very great change for the mail carriers, for they often carried not only lanterns, but also small stoves for warmth and light on the cold, wintry days.

The only other change noted in the postal department during the final years of the period was a note about postal rates in 1917, which might come as a surprise to those of us accustomed to the much higher rates today.

> The new war tax bill has affected postal rates, and after November 2nd, it will cost three cents to mail an ounce letter and a 1 cent stamp must be affixed to a postal card to insure its transmission. Drop letters will require a 2-cent stamp instead of one as heretofore.[45]

Law Enforcement

Crime did not rage rampant during these decades. The year 1909 seemed to bring the greatest offenses; however, today these incidents would seem relatively minor ones. In fact, Rhome has remained a very quiet town throughout the years.

1901 brought another suit for trespassing. This time it was the same old offense: that of lovers going through pasture gates and failing to close them after passing through. 1905 brought the story of a burglary. "Some parties entered in the back door of Logan Bros.' general merchandise store last Tuesday night, taking all the watches and chains and some few other articles thought to amount to $38 or $40 worth."[1] Two young boys were arrested in Fort Worth for selling jewelry supposed not to belong to them. The constable, John H.

Davis, went to Fort Worth and brought the boys back to Rhome, where they both acknowledged their guilt.

By 1907 Rhome had a new constable, Claude Shaw. On January 1, 1907, Mr. Shaw arrested a Haslet man accused of stealing a purse from the home of Mr. Hudnall of the Rhome vicinity. "This was Mr. Shaw's first arrest since he has become the peace officer of Rhome."[2]

The *Decatur News* lists two different justices of the peace for Rhome: Justice Brown in 1904 and Justice Hambright in 1908. On April 30, 1909, the *Messenger* recorded Sheriff John Branch as holding a 19-year-old burglar in the "county hostelry." The young man was charged with burglarizing the store of W. W. Morris at Rhome.

> He was captured by officers after an exciting chase near Valley View, in Cooke County, last Saturday morning. He was brought to Decatur and jailed. At a "reception" held by County Attorney Ratliff Monday morning the young man went into details and told an interesting story about the affair. . . has a cheap novel hero air about him and seemed to heartily enjoy the notoriety gained by his deed. He implicated a farm tenant living near Rhome . . . but the tenant bitterly denied any connection with the burglary. He is also held in jail.

The story is further related by the young man as follows:

> . . . "We went to the blacksmith shop that fronts to the railroad and hitched our horses and went to the depot. We went over to the depot to do our planning. We had made arrangements to sell the stuff to a man . . . he lives at Marieta, Oklahoma. He had seen the stuff and said that he would give us $100 for what we got" . . . he says they proceeded to the Morris store. Entering the store through a rear window . . . they went about their work.[3]

A long list of what they took follows in the article: guns, jewelry, razors, knives, pants, gloves, and sardines and crackers. The last two items were probably insurance that they would not go hungry on the trip to Marietta. The story ended on June 12, 1909, with the young man, now referred to as being only seventeen years old, pleading guilty to burglary in the district court and being sentenced to two years in the penitentiary.

The next occurrence in 1909 was another burglary, this time occurring at the depot. Three young men, two of them from prominent families in Rhome, broke into the depot. ". . . taking therefrom a supply of drunk producing fluid. . ."[4] Although the case went to court, the young men were all acquitted of the crime, two of them having turned state's evidence.

On June 14, 1912, Rhome was the center of considerable excitement when Officer Tom McCurry arrested a youth who allegedly had stolen an automobile at Newark a few minutes previously.

> A short time after the arrest of the boy, about 16 years old, the owner was brought to Rhome by Dr. Huddleston of Newark, in the latter gentleman's car. The owner then took Officer McCurry and the youthful prisoner to Decatur in his own recaptured car. The boy wore knee pants, was well dressed, and began shedding copious tears, though the sympathy he longed for never came . . .[5]

Other than feuding of a relatively mild nature, little happened to disturb the quiet and peace of Rhome.

Banking Affairs

The first mention of a bank for Rhome came in a report by the correspondent to the *Wise County Messenger*. "Rhome is to have a national bank soon."[6] By the next week it was announced that Mr. C. E. Martin of Decatur was to be cashier of the new bank.

> Since our last communication we are now able to say that Rhome has a bank, an institution that has been badly needed at this place for many years; it is now running in a small building belonging to Judge Hambright.
>
> A new brick building is now under course of erection, when complete it will be very acommodious and imposing structure.[1]

This building, owned by Judge Hambright, is probably the same small building which served him as an office when he was the justice of peace and later served as a post office. One month later there was a report that the new bank building was almost complete. Then in 1906 came further news that the bank had acquired a new safe.

> The new time lock safe was received last Monday by the First Bank of Rhome. The safe is the latest design, burglar proof, and weighs a good many hundred pounds.[2]

This safe was purchased from Yale and Towne Manufacturing Company of Stamford, Connecticut. Today it is still in use in the Rhome

City Hall, which now occupies the brick building that was built in 1904.

From an old letterhead, on which was written an agreement concerning shares of stock in the Rhome Creamery Company, comes the information that W. T. Waggoner was president of the bank, T. B. Yarbrough was vice president, and C. E. Martin was cashier. It was an unincorporated institution with an individual responsibility advertised as five million dollars. From a list of information about the bank, compiled by Joel R. Chambers, a later president of the bank, comes further information that their bookkeeping system was the "Old Boston Loose Leaf Ledger, pen, ink, and elbow system."

In 1914 the First Bank of Rhome was nationalized to The First National Bank, Rhome, Texas, with a capital stock of $25,000.00.

> The news comes that the First Bank of Rhome will be changed to a national institution, application having been made to the federal government. The First Bank of Rhome, owned and operated by the Waggoner interests, has been a splendid asset and "feeder" of the Waggoner First National Bank in Decatur. In passing to a national bank, the Rhome institution loses the distinction of being one of the strongest financial institutions in the South; as a private bank of Mr. Waggoner, it had the backing of this many times millionaire's wealth. In the change, doubtless some of the citizens of the great Rhome country will be admitted into the list of shareholders of the national.[3]

Two months later there was a notice that the bank had been nationalized:

> The thriving little city of Rhome now boasts a national bank, the U. S. government having granted a charter to the First National Bank of that place. For some years Rhome has had a private banking institution, which was owned and controlled by Messrs. Waggoner and Yarbrough of Fort Worth, and was linked with the gentlemen's First National Bank of Decatur . . . but in becoming a national bank, it ceased to be a "feeder" bank. . .[4]

In February, 1915, came the news that C. E. Martin was resigning as cashier in order to accept the position as first assistant cashier of the First National Bank of Decatur, Texas. Upon his resignation, A. C. Alexander became cashier with L. R. Douglas as assistant cashier. A. C. Alexander served from 1915 to 1919, using what was known as the Jones Loose Leaf Ledgers, their work being done with pen and ink until 1929. In 1915 when C. E. Martin resigned, the directors of the bank were W. T. Waggoner, Z. B. Bobo, C. E. Martin, A. C. Alexander, J. H. Rowan, J. T. Day, and W. W. Morris.

Medicine and Drugs

During these two decades Rhome could boast of several doctors, a druggist, a veterinarian, and a dentist, who practiced part-time in the town. These people concerned with the health of the community were Dr. J. D. Burch, who lived in Aurora, but for a time took care of most of the people of Rhome; Dr. J. W. Dossey; Dr. G. P. Cherry; Dr. D. A. Carpenter; Dr. B. M. Jones; Dr. W. L. Russell; Dr. Payne, dentist from Decatur; Z. B. Bobo, a druggist; Roy B. Edwards, a druggist's assistant, who later went on to study pharmacy in Galveston; C. K. Wilkerson, who drove the hearse for Rhome; and S. L. Leonard, who served as veterinarian.

Despite the wealth of care in the health field, Rhome still suffered through several sieges of illness. Dr. J. D. Burch lived in Aurora, but the Rhome residents knew him well and called upon him often during this time. "Dr. Burch is curtailing his rye patch and enlarging his orchard. The Doctor believes in vegetables, fruit, and flowers, and knows that the 'home grown' varieties are by far the best and most convenient for use."[1]

At this time when Dr. Burch was preaching the efficacy of fruits and vegetables for health, Rhome was in fear of a small pox epidemic.

> The smallpox situation was unchanged at Rhome last reports only one case and it under guard, and I hope there will be no other cases. The people at Rhome and vicinity and here (Aurora) have very generally acted quite sensibly by going on about their business and avoiding getting excited and are awaiting developments. I presume all necessary precautions have been and will continue to be taken in avoiding contact, and that all necessary sanitary regulations will be observed. The section house, where the case is, being distant from the resident and business part of town, made isolation convenient.[2]

Rhome lost one of its very much respected doctors in 1905 with the death of Dr. J. D. Burch. "Dr. J. D. Burch, a prominent physician, died very suddenly at noon Sunday at his home at Aurora. He was well-known all over Northwest Texas. He was buried by the Masons and Odd-Fellows."[3]

Another well-known physician of this early period in Rhome was Dr. J. W. Dossey, who married one of the daughters of Colonel Benjamin Morris.

> Rhome is peculiarly fortunate in the personnel of her physicians. Dr. J. W. Dossey, who has been practicing here for about six years is a gentleman of thorough education and experience.

THE HOME OF Dr. and Mrs. W. L. Russell. It was one of the houses moved to Rhome from Aurora. Mrs. Russell still lives in the home.

He is a well-read, able, and careful physician, who inspires confidence in his ability and has proven himself a very successful practitioner. Aside from his profession, he is a cordial progressive citizen, who is counted among the foremost citizens of Rhome.[4]

About a year before this time, it was reported that Dr. Payne was in Rhome, taking care of the dental problems of the citizens. He came to Rhome every other week and carried out his practice in a back room of Dr. Carpenter's office.

Another early physician was Dr. G. P. Cherry. The first newspaper mention of Dr. Cherry tells of a fire which destroyed the Cherry family's barn. "The barn of Dr. G. P. Cherry, living seven miles northeast of Rhome, was destroyed by fire Sunday night about 12 o'clock."[5] On June 1, 1906, there was a quote from the Rhome newspaper, the *Light*, which stated that Dr. Cherry had announced his intention of taking up the profession of medicine in Rhome. His home in Rhome was moved there from Aurora, and is the house in which Mrs. W. L. Russell lives today. He continued practicing medicine until after 1923, according to the newspaper references.

Z. B. Bobo had been Rhome's only druggist for many years. A 1902 edition of the *Decatur News* carried a good description of the store which he ran.

> One of the most attractive establishments in Wise county is the store conducted by the popular and enterprising citizen, Z. B. Bobo. It is indeed a credit to the town. Mr. Bobo sold drugs in Aurora when that was the principal trading point of Wise county, and has been identified with the people of this section for many years, sharing their joys and sorrows in good season and bad, and today is doing a lucrative business, which fact attests to the excellent standing and correct business methods of the man. Ten years ago he moved to Rhome and has ever been found ready to do his part toward public enterprises of all kinds. Mr. Bobo's stock consists of drugs, patent medicines, toilet articles, perfumes, paints, oils, etc., and nothing but the purest drugs are handed over the counters. In addition to drugs Mr. Bobo has two rooms filled with furniture and undertaker's goods.[6]

In 1905 it was reported that one of Mr. Bobo's assistants, Roy B. Edwards, was going to continue his education in pharmacy. "Roy B. Edwards left this morning for Galveston where he will enter the State University and study pharmacy. Roy is a good bright boy, having been assisting in the Bobo drug store here a long while. We will miss him during his stay at Galveston."[7]

Early in the year 1906 Rhome was still worried about the disease, smallpox.

> Nine cases of smallpox are reported at Boyd. If the report is true and the cases are smallpox, a strict quarantine should be raised by all other towns in the county to prevent its spread, without all such cases are put into quarantine camps and kept there under strict provisions of the law.[8]

In May of that same year it was reported that many people had died of the measles in the area.

Dr. D. A. Carpenter was another of Rhome's earlier physicians. His name first appeared in the newspaper files in 1902.

> Rhome has ably sustained her reputation as a healthy town, not only because of its high location but also because of her excellent corps of physicians. Among them is Dr. D. A. Carpenter, a physician of ability and withal a genial, social gentleman who always has a good word for his adopted home and ever ready to aid in any enterprise. Dr. Carpenter is a native of Kentucky, that grand old state of mint juleps and truest aristocracy. He located in Texas as a matter of preference and lived for awhile at Clifton, Bosque county; about three years ago he came to Rhome and cast his lot among the clever people of Wise. Dr. Carpenter is a student of his profession, and by his careful conscientious labor has endeared himself to the people.[9]

In 1907 Dr. Carpenter was on his way to Chicago to further his medical studies. "Dr. D. A. Carpenter left last week for Chicago. He proposes remaining several months while completing his study of medicine."[10] Dr. Carpenter's family biography states that he left Rhome to move his business to Decatur in 1910.

It was in 1910 that Z. B. Bobo, the druggist, started construction of his new drug building. "Our clever druggist, Z. B. Bobo, is having erected in the place of his old drug building a handsome brick structure, which will add materially to our little town's good welfare."[11] According to one of his daughters, Mrs. C. E. (Ann) High, the building was cut in half and the two halves were moved to the west side of the stone building which served as a grocery store for the Leonards. Later one half of the building was to be Rhome's first garage business.

For a time Dr. B. M. Jones was a physician in Rhome. On December 17, 1915, the *Decatur News* reported that Dr. Jones had been elected president of the Wise County Medical Association. Shortly after this time both of the newspapers in the county reported that Dr. Jones was contemplating a move to Burkburnett. His family was to follow him about the 15th of January, 1916. "This is one of Rhome's most prominent families and their large circle of friends wish them much success and happiness in their new home."[12]

Dr. W. L. Russell came to Rhome about 1911. He purchased the home which had been occupied by Dr. Cherry. This is the same home in which his widow lives today. The first mention of Dr. Russell in the newspapers came in connection with a story about illness in Rhome. "Dr. W. L. Russell is very busy these days with la grippe patients. He reported Tuesday morning a hundred cases in and near Rhome."[13] From Dr. Russell's own records comes the fact that he did not deliver any babies during 1911, but his first recorded obstetric case was August 11, 1912. His first country call was a visit to Mrs. Rhea Hudnall in July, 1911.

C. K. Wilkerson served as hearse driver for Z. B. Bobo, who owned the first and only hearse that Rhome could claim. This hearse is on display today in the Wise County Historical Museum in Decatur, Texas. "C. K. Wilkerson made a hearse drive to Justin, Sunday."[14] From this report it must be assumed that the fine old hearse with the glass sides served a wide area surrounding Rhome.

Although the doctors were sometimes called upon to perform veterinarian services, S. L. Leonard provided this service for Rhome's farmers and ranchers as well as for those in vicinities as far away as Bowie. "S. L. Leonard was in Bowie Monday doing veterinary work."[15]

FIRST HEARSE USED in Rhome. Owned by Z. B. Bobo.

By the fall of 1918 the plague of Spanish influenza was in full force in the United States. The following proclamation by the mayor of Decatur indicates the seriousness of the situation:

> On recommendation of the City Health Officer, I hereby order that all places of public worship, amusement, and the public schools be closed from this date Friday, October 11, 1918, until Monday, October 21, 1918; also that all people shall refrain from gathering in crowds or assembling together for any purpose. This action is deemed necessary that this community may avoid the epidemic of Spanish influenza now raging in the State and Nation, and the people are warned to strictly observe this order.
>
> A. C. Bennett, Mayor[16]

Since this situation prevailed in Decatur, it is certain that the same was true of the surrounding communities. The following week, October 25, 1918, the newspapers were filled with notices of the deaths of influenza victims all over the county. That same week there was also a notice about a state food inspector being in Decatur, checking all the eating places:

The pure food man was in town looking after the restaurants, cold drink stands, and other places where food was offered and displayed for sale. He imposed fines on some and ordered others to clean up and stay clean. Mr. Portwood says the good work must go on, and if he comes again and finds similar conditions, other and heavier fines will be imposed.[17]

Possibly the most destructive single incident ever to happen in Rhome was the storm which struck the town in June of 1907. Ann High states that after the storm had abated, Uncle Zack and Aunt Betty Bobo took a lantern and all the children in their night clothes to walk to Grandpa Morris's house and then to the houses of all the other relatives to be certain that they were safe from harm.

Following is the *Decatur News* account of the storm:

DESTRUCTIVE STORM Does Considerable Damage in Towns of Rhome and Justin. No Lives Lost.

Threatened twice in its existence, from destruction by cyclone, Rhome was visited last night at 12 o'clock by a real twister, which swooped down without a moment's notice. Most of the people were caught asleep, but when the furious gusts fell upon the town, all made an effort to gain refuge and several were stunned by lightning before reaching their cellars. Almost by the time all had gained admission to storm cellars the whirling mass of clouds had finished its work and gone on in a southeasterly direction. The rain and hail which came at the same time and for several minutes after, drenched everything. Nearly every house had from a quarter to an inch of water in its rooms.

So far as reports have been received no life was lost and no body injured beyond a few scratches. Following is a list of property damage:

Colonel B. Morris' large warehouse unroofed and building otherwise badly damaged. The roof was carried some distance by the wind and smashed to splinters.

The Fort Worth and Denver Railway's large water tank, which was full of water, had its top twisted off and was hurled all over town, pieces of which were hurled against other houses, breaking through windows. Three box cars standing on the siding were unroofed and twisted, pieces of 2 x 6 scantling which were picked up out of Rowe's lumber yard by the wind were driven entirely through both sides of one of the box cars.

Eight windmills were blown down and wrecked.

The Rhome Milling Company's plant was badly damaged, the roof being raised by the wind, and the large smokestack blown entirely away and crushed.

The Presbyterian and Baptist churches were blown from their foundations and badly wrecked. The Methodist and Christian churches were also blown off their blocks and damaged.

The public school building in the northeast part of the town was blown several feet, but remained intact. A new residence which was being constructed by Pugh Morris east of the railroad was blown down and reduced to splinters.

In the very middle of the storm's fury lightning struck Judge Hambright's barn which is located at the back of a long row of wooden store buildings, and it took fire.

The entire block of business houses would have been consumed by the fire had it not been for the timely aid of citizens who braved the storm and with fire extinguishers and tin buckets subdued the flames. Several smaller outbuildings were completely demolished by the wind.

An accurate figure on the property loss cannot be had at this time.

Two men, who saw the cyclone approaching, endeavored to alarm the town, but the dark ominous whirling cloud which proved to be a real tornado beat them to the scene. The rain was the heaviest ever seen. Crops are badly damaged.[19]

Politics and Government

Today it is difficult to imagine what excitement a simple candidate speaking could generate in our forefathers. One of the big entertainments of the town was to gather on Main Street to listen to the men desirous of public office debate each other for the post. "The election yesterday was a little exciting, as the candidates' friends were working hard all day and everyone was confident of his friend's winning."[1] One of the leading Democrats of the Rhome precinct was Mr. H. H. H. Hambright. "Mr. H. H. H. Hambright is notary public for the Rhome precinct and attends to all business of the office in a correct manner. He is also Democratic chairman of the box and an old resident, having lived here about 25 years."[2] Mr. Hambright also served as justice of the peace for Rhome for many years. A typical example of the candidate speaking was given in 1908 when T. J. McMurray of

Decatur spoke in Rhome. One hundred and fifty farmers came into town to hear Mr. McMurray. "Hon. T. J. McMurray of Decatur will speak here Saturday, May 18, in defense of Senator Bailey and arrangements are being made for a big crowd. A canvass of this voting precinct reveals the fact that Bailey will carry it by five to one."[3] In July of this same year there was a second candidate's speaking.

The Democratic party was not the only choice for the southerner of this time. The Socialist party was also active in the county. On October 2, 1908, the Socialist party platform was published in Wise county. The party had candidates for most of the county offices, even for commissioner.

Interest in politics was shown by the list of poll tax payments made in Wise county. In 1906, Rhome had 93 persons to pay the poll tax so that they could vote in the coming elections. By 1908 the number had jumped to 109 persons. The interests were many, but taxes, land assessments, prohibition, income tax and women's suffrage took the lead among the issues.

In 1902 when a county prohibition election was called, a list of about sixty-five names appeared in the paper under a listing of the beneficial effects of prohibition for Rhome.

> A County Prohibition election having been ordered for Saturday, May 15, 1902, the undersigned think it proper to give the following facts to the people in regard to the working of the prohibition law as applied to the town of Rhome:
>
> 1st   Prohibition has prohibited in Rhome.
> 2nd   Church, school, and social interests have prospered wonderfully during the reign of prohibition.
> 3rd   Prohibition has in no wise hurt the business of the town.
> 4th   Law and order have ruled here since the open saloon has been voted out.
> 5th   Intemperance in town and community has greatly decreased.
> 6th   Though it is true that some liquor has been shipped in by express, the amount is small, compared with the amount that would be handled with the open saloon.
> 7th   The prohibition law has proved a blessing to our community, and we would be sorry indeed to have it set aside and "rum shops" forced upon us.
> 8th   We would especially appeal to the people around us who would not have saloons, even if prohibition should be defeated to lend us their aid to keep

saloons out of Rhome. To this end we urge that every prohibitionist in this part of the county go to the polls on March 15th and vote for prohibition.

Signed:

H. H. H. Hambright	D. R. Wade	D. P. Shaw
D. C. Caldwell	A. Fairchild	J. E. Rieve
G. W. Morton	W. C. Huddleston	F. M. Hatler
E. W. Byars	L. Benton	W. S. Alderson
H. J. Taylor	F. E. Shanks	C. M. Huffines
C. J. VanMeter, Jr.	W. A. Rogers	T. S. Mount
J. W. Morton	J. B. Simms	C. W. James
W. H. Harris	J. J. Hudson	E. A. Harrison
A. B. Witt	T. M. Poteet	S. H. Mount
J. A. Troxell	T. E. Callahan	Geo. W. Watkins
A. A. VanMeter	Wm. Lockridge	J. M. Ford
T. J. Rogers	P. M. Smitherman	C. C. Newberry
Edgar Byars	H. K. Powell	John West
W. J. Dossey	T. H. Wilkerson	B. Morris
R. W. Stanfield	B. W. Logan	W. Keele
J. D. Johnston	T. H. Witt	W. W. Morris
J. F. Thurmond	Wm. O'Neal	J. H. Davis
H. I. Watkins	I. L. Lewis	Allen Hill
Noah Reeves	J. R. Purcell	M. T. Oates
J. H. Rowan	F. D. Talbert	J. P. Morris
H. B. Barker	Aug. Thorell	J. W. Yokley
E. L. Smitherman	A. N. Rives	Char. Morton
Z. B. Bobo	A. J. W. Jennings	

Since nationwide prohibition did not come for many years, it may surprise many descendents of these people to know that their fathers and grandfathers in this early day had the courage to oppose a practice which had existed openly over much of the nation. It is significant that today Rhome is still a "dry" town.

In 1908 one Rhome tax payer felt called upon to oppose the property taxes being assessed on the farmers. His name is unknown to the writer, but perhaps many opponents of the property tax will sympathize with his letter to the *Messenger*:

> I was glad to see that paragraph in the *Messenger*, calling attention to the enormous assessments of farm property in this country. In view of existing conditions this is more extortionate and unjust than it would ordinarily be. We have again suffered an almost entire failure in our wheat and oat crops, and with the prospects of our taxes being doubled, and in some cases trebled,

the outlook is anything but promising. Is there no remedy for this state of affairs? Have we no recourse whatever to relieve outselves of almost unbearable burdens? . . .

TAXPAYER⁵

The farmer of Rhome today can certainly sympathize with this poor tax payer since the payments have grown enormously since the letter was written.

By 1914 it was of interest to the citizens of Rhome to know who the big tax payers were. Thus a list of those who paid over $100 to the tax funds was given. From the list of the entire county it was noted that the Lillard interests paid more taxes than any other coporation, while J. J. Hudson of Rhome paid more than any other individual in the county. The "over $100" list for Rhome citizens was given as follows: "L. B. Barker, R. L. Bryan, J. T. Day, Z. B. Bobo, E. P. Carpenter, J. J. Hudson, Mrs. R. Morris, W. J. and B. W. Logan, C. C. Leonard, Morris Mercantile Company, L. Renshaw, Rhome Milling Company, A. A. VanMeter."⁶

Rhome's young attorney, M. W. Burch, was beginning at this time to gain county-wide recognition in the field of law.

> Attorney M. W. Burch of Rhome, one of the coming legal lights in Wonderful Wise, was in to see the *Messenger* a few days ago, and gave a good account of the great Rhome country. Prospects, said Mack, were never better for a bumper wheat crop, and trade conditions were flattering. This young attorney is a progressive and a big booster for his town and county.⁷

By 1914 Mr. Burch was listed among the candidates for office of county attorney in Wise county.

> The announcement notice of M. W. Burch's candidacy is published this week in the county papers. He is a candidate for the office of prosecuting attorney. Mr. Burch comes from one of the pioneer families of Aurora, Rhome country; he is industrious, a young man of strict integrity, honorable in his dealings, and a close student of the law. If the voters of Wise county appreciate this stalwart young man's fitness for the position he seeks, and elect him, the responsibilities of the office will rest in safe hands and he will put forth the best there is in him to merit the confidence of the people.⁸

The year 1913 brought about changes in the National Constitution which allowed the passage of a bill to introduce the federal income tax legislation. At this time, however, the individual tax payer

THE HOME OF Mac and Belle Burch, which was moved from Aurora, circa 1902. This house was located about one block east of the school, facing south.

was not particularly concerned about the tax that was to become later the chief source of revenue for the government.

> The income tax is an imposition over which very few of us are privileged to get angry. A man has to have an income of at least $3000 a year before he can get mad at the income tax. Even then, he cannot really complain, except, of course, in order to show that he is in the down-trodden upper class . . . .[9]

Toward the end of the period came the women suffrage movement. It was in 1920 with the adoption of the Nineteenth Amendment, that women's right to vote was written into the Constitution of the United States. However, by 1918, the women of Wise county were ready for their voting rights. The states were gradually voting in woman suffrage rights, and June, 1918, found the women of Wise county organizing.

> A meeting of the ladies of Wise county was called to order Saturday June 15 at 3 o'clock in the district courtroom by Mrs. B. B. Sellars for the purpose of hearing Mrs. Curtis of Dallas speak on "Woman Suffrage" and also to organize a woman's Democratic league of Wise county . . . The next thing was to elect officers of the various precincts, the following being elected . . .

MRS. JANE HATLER, one of Rhome's very first citizens.

Rhome—Mrs. C. E. Shaw, chairman; Mrs. Tom Leonard, secretary.[10]

In July, 1918, came a call for the women to register for their right to vote. "The Wise county tax collector's office has been an unusually busy place since registration day. There have been about three hundred ladies registered since the 26th. Ladies, don't wait too long. The 12th is the last day."[11]

Rhome's Churches

Although only a small town, Rhome has always been well represented by religious organizations. The situation might well be described by a report found in the *Decatur News* of 1902:

Rhome Has Four Church Organizations

The Baptist church was organized about 14 or 15 years ago. Present pastor is Rev. S. M. Edwards of Decatur. They have their own church building, Sunday school every Sunday at 10 a. m. with F. M. Hatler as superintendent. The resident ministers are Revs. G. W. Martin and Wm. Keele.

The Methodist church was organized about twelve years ago. Their present pastor is Rev. J. B. Simms, who resides in Rhome. Sunday school every Sunday at 10 a.m. with F. M. Poteet superintendent. They also own a church building.

The Cumberland Presbyterian church was organized about three years ago. Their pastor is Rev. W. E. Robinson of Ringgold. Preaching every third Sunday in the Methodist church. Resident minister is Rev. R. W. Stanfield.

The Christian church was organized about two years ago. Their present pastor is Rev. Young of Sunset. Sunday school at 10 a.m. at the school house.

All churches are in very good harmony. The Baptists and Methodists have each held revival meetings this season with splendid results.[1]

A seeming discrepancy in dates may be accounted for in the fact that the churches usually organized several years before they were able to build a church house.

In May of 1900 the Rhome Missionary Baptist church was growing by leaps and bounds. A report from the *Wise County Messenger* confirms that growth. "The recent Baptist meeting at Rhome resulted in 17 additions to the church, 13 by baptism, 3 by statement, and 1 by restoration."[2] The next year a big revival was held at the Baptist church. The meeting was conducted by Reverend J. B. Tidwell and Missionary Edwards. This time there were six conversions and four accessions to the church.

Organizations within the church were also being formed, including a Sunday school a training union, a Sunbeam Band, and a Ladies' Aid Society. "The Women's Missionary Union of the Rhome Baptist church was first called 'The Ladies Aid Society', and was organized in 1903, thirteen years after the church was organized. Mrs. Edwards, who was then the pastor's wife, was the first president."[3] In November of 1909 it was reported that the ladies were planning a dinner. "Only a few more days until Thanksgiving. The Baptist ladies are to have a dinner on the main street of Rhome to get up funds for Buckner's Orphan's Home at Dallas."[4] The charter members of this organization were as follows: Mrs. Z. B. Bobo, Mrs. H. C. Hazen, Mrs.

Hodges, Mrs. Booker Witt, Mrs. F. M. Hatler, Mrs. West, Mrs. Edwards. In 1918 the name of the Ladies' Aid was changed to Women's Missionary Union.

The original church building belonging to the Baptists was demolished by a tornado in 1912; however, all the church records were rescued. A new church building was started as soon as the new plans could be made. "Preparations are being made for the erection of a $5000 church here. The site is located and work will begin immediately."[5] A new location was chosen for the building. This new red brick church was erected in the heart of town, one block from the business center. "This building has an adequate auditorium, a baptistry, study and office, and six classrooms. The cost was approximately $7000."[6]

The new church served as the site of many religious, as well as social, events for the young town. One of the most notable of these events brought greetings from one of the oldtime families.

> The Lois Class of the Baptist Sunday School entertained the "grandmothers" of the different churches in town on Thursday evening at the Baptist church. The classroom was effectively decorated with Christmas bells, ferns, holly, and American beauty roses. Those who received the guests were Mmes. B. Casey, R. E. Leonard, B. M. Jones, C. E. Shaw, and W. L. Russell. Among the diversions of the evening was an old time spelling match which was enjoyed by all the grandmothers. Mrs. W. Morris received first prize; Mrs. M. F. Cates, second. Col. and Mrs. B. C. Rhome of Fort Worth sent each guest a carnation as a reminder of the happy days gone by and wished each a Merry Christmas and a Happy New Year. At the close of the evening a two-course luncheon was served.[7]

A report from the *Decatur News* of the same date gave the following list of grandmothers who were guests at the luncheon: Mmes. J. W. Prunty, N. G. Holt, Sarah Long, M. Troxell, Bryant, Douglas, Privett, VanMeter, D. P. Shaw, W. J. Finlayson, Charles Hudnall, and M. T. Oates.

Another occasion provided an innovation in the installation services for the officers of the Baptist Sunday School.

> A very unusual but appropriate service was held at the Baptist church last Sunday. The Sunday school teachers were installed by a formal ceremony. The newly elected teachers and officers of the Sunday school were as follows: R. E. Leonard, Supt.; Mrs. W. E. Horton, Sec. Treas. and classification officer; Mrs. Harry Wilson, Supt. of Home Department and Cradle Roll; C. C. Hudnall, teacher of adult men; Mrs. Mary Morris, teacher of adult

THIS BUILDING WAS the second structure built by the Missionary Baptist Church. It was demolished to make way for the building which houses the First Baptist Church of Rhome.

women; Rev. E. J. Thompson, teacher of senior boys; Mrs. C. E. Shaw, teacher of senior girls; C. K. Wilkerson, intermediate boys; Miss Mattie Neal, intermediate girls; Jarrett Hudnall, junior boys; Miss Adran Ash, junior girls; Miss Nona George, primary; Miss Lela Jenkins, beginners.[8]

Mrs. C. E. Shaw changed her assignment three years later when she accepted charge of a new organization, the Sunbeam Band, a position which she occupied for thirty-five years. Her assistants were the Misses Lula and Lela Jenkins. The Sunbeam Band had been organized in December, 1918, by Mrs. C. P. Morris. On January 19, 1919, Mrs. C. E. Shaw was elected leader. Flora Leach served Mrs. Shaw as assistant.

With the turn of the century, the Methodists were still only dreaming of the time when they would have their own church house for meetings. Their meetings were held in the school house, under brush arbors, and even in a tent. "The Methodist meeting closed Wednesday after progressing nicely for ten days. The tent was moved to Rhome Friday and Bro. Sherwood will begin a meeting there, and we hope will do much good."[9] This situation was not to last for long. The Methodist ladies began working on funds for a new church structure. "The ladies of the Home Mission society are going to begin soon to raise money to build a Methodist church in Rhome. We hope they will have success. Would be a good idea to have a supper, ladies."[10] It certainly did not take long for the ladies to put that suggestion into effect because before the end of the month there was a report of the supper. "There is to be a supper at the school house Thursday night for the purpose of aiding to build a Methodist church in Rhome. This is a very important entertainment. Ye editors are invited to come down."[11]

The ladies must have succeeded in their efforts, for in April, 1902, came a report of the building of the new church. "The new Methodist church is moving up rapidly and it will not be long until Rhome can boast of two good churches . . ."[12]

The new building was not without its tragedies. First, in May, 1902, came the report of two workmen who were injured while working on a scaffolding which gave way and dropped them about twelve or fifteen feet. Then in another few weeks, there was a heavy storm which almost destroyed the partially finished building. "We can report plenty of rain and more wind than nervous people like to see. Last Sunday the heaviest storm passed over Rhome that has ever been known right in this town. The wind came mainly from the west and struck the new Methodist church moving it about four or five feet due east and then came very near turning it over. It was so badly wrecked that it is doubtful if it can ever be straightened without tearing it entirely down."[13] Apparently, the damage could be repaired; however, it was another year before the dedication of the structure.

> Last Sunday was the most pleasant day, in many respects, that we have had in Rhome for a long time. This was the day appointed for the dedication of the new Methodist church. The weather was clear and beautiful. The dedication service began promptly at 11 o'clock. Opening song, "All Hail the Power of Jesus." After the song, prayer was led by Rev. W. S. May, one of the former pastors, who had much to do in originating the enterprise. Then followed a scripture reading by Pastor Sims. Then followed a most interesting and instructive sermon, if heard without prejudice, would do any Christian good. After the sermon, the house was formally dedicated; the prayer was offered by Brother Miller.
>
> As alluded to above, one of the most conspicuous personages was Rev. W. S. May. It might be truthfully said that he is the father of the enterprise, for it was during his ministry that the plan to build the church was begun. Like David, he planned to build a house for the Lord, but it was left for his son to do the work.

THIS WAS THE first building that was erected by the First Methodist Church in Rhome. The bell is now hanging in the bell tower of the present church.

The older citizens were delighted with the presence of Rev. Shrader, who was pastor here in 1893. One of the greatest revivals ever known at this place was led by him during that year.

We were glad to see quite a number of people from Boyd, Newark, Fairview, and other places.

SCRIBBLER[14]

The Quarterly Conference records of October 13, 1902, records a letter from the trustees confirming the building of Rhome's First Methodist Church building:

Our church house is now complete and is a thing of beauty, the value thereof is $1700. We have it insured in the Fire Association of Philadelphia for $500 . . .[15]

This new church building served the congregation until the year 1940. It also served the entire community at various times, such as being the site for the Community Christmas tree. Children of the community watched with eagerness the comings and goings on the day of the party. That night it was a tremendous thrill to have one's name called out, with Santa Claus holding out a lovely doll or a bright red wagon.

On April 23, 1900, Pastor F. M. Sherwood reported that Rhome had a Senior Epworth League of about thirty-six members. On November 13, 1901, Mrs. Lou Morris, president of the Women's Home Missionary Society, reported that the society had eleven members, and that they had sent a box of clothing and money to the Waco Methodist Orphanage. Mrs. F. E. Shanks was the vice-president of the organization.

One of the more interesting customs of the early Methodists was called "pounding the preacher," a procedure in which the members brought gifts of food and money for the pastor and his family. A description of one of the poundings at Rhome was given by the pastor, I. A. Thomas, on December 21, 1910. "We were severely pounded at Rhome, Tuseday night and the pounding was the most elaborate one we have ever received on a circuit. To us it was very encouraging and makes us hopeful for the future . . . ."[16]

The year 1902 brought a large number of transfers from the Methodist church at the village of Aurora.

Like the Baptist church, the Methodist church also had social functions similar to the one described in 1915.

> The Philatea Sunday school class of the Methodist church entertained at Mrs. J. R. Troxell's Thursday afternoon, honoring their teacher, Mrs. O. H. Barker, who will soon leave for Burkburnet to reside. The evening was delightfully spent in conversation, music, and diversions. A delicious salad course was served to the following guests: Mmes. O. H. Barker, Clyde McCurdy, E. L. Smitherman, W. T. Leonard, Tom Green, C. E. Shaw, J. R. Troxell, and Misses Nora and Pearl McCurdy, Winnie Mae Morris, Lucile Dohnan, Beulah Mullinax, and Kate Barker.[17]

In 1906 the Rhome Methodist church entered a new venture which probably has not been attempted by any other Rhome church before or after this time. "The *Light* this week sold to Rev. O. J. Reed, a job press, type and other material, and the *Young People's Friend* will be published at the Methodist Parsonage from this time on."[18] This writer was unable to find out how long this church paper was published.

One of the many traditions of Rhome has been the picnic at the Falls. While today it might be difficult for young people to imagine, it was the big event for young people in Rhome's earlier days. "There will be a union Sunday school picnic at the Falls on Friday, May 10. A

THE CUMBERLAND PRESBYTERIAN Church at Rhome.

PRESBYTERIAN CHURCH AFTER the cyclone that hit on August 8, 1912.

nice program will be rendered and everybody is insured a pleasant time. Dinner served on the ground."[19] This writer can recall many good times while picnicking or swimming at the Falls, a water hole about a mile from the center of Rhome on the present Highway 114.

The Cumberland Presbyterian church was not far behind the others in acquiring a church building. Their first home was a building which was moved from Aurora to Rhome in 1904. "The Cumberland Presbyterian church of Aurora will be moved to this place next week. Contract has been made for its removal."[20] The work was not completed until sometime in May. "The C. F. Church that has recently been moved from Aurora to Rhome is being papered and painted and is looming up nicely."[21]

The first church was destroyed by a cyclone in 1912. "The Presbyterian church which was wrecked by cyclone is being rebuilt. It will be completed in a few weeks."[22] The Presbyterian church held revival meetings, mothers' day services, and other special events within their church. "The members of the Union Bible class entertained with a moonlight picnic on the lawn of Judge and Mrs. Hambright Thursday evening. About one hundred were present. Several readings were given by Mrs. Casey and her class in elocution. After the formal program a variety of games and levity were engaged in until luncheon was spread at ten o'clock on the lawn."[23] One of their most interesting events was their "dollar tea." "Mrs. J. W. Beard entertained the Presbyterian Ladies Aid society last Monday afternoon. The occasion being their dollar tea. Each member told in rhyme how they made their dollar. The evening was pleasantly spent. Delicious refreshments were served."[24] Before the end of the decade one of the most popular of all the Presbyterian ministers, W. A. Binyon, came to the Rhome church. "Rev. W. A. Binyon will preach at the Presbyterian church next Sunday morning and night. Everybody invited to attend these services."[25]

Not far behind the Presbyterian and Methodist churches was the Christian church of Rhome in building its congregation a home. "There is some talk that the Christian church of Rhome is about to buy the old Union church at Aurora, and if they succeed in buying it, they will move it to Rhome."[26] In August of 1904 there was a report that the new Christian church was almost completed.[27] This last report leaves the writer in doubt about the origin of this first church building. Since the report came almost two years later than the original report about a church building, it is more probable that the church body decided to build a completely new church house.

There was a report of a revival in 1908 which was very successful for the church. "The Christian revival which has been in progress here

FIRST BUILDING BELONGING to the Church of Christ. Probably the building which was moved from Aurora, Texas.

for two weeks closed last night leaving a good work accomplished. The meeting was conducted by Rev. Carter of Whiteswright. A Mr. Taylor of Chicago led the singing. The meeting was well attended and several accessions to the church were made."[28]

Choir practice was a regular weekly event in 1916, as reported by the *Wise County Messenger*. "Rev. W. A. Bentley will fill his regular appointment at the Christian church the second Sunday, Februray, 13th. Choir practice every Friday night. Everybody invited."[29]

However broad-minded and tolerant the churches of Rhome may have been toward each other, they did not encourage the growth of other faiths, as shown by the following quote:

> There have been two men claiming to the be Mormon elders tramping this section for the past few days, but they are getting rather cool receptions where they go. They went to two places on the prairie and were driven away by both men and women. Last Sunday they were at church, and after services they remained at the church until about two o'clock. On Monday they returned, and we regret that our trustees allowed them to preach in our school house. The trustees, however, think they are doing right.

This is a system of doctrine that is pernicious and dangerous to our civilization as well as our Christianity. The very fundamental principles of that system of doctrine strike at the very tap root of all that is most sacred and holy in our land and homes. It seeks to enter our homes and poison the minds of the inmates and to estrange wife from husband, daughter from mother; in fact, it destroys all that is most sacred of our Christian homes. At the same time it seeks to destroy Christian churches of our land.[30]

Education and Educators

During these years education in Rhome made great strides, advancing from a small, wooden one-teacher school to a two-story brick building with five or six teachers. In 1901 Rhome had a subscription school with one teacher. In June of the same year there was concern over seating for the school house. "The young people had an 'I scream' supper at the school house last Saturday night, part of the proceeds to be used toward seating the school house."[1] By November of the following year, there were two teachers for the school. "The school is progressing nicely under the management of Prof. Huddleston and Miss Becker. At the present writing there are over one hundred pupils in attendance."[2] During 1902 SCRIBBLER, the Rhome reporter, was concerned about the quality of textbooks, especially since the question of uniform adoption of textbooks had arisen. ". . . But SCRIBBLER is of the opinion that of all frauds that were ever palmed off on an intelligent people, the new arithmetic is the greatest of all, and the grammar is not far behind . . . "[3]

Many people today will remember the addition to the school house, making it an L-shaped structure. "The addition to the house is almost complete, and school will open Tuesday, Prof. Bain as principal and Miss Annie Wilkerson, assistant."[4] During the previous school year there was a suggestion that the citizens were not really going to be satisfied with the l-shaped addition to the building. "The citizens are now agitating a $50,000 school building, and if this enterprise is carried through, it will no doubt settle the question that Rhome is to be the largest city in Wise county."[5] Without a doubt the reporter was excited because he certainly must have added an extra zero. Five thousand would have been more like the suggested amount to be spent for a building at that time.

In 1905 the old building was partitioned. "The public school building is being partitioned so as to give more different departments for the school."[6] This development also tells us that the school was growing and that more teachers were being hired. "Rhome public school will open the 18th of Sept. under the management of Prof. H.

H. Bain. Miss Annie Lyle of Boyd will have charge of the intermediate work and Miss Allie Renshaw of Decatur, the primary work."[7]

A report from the *Light* gave the scholastic population for the Rhome school in 1905. "C. J. VanMeter, Jr., finished taking the scholastic census for the school district last Monday. He has on his reports 124 within the scholastic age."[8] One successful teacher who came to Rhome and remained for several years was J. Wesley Bailey.

> J. Wesley Bailey and family are this week moving to Rhome, where Mr. Bailey will have charge of the public school. Several years successful work here have proven his efficiency and our friends at Rhome are to be congratulated, as are also Mr. Bailey and family, who are going to a fine community.[9]

Professor Bailey did more for the community than just teaching in the public school. He also taught Normal Courses for those interested in the teaching profession. "Professor Bailey began teaching a Normal Course in the public school. The following students were enrolled: Sallie Bobo, Roxana Morris, John Bobo, Earl VanMeter, Ollie Mae Fairchild, Robert NeSmith, Robert Leonard, Kate Troxell, Mary VanMeter."[10] Mrs. Kate Troxell Shaw told the writer that several of these students took the state examinations in 1910, received certificates, and taught school.

The first real hint of a new school building came in 1909. "An educational sentiment is growing in this community, and we hope to be able in the near future to report the arrangements for a new school building."[11] In 1910 there was an even more positive report. "Location for our new school building is being discussed. Work will begin on it early in the spring."[12] The new building, according to stories in the Morris family, was built on land that originally had been dedicated by the family as a cemetery. At the death of little Allie Morris, a daughter of W. W. Morris, it was found that the soil covered almost solid rock formations, thus making it impractical as a cemetery. The plans for the site were changed to school purposes. "Our beautiful new school building costing $8,500 is nearing completion and will be ready for school opening by the 15th of September."[13] The first week in September brought the following announcement:

> The school building will be ready for the opening term of 1910 on Sept. 12. Faculty: Frank Wallace, principal; Mrs. Etta Wallace, 1st assistant; Miss Amanda Hildreth, 2nd assistant; Miss Mable Call, 3rd assistant; and Miss Cresidus Reese, music. Miss Ruth Ward, 4-5 grades.[14]

CLASS PICTURE IN front of the old school house at Rhome, approximately 1905. Front row: John Browning, Lloyd Douglas, Hirem Burrows, Hugh Burrows, Dennis Ford, Joe Taylor, Hugh Porter. Second row: DeWitt Morris, Etta Simmons, Ellis Troxell, Earl Shankle, Euna Wright, Sol Lynch, Alice Sullivan, Basil VanMeter. Third Row: Ollie Mae Fairchild, Bill George, Virginia Bobo, Marie VanMeter, Vance Beauchamp, Susan Burrows, Roxana Morris, Earl VanMeter, Ada Sullivan, Prof. Bailey. Fourth Row: Amanda Hildreth, Bob Leonard, Sally Bobo, Forrest thurmond, Rena Morris, Robert NeSmith, Kate Troxell.

CLASS PICTURE IN front of old school building at Rhome, approximately 1905. Front row: Homer Bryan, ___, Fred Vance, Hayden Looney, Charlie Morris, ___, Fletcher Barnes, ___. Second row: Marvin Poteet, ___, ___, Wendell Morris, Jeff George, Leonard Robertson, Tom Bobo, ___, Olan VanMeter. Third row: ___, Merle Newman, Velma Robertson, Jewel Looney, Velma Carpenter, ___, Lois Newman, Opal Barker, Jennie Bryan, Naomi Scott, ___, Ella Burch Barker, Ruth Scott, Ann Bobo, Bessie Barnes. Fourth row: ___, ___, ___, Glenn Barker, Meda Browning, ___, ___ Ussery, ___ Logan, Nona George, Jack White, Zack Bobo. Fifth row: ___, John Browning, Bessie VanMeter, Edith Taylor, Winnie Mae Morris, Bessis Bobo, Gabie Sue Carpenter, Virginia Bobo, Joe Naylor, Paul Scott, John VanMeter, Carl Carpenter, Ernest Poteet.
Sixth row: Owing Herring, Earl VanMeter, Mary Shankle, Maude Taylor, Mary VanMeter, Eddie Simmons, Newt Barker, John Bobo, Basil VanMeter, Bob Leonard.

RHOME'S SECOND SCHOOL building. This building burned in 1929.

VIEW LOOKING EAST from school building. Early Rhome basketball team.

Today an Etta Wallace Scholarship is given each year at Northwest High School by Dr. Zack Bobo, Jr., of Arlington, Texas. Dr. Bobo was a student of Mrs. Wallace at the time she was teaching in Rhome.

With the advent of the new building, Rhome school began to be active in the University Interscholastic League events. In 1915 Wise county had only two schools entered in the League, Rhome and Greenwood. The events which they entered were essay writing, declamation, debate for boys and girls, tennis, basket ball, and track. Robert Leonard was elected superintendent of Rhome school in 1915. Mr. Leonard worked very hard to improve the school, and as a means of interesting the citizens, he wrote a page for the *Decatur News* each week, chiefly concerning the activities of the school.

> School interest has perhaps never before been to the height it has now reached . . . Some of the things which have been done in the past year and are planned for the coming year:
>
> 1. The school has come from a three-teacher to a six-teacher school.
> 2. The establishing of the Departments of Agriculture and Domestic Science.
> 3. The expenditure of several hundred dollars in setting the school grounds in Bermuda grass.
> 4. Fencing the school grounds with an iron net woven wire fence.
> 5. The equipping of science laboratories.
> 6. The donation of three hundred volumes to the library by Superintendent Leonard.
> 7. Establishing a high school of eleven grades.
>
> Most of the money for carrying out the above work has been given by the citizens of Rhome. They are ready to help in any movement which means a better school and a better town.[15]

A note on the growth of the school was given in October of 1915. "Every foot of space in the public school building is now in use. When this building was erected, it was supposed that half of it would accomodate the student body for the next ten years."[16] Thus our parents suffered from the same problems which we still face today—school growth.

The honor roll for October, 1915, was given as follows for Rhome school: Aleeta Svenson, Glenn and Opal Barker, Marvin Poteet, Tom Bobo, Wayne Renshaw, Comer Dossey, Anna Bobo, Maggie Svenson, and Beulah Mullinax. On the same week in October there is an account of the Rhome participation in the Wise County Fair:

Last Friday the public school was dismissed so that all the students would have a chance to attend the Wise County Fair. About sixty took advantage of this opportunity. They met at the public school building after arriving in Decatur and paraded through the town with other students who represented the various schools of the county. After this they all marched to the fair grounds and immediately began to view the exhibits and attractions with pleasure and anxiety. Three of the teachers accompanied this crowd of youths and maidens on the outing.

The time came in the afternoon for combat for honor. Four races and a basketball game were listed in which Rhome had representatives . . . The first race listed was a hundred yard dash for boys between ages of 15 and 21 . . . Jeff George represented Rhome, and as he had not illustrated to the outside world his capacity for running, little was said or thought of his appearance on the track in the warm-up . . . Jeff led the race from start to finish . . . when the race was over, shouts and hats went up for the "big blonde" from Rhome who had set a new standard and record for Wise county.

The second race was a 100 yard dash for the school teachers of the county. The judges called this one a tie between Robert Leonard and Aston D. Turner. They called for the race to be run over, but Turner didn't care to take a second chance.

The third race was a 220 yard dash for all boys. Jeff George won this race with more ease than the first. The 400 yard race was won by Paul Bobo, who had had neither practice nor coaching. This is some record for Rhome on foot.[17]

They were in for disappointment, however, because Rhome lost the basketball game.

Many innovations were taking place in the school system. In 1915 there was a report on a project for the agriculture department in which the boys experimented with the effects of different fertilizers on corn, as prescribed by Texas A & M College. Rhome school was gaining a reputation in the county, so much so that students from other parts of the county were being sent to school in Rhome. "Tom Ewing of south of Decatur was here Sunday. He brought his son J. C., who entered school here Monday . . . Jack Robertson, from south of Boyd, also entered school Monday."[18]

In November of the same year there were other innovations. "Mrs. Casey of Rhome is inaugurating physical culture in the various schools of the county. Mrs. Casey teaches the students for 25 cents for a series of ten lessons."[19] Three weeks later it was reported that the state was giving Rhome a sum of $500 for the purpose of maintaining industrial work in the school.

Declamation contests were sponsored by the school. "A silver medal contest was given in the High School auditorium last Saturday night. The medal was won by Miss Roe Morris . . . We feel that it is well to say that little Miss Maude Morris showed splendid ability in expression."[20]

The graduating class of Rhome High School in June, 1915, included the following: Misses Letta May Svenson, Glenn Barker, Opal Barker, Will Hoge, Hannah Brammer, Odie Oates, Marvin Poteet, and Wendell Morris.

Arbor Day was celebrated in February, 1916, by the Rhome school. The following description of the day gives the reader an idea of school life at that time:

> Tuesday, February 22, was observed as a holiday at school. All the children and teachers gathered at the school house about nine o'clock and spent the day planting trees. Dinner was served to all. In the evening at 7:30 the students rendered a splendid program in the auditorium for Arbor Day and Washington's birthday. Perhaps the largest crowd attended the program that ever attended any entertainment in Rhome . . .
>
> Program
> A Hymn for Arbor Day . . . . Seventh and Eighth Grades
> Welcome Address . . . . Jeff T. George
> Tribute to Trees . . . . Ray Ellars
> The Destruction and Preservation of our Forest . . . . . Willie Oates
> Why We Should Observe Arbor Day . . . . Hannah Brammer
> Governor Hogg's Dying Request . . . . Clarence George
> The Kind of Trees to Plant . . . . Drummond Dill
> Life and Character of Washington . . . . Russell McCurdy
> Song "George Washington" . . . . Seventh and Eighth Grades
> The Liberty Bell . . . . Glenn Barker
> "Tis Splendid to Live So Grandly" . . . . Zaeta Morris
> Words from Washington . . . . Waymon Rogers
> Tommie's Queries . . . . Earl Van Meter
> The New George Washington . . . . Jack Lisby
> In Memory of Washington . . . . Prof. Comer Dossey, Zack Barton, Boyd Logan, Chas. Robertson, Harry Logan, Dave McCurdy, and Joe Sparks.[21]

Despite the rosy reports about school conditions, not all was well with the county schools, as a report from Decatur shows:

> In this county 67 teachers are teaching on second grade cer-

tificates, and only three in the entire county hold degrees from a college or university. The teachers of the county, on an average, are paid less than $20.00 per month, counting twelve months to the school year. This is less than is paid a hired hand.[22]

The first levying of a tax to support the local school district was accomplished in May, 1918.

ELECTION NOTICE
Be it ordered by the board of trustees of the Rhome Independent School District that an election be held in the building in which the First National Bank is located in the town of Rhome . . . to determine whether the board of trustees of said district shall have the power to annually levy and collect a tax upon all taxable property . . . for the support and maintainence of public free schools . . . of and at a rate not exceeding fifty cents on the $100 valuation of taxable property . . . such tax if voted to be levied and collected for the year 1918 and annually thereafter unless it be discontinued as provided by law . . . [23]

The graduation class of 1919 listed five members: Leta Janice Smith, John Gordon Barker, Dottie Daye Lowance, Etta Mae Hutchison, and Mildred Madeline Reid.[24]

Amusements, Recreation, and Social Life

The two decades before 1920 saw a great growth in all aspects of life in Rhome. New organizations, new types of entertainment, extensive social affairs affected Rhome's citizens. "There is also some talk of organizing a Chautauqua Literary and Scientific Circle at Rhome. This is one of the best institutions of the kind of which we are acquainted."[1] Whether this organization ever materialized is not known, but at least there were citizens who were interested.

An organization which did develop was the Odd Fellows Lodge.

Rhome had an Odd Fellows Lodge organized on July 28th with T. J. Weems, N. G. Holt, and W. W. Morris . . . The lodge is very grateful to L. C. Slimp for his untiring efforts to make the organization a brilliant success, and the lodge now has a school of instruction in the work of the order taught by Mr. G. C. Newton of Fort Worth. The school is taught each Saturday night, which is the regular meeting night.[2]

This lodge evidently proved successful in Rhome. A barbecue was planned by the Odd Fellows Lodge to be given April 6, 1906, in

Rhome. "This will be a public out-door barbecue, and a big day will be enjoyed here by everybody who wants to come."[3] In March, 1910, H. I. Watkins and Mrs. M. W. Burch attended the IOOF convention in Austin as delegates from Rhome.

Hunting was one of the sports which occupied the younger men of Rhome.

> Some of our townsmen have been taking up arms against the squirrels in the Trinity river bottoms and wild ducks lately. Knowing these notorious hunters, however, the squirrels and ducks have been "hiding out" and not a shot has been heard to ring out its echo through those lofty woods.[4]

The next week's report brought a story about cowboys hunting in the area surrounding Rhome:

> The boys from the Caldwell ranch are having some fun chasing and killing wolves. Latter part of last week they succeeded in killing two more large grey wolves. One young fellow clubbed one in the head while the wolf was standing on a log out in the water away from the dogs.[5]

The first mention of motion pictures as entertainment for Rhome came in the year 1906; however, it was near the end of the second decade before Rhome finally acquired a picture theater of its own.

> There were two young fellows here last Thursday with a moving picture show. After trying nearly all day to get a house in which to show, and failing, they left for some other place. Our town is without amusement for the young and old. If it only had a city hall, it would not be so. Where is our enterprise?[6]

It was 1918 before the motion picture business came to Rhome. The first theater was located on the lot just west of the present Masonic Lodge building.

> Ellis Troxell started the picture show, later called the "Lyric Theater" about 1918. He sold it to Jim Troxell when Nelma was about two years old in 1920. Wayne Renshaw once refused to go on a trip with his family because of a movie serial, "The Perils of Pauline," with Pearl White. Pearl was tied to a railroad track and the train was about to run over her. Wayne didn't want to miss the outcome.[7]

Mr. Jim Troxell operated the theater until about the late 1920's when

RHOME TENNIS CLUB, 1910. Front row: L. W. Renshaw, M. W. Burch, John Bobo, and Claude Shaw. Back row: Mrs. M. W. Burch, Kate Troxell, Bennie Bobo, and Claude Coleman.

the new school gymnasium brought about too much competition for the small crowds that Rhome could provide.

Rhome had a tennis club in 1910. The accompanying picture shows the members of the original club: Mrs. M. W. Burch, Kate Troxell, Bennie Bobo, Claude Coleman, L. W. Renshaw, M. W. Burch, John Bobo, and Claude Shaw.

Baseball continued as a very popular sport for Rhome. In 1913 there was a story about the Rhome team. "The King's Candy baseball team of Fort Worth played the Rhome team here Saturday. Game was called at the 14th inning on account of darkness, the score standing at 1 to 1."[8]

Not all pastimes were as vigorous as the baseball and tennis activities. There was also in the county a great interest in the game of checkers. The following report is of a tournament that took place in Rhome during the Christmas holidays in 1915:

> The great monotony of the daily routine of life was solemnly
> disturbed from its peaceful slumbers during the Christmas week

when our native townsmen burst forth in a wild stampede, each one desperate with the other; the question which had arisen in their minds . . . "Who is the best checker player in Rhome?" In order to check the wild pulsating . . . a series of games must be scheduled . . . By common consent it was agreed to let G. C. Hill arrnage the schedule. Those combatting . . . were: Ben Morris, Claude Shaw, Julian Ward, C. C. Ramsey, Jim Troxell, and G. C. Dill. In as much as Ben Morris had waved forth this honor for some time . . . it was almost a conceded fact that he would win the high score. After the game had started, no one rested day or night until the situation was brought to a clear finish. Long before the series had ended, an underground current began to prevail that C. E. Shaw was demonstrating some unforseen skill in the game . . . At the close of the game, no one was near Mr. Shaw; it was clear that honor, praise, and fame should be given him . . . Ben Morris for many years has shown the greatest skill, but it was supposed that old age and bad eyesight prevailed on him during this time . . . Jim Troxell demonstrated a magnificent type of player, but was too light for the champion of the tournament.

Dr. Petty of Decatur will have to fight for the lover's cup yet. C. E. Shaw is ready to choose him at any moment that the Dr. feels equal to such a task.[9]

Mrs. Jim Troxell, mother of this writer, often told of the zeal and dedication of the checker and domino players. Once during an especially intriguing game, a storm blew out a window of the Troxell home. The players calmly stood a mattress against the window and continued the game until morning.

The first mention of the women's study club of Rhome came in 1914 when the organization was referred to as the Thursday Book Club. "Miss Nell Troxell was hostess to the Thursday Book Club at the home of her aunt, Mrs. James Troxell. In a diversion of modern authors, Miss Vida Dolman was prize winner. Lovely refreshments were served to the following members: Mmes. Martin, Shaw, Burch, Wilson, Troxell, Renshaw, Misses Addie Hambright, Mattie Neal, Vida Dolman, and Velma Neal."[10]

Literary efforts were furthered by the presentation of a Greek play, *Thesus and Ariadne,* in the Rhome High School auditorium. The cast was listed as follows:

Thesus—Mr. Sparks
Youths—Messrs. Hudnall, Taylor, Troxell, Douglass, Sparks, Burch, and George
Ariadne—Miss Zorns

Maids—Mmes. Barker, Troxell, Burch, Green, Leonard, and Misses Chambers, Barker, George, Morris, Wright, McCurdy, and Fairchild.[11]

Checkers was not the only contest that took place in Rhome. There were many other types of competition.

> A decided innovation in the cotton picking realm of this community took place in the Bill Brown cotton patch . . . when H. R. Hambright and Charley and Frank Morton . . . took to the field at 6 a.m. and left when Old Sol had bid farewell to the golden gate of the west. When the figures were made at the close of the day, H. R. Hambright was in the lead, and received the pennant, having bagged 742 pounds of strict middling; Chas Morton was next . . . with 721 pounds, and Frank Morton with 718 pounds. The money derived from the picking will be sent to Buckner's Orphans Home . . .[12]

A very different type of contest was sponsored by the *Decatur News*. "The Decatur News sponsored an automobile and piano subscription contest. From Rhome the nominees were Miss Kate Barker, Miss Bess Bobo, Mrs. Drummond Burch, Miss Irva Lee Fairchild, Miss Nona George, Miss Addie Hambright, Miss Pearl McCurdy, Miss Kate Leonard, Miss Mattie Neel, Miss Katherine Taylor."[13] This contest stirred up a tremendous amount of interest throughout the county. There was a notice to this effect during the next month. "Miss Kate Taylor is going to be hard to beat in the Ford Automobile race. Ten thousand votes on one day shows there is somebody at work."[14] In May it was reported that there were only two left in the contest, Miss Katherine Taylor of Rhome and Miss Myrtle Huddleston of Decatur. The final count was reported on May 12, 1916, with Huddleston, 281, 250; Taylor, 219, 150.

Rhome citizens attending the Wise County Fair were treated to a demonstration by an aviator in 1915. "Aviator LaVivian made his first flight Tuesday afternoon at 5 o'clock, the weather conditions fine. The crowd was awed by the skill of this masterly birdman, and his daily flights during the remaining days of the fair will be the most interesting part of the program."[15]

Rhome social life saw many weddings during this time. Sometimes the young couples stole a march on their elders and married before the appointed time. On a Wednesday afternoon at the end of August, Miss DeAlva Greer of Decatur gave a party at the home of Mrs. David Dickson, announcing the wedding on the coming Tuesday of Miss Ruth Scott to Mr. Ones Finlayson. "Miss Ruth is one of

THE HOME OF Zack and Bettie Morris Bobo, which still stands in Rhome today.

Decatur's very sweetest and prettiest girls and a great favorite with *The News*. Mr. Finlayson is a member of one of Wise county's most prominent and highly esteemed families, living in the Rhome community."[16] The next week's paper brought the news that the young couple had slipped up on their friends and married that Saturday evening at the home of Mr. and Mrs. Arthur Simmons in Decatur. They were then on their honeymoon in Galveston. Among the other couples who were wed during this time were Mr. Ocie Thorell and Miss Dollie Brammer, Mr. Everitt McCurdy and Miss Winnie Mae Morris, Miss Blanche Hutcherson and Mr. Joseph F. Day, Mr. Ellis Troxell and Miss Katherine Taylor.

Many different types of entertainment were enjoyed by the young people of Rhome, including an oyster supper, an ice cream social, a Chinese tea, card parties, 42 parties, and a "Quilting Bee." The townspeople were not bored by a lack of things to do. "J. R. Troxell and wife, Pugh Morris and wife, and John Postum Whitehead and family spent one day last week pecaning. They report an excellent pecan crop this year."[17] One interesting party was that given in the Zack Bobo home.

> Miss Bessie Bobo entertained a few of her friends Saturday night with a leap year Valentine party at her lovely new home on Penn street. She was assisted in entertaining by her sister, Mrs.

Carl Christian of Decatur and also Mrs. Jim Troxell. In the progressive game of mending broken hearts, the high score prize went to Everitt McCurdy. After various games and contests, Misses George and Wright played several piano solos. Miss Katherine rendered a vocal number in a very charming manner. A delicious salad course was served to the following: Misses Nona George, Winnie Mae Morris, Adrain Ash, Katherine Taylor, Euna and Midget Wright, Ollie Mae Fairchild, Pearl McCurdy, Katherine Barker. Messrs. Budge Sparks, J. Hudnall, Jeff George, J. C. Ewing, Lloyd and Gladys Douglass, Arthur Simmons, Louis Sparks, Basil VanMeter, and Everitt McCurdy.[18]

Another party which was very successful was a card party at the home of Mr. and Mrs. Tom Green, in honor of Miss Bess Joyce of Fort Worth. "One especially pleasant feature of the evening was music furnished by Mrs. Green, piano, and Mr. Russell, violin. Refreshments were served to Messrs and Mmes. M. W. Burch, C. E. Shaw, J. W. Russell, and Mrs. H. I. Watkins, Misses Bessie Austin, Roxana Morris, Willie Ford, Polly Harrison, Ollie Mae Fairchild, and Mary Shankle; Messrs. Burge and Tom Sparks, Drummond Burch, Joe Taylor, and Jim Sparks."[19]

The Thursday Book Club was especially important to the ladies of Rhome. On different occasions it was entertained in the homes of Miss Addie Hambright, Mrs. Terrell Lillard, Mrs. M. W. Burch, and Miss Ollie Mae Fairchild. Generally, the club colors of white rose buds, pink carnations, and fern were carried out in the decorations and refreshments.

As a final note of the social life, there was a story in 1918 of entertainment for the boys in uniform. "Mr. and Mrs. Z. B. Bobo had as dinner guests Sunday twelve aviators from Camp Hicks. The boys were loud in their praise of the hospitality shown them and the pleasant day spent in the Bobo home."[20]

Military Obligations

The headlines on April 6, 1917, read "WAR—The United States Senate has declared a state of war exists at this time." The citizens were ordered to drill. All men between twenty-one and thirty-one were ordered to appear at their voting boxes and register on June 5, 1917, for the draft. "No matter what you claim you have for exemption, you must register."[1] One young man living south of Decatur shot himself to death in an effort to resist the draft. Texas was called upon to furnish thirty thousand men under the draft. Rhome had seventy-two young men to register for the service. There was also an appeal to the young women of the county:

> The patriotic girls of Wise who wish to "do their bit" should "adopt" the soldiers of Capt. Lillard's Wise county company. These patriots have volunteered to fight for Uncle Sam against the common enemy in protection of the most sacred and glorious principles, and as they are entering upon this great task . . . it would greatly cheer and please each of them to know that he was being remembered by a lassie back at home who sends him some material comforts and nick-nacks which soldiers enjoy so much . . . . If you can visit the camp, write Capt. Steve Lillard at Decatur, and he will try to please you in the selection of a soldier for "adoption."[2]

The ladies also helped through the Rhome Red Cross auxiliary by knitting sweaters and mufflers for the soldiers. The following persons were named in a list of Red Cross personnel from Rhome. Mrs. Z. B. Bobo, Mrs. M. E. Simmons, M. E. Simmons, Mrs. W. W. Morris, Mrs. H. I. Watkins, Mrs. W. J. Mullinax, Mrs. Laura Holt, J. J. Eagan, Mrs. Charlie Hudnall, Mrs. L. W. Renshaw, Mrs. W. T. Leonard, Dr. W. L. Russell, and Mrs. Earl VanMeter. A Junior Red Cross class was organized by Mrs. Tom Leonard.

The first draft of soldiers was reported in July, 1917, and the following Rhome men were listed: Guy Hudnall, Sidney McGoodwin, Grover C. Brown, Milen Frank Thurmond, H. T. Brammer, J. F. Balch. The second call in August, 1917, listed Luther Baugh, Willie R. Oates, Homer F. Brammer, Gillian D. Bryant, Elzey E. Simmons, Solomon Carpenter, and Robert A. Stephens.

The government rationed food by setting aside certain days of the week for conservation of certain foods. There were wheatless days on Monday and Wednesday, meatless days on Tuesdays and one meal each day was meatless; porkless day was Saturday when no pork could be served including lard. Potato Friday was set as a day when the house holder was urged to serve copious quantities of potatoes. Retailers could sell no more than five pounds of sugar to a city customer at one time nor more than ten pounds to a country resident. Flour was sold no more than one-quarter barrel to city folks and one-half barrel to country folks. One of the most interesting directions was that no housewife was to have in her possession at one time more than thirty days supply of any other food commodity. It was considered hoarding which was punishable by a fine of $5000 or two years imprisonment or both! The *Decatur News* carried an article on the jackrabbit as a war meat. Five or six recipes were given for rabbit sausage, rabbit chili con carne, and others.

Accounts beginning in October of 1917 carried the news of Rhome's young men and women who had enlisted in one service or another. Jarrett Hudnall and John Bridges came home from Camp Bowie to spend Sunday in Rhome. In May, 1918, Thurman Hudnall and A. C. Alexander were stationed at Camp Travis. During July, 1918, there was a report of Rhome's first nurse: "Miss Mary Thurmond of Dallas is here for a few days to visit with homefolks. Miss Mary has enlisted as a Red Cross nurse and will probably to to France soon."[3] Luther Baugh and Otis Oates were called into service in July, 1918. By July, the boys were being sent overseas. "Word has been received by relatives that Lloyd Douglass, Sid McGoodwin, and Thurman Hudnall have landed safely in France."[4]

Both newspapers carried dozens of letters from soldiers all over the world to their parents and friends. A letter from Thurman Hudnall to his parents was one of those printed in the *Messenger*.

> The following letter was received by Mr. Chas. Hudnall of Rhome from his son Thurman who is now in "Sunny France." "Dear Mother and Father: I have been pretty busy this past week, but will now take time to write you a few lines. I like everything over here very well, but I can't say I think as much of France as I do of the United States.
>
> "We haven't had any hard luck yet as I had expected us to have. We will leave here pretty soon and if you don't hear from me in three or four days, don't worry, because I won't have time to write . . . Don't think I will be over here very long because I feel like I will be home pretty soon. I have never gotten homesick because I haven't had time to worry about that . . . Thurman Hudnall."[5]

A report from Fairview in 1917 noted that the aviators from Hicks Field were busy training over the area. "Airplanes are seen daily now flying all around in this vicinity. J. F. Thurmond and family motored to the aviation camp Sunday afternoon and saw a great number doing all kinds of stunts."[6] The *News* was enthusiastic in its approval of the use of the airplane in the war. "People are waking up to the fact that aviation will play no small part in helping to win the war."[7]

The residents of the area were very pleased to have the young aviators visit in their homes. It was a custom of the time to invite them for Sunday dinner.

> Mr. and Mrs. J. F. Thurmond entertained eighteen of the aviators of Camp Hicks with a dinner Thanksgiving . . . The boys of the 17th have finished their training and are only waiting their

commission before going to France. It was a great pleasure to Mr. and Mrs. Thurmond to have the boys present and the dinner was greatly enjoyed by them. Others present besides the aviators were Miss Mary Thurmond, Miss Davis, and Miss Murl Brymer of Dallas, Forrest Thurmond and family, J. H. Troxell and son Charley, J. H. Rowan and family, Miss Alice Small and Miss Audrey Petty.[8]

Another branch of the service was also enlisting Rhome men. "J. H. Troxell and son Clarence were up from Rhome Tuesday, and made the *News* a pleasant call. Clarence joined the navy and has been away for about two years. He came in Sunday on a twenty-five days' furlough. He was in South America in seven months' duty, but is now on convoy duty and has made six trips across the ocean. He is looking well and has made good since being in Uncle Sam's service."[9]

Rhome was asked to push the sales of Liberty Loan Bonds to the amount of $15,000. They were also very generous in their contributions to the Red Cross. One quota named was $800, and Rhome had exceeded that in a few weeks' time.

The in October of 1918 came news of an epidemic which struck all over the country. Hundreds of persons died in the United States of this fever. Spanish Influenza was the scourge that crippled the country. "On account of the Spanish influenza epidemic, the public school was dismissed for this week. There are several cases in town and the surrounding country."[10]

The next week brought news from the boys in service. The headlines read as follows: "Wise County Boys Whipping the Huns—Fighting Like Veterans!" In December there was cheering news to one of the Rhome families. "Thurman Hudnall of Rhome returned this week from France, where he has seen service for several months with the signal corps of the 90th division. Hudnall is the first Wise county boy to return from the front."[11]

The women of Wise county enlisted in the drive for the Victory Loan. Rhome women organized on Monday morning, April 21, 1918. The chairman was Miss Virginia Bobo with her committee of Mrs. Jim Douglass, Miss Bess Bobo, and Mrs. Tom Leonard. Miss Aleen Rowan represented Fairview in the drive. "The ladies are making a house-to-house canvass over the county and a large number of bonds have been sold up to date."[12]

Chapter 6

Boom and Depression Years — 1920 to 1945

During the early 1920's, business in Rhome was "off and running." There were four or five groceries, several cafes, black smith shops, barbershops, two hotels, and other businesses. Rhome was booming. Oil was on everyone's mind. "W. T. Leonard is making a tour of the several oil fields in Texas."[1] Also, Rhome had visitors because of the possibility of oil. "Messrs. Coleman Benton, W. D. Richardson, and C. W. Borden of Irvine, Kentucky, who are in Texas in the interest of their oil holdings, were guests for a few days last week of Luther Benton and family."[2]

One enterprising young business man started an interest which is continued by his youngest son, William Troxell, to the present day in Rhome. "E. C. Troxell, who has made the construction of radio and receiving sets a special study and can tell you some new things about its possibilities, has installed eighty-seven receiving sets in Rhome and community."[3]

In April of 1923 came one of the most stirring events of Rhome's business history. Rhome was planning to have a monthly "trades day."

> The businessmen and citizens of Rhome have established a monthly trades day for this town and have set the day as the first Saturday in each month. Arrangements are now underway to make the first trades day a big success on Saturday, May 5th. A baseball game and a free bronc show will be among the entertaining features, while all who are in Rhome on this day will participate in the event of giving away of forty-five dollars in cash by the businessmen. Ten dollars, five dollars, and three dollars will be given away, and the following cash premiums will also be offered as follows: First bronc rider, $5.00; bull-dogger of steer, $5.00; largest family attending trades day, $2.50; winner of boys' foot race of one hundred yards, $1.00; winner of the tuniman race, $1.00; ball and bat for winning baseball team, value $4.00.[4]

May 11, 1923, brought a joyful account of the success of this first trades day. A large crowd attended; the streets were crowded with cars, wagons, and the old 'one hoss and shay'. The merchants and citizens

SATURDAY STREET SCENE in Rhome, Texas, in the 1920's.

were so pleased that they promised a bigger and better day to come in June. In fact, most of the business news of this period ran to reports of the success of trades day. June 2, 1923, promised an even better rodeo than the past month's affair. "Beginning promptly at one-thirty o'clock will be the rodeo. Ones Finlayson, director of the event, assures the public interested in this phase of the program that some of the best riders and horses in the country will take part."[5] Mr. Finlayson remembers that the rodeo grounds were in the first block southeast of the present day Fort Worth and Denver railroad crossing. It was in this same location where many years before the town had held horse races.

The report of the success of this second trades day was lengthy indeed. Rhome was glowing with the feeling of success. Seemingly, the greatest interest was in the rodeo events.

First money for the bronc riding contest was taken by Stuttering George of Fort Worth, who with his wife, is a feature of the fat stock show of Fort Worth each year; second money went to Sid McGoodwin, a local man; third place was taken by Cowboy Baker, the well-known rider from Boyd . . . The prize for best cirsingle rider was taken by Buck Peterson of Justin. Peterson, though only eighteen years of age, is a daring and skillful rider and finished one of the best thrills of the entire event . . . The saddle race was won easily by Sid McGoodwin of Rhome. The prize money for the best bucking horse went to Alva Dunn of Newark. Cowboy Baker brought two of his best mounts, "Grey Devil" and Black Diamond" . . . We would not fail to mention the riding exhibition given by Mary Berier of Miles City, Montana. Mrs. Berier is a rider of no mean ability, and she promises us another attraction July 7th . . . At five-fifteen o'clock the cash prizes were given away. A. J. Cagle won the first prize of five dollars; Blanche Butler, three dollars; and Jim Byrom, two dollars. The following people won one-dollar bills; Leslie Coates, Richard Byrom, Mrs. J. E. Norman, Sarah Byrom, W. Beauchamp, Mrs. Floyd Byrom, Marco Terry, and W. H. Miles.[6]

At the end of the article was a plaintive request: "Ladies, what about a rest room for trades day?" Although the exhibit was not described, the Aurora girls' club was complimented upon its interesting exhibit at the trades day.

Another interesting feature of trades day was started during the July trades day. "The ladies of the Baptist church will give Saturday market on next trades day. Every member is solicited to send cake, pie, or other eats that are suitable for a market."[7] From this time on it became the custom for each of the churches to take turns in providing food for sale to the participants in Rhome's ever-growing trades day affair. The post-office building was the place where the food was displayed and sold. The Methodist ladies announced that they would hold the food market for August.

The trades days continued throughout the year 1923 and probably into 1924. Baseball games also provided high points for those days. "The baseball game, Rhome vs. Paradise, under the leadership of Mr. J. H. McGlothlin, held the crowd's interest from two-thirty to four-thirty. Automobiles formed a grand stand from which great volleys of "rah and hurrahs" came occasionally. It was a hard-fought battle, but the skinny Rhome nine lost the fight."[8] Approval came from Aurora on Rhome's trades day.

> A large number of our folks were present at the trades day in Rhome Saturday. We appreciate the effort Rhome is making in our behalf and are always glad when the first Saturday of each month rolls around. Speaking of trades days reminds us that Boyd is extending invitations to her initial trades day July 21st.[9]

The advertisement for the August event contained a sure-fire draw for the rodeo fans:

> A special attraction of the rodeo for next trades day in Rhome will be the appearance of "Peaceful" Henry, owned by

> Cowboy Baker. This is a seven-year-old one thousand percent dynamic bronc coming from the famous four-six ranch who seldom fails to throw his rider. Also, Gray Devil and Black Diamond will be here.[10]

Also, among the new enticements were different contests for participants. For example, there was an offer of a fifty pound sack of Queen Quality flour for the best loaf of bread made from the flour. There was even a ladies' wood sawing contest. The culinary contest was to be in the bank building. Some of the winners of the contests were listed as follows:

> The one dollar prize for the largest watermelon was taken by Mr. Tom Byrom of Aurora; Mrs. W. M. Slimp took first prize for the best cake; Mrs. L. T. Green won the forty-eight pound sack of Queen Quality flour . . .; Mrs. B. W. Stephens took first prize with her plate of light rolls . . .; the ladies wood sawing contest was won by Mrs. J. A. Evans, first; Mrs. W. M. Slimp, second; Mrs. Sam Brammer displayed the best gallon of tomatoes.[11]

One of the important business establishments in Rhome was the Rhome Milling Company. The extent of their markets may surprise the reader.

> The Rhome Milling Company has a mill force that is probably unsurpassed anywhere, especially engineer W. E. Horton and miller J. L. Stone.
>
> This great enterprise represents a large sum of money, and the pay-roll helps the town—some really interesting things for you to think about. There is a reason for this mill shipping to Cuba and to Old Mexico quite a number of their products and furnishing two of the largest hotels in Texas.[12]

One of the largest fires of this period in Rhome occurred in 1923. "Last Sunday morning about three o'clock fire broke out in the post office building which burned five business houses on the south side of the town which were the post office, Jim Spark's hamburger stand, P. S. Bost's barbershop, S. L. Leonard's meat market, and Dr. Childress' office. The cause of the fire is unknown."[13]

A new business enterprise was begun in November, 1923. "Mr. P. S. Bost is now in charge of the filling station in the Leonard addition. Mr. Bost is having a new tonsorial shop built adjoining the filling station, which when completed will add much to Rhome's new business district."[14] At this same time new cars were important and new enough in the community for the reporter to list the owners of new automobiles. Among these owners were DeWitt Morris, C. E. Shaw, Thurmond Hudnall, E. P. Carpenter, Luther Benton, and Robert West.

The great success of the trades days must have spurred Rhome's business leaders to new heights. In 1925 came news of a new attempt to continue the good work done in the little city.

> A committee from the Decatur Chamber of Commerce, composed of C. P. Dodson, W. M. Love, S. M. Ward, and Cliff Cates, were invited to Rhome last Monday night to assist in the organization of a chamber of commerce movement for that town and community.
>
> As a result, the Rhome Civic League was created with L. W. Renshaw as president and Joe Wren, secretary. The Rhome people are quite enthused and have adopted a program looking to the general development of one of the best sections of North Texas.[15]

This writer was unable to find any further news of the Rhome Civic League, but at least the attempt was made to improve the town.

In the fall of this same year, 1925, came the news of the death of a gentleman well known to the merchants of Rhome. "W. A. Brooks, traveling salesman for the Waples-Platter Grocery Company of Fort Worth, for many years a member of the old school known as 'drummers', died Sunday morning at his home in Fort Worth . . ."[16] Mr. Brooks had been coming to Rhome for many years, and he was the best known traveling salesman in this section. He was so well-liked by the Morris family that Grady Morris named his youngest son, Brooks Morris, for Mr. Brooks.

There is a long gap in the news from Rhome's business section. This is not difficult to understand if one remembers the history of the early 1930's. Businesses were failing, not growing, after the business slump and the failure of the stock market in 1929. It was not until 1933 that a new report of Rhome's business health was given. At that time the *Wise County Messenger* gave a review of the businesses in many of the towns of the county. The following Rhome businesses were described:

> McKINNON BROS.—A welding and machine shop and garage at Rhome that is well worth mentioning is that of McKinnon Bros., who started here in 1927. When they do your work, it is

RHOME'S FIRST GARAGE, owned by Marvin Holt. Left to right: Mr. McCloud, Sid McGoodwin, Waymon Rogers (a grandson of Mrs. Jane Hatler), Marvin Holt, a driller (unknown), Curtis Wilkerson, Carl Buerbaum, Mr. Ramsey (Carl Ramsey's father) S. A. "Abe" Brammer, Nathan Green Holt, (unknown).

P. L. HARVEY'S second grocery store building in Rhome.

done right and the charges are very reasonable, too. Magnolia products and acetelyne and electric welding are featured here.

L. C. SLIMP—One of the most reputable firms in Rhome is that of L. C. Slimp's garage and grocery. Mr. Slimp has operated these businesses since 1920. Here you may purchase staple and fancy groceries, gas, and oil, Goodyear tires, Willard batteries, and store your car and at prices you can afford. This is truly a house of service and cooperation in the progress this county is making, and is deserving of your cooperation. Mr. Slimp has been in business here in Rhome since 1920 and has always taken an active interest in all of Rhome's social and business interests. The motto: Select quality and personal service is really lived up to.

HOLT'S GARAGE—One of the finest garages in this entire vicinity is the one at Rhome conducted by Mr. M. Holt for the past 19 years. Mr. Holt himself is an expert mechanic with many years of experience in this line of endeavor, and he personally inspects every job. Gulf gas and oil, Federal tires, and Hawkins batteries and wrecking service are some of the many features of Holt's garage . . .

W. W. MORRIS—There's a record of fifty years of reliable service and square dealing behind this general merchandise store and lumber yard which W. W. Morris took over in 1882. In these years, Mr. Morris has seen new business houses come to Rhome and he has seen them go—but he has always been able to hold old patrons and add some new ones—and there's a reason, for satisfaction is always guaranteed to W. W. Morris' customers.

Mr. Morris has lived in Wise county for fifty years, having come here from Alabama when he was 24 years old. The unique truth is that Mr. Morris has lived in the same house fifty years, had the same store fifty years in the same county fifty years and has been an ardent booster for this county fifty years.[17]

In August of the next year, 1934, Mr. and Mrs. John Petros came back to Rhome after a few months absence and started their restaurant business in the White House Cafe.

P. L. Harvey also came to Rhome about 1934. He started his first grocery store in the old ice house building that was moved from its location on the railroad right-of-way to the corner on which a Fina station was later built. He added to this building to make it into a grocery store. Sometime later Doctor Russell built the building which became the second grocery store that P. L. Harvey operated in Rhome. He started his present building about 1942 and moved into the building in 1943. Since that time the structure has been expanded to its present size.

The Harvey Grocery and Hardware store stands today on the corner which once held the Hambright Cottage Hotel. It was about 1933 or 1934 that Phil S. Bost dismanteled the Hambright Hotel building, using the wood to construct forms for the solid concrete building which belongs to Florence Bobo Huddleston today. At that time Mr. Bost installed the White House Cafe and a barbershop in the building. During one period Claude Sledge ran the White House Cafe. The old building which today is referred to as "The Alamo" was built by Mr. Bost after he completed the White House Cafe. Sometime during the 1930's Mr. Livengood built his home and his shoe shop between the two buildings.

Another disastrous fire struck Rhome in the early 1930's. In fact, the 1930's were tragic for Rhome. Fires and murder almost wiped out the business sections of the town. This first fire of the 1930's destroyed the building which had been known as the "old stone building." It had been built by Colonel B. C. Rhome in the very first days of the town's existence. "The stone for the building was hauled by Andy Mellon using six yoke of oxen. The stone was brought from the Wells Stephens place west of Rhome. The completion of the building was celebrated with a grand ball for all the settlers far and near. Musicians were hired from Fort Worth for the gala occasion."[18]

> Early Tuesday morning about 2:30 o'clock, fire was discovered in the Morris Mercantile Co. building in Rhome, and completely gutted the stone structure, and for a time threatened to spread to the east section of the town. It is estimated that the loss will be above $25,000. Half a block of business property was destroyed.
>
> The blaze razed Rhome's first stone building . . . Flames spread rapidly to a frame warehouse in the rear of the stone building and leveled it to the ground.
>
> Of the Rhome building only the east and west walls remained standing at daybreak. The structure housed the Morris Mercantile Company, owned by W. W. Morris and DeWitt T. Morris and the Rhome Mercantile Company owned by Joe Wren.
>
> The Morris firm occupied two of the four store spaces, Wren occupied one, and a fourth was vacant. Three of the spaces were owned by Mrs. J. W. Logan, and the other by W. W. Morris. The warehouse was owned jointly and was used by the Morris company . . .
>
> Sparks carried by the wind from the southwest ignited several other buildings, but a quickly formed bucket brigade kept these blazes from doing any damage. Only the thick east wall of the Rhome building prevented the flames from spreading to a barbershop and grocery adjoining. It was in this barbershop that Deputy Joe Brown was shot to death by Glen Hunsucker and Ed "Perchmouth" Stanton.
>
> . . . Origin of the fire had not been determined several hours later, and officials planned an investigation on the conjecture that robbers might have fired the building to cover traces of their crime. . . .
>
> The vacant store space in the Rhome building was usually used as a polling place and election officials set up the voting box in a downtown business house for Tuesday's election.[19]

Between the time of this fire and the third very destructive holocaust, some new businessmen located in Rhome. Mr. R. M. Vandiver was the owner of a Rhome grocery store. Mr. P. L. Harvey was mentioned as Rhome's ice man. Mr. Orville Ewing owned a restaurant and bus station. This bus station was first located on the corner where the Ham-

"MOM" AND G. Sledge with their son, Ira, in front of the family-owned restaurant in Rhome.

RUINS OF THE old stone building after it burned.

bright Hotel had stood. Then it was moved to the new highway on the corner opposite the Masonic Building.

The McKinnon Brothers Machine Shop made the news during this time because of a new first for Rhome. "Jim and John McKinnon . . . received the first load of tank steel ever to be shipped to Rhome. The Birmingham steel was sent here by rail and water."[20] The preceding quote seems particularly important because the three largest industries in Rhome today are shops that use large quantities of steel.

The second fire to wreak havoc on Rhome's business area occurred about one o'clock in the afternoon on July 20, 1939.

> An oil stove exploded in the cream station at Rhome shortly after 1 p.m. Wednesday and the fire that followed destroyed seven buildings. Two volunteer fire fighters were overcome while fighting the blaze.
>
> After raging for more than an hour, the fire was brought under control by the Decatur and Bridgeport fire departments and scores of Rhome residents who were called to the scene by Mrs. Glen McCrary, telephone operator.
>
> In addition to the cream station, buildings destroyed were a

1929—E. E. RICHARDSON Cotton Gin in Background. Picture of original shop and filling station. Founded by J. R. McKinnon in 1928. Acquired by Star Tank and Trailer Mfg. Company in 1945. Left: Warner Walker. Right: Wayne Ash.

JARRETT HUDNALL'S

STORE building.

"RHOME BUSINESSMEN OF THE 1930's"
HAROLD BOST AND Aaron Payne.

RHOME GROCERY STORE during the 1940's.

GARLAND MOORE, WORKING at Rhome's Ice Depot.

hotel, grocery store, barbershop, garage, and two empty buildings.

Rhome residents formed a bucket brigade to fight the blaze since there is no organized fire department here.

The volunteer fire fighters who were overcome from the intense heat were Claude Russell and Leroy Mays, both of Rhome. The Rhome residents' work was credited with keeping the fire from spreading across Highway 81.[21]

The residents of the town made up a purse for the fire department to show their appreciation for help in putting out the fire that threatened to destroy the town. J. T. Richardson took the funds to present to the fire departments. A related note adds to the story. P. L. Harvey said that with one bucket of water at the time the fire began, it could have been put out.

For quite some time Dr. W. L. Russell was the only doctor practicing in Rhome. However, in 1923 there was mention of a new doctor coming to town. "It is reported that Dr. Childress, formerly of Boyd, contemplates locating in Rhome."[22] By the first of the next month Dr. J. M. Childress and his family had arrived in Rhome to begin his new practice here.

In the middle of June, Dr. W. L. Russell, as secretary of the Wise County Medical Association, was attending the meeting of that association in Decatur.[23] Mr. Z. B. Bobo was still the only druggist in the town, and his son, Tom Z. Bobo, was a third year medical student of Baylor Memorial College, of Dallas. "Tom is studying this summer with the medical army corps of Fort Sam Houston. Tom is with the second company R. O. T. C. camp. This student medical department is a recent addition to the army work of our government."[24]

A former doctor in Rhome, Dr. G. P. Cherry, was now practicing in Fort Worth, but he made a business trip to his old town on November 17, 1923. In 1924, Dr. W. L. Russell began erecting a new office for his practice. "Dr. W. L. Russell is erecting a handsome little stucco office building on his lot on South Main street. This will be a pleasing addition to our city."[25]

The review of the businesses in Rhome which was published in 1933 gave the following account of the drugstore in Rhome.

Z. B. BOBO—Today the modern drug store like Z. B. Bobo's carried a very diversified line of merchandise. Drugs, toilet articles, stationery, etc., comprise the contents of the store, all

OFFICE BUILDING OCCUPIED by Doctor W. L. Russell.

tastefully arrayed and well displayed to make your shopping easier and more pleasant.

> Prescriptions are filled in the most careful way, no effort being spared to assure the use of only the purest drugs and chemicals. Mr. Z. B. Bobo, registered pharmacist, attends to this department himself, with the utmost care. Our health is his wealth, and it is the business of a drug store to safeguard health. Since 1891 Mr. Bobo has been giving "quality and service."[26]

Even in the days of the horse and buggy there was a definite need for some kind of assurance that pasture gates would be shut, particularly before the time that Rhome had good highways to all the outlying communities. With the advent of the automobile, the need for some kind of self-closing gate was even more important. Mr. S. A. Lowance came up with an invention designed to solve this problem of the gate closing. "S. A. Lowance of the Rhome community has applied for patent rights on an automatic automobile gate that he has recently made, and prospects look bright for a big demand for the invention. In the opinion of all who have seen the gate in operation, it fills the demand."[27] One of the gates was installed on the Bill Logan farm near Rhome. A description of the gate and its operation was given in the next month's paper:

> . . . the gate can be opened by passing automobiles and will automatically close after the machine has gone over it. The gate is pressed down to the ground as the auto comes into contact with it, and stays in that position until released from the pressure, when it is restored to the closed position. . . For years, since the automobile has come into its own and become the chief manner of travel, such a gate has been in demand by the public on wheels, and in Mr. Lowance's patent this demand has been met.[28]

One other feature that made the gate device desirable was the fact that it was movable; if the farmer saw a need to move his gate, the operation was very simple and economical to accomplish, since it was not complicated in its make-up and was economical to manufacture.

Cotton was still being grown in the Rhome community during these years. The year 1923 gave a glowing account of "King Cotton." "772 bales of cotton have been ginned by the Rhome gin up to this time. The gin is running night and day and cotton is selling for a good price."[29] At this time there was only one gin in Rhome, that owned by L. W. Renshaw. By 1926 there were two gins here. E. E. Richardson, who had had considerable experience in ginning in the county, moved to Rhome and built the Farmers' Gin. That year the cotton reports were still glowing with success. "Cotton is opening rapidly with not enough pickers to gather it. The gins have turned out 406 bales to date."[30]

Today, 1978, Rhome is still waiting and hoping for oil; however, although wells are getting closer and closer, there have not been any wells nearer than a couple of miles or more. Hope beats eternal, and there are those of us who feel certain that the oil or gas must be here, especially since reading stories of the artesian water well that ran oil down Elizabeth creek, according to old timers.

At any rate, rumors were rife in 1923 that the Scott-Hunter well would be a producer, and Rhome wanted to tell the world that it was the city located nearest the well site:

> To begin with, we want the world to know that the Scott-Hunter drilling well is located less than seven miles from Rhome by road—air line, five miles—and in talking to some lease hounds, it is closer. Now to be honest, the well is nearer to Rhome than any other town and the drillers with their families live here—a fact of which we are proud, for they are a fine bunch of people. The men sure are on the job. Giving out information is a lost art with them; on the other hand, after the boss gives orders

to let people know the truth, these men will give the seat-warmers a pleasant "yes" or "no" . . . The oil situation has helped Rhome, and she is fast awakening from a slumber of many years to the golden opportunity she has at hand.[31]

There was a report of a visit by the general superintendent of the Fort Worth and Denver railroad. The Denver was prepared to take care of any situation which might develop in the Rhome oil situation. "At present, the local crew tie-up here turns for Wichita Falls, Rhome has ample switch track, passing track, and a "Y" for turning purposes, and she is ready for the long looked for oil gusher."[32]

Glowing news of the Scott-Hunter well kept coming from Rhome and Fairview as well as from Decatur, which also claimed the well site in its territory. Leasing land was big at the time. Most of the farmers were leasing or had already leased part, if not all, of their land. ". . . so we are expecting to be 'running smoothly' soon with oil instead of rain watering our crops."[33]

The reports took on a note of humor, however, as the days went on without bringing in any definite news.

> Some acreage owners were so enthused over the report of the Hunter-Scott Sunday they kept the Southwestern hot calling friends on long distance and trying to get in touch with their agents to raise the price of acreage. However, by Monday, they were back on par basis.

> A large percentage of the inhabitants of Rhome and vicinity with hundreds of visitors from afar went out to the Scott-Hunter Sunday afternoon, chasing the rose-hued bubble that she was "coming in". We are informed that things got so warm they decided to postpone the event for a day or two.[34]

Things were still exciting the next week when a report came from one of the Rhome citizens: "J. L. NeSmith, self-claimed geologist, asserts that the Hunter-Scott is drilling over a huge pool of oil. Hope your knowledge is well seasoned, Parson Jim."[35] Excitement about the Scott-Hunter died out, but not the eternal hope for oil.

The next enthusiasm over oil came for a section south and southwest of Rhome. M. T. Oats visited the *Messenger* office with news of oil activity in 1925. He stated that representatives of oil companies located in Dallas had been in the community and that they were reporting the possibility of opening up operations south and west of Rhome.

> "These geologists," said Mr. Oats, "told me they were con-

fident something big and sensational would be found in our section, and within a few days we are expecting other geologists to come and make examinations. The gentlemen in our section this week came unsolicited and after days of study and close examination, they were out-spoken in the predictions that Rhome and the sections west and southwest would soon be enjoying one of the greatest plays in the oil spheres."[36]

When more activity did come to the Rhome area, it was in 1929 on the Dorn Beauchamp survey. "Reports come from the test well near Rhome, on the Dorn Beauchamp survey, is making a slight showing of oil at 165 feet, and much interest is manifested."[37] They were quite excited about the fact that the artesian water sand in the area showed no water. In February of the next year there was a statement that a good gas and oil sand was hit at a depth of 835 feet. The well was being drilled by the D. & L. Company. The test was contracted to go 2000 feet and was located on the D. C. Slimp farm in the Dorn Beauchamp survey.[38]

Although there was again some excitement in the 1930's about the old Keystone location, nothing came of the rumors.

Transportation

Although the highways were coming into their own, the railroad still remained the main artery of transportation for Rhome. In May, 1923, after a visit from the officials for the railroad, it was decided to add more trains to the schedule for the Fort Worth to Wichita Falls run.

> Two new trains have recently been added to the equipment of the Fort Worth and Denver road passing through Decatur, which gives the best train service to the town she has ever received. The city now has four trains each way each day. The mail delivery has also been made more efficient.[39]

About this time it was also that all mail for dispatch from each town should reach the post office at least thirty minutes before the train time. It seems apropos to note here that today Rhome has only one mail delivery. Progress in indeed strange.

There was one other note in 1923 involving the railroad and the depot. "F. E. Bailey, operator at the North Yards, was acting agent for the Fort Worth and Denver railroad at Rhome last week, relieving Mr. J. H. McGlothlin, our wide-awake well-known agent who was confined to his home with a severe attack of sciatic rheumatism. He is much improved at this writing and was on the job again Monday."[40]

J. H. "MAC" McGlothlin and Jarrett Hudnall with the Masonic building in the background.

Despite the dominance of the railroad, the automobile was coming into its own, and the highways of the area were a central focus of attention. In 1921 there was a warning given to drivers of all automobiles.

> ... they must have their cars registered by midnight of the 23rd day of March, 1921. All cars not being registered by the above date will be fined as the law prescribes. This notice is given for the benefit of those who have not had the opportunity to register their cars.
>
> And notice is hereby given to violators of the traffic law with reference to lights, mufflers, speeding, number plates and seals in their proper places on the car ... By order of Geo. Gage, Traffic Officer.[41]

Another note about what constituted automobile laws might also surprise some readers, as a notice in Decatur calls to mind:

> The *News* is requested to call the attention of automobile owners and drivers to the fact that the law governing automobiles will after April 16th be strictly enforced in Wise county. If you exceed the speed limit, either in town or on the public highway, or go off and leave your car or truck with the motor running, or you run without sufficient lights, or do any of the various things prohibited by law, don't be disgruntled if you have to pay a fine, for that will be the result if the traffic officer gets you. Mr. Dalton, an experienced motorcyclist, and an ex-ranger and deputy sheriff, has been employed to patrol the MERIDIAN highway, and he says that the law will be fearlessly enforced. Run on the safety first principle and avoid accidents and fines.[42]

In May and June of 1923 the Meridian Highway was being repaired. "The south end of the Meridian is in better condition than ever, which is the result of the maintenance crew being constantly at work."[43]

In the regular session of the Texas Legislature came a surprise for most automobile drivers and other users of gasoline.

> More than two hundred and fifty thousand dollars has thus far been collected by the comptroller's department under the original one cent per gallon tax on gasoline act as passed at the regular session of the thirty-eighth legislature. This money is being held by the comptroller instead of being deposited in the state treasury due to a resolution adopted by the senate sometime ago requesting the comptroller to withhold depositing the money in the treasury until it has been determined who is to pay the tax. . . [44]

As early as February, 1925, a story came out of the *Decatur News* that brought the entire county's attention. For years the only routes to Dallas were long, round-about, and now it was proposed to open up a new route that would go directly into Dallas from Rhome. More than that, it would make Rhome a crossroad town again almost a century later than its first experience as a crossroad village. Two major highways would cross in Rhome.

> Presiding Elder C. L. Bounds visited Dallas and S.M.U. Tuesday. While at the University, talking with the Mayor of University Park, the Mayor pointed out a number of workmen near White Rock, about ½ mile north of S.M.U., and said, "See

those men working over yonder? They are building a highway to Wise county to intersect the Meridian road a short distance below Rhome." Bro. Bounds replied, "Yes, I heard about that at the Chamber of Commerce meeting last night, and they were going to use the grade of the old Dallas and Northwestern railroad, which was graded into Wise county a number of years ago, but didn't know it was a certainty."

This looks very much as though this highway was going to be built right away, and if it is, it will be a great convenience to Wise County people and travelers over the Meridian road who wish to go directly to Dallas in a commercial way, bringing her wholesale houses nearer and making them more convenient to the merchants of this section.[45]

Dallas county took the lead in proposing the highway to the state. "Dallas county officials and chamber of commerce representatives will go to Austin again soon to try to get designated as a state highway of the Dallas-Rhome road that cuts across the southwest corner of Denton county from east of Roanoke to beyond Justin, following the line of the old Dallas, Pacific, and Southwestern Railroad embankment built in the 1880's."[46]

Mr. Fate Renshaw headed a delegation from Rhome meeting with the commissioner's court in behalf of the movement of the Dallas Chamber of Commerce to get a permit to construct the highway out of Dallas to intersect with the Meridian highway at a point near Rhome. On April 14, 1926, it was reported that the highway was assured by action in Austin. "An airline route from northwest Texas to Dallas was assured today when the highway commission designated as a state highway a 50 mile road that will run from a point seven miles northeast of Dallas northwest to Rhome in Wise county, linking state highways 1 and 2 . . . A telegram from Fort Worth Chamber of Commerce was the only unfavorable communication . . . It was proposed that Wise county build her part of the highway after providing the right-of-way from Rhome east to the county line, about four miles, as a first inducement to securing the completed road."[47]

These reports sounded very good, but trouble was brewing because there were still people who had a vested interest in the old, Gulf, Texas, and Western Railway. Actually, several different names had been used to designate the grading that had been done for the now defunct railway effort.

Dallas, Texas—Court action may be taken by the Gulf, Texas, and Western Railway to prevent the construction of the Dallas-Northwest highway between Dallas and Rhome, in Wise county, along the route of the old Dallas and New Mexico railway, it was indicated in Dallas this week.

>Frank Knox, receiver, said his company denies the right of the highway to occupy the 100-foot strip of right-of-way between Dallas and Jacksboro, claiming the Gulf, Texas, and Western is the owner.[48]

Apparently, the quarrel produced little substance because a report came from John Boswell of Dallas: ". . . He brought the reassuring news that the construction of the Dallas Northwest Highway from Dallas to Rhome will be started as soon as several minor hindrances may be removed. He said that Dallas is anxious to connect in directly with the producing territory of this section, and wants more and more of the dairy and poultry produce of this region."[49] In November, 1927, a delegation from the entire area who appeared in Austin were reassured by the State Highway Commission. ". . . as soon as they would appear before the commission with money in hand, 'we will talk business with you and help you to get your road'."[50] The total cost of the road was estimated to be $2,373,030. Dallas county offered to pay sixty percent of the cost.

The highway was completed by May, 1932, and a great celebration was held first in Rhome in the morning and then in Grapevine in the evening. Stirring headlines appeared in the county newspapers lauding the great benefits to be gained from the new highway.

CELEBRATION AT RHOME, MAY 19

>Rhome citizens invite the whole of Wise county to join them in celebrating the completion of the Great Dallas and Northwestern Highway next Thursday morning, from 9 until one o'clock, when the Grapevine celebration will be visited and participated in by all. In view of the fact that the great Rhome-Dallas road intersects the Meridian at Rhome, it is fit and proper that a celebration be held, and the enterprising citizens of Rhome and community promise all visitors a royal time. Immediately at the close of the festivities, all present will journey to Grapevine and take part in the celebration at that place.
>
>An interesting program has been arranged; prominent speakers will be present and two bands will furnish music.[51]

The writer is certain that there will be many who will remember this great celebration, particularly the speeches, the ribbon cutting, and definitely the street dance held in Grapevine that night.

Because of the two great highways through Rhome, there was another innovation in transportation. Marvin Holt remembers early in the 1920's driving a jitney to Fort Worth and back once each day, where he waited for his passengers near the courthouse for the return trip to Rhome. In 1923 there was an advertisement of an auto stage line from Rhome to Fort Worth: "Ride the Sedans. During December and the holidays. Regular trips on schedule. No matter what the weather is you will have a comfortable ride to or from Fort Worth if you ride with us. CONLEY'S AUTO STAGE LINE."[52]

By 1926 a regular bus service had been started from Fort Worth to Wichita Falls. This service was a forerunner of the bus service which Rhome has today.

> Mack Bus Company, or North Texas Coach Company, operating out from Fort Worth and Wichita Falls, has inaugurated a transfer system that is appealing to the traveling public, and expenditure in handsome equipment is proof positive that the company intends to give their patrons the best that money can buy.
>
> Five big, roomy cars, with appointments like a modern Pullman car, have been placed on the Meridian highway, each car carrying twenty-four passengers. The cars will carry the names of the towns along the highway, and "Miss Decatur" made her appearance yesterday.[53]

R. C. Bowen had purchased the company by 1935, and he was soon announcing new, improved service for bus patrons of the area.

> R. C. Bowen announces the purchase of a new streamline yellow coach for service . . . this new car is the last word in motor coach construction. It has all the latest improvements and is the most luxurious and easy riding coach built in America. It will have a seating capacity of 29 passengers. There are no aisle seats. Each passenger is assured of a real individual reclining seat of the latest aeroplane type . . . [54]

From the Bowen Bus Company came the Continental Trailways Coaches of today.

Despite the new highways and the modification of those in existence, there were still problems such as the dangerous curve just south of downtown Rhome. In 1937 the Texas Highway Department raised the railings around the curve. They seemed to be taller and stronger, but the curve was still dangerous, and motorists were warned to approach it with caution. Because of this situation, it became evi-

(L to R) CHARLIE MONDRICK, WOODROW Wylie, Gussie Mondrick, Lonnie McKee, Dr. W. L. Russell. Mondrick's filling station on new highway.

dent that a change had to be made in the route of the highway.

> Down in Rhome there seems to be somewhat of a controversy among some of the citizens as to the new highway. The highway department wants to construct through the town. The *Messenger* is not familiar with the merits of either route, but we would suggest as a friend and booster for Rhome that the good citizens of the town get together on some route and get the building contract from the highway department. Delaying may see nothing done for months, even years. The department may spend the money some other place; hundreds of places are clamoring for highway money.[55]

P. L. Harvey says that the controversy was strong in Rhome. He also said that one venerable old lady asked him how he was going to vote on the referendum about the highway. He answered, "Just the way you are, ma'm." She left the store, but moments later returned. "But just how are you going to vote, sir?" she asked. "The way I want to vote," P. L. replied.[56]

The decision was made to move the highway one block west of the original highway. As a consequence, many of the businesses which were left on the old highway made the move to the new location.

The columnist called "Dr. SkyGak" of the *Messenger* had a little good-natured kidding about the situation: ". . . the little city of

Rhome is having a highway paved right down her midriff and is going through the painful process of having her face uplifted and a permanent wave. When the road is open to public travel and all the debris is cleaned up, the little town will put on her Sunday britches and go places."[57]

At the beginning of this period of Rhome's history, Mr. Tom Stephens still owned the telephone company, but soon it was purchased by Mr. Charlie Hudnall. "Charles Hudnall attended the district meeting of the of the Texas Independent Telephone Company held at the Hotel Texas at Fort Worth Wednesday."[58] In 1925 Mr. Hudnall leased the telephone company. "Charlie Hudnall, who for many years has been owner and manager of the Rhome telephone exchange, has leased same to Mr. B. F. Ferguson. Miss Ollie Smith is the present capable operator and the new management is already giving very efficient service."[59] Mr. Ferguson gave up his lease after three years, and Mr. Hudnall returned to the business. According to information from Robert Owens of the present telephone exchange office, Mr. Hudnall leased the exchange to a Mr. Tom Bearden from Baird, Texas. Apparently this lease lasted for about ten years. After Mr. Hudnall's death in 1941, the heirs sold the business to Mr. T. P. Bearden, who hired his brother J. P. Bearden to manage it. The name of the exchange was changed to the Home Telephone Company.

On August 1, 1947, the Rhome exchange was purchased by Mr. C. P. Owens from the Home Telephone Company. The exchange then became the Rhome Telephone Company, and the lines were extended to the Aurora community. In 1949 lines were also extended to Fairview as a part of the Rhome Telephone Company.

Mr. Robert W. Owens purchased the business on November 1, 1953. The business was incorporated on October 26, 1960. On June 3, 1961, the old central operator was dispensed with, and Rhome Telephone Company was cut over to the dial system. By July 1, 1970, Direct-Distance-Dialing equipment was installed, and Rhome joined the nationwide system of direct dialing.

Over the years Rhome has had many different telephone operators, and among them were found the following names. The writer was unable to establish dates of service for each. Allie Douglas, Ona White Lattimore, Adrian Ash, Gladys Boyd, Okie Sparks, Glenice Naugle, Inez Hall, Marie Logan, Mrs. W. L. Russell, Mrs. Lucille Winfrey, Mrs. Hays, Nova Caldwell, Joanne Rucker, Trilby Hudnall, Ruth Hall, Estelle Herring, Pauline Ford, Mary Jane Bennett, Darlene Reid, and Carol Burk. Some of the linemen who have served the company have been Bert Deaman, Ed McCrary, Joe

Childress, E. P. Carpenter, and Thurman Hudnall. (Most of the preceding material was submitted by the present owner and manager, Mr. Robert Owen.)

One of the Rhome's successful manufacturing concerns was started by Mr. Joe Baker. Shortly after Mr. Baker returned home from the armed services, he started manufacturing cattle feeders. In 1947, Mr. Baker purchased a vacant lot. He had an electric meter installed on a pole and was in business. He welded anything that needed to be welded. He designed and built the first commercial cattle feeder of this kind. He sold and delivered them in all states of the United States except five. He also manufactured creeps, half-creeps, troughs, hay racks, and calf pens. Anything that had to do with livestock, he built. He also built barns, corrals, cattle guards, and fences. He built some of the first and largest commercial feed lots in this country. Purina Feed Mills helped him to promote and sell his products. In a few short years his business grew into a million dollar concern.

Mr. Baker has contributed much to the community in which he lives. He has served as Mayor of Rhome for several terms. He also contributed his time and labor to building the bleachers and corrals for the Youth Fair of Wise County.

In 1977, Mr. Baker turned his business over to another party, which is still manufacturing Baker Built Feeders.

Although it seemed that the radio was just coming into its own, in 1927, Rhome citizens were reading about another startling, almost unbelievable invention. "Television was back in the laboratories of the American Telephone and Telegraph Company Saturday marked 'condition for commerce.' How long it will take before this order is filled, engineers refused to prophesy, but admitted that they had a big job ahead of them. One of the serious problems in perfecting the invention for general use is that of cost."[60]

The bank was growing steadily during these years. Changes were being made.

> Our First National Bank has been 'spring house cleaning" under the expert hands of Simmons and Samuels. The interior has been painted, powdered, and marcelled, with a new sign in front, which is a joy to behold. Our genial cashier, Mr. Douglas, and Assistant Cashier, Mr. Stevenson, are dispensing with new vigor.[61]

According to a report written by Mr. Joel R. Chambers in later years, Mr. A. C. Alexander had been succeeded by Mr. L. R. Douglas as cashier and Mr. F. T. Stevenson as assistant cashier. In the year 1924

Mr. Stevenson was succeeded by Mr. Joel R. Chambers as assistant cashier. "Joel R. Chambers has accepted the position of assistant cashier with the First National Bank. Mr. Chambers is a capable, progressive, young man, well fitted to fill this position."[62] Miss Ella Mondrick was employed as a bookkeeper for the bank. L. D. Harbin assumed a position with the First National Bank of Rhome in July, 1928.[63]

In the year 1925 the Burroughs Posting machines were installed and a change was made from the Jones Loose Leaf Ledger to the I. P. Loose Leaf Ledgers. An increase in business saw a second posting machine installed.

Bank news during this time was not very colorful except for the numerous burglaries the bank suffered. The years 1927, 1928, and 1929 all brought news of burglaries. Each time the burglars attempted to break into the brick vault. On the last occasion they succeeded in digging a hole into the vault, but their attempts to get at the strong box which held the bank's money was unsuccessful. They abandoned the job after all their efforts. They secured only a small amount of change after scattering customers' papers all over the floor.[64]

The depression of 1929 hit the country and many banks were closed because of the lack of confidence in the ability of the individual banks to pay out their deposits. Apparently, Rhome weathered the storm because no report of closing was made until the national Bank Holiday closed every bank in the country. Rhome's people and others took that process with good humor according to a report in the *Wise County Messenger*:

> New York, March 7—Quips, grins, and tall stories were on the lips of Americans today as they went to a well they had not tapped since war days.
>
> It was a well of extra resourcefulness, of ingenuity, of good humor—Human life, in spite of the shortage of cash, was finding ways of carrying on . . .
>
> Tales of millionaires beseeching butlers for a spare dime, of folk with 1000 dollar bills being snubbed by change guarding clerks, went the rounds. Ladies who used to talk about their operations now had a new topic—of how that nasty groceryman would not give them change for $20.00 when they bought a ten-cent can of beans.[65]

The Bank Holiday was a shock to the people of Rhome, but fortunately, here no one had to go without necessities because the grocery stores, restaurants, drug stores, and other businesses provided the necessary credit to tide the people over the hard time. This care and thought are the result of being a small town where everyone knew everyone else.

The health of the Rhome bank is attested to by the review of county businesses given in the *Wise County Messenger* in 1933.

> FIRST NATIONAL BANK, RHOME—Every person who enters this bank—man, woman, or child, depositor, borrower, or stranger—is entitled to all we can do in the way of service, courtesy, and cooperation. If we give less, we are negligent in our duty to you, and the First National bank tries not to be negligent in anything.
>
> When we organized this bank eighteen years ago, we installed in our various departments the most up-to-date facilities and conveniences for giving our patrons prompt and efficient service. But we cannot always determine how well we are measuring up to the ideals we have set as standards for ourselves . . . We welcome constructive criticisms at all times.
>
> The present officers are W. T. Waggoner, President; J. H. Rowan, Vice-President; and Joel R. Chambers, Cashier.[66]

That same week in March, 1933, brought news of banks all over the nation being carefully examined by employees of the Reconstruction Finance Corporation with a view to purchase of preferred stock by that government agency so that the institutions might be reopened. Rhome can be proud of the fact that it has always had a sound banking organization.

The year 1935 brought about incorporation for the city of Rhome. On August 14, 1935, the Commissioners' Court of Wise County authorized an election to be held in Rhome, Texas, on September 17, 1935. The Court also specified that Rhome should adopt the Commission form of government. Joe Wren and P. S. Bost were appointed judges for the election. Incorporation carried by a vote of 66 for and 10 against.

Early in the 1920's the post office location was moved to the ground floor of the Masonic Lodge building. In 1922 the postmaster was Mr. Joe R. Taylor. About this time the carriers gradually changed from horse and buggy to the automobile. Mr. Troxell's first automobile was remodeled from an old Model T Ford which he rebuilt to his own specifications to haul the mail.

JOE THURMOND, LUTHER Benton, and Bud Logan in front of Rhome post office.

In 1932 the price of a postage stamp went up again. This time the new stamp cost three cents. "Citizens will start using the new 3-cent postage stamp and help to get the Government out of the red."[67]

Charles Blair Morris became postmaster in 1933 and served until 1940. The post office remained in the Masonic Building during these years. In 1934 the Rhome routes one and two were combined. A toss of a coin decided who would remain in Rhome and who would accept the transfer to a new route in Decatur, Texas. Mr. Whitehead was the winner and remained as carrier for the Rhome routes. Mr. Troxell moved with his family to Decatur, where he finally retired in 1948. In 1958 the Troxell family began its plans to return to Rhome.

Mrs. Kate Shaw began her service in 1940. She served in this capacity for over seventeen years. The post office building remained in its location in the Masonic Building until some time during World War II, when the office was moved to the back of the Bobo Drug Store building. "It was during her tenure that carrier John Whitehead retired and was succeeded by John Will Finlayson in 1946."[68]

THREE RHOME GENTLEMEN sitting on the postoffice steps. Left to right: Charles Sparks, Tom Leonard, and George Sullivan.

Mrs. Shaw was succeeded in the office of postmaster by Mrs. Cassie F. Hudnall, who began her service in 1957. In 1962 the post office was once again moved. This time it was to the first permanent post office building to be built in Rhome. Mrs. Hudnall served as postmaster until her retirement in 1971, when Mr. Bill Blaylock was appointed to replace her.

The 1920's were booming years for the farmers of Rhome. The reports from that period show a tendency for diversifying their farming efforts. Lecturers and seminars were being brought to the county to help the farmers better their work. An example of this effort is shown by the following: "Bruce Oates, the agricultural agent for the F. W. and Denver will be in Rhome on Wednesday morning, April 16th to lecture on poultry and care of eggs."[69] That same week there was also a report on a future lecture on livestock farming. "C. C. French, industrial agent for the Fort Worth Stock Yards Company, will lecture for us on livestock farming sometime in August."[70]

The lectures apparently spurred the citizens on to greater efforts. On the 18th of May there was a report of the organization of a live stock association:

> The Pure-bred Live Stock Association—what is it for? First, to encourage better breeding in all lines of stock raised on the farm . . . Second, to encourage the community fairs to assist in holding sales of livestock to advertise the county. Third, to assist all who want to show their best to the best advantage; carry the winners to the state fair and put Wise county on the map where she justly belongs.
>
> We ask the support of all in this work.
> P. S. Bost, President
> M. M. Love, Sec'y-Treasurer[71]

Of particular interest to Rhome will be the fact that the president of the association, Mr. P. S. Bost was a Rhome citizen.

The glowing reports of farm produce from Rhome filled the newspapers for 1923. "Grain threshing will soon be in full swing in this vicinity. The best wheat crop since 1917 will soon be moving . . ."[72] In August a report of the hay harvest sounds almost miraculous.

> Bill Carpenter, a Rhome farmer, made hay while the sun shone to the extent of nine tons and four hundred pounds from a fraction less than an acre of Rhome black land at one cutting. The statement is vouched for by the balers, who received twenty-seven dollars for their work.
>
> A wonderful crop! Doubtless it has not been exceeded in all Texas. What's the use of going to the magic valley . . . when this can be done in Wise county?[73]

September brought a good report on the cotton crop for that year. "To date, Tuesday, September 11th, the receipts of the local gin are eight hundred and eleven bales, ginned with twenty-eight more wagons on the yard at four o'clock. Two crews are hardly sufficient to meet the demands made upon them. The best price yet paid here was twenty-seven and a half cents."[74]

When the depression began, Rhome was still basically a farming community, and the hard times were a blow for the farmers of Rhome. Bankruptcy became a familiar term to many of the people of the community. But a tenacity and an urge to survive dominated the spirits of these hardy pioneers, and survive they did.

In the year 1923, Rhome lost one of its longtime, faithful officers of the law. C. C. Leonard resigned his office as Justice of the Peace of Precinct No. 5 after serving many years in that capacity.

> "Squire" Leonard, as he is familiarly known, has served the people of Wise county for 35 years as an officer, being first elected Justice of the Peace in 1869. He has filled the offices of County Commissioner one term and Tax Assessor four years, but his main business has been as Justice of the Peace. During his long term of office he has enjoyed the perfect confidence of all the people, and not one breath of scandal has been attached to his career as a public officer.
>
> Advancing years and failing eyesight have compelled him, against the wishes of his many friends, to cease his public duties; and he wishes here to express his thanks for the confidence Wise county people have reposed in him during his long career as a public officer . . .
>
> L. R. Douglas of the First State Bank has been appointed as Mr. Leonard's successor.[75]

The crimes which occurred in Rhome during the 1920's were relatively minor ones compared to those that happened in the 1930's. One rather amusing story was told about a chicken thief.

> Last Friday night as Deputy Sheriff George Gage was returning from Fort Worth and when near Rhome, he saw a car standing empty by the roadside. His suspicions being aroused, he waited awhile and soon two men came running up with a bag of chickens and placed them in the car. After questioning them, Mr. Gage placed them under arrest, brought them to Decatur, and placed them in jail. The chickens were identified by Mr. Benton of Rhome as his. Examination of the car showed it to be fitted with a wire coop concealed under the back seat and it looked as though it was prepared for a regular chicken business.[76]

Another Rhome man ran into trouble somewhere along the same road about two years later than the chicken incident. This time Knox Hutchison was robbed.

WALTER LOONEY

> While traveling the Meridian Highway this side of Rhome Tuesday morning about eight o'clock, Knox Hutchison of Newark had a stranger, who was walking along the road, board his car, and at the point of a pistol, demand his money. Hutchison told the man he had only $1.03, but that he could help himself to the money. After taking it, the stranger, who appeared to be Italian, jumped from the car and ran across the railroad track. The hold-up was reported to Sheriff Workman, and officers went to the scene. An arrest was made, but Hutchison said he was not the man who held him up.[77]

As was previously stated, nothing of importance occurred during these years. A few bogus checks were passed, an auto was stolen, a Rhome girl disguised herself as a man and ran away from home for awhile, but she returned home sadder but wiser for the incident.

Our deputy sheriff was Joe Brown. He had occasion to arrest a few drunks; however, one particular arrest was funnier than the others:

> Aside from being the village constable, or deputy sheriff, Joe Brown is a tonsorial artist at Rhome, and he is frequently called upon to shave travelers who arrive in Rhome, tired, happy, and unshaven. They say Joe is a good barber, and for many years he has been known as a good officer of the law. So, and by, one day recently a traveler, by automobile, arrived in Rhome, wanting a shave. He went to the Brown shop on Main Street. After applying a hot towel, followed by a goodly portion of lather, Joe sniffled the man's breath, and he detected the odor of strong drink; drink that is forfbidden by law. Joe proceeded to give the man one of his best shaves, and when he was rounding out with the bay rum and talcum powder, he asked the customer if he had anything to drink. The man replied, "No." Joe insisted that the fellow surely had a little to sell to a dry and thirsty man. Again, the stranger stated that he had none for sale. "Probably not," replied Joe, "but I believe you have some in your car, and with the authority of the law, I am going to see." Brown went out to the car, which had been parked immediately in front of the barbershop, and there under the seat, were two partly filled pints of liquor—white and red. The stranger, bewildered and handcuffed by the officer, marched back into the shop. "Take a seat over there," commanded Brown, "and we will go to Decatur in a few minutes. . . ."[78]

The remainder of the story tells how the man was taken to the Decatur jail, how he had purchased the bottles earlier, and the fact that if he hadn't stopped for a shave, he wouldn't have been caught. ". . . who would think of finding an officer and a good barber in the same man," the prisoner related, with a merry twinkle in his eye.

The preceding story was told to let the reader know a little about the gentleman who was shot down by merciless desperadoes in less than four years time from the date of this story.

> Staging one of the most brutal murders ever enacted in Wise county, at high noon Friday in Rhome, a young desperado shot down Deputy Sheriff Brown, firing two 45 calibre bullets into his body, and deliverately leaving town on the public highway with companions in their automobile.
>
> Leaving behind the driver of their car, Doyle Meeks, 27, of Hedley, the trio sped from the scene of the shooting toward Dallas, leaving Deputy Joe Brown dying from a fatal bullet wound in the neck; he was struck also in the arm.
>
> Meeks surrendered after running a short distance from the office and was taken by Sheriff Faith of Wise county to Fort Worth for questioning. Meeks denied he knew either of the two men except as "Wayne" and "Joe," the names they used in conversation on the way from Quitaque, Briscoe county, which they had left at 3 a.m. yesterday.
>
> He gave the name of the woman, saying she was the proprietress of a tourist camp at Quitaque at which he formerly was employed. He went Tuesday from Hedley to Quitaque at which he formerly boarded with the woman, he told officers. He was awakened early Friday morning by the woman, who told him she wanted him to drive her car with the two men to Fort Worth. They left at once . . .[79]

According to reports, the group had been suspected of stealing some oil in Decatur. The *Decatur News* carried pictures of the scenes of the slaying. The captions under the pictures gave a vivid picture of the scene.

> In the doorway of a little, stuccoed barber shop at Rhome before which a curious crowd soon gathered, Deputy Sheriff Joe Brown of Wise county was shot down Friday by the gunfire of a member of a group of theft suspects he had just arrested . . . Below is Walter Looney, demonstrating how Brown was standing at the telephone, attempting to communicate with the sheriff's officer at Decatur when one of the group under arrest suddenly drew a gun and tried to abduct him. Looney, standing near the door was also menaced by the gun, but ducked out the door and escaped. Brown was shot a few moments later at the same spot where Looney had been standing.[80]

Texas was beset with criminals and desperadoes during these early years of the 1930's. A statement from the sheriff of Atoka, Oklahoma, makes the situation stand out very vividly. ". . . Joe Brown was one of four officers, sheriffs, and deputy sheriffs who lost their lives in the discharge of their official duties last week in Texas alone at the hands of the criminal underworld . . ."[81]

While the law enforcement officers of Texas were still searching for Glenn Hunsucker and his companion known as "Perch Mouth" or "Parrot Mouth" Stanton, Mrs. Ida Hunsucker went on trial in the district court at Decatur, Texas. She was sentenced to two years imprisonment on a murder charge in connection with the slaying of Deputy Sheriff Joe Brown. Along with the other charge, Mrs. Hunsucker was to serve three years in prison for receiving stolen goods at the tourist camp she operated in Quitaque. That sentence had been suspended, but with the new conviction, she was required to serve the first sentence also.[82]

One week after Mrs. Hunsucker's conviction, it was reported that Glenn Hunsucker had been fatally shot in New Mexico.

> Carrizozo, New Mexico, July 17—Sheriff A. S. McCammant of Lincoln county today advised Tulia, Texas, authorities that their description of Glenn Hunsucker, wanted in connection with the murder of an officer there several months ago, tallies exactly with that of a man killed near Ramon, N. M., in a gun battle with officers yesterday.
>
> Hunsucker and his companion whom officers believe to be "Parrot Mouth" or "Perch Mouth" Stanton were surprised by officers yesterday afternoon at a lonely spot near Ramon, New Mexico, 60 miles northeast of here.[83]

The same newspaper that told of Glenn Hunsucker's death also carried a story which is still unexplained according to the law officers at that time, but which seems to have some bearing on the slaying of Deputy Sheriff Brown. Walter Looney, the only witness to the slaying of Deputy Brown, was waylaid and beaten near Saginaw, Texas.

> Severely beaten about the head by two men, a man giving his name as Budd Looney of Rhome was found unconscious on a side road near Highway 2 about a mile south of Saginaw late yesterday afternoon. Looney witnessed the slaying of Deputy Sheriff Brown at Rhome last January.
>
> Matt Markum . . . reported to the sheriff's office that he was driving on the main highway when he saw two men drag the un-

conscious form of another man out of a coupe. After taking the man from the automobile, both men began beating him on the head, apparently with blackjacks.

Markum turned his car around to investigate the trouble, but the men fled as he approached, leaving the man unconscious on the highway. Markum took the man to the Saginaw where he was treated and revived at a drug store.

On regaining consciousness, the man told Markum his name was Budd Looney of Rhome. He said that he was a witness to the killing of Deputy Sheriff Joe Brown of Rhome last January, and the men had told him that he "knew too much," according to Markum.

Markum said that the man told him that he either was forced into the automobile or hailed a ride with the men at Saginaw. Markum was not positive about the details concerning how the man happened to get into the automobile . . . Jennings Brown, county attorney of Wise county, said that he would go to Rhome and make an investigation of the slugging.[84]

During this same year the Urschel kidnapping took place and there were also headlines that proclaimed Machine Gun Kelly was roaming Wise county. Then in the spring of 1934, Clyde Barrow and Bonnie Parker shot and killed two highway patrol officers near Grapevine, Texas.

March 15, 1929 brought a new surprise for the Rhome, Texas, community, just as it shocked the rest of the nation. The government had set up a new agency which was responsible for collecting a tax on the income of most people. The announcement of the new tax was made as follows:

> **Who?** Single persons who had a net income of $1000 or more for the year 1920; married couples who had a net income of $2000.
> **When?** March 15, 1921, is the final date for filing returns and making first payments.
> **Where?** Collector of Internal Revenue for the district in which the persons resides.
> **How?** Full directions on Form 1040A and Form 1040; also the law and regulations.

During this same year the Urschel kidnapping took place and there were also headlines that proclaimed Machine Gun Kelly was roaming Wise county. Then in the spring of 1934, Clyde Barrow and Bonnie Parker shot and killed two highway patrol officers near Grapevine, Texas.

March 15, 1929 brought a new surprise for the Rhome, Texas, community, just as it shocked the rest of the nation. The government had set up a new agency which was responsible for collecting a tax on the income of most people. The announcement of the new tax was made as follows:

> **Who?** Single persons who had a net income of $1000 or more for the year 1920; married couples who had a net income of $2000.
> **When?** March 15, 1921, is the final date for filing returns and making first payments.
> **Where?** Collector of Internal Revenue for the district in which the persons resides.
> **How?** Full directions on Form 1040A and Form 1040; also the law and regulations.
> **What?** Four percent normal tax on taxable income to $4000 in excess of exemption. Eight percent on balance of taxable income. Surtax from 1 percent to 65 percent on net income over $5000.[85]

Many objected to the tax, but pay they did.

Two years later a huge crowd witnessed the largest parade that Decatur had ever seen. It is almost certain that Rhome helped to swell the crowd of on-lookers. The *Decatur News* estimated that twelve hundred people witnessed the strange parade and six hundred persons took part in the parade.

> A crowd estimated to be the largest ever in Decatur witnessed a parade of the Ku Klux Klan in Decatur last Wednesday night at nine o'clock. The crowd began gathering early and by eight o'clock the square was crowded with people waiting for the marchers. People were here from all sections of the county, while many came from Fort Worth and other nearby counties.
>
> Promptly at nine o'clock the parade came into the square, led by fiery cross, electrically lighted and carried by a klansman on a horse. Next in line came a number of unmasked klansmen wearing special regalia, supposed to be worn by officers of the order. Next in line came a quartette which sang religious songs as they marched around the square. Following came the klansmen

in twos. The line of march came from the old oil mill; it is said that the leaders of the parade returned to the starting point before the last of the marchers had started to march. The visitors were members of the Fort Worth klan and carried several banners with inscriptions telling some of the things the order stands for. One banner bore the inscription: "One government, one flag, and one wife." These signs drew applause from the various sections of the crowd as they passed.[86]

The men from Fort Worth certainly did make a big bid for their organization at this parade, but since there were no more news reports about the group, it is to be supposed that there was no vigorous movement among this county's citizens. It just seems to have died out as far as Rhome was concerned.

As far as support or opposition to prohibition, Rhome was divided. In 1923 there was a story about the capture of a large still manufacturing corn whiskey:

> .... Sunday morning the same force accompanied by Deputy Game Warden Hugh Breedlove, bagged the biggest still ever captured in Wise county. It was a 75 gallon boiler and had three worms, and there were 475 gallons of mash. The still was on a place . . . east of Rhome.
>
> The officers have had knowledge of this still for some time, and were aware that it was furnishing booze to be sold in Fort Worth and Dallas.[87]

The churches of Rhome were fighting strongly against the sale and use of liquor. "Mrs. Bobo at Rhome has invited the Loyal Temperance Legion of Decatur and any one else who can come, to attend a public speaking there Saturday afternoon, September 29, at 2 o'clock. The children will render a short program."[88]

Social Affairs and Other Activities

Many delightful parties and entertainments were enjoyed by the Rhome citizens during these two decades. Mr. and Mrs. Wood Russell almost made an annual celebration of Hallowe'en. At least two years in succession they gave parties for their daughter, Cassie Frye Hudnall, who also says that they celebrated her birthdays in almost as festive a manner.

A Hallowe'en party which was delightful in every particular

was the one given by Mr. and Mrs. J. W. Russell, and daughter, Miss Cassie Fry, on Friday evening, October 28. The home was decorated in a most artistic way in keeping with the approaching holiday. Black cats, hoot-owls, and witches were everywhere. Music, games, and merry conversation were followed by delicious refreshments consisting of sandwiches, cake, and punch. Those attending were Mr. and Mrs. Marvin Holt, Mr. and Mrs. J. R. Troxell, Mr. and Mrs. C. E. Shaw and son; Misses Velma Carpenter, Omadelle Sparks, Lena and Lillian Rickman, Nona George, Gypsy Coates, Ozelle Hamack, Zaeta Morris, Glennace Looney, Glenn Barker; Messrs. Horace Barker, Chas. Morris, Dale Maeyers, Loyd Douglas, Jarrett Hudnall, Chas. Troxell, Thurman Hudnall, John Naugle, and Marvin Lehew of Fort Worth.[1]

The foregoing was certainly not the only party given, but was included because it seemed to be one of the more elaborate and different parties for the young people. Another such party was given a couple of years later by the Bobo family for their daughter, Ann Bobo.

> Miss Ann Bobo entertained with a slumber party last Thursday night complimentary to Misses Zaeta, Roe, Roxie, and Maude Morris, who left Saturday for their new home in Fort Worth. The young ladies who "rioted" through the night in this beautiful and hospitable home topped off with a sunrise breakfast in the woodsy vale were Misses Cassi Russell, Dannie Sampson, Zaeta Morris, Ethel Horton, Virginia Bobo, Maud Morris, Merle Van Meter, Mary Jo Troxell, Gertrude Horton, Roe Morris, Gladys Troxell, Florence Bobo, Loretta McGhee, Eula Mae Renshaw, Roxie Morris, and Ann Bobo.[2]

That same year in August the "Star Class" of the Baptist Sunday school entertained at the home of Mr. and Mrs. C. E. Shaw on a Friday evening.

> The gay, happy guests came dressed in children's costumes, and games and refreshments were planned to please and interest the juvenile mind.
>
> After an enthusiastic vote by all the guests, prizes were given to Miss Omadell Sparks and Mrs. J. H. McGlothlin as being the "cutest" children; Mrs. McClothlin and Zack Bobo, Jr., tied on this vote, but the prize was finally won by Mrs. McGlothlin.
>
> The personnel of the class, with honorary members present, were Misses Margaret and Alleta Mae Svennson, Virginia and Ann Bobo, Flora Leach, Omadell Sparks, Eula Mae Renshaw,

NELMA TROXELL'S BIRTHDAY party. Standing: Lorene Simmons, Frances Taylor, Bernice Simmons, Lorene Smitherman. Back row seated: Marie Chambers, holding Joel, Jr., Mary Ruth Simmons, Helen Payne, Roberta Nichols, Ruth Harlen Brammer, Blanche Evelyn Thompson, ____, ____, ____, Mary Jane Bost, Helen Stewart. Front row: Vivian Troxell, Nelma Troxell, Kenneth Brammer, "Sonny Boy" Thompson, Carl Thorell, Arthur Nichols, Charles Stewart, Billy Taylor, ____.

> Mrs. L. R. Douglas, and Zaeta Morris; Messrs. Charles Troxell, Zack and Pat Bobo, Jarrett Hudnall, Dale Maeyers, and Charles Sparks; friends of the class who were present were Misses Gladys and Mary Jo Troxell, Burch Barker, Etta Mae Hutchison, Florence Bobo, Mr. Gordon Barker, and Mr. and Mrs. J. H. McGlothlin.[3]

During 1926 the outstanding party seemed to have been one given by Mr. and Mrs. Carl Slay.

> Mr. and Mrs. Carl Slay entertained with one of the loveliest parties of the season, at their beautiful country home on last Thursday evening. Valentine motifs were used in the decorations and the diversions were suggestive of Valentine. The following guests were present: Messrs. and Mmes. J. H. McGlothlin, Joe Wren, Marvin Holt, John Naugle, C. E. Shaw, Joel R. Chambers, J. R. Taylor, Dale Maeyers, Charlie Payne, O. T. Finlayson, C. A. Nichols, Lloyd Douglas. Mrs. Dewey Ellis, L. C. Slimp, and Misses Mamie Trussell, Verda Logan, Lucille Richardson, and Nona George; Messrs. Boyd Logan, Thurman and Jarrett Hudnall, and the very young society buds, Alice, Inez, and Isla McGlothlin, Calvin, Frances, and Billy Taylor, Arnold Shaw, Joel and Marie Chambers, and Jackie Douglas.[4]

Many kinds of entertainment occupied the Rhome citizens from this time on. For example, the Masonic Lodge of Rhome entertained with an annual George Washington birthday party on February 22. On March 1, 1929, between seventy-five and one hundred guests were entertained with a patriotic program and grand eats.[5]

During the late 1920's Rhome also had another type of entertainment that is probably little remembered by many of the younger citizens. For some years Rhome boasted of a golf course of nine holes. Mr. E. E. Richardson lent the use of the pasture behind his house for the course, and many happy hours were spent there playing golf *and* tending greens by the golf enthusiasts of Rhome. Sometimes caddies slipped off and enjoyed a "swim" in one or other of the little water holes that occupied the course.

Vacation trips also occupied the minds of younger Rhome citizens. One memorable trip was that taken by Pat Bobo and Wayne Renshaw.

> The majority of friends said that the plans would not materialize; the parents rather suggested that it would not be permitted; a very few who have dreams of a motor trip to the Pacific coast wished a good luck and God speed, and on Tuesday afternoon, June 19th, of 1923 in a "King Tut" racer well-equipped for camping two of our most prominent young men shook the dust of their native village and departed for a well-planned tour which includes the cool heights of Colorado Springs and Denver, Salt Lake City, Yellowstone National Park, San Francisco, Los Angeles, and minor points.
>
> Look for glowing reports of the motor tour through our great northwest from the versatile pens of Pat Bobo and Wayne Renshaw, who are the heroes of this educational trip.[6]

During the 1930's the social events were for the most part a result of activities of the Thursday Study Club and the very active school events, with the exception of one announcement soon after the Democrats took office in 1933. "Beer, in all its old-time foaming, amber-hued glory, will be legally on sale by July 4, August A. Busch, Jr., owner of the world's largest brewery, predicted today . . ."[7]

In 1936 the Rhome businessmen revived the old enthusiasm of the trades days of the 1920's. Music furnished the beginning attraction:

> A musical program, arranged by Cleo Rann of Decatur and sponsored by the businessmen of Rhome was enjoyed by a large crowd at Rhome Saturday night, May 10th. A two-hour program

of trio, solo, and quartet singing, together with the Greenwood Racketeers string band, furnished plenty of entertainment for everybody. Most all of the candidates of Wise county were present, and an invitation is extended to all candidates and others to be present again next Saturday at which time another program will be held on the streets of Rhome. The movement has adopted as its slogan, "Follow the crowds to Rhome Saturday night."[8]

The enthusiasm may have continued until the next week, but there was no mention of the candidates or a music program for the next week. Nevertheless, Rhome was not content to give up on its ideas. Another report came in March of 1937. "The Rhome Rodeo, which was sponsored by the businessmen every Saturday night of each week last year will probably reopen as soon as the weather permits."[9] The rodeo grounds were located east of the depot in the same place that they were held a decade before. Charlie Morris was in charge of these rodeo arrangements.

The end of the 1930's saw the organization of both the Boy Scouts and the Camp Fire Girls. Both groups were energetic in providing activities for the youth of Rhome and community. 1938 brought news of a Boy Scout project involving almost the entire community:

> A cast of about 60 local business and professional men and women assisted by the Rhome community, will parade before the footlights on Friday and Saturday nights, December 16 and 17 in presenting "The Laff Round-Up," a hill musical review for the Boy Scouts' Christmas fund. The production is packed full of fun and clean entertainment. Below appear the names of some of the folks taking part:
>
> J. W. Inman, B. H. Hartman, Jerry Hudnall, Joe Taylor, Rev. Walters, J. H. Summers, J. R. Chambers, T. F. Ballew, Nelsie Hayes, Clayton Little, Joe Day, Claude Shaw, Walt Looney, Mrs. Naugle, Mrs. Pendleton, Mrs. Looney, Miss Walker, Miss Dougherty, R. B. Brown, W. C. Looney, H. B. Van Meter, Mrs. Van Meter, Chas. Hudnall, Bryant Vandiver, Betty Richardson, Ada Mae Whitehead, Pearl Erwin, Mary B. Hudnall, Vivian Troxell, Estelline Smith, Betty Thurmond, Beatrice Mood, Florence Jackson, Pauline Anderson, Harold Bost, Ralph Idell, Slick Summer, M. P. Taylor, Miss Russell, Marys Fuqua, Jesse Coker, Joe Wren, C. A. Nichols, Mrs. Nichols, Beverly Wren, Peggy Ewing, Wanda Naugle, C. W. Slay, Pete Sparks, H. H. Anderson, Mr. McGlothlin, Oleta Mason, Lucy Sparks, Francis Bost, Mrs. W. T. Smith, Alma Ruth Day, Thelma Wren, Jackie Douglas, Cora Emma Simmons, Jerry Looney, Geneva Fuqua,

Ida Mae Nehymer, Fred Boyd; the names of the square dancers will be supplied later.[10]

Unfortunately, the names of the square dancers were omitted from the next week's news. However, the girls were not to be out done by the boys. They had already organized a group of Camp Fire Girls in Rhome. Their first event came in January of 1939.

> The Ta Wan Ka group of Rhome Camp Fire Girls had a Christmas party at the home of Jackie Douglas. After a candle lighting ceremony, gifts were distributed from the Christmas tree. Games were played and refreshments of home-made candy, fruit, and soda pop were served to the group.
>
> The Christmas project of the Ta Wan Ka was to donate five dollars to the Community Christmas Cheer fund. This money was earned by the girls. They also decorated the tree and the church for the Christmas pageant. Eight of the girls taking part in the pageant presented by the school.[11]

In April of 1939, the Boy Scouts were planning a trip to the Boy Scout Circus. "The Rhome Scout Troup (152) is looking forward to the Boy Scout Circus April 15 in Fort Worth. Joel Chambers, Jr., Ralph Wren, and Mays Fuqua are going to decorate their bicycles to ride in the Bicycle Parade. Alfred Nichols and Joel Chambers are entering model airplanes. Six scouts are taking part in the scout ramble."[12]

In July of 1939 Mr. J. W. Inman took a group of his boy scouts to the New York World's Fair. "The boys, Joel Chambers, Jr., Ralph Wren, and Ralph Huddleston, all of Rhome and Lawrence Goodger, Jr. of Boyd told of visiting many points of historic interest . . . Joel Chambers, Jr. surprised Rhome with a telephone call from the fair ground."[13]

The next activity to be brought to Rhome provided fun for all ages. "Rhome will have a skating rink here soon. Mr. Orville Ewing is going to build one of forty by sixty-four feet. It will be opened in three weeks. The rink is to be a permanent project."[14] Mr. Ewing was the gentleman who owned the first bus station cafe in Rhome. Within three weeks the rink was completed and opened to an excited crowd of Rhome folks. "The Rhome people aren't amateurs any more at this skating business. An open session was held for the women who were learning Monday afternoon. The merchants say their silk stocking business has almost doubled in the last week."[15] In the same issue

BUS STATION CAFE, owned by Orville Ewing.

came a report of one of Rhome's barbers. "Mr. Allan Cobb believes he will quit the hair cutting business and start cutting the figure eight. The barber is the champion roller in the community. He has accomplished as much in the last two weeks as many skaters do in two years. Mr. Cobb says his best friend now is not his skates, but a bottle of rubbing alcohol."[16]

Plans for a tacky party at the skating rink were in progress by the end of June, 1939.

> Mr. O. R. Ewing plans to have a tacky party on the skating rink next week. The date is indefinite, but will be announced soon. A prize will be given for the most ridiculous costume. Ferdinand the Bull will be there. Come see him.[17]

Along with this announcement was the news that another Rhome businesman had tried the thrill of skating. "Mr. DeWitt Morris tried his skill on skates for the first time in twenty-six years Tuesday night. He wasn't doing so bad."[18]

There was another announcement of a type of entertainment for Rhome citizens. This writer was unable to obtain much information about the location of the shows, but surely some will remember attending the open air theater. "The show-going people in Rhome have been enjoying the open-air theater here. The show operates ever Tuesday night."[19] An earlier type of entertainment was the tent show.

A PLEASANT SUNDAY afternoon pastime. Frances Bost, Lois Hicks, and Catherine Troxell with two younger ladies.

Every year the Haverstock Tent Players came to Rhome for a few days of entertainment. Many will remember these as well as the earlier medicine shows.

For the women of Rhome the greatest achievement was the organization of a group that lasted thirty years. Much of the following material was taken from a speech given by Mrs. Pugh Morris in 1952, at the 25th Anniversary party of the club. Mrs. Isla Finlayson was kind enough to lend the writer the scrapbook which she had compiled during the club years.

In May of 1927 a small group met in the Masonic Lodge Hall for the purpose of organizing a study club. They felt the need for such a club to promote mental development and social intercourse among the women of the town. Mrs. J. P. Morris invited the group to meet with her for the first regular meeting.

Twenty-one ladies met at Mrs. Morris' home, organized the club, selected a name, The Thursday Study Club, and a study course that day. Mrs. Carl Slay was elected president. Texas history was to be the program for that summer. The charter members of the club were as follows: Mmes. Drummond Burch, Joel Chambers, Loyd Douglas, Ones Finlayson, Marvin Holt, Thurman Hudnall, Boyd Logan, Verda Logan, Dale Maeyers, J. H. McGlothlin, Pugh Morris, John Naugle,

C. A. Nichols, Wayne Renshaw, Claude Shaw, Carl Slay, Clyde Slimp, Forrest Thurmond, W. A. Tomlinson, J. R. Troxell, and Joe Wren.

The *Decatur News* carried a story that fall about the club, since that publishing company printed the first yearbook for the society.

> The News completed and delivered last week, the "Year Book" for the Thursday Study Club in Rhome, Texas, an organization for mental development and social intercourse. The course of study is English literature, with current articles interspersed throughout the entire program. The officers are as follows:
>
> President . . . . Mrs. Carl Slay
> Vice-President . . . . Mrs. C. E. Shaw
> Recording Secretary . . . . Mrs. J. P. Morris
> Corresponding Secretary . . . . Mrs. O. T. Finlayson
> Treasurer . . . . Mrs. Boyd Logan
> Parliamentarian . . . . Mrs. C. A. Nichols
> Critic . . . . Mrs. Wayne Renshaw[20]

This same year the club was very proud of the fact that it had become a federated club. When they were admitted to the General Federation of Women's clubs at the State Convention in Denton, Texas, Mrs. J. H. McGlothlin represented the Rhome club.

One of the chief projects of the club was the presentation of a Majestic Vaudeville program at the school auditorium, where they "took in the neat sum of $200.00," which they presented to the school library. This marked the beginning of many social and civic occasions, many of which were planned for the husbands of the club members.

The Thanksgiving banquet was made an annual affair for the club, as was the spring luncheon given at the close of the year by members having the lowest attendance records. The county newspapers carried many accounts of delightful club meetings for these women. The children of club members, the writer being one of the said children, remember with delight and pleasure the day upon which his particular parent was hostess. On that day the family always shared in the "goodies" planned for dessert for the occasion such as chicken salad, fruit salad, and angel food cake.

In 1928 the club initiated two new club members, Mrs. Oscar Barker and Mrs. C. E. Payne, to replace departing members who had moved away. This was also the year in which the club entertained the

First District President of the Texas Federation, Mrs. Mack Burch, a former Rhome citizen.

In July of 1928 the Thursday Study Club started a project to beautify the town:

> "The Yard Beautiful Contest," conducted by the Thursday Study Club, closed Monday, July 9th. Our County Agent, Miss Sims, was here Monday afternoon and judged the yards. She awarded first prize of $5.00 to Mrs. J. M. Brammer; second prize of $2.50 to Mrs. J. M. Childress. The club expects to make this contest an annual affair. We hope to have more yards entered in the contest next year, with more and better prizes.[21]

On November 2, 1928, the Thursday Study Club entertained their husbands with a moonlight picnic at the Finlayson Ranch, where the group of fifty guests engaged in "lively games and very satisfying refreshments."

In 1929 Mrs. Earl Simmons and Mrs. Fate Renshaw were voted in as new members. That year they presented a flag to the school. The same year the club engaged in a project to beautify the school grounds. "Mr. Baker of Baker Floral Company met with the Thursday Study Club and discussed plans for landscaping the school grounds."[22] The following year, 1930, the club began a study on travel in the United States, and they also planned a program of highway beautification for Rhome.

The club voted in two new members in 1931. They were Mrs. Harold Van Meter and Miss Ruth Van Meter. The club history reads as follows: "Thanksgiving banquet was given at the Masonic Hall, where most of us ate our first oyster cocktail." This year was also the time when the club decided to make the school teachers associate members. The teachers were Ella Fay Kendell, Jane Hoyl, Louise Scott, and Katy Ruth Anderson. This year the civic project was playground equipment for the school.

In 1932 Mrs. Clarence Greer became a new member of the club. The club carried out several civic projects. They sent baskets of fruit, nuts, and candy to the shut-ins; they presented two programs for the high school students, "Texas," and "A Health Program." The club also assisted the Red Cross in distributing typhoid serum and paid a nurse to care for typhoid fever patients.

Mrs. J. P. Morris was re-elected president of the club for the third time in 1933. The membership of the club was enlarged to twenty-four with the addition of Mmes. Foy Byrd, O. C. Clark, Sy Gaston, and Mrs. Webb. Among the club civic projects were a clean-up campaign for the town, a marionette show to benefit the school library,

THE THURSDAY STUDY Club gave a handkerchief shower for Mrs. J. R. Troxell at the home of Mrs. Joe Wren. The honoree was moving to Decatur, Texas.

and a visit to a Dallas art museum. In 1935 the club was interested in art in the home and many programs were on interior decorations. They also sponsored Miss Dorothy Finlayson for queen at the Wise County Fair. For their civic project they gave a large unabridged dictionary to the school. Mrs. H. F. Malone became a new member of the club.

In 1936 two new members joined the club, Mrs. Tom Dodson and Mrs. A. B. Van Meter. This year the club was privileged to hear Miss Oppenheimer of Dallas in a book review. The new member in 1937 was Mrs. Joe Day.

The club year book was printed by the *Wise County Messenger* in 1939.

> The job department of the Messenger is this week printing the annual yearbook of the Rhome Thursday Club, and is one of the most attractive and beautiful books we have ever published. The Rhome club is one of the most outstanding literary organizations in the state, composed of ladies living in the vicinity of Rhome. The officers of the progressive and wide-awake club are as follows: President, Mrs. Harold Van Meter; Vice-President, Mrs. C. E. Shaw; Secretary, Mrs. L. Wayne Renshaw; Corresponding Secretary, Mrs. J. W. Finlayson; Treasurer, Mrs. J. P. Morris; Parliamentarian, Mrs. J. D. Burch; Critic, Mrs. Carl Slay.

Members of the club are as follows: Mmes. J. D. Burch, Joel R. Chambers, John R. Dunn, Lloyd R. Douglas, J. W. Finlayson, O. T. Finlayson, S. H. Gaston, Marvin Holt, Thurmon Hudnall, Harry Logan, Dale Maeyers, J. Pugh Morris, J. H. McGlothlin, John W. Naugle, C. A. Nichols, L. W. Renshaw, L. Wayne Renshaw, C. E. Shaw, Carl W. Slay, A. B. Van Meter, H. B. Van Meter, D. O. Wilbur.[23]

This year for the first time a sad note entered the club report. "Our Circle was broken when our beloved Mrs. Mac (Mrs. J. H. McGlothlin) was taken from us." In 1940 the new members were Mrs. Joe Thurmond and Mrs. Cherry. The year book also carried its first memorial page for Mrs. McGlothlin's death.

It was in June of 1942 that a special call meeting was held in Mrs. Hudnall's home. At this time it was thought expedient to disband the club for the duration of the war so that the club members might answer the need for "an all-out effort to win the war." Four years intervened. The war was won. On January 23, 1947, Mrs. Finlayson called a meeting at her home to resume club work.

In 1947 the new members were Mrs. Robert Bennett, Mrs. Hans Schluter, Mrs. Loyd Browning, Mrs. Roy Montgomery, and Mrs. Joe Taylor. It was in 1949 that the club adopted a French family, Monsieur and Madame Locquet and their two sons, Gilbert and Barnard, to whom they sent food and clothing. The club year closed with a yard improvement contest.

In January, 1950, the local school board gave the club permission to take over the old home economics building and to convert it into a community center and club house. The men and women of the town and community began work remodeling the building, and on February 22, 1950, the Thursday Study Club had its first meeting in the center by sponsoring a George Washington Tea.

The Thursday Study Club met in the home of Mrs. J. P. Morris in 1951 for a plantation luncheon. Everyone came dressed in costume. The tables were laid with white linen cloths, centered with corsages of violets, which were presented to each member after the luncheon. A typical Southern menu was served: fried chicken, gravy, creamed potatoes, string beans, pickled peaches, potato salad, hot rolls, pecan pie, and coffee. After the luncheon, slides from the Natchez Garden Club were shown and thoroughly enjoyed. Each member modeled her costume before the group, and Mrs. Joe Thurmond's costume was judged most typically southern. Letters received from ex-members of the club who had moved away were read to the group.

In March of 1952 the club was awarded first place on its 1951 year book by the Convention of Federated Clubs in Fort Worth. From the

Wise County Messenger came a report of the twenty-fifth anniversary of the Thursday Study Club of Rhome, which was celebrated on the afternoon of November 6, 1952, at the Community Center in Rhome.

> The club room was beautifully decorated with the color scheme of red and white with red carnations used as the cut flowers.
>
> Mrs. Robert Bennett, the program chairman, introduced Mrs. Morris of Rhome who gave a summary of the activities of the club for the past quarter century . . . The club's charter members were honored as well as the ex-members. Delicious refreshments were served to about forty members and guests.[24]

At the end of the history of the club was a touching comment by Mrs. Morris:

> It makes me very happy to have you past members here to help celebrate our 25th Anniversary. The club has meant much to me and I feel we have accomplished many worthwhile things during the years. I hope during the coming years we will be able to accomplish even greater things.[25]

The Thursday Study Club received one of the highest honors when one of its members, Mrs. J. W. (Isla) Finlayson, was named the "Outstanding Clubwoman" of the First District, Texas Federation of Women's Clubs for 1954-55. This award was made at a meeting in Vernon on March 30, 1955.

> The honor that was bestowed on Mrs. Finlayson at the 53rd annual convention of the district, held last week in Vernon, has been a matter of community pride because the recognized accomplishments involved community projects.
>
> And Rhome citizens of all ages are pulling for their outstanding clubwoman to win the statewide award at the TFWC convention in Galveston in May.[26]

The Thursday Study Club of Rhome finally closed its activities at the end of the club year, 1956-57. Mrs. Barney Wright was the last president of the club. Apparently, the group was willing to give over the reins of club work to a younger group of women who were organized in 1957.

This new Junior Women's Club of Rhome was organized in 1957. However, notice must be taken of an earlier group which was organized in 1935.

A Junior Women's Club was organized on Wednesday, May 22, 1935, in the home of Mrs. J. E. McDaniel. Officers elected were the following: President, Mrs. A. G. Ray; Vice-President, Mrs. E. P. Carpenter; Secretary-treasurer, Mrs. Emmett Anderson; Reporter, Mrs. Reese Anderson; Social committee, Mmes. Harold Simmons, Thomas Clark, Irwin Kennedy, Walter Looney, Joe Childress, and J. E. McDaniel.

There was a report in June 1935, of the members entertaining for their husbands with a picnic at Forest Park and Lake Worth. The last information this writer was able to obtain on the group was the following from the *Wise County Messenger*:

> The Junior Women's Club met at the home of Mrs. E. P. Carpenter, Jr., on January 15th. The program of the day was . . . household hints. Menus are given at each meeting. Plans were discussed about a St. Valentine Party. On the anniversary of each member the club presents her with a most useful gift. Several new members have been added and old members and new ones who would like to join are especially invited to attend the next meeting at the home of Mrs. Joe Childress on January 29th. At that time "dressings" will be discussed. Refreshments were served to Mmes. Ed. McCrary, Joe Childress, Odis Stegal, LeRoy Beauchamp, Harold Simmons, Mary Ray, J. E. McDaniel, Jr., D. Rucker, Bill Troxell, Louise Kennedy, and the hostess.[27]

It is likely that this club, like the Thursday Study Club, felt it expedient to disband during the war days. The members were probably scattered by the time the war ended, and it was never called back into session.

The new Junior Women's Club was organized on September 5, 1957. The first officers were as follows: President, Mrs. John T. Livengood, Jr.; Vice-President, Mrs. Paul "Pat" Logan; Recording Secretary, Mrs. Harold Harvey; Corresponding Secretary, Mrs. Jerry Harvey; Treasurer, Mrs. Arlis Haun; Parliamentarian, Mrs. Mays Fuqua; The charter members were as follows: Mmes. Al Allen, Joe Baker, J. W. Finlayson, Mays Fuqua, Darrell Green, Pete Hale, Jerry Harvey, Harold Harvey, Arlis Haun, John Livengood, Jr., Paul Logan, Dan Maeyers, Ivan Matthews, Ervie Motley, Robert Owens, Herman Pepper, Carl Schluter, M. L. Smith, M. P. Taylor, Clarence Walker, Elmo Wise, John J. Wilson. This group is still in existence and is very active today. It has replaced the original Thursday Study Club in its activities and projects that are carried on today.

Education

The Parent-Teacher Association for the Rhome school was quite active in 1920. This was the first mention of such an association for Rhome; thus it must have been organized about this time.

> The parent teachers association held its first open house to the citizens and patrons on Tuesday evening October 12. An interesting program of readers and music was rendered, and the debate by Messrs. Handley, Gribble, McGlothlin, and Shaw was the climax of the evening. Thanks are especially due to the members of the Rhome orchestra: Mr. McGlothlin, cornet; Miss Midget Wright, clarinet; Miss Velma Carpenter, drum; Misses Rickman and Stone, violin; and Mrs. Rena Troxell, piano, for their many delightful selections. Refreshments were served and many new members were added to our list.[28]

School opened in 1921 with glowing reports of its achievements and future hopes. "Rhome high school opened Monday with the most auspicious outlook of its history. A more hearty cooperative spirit among the school patrons has never before been demonstrated. An enrollment on the first day of a hundred and twenty students evinces an interest that means achievement . . ."[29]

The school news from Rhome was quite extensive for the 1920's. A very interesting reporter was found in the person of the Wise County School Superintendent, Wallace Gregg. Mr. Gregg wrote lengthy columns each week on all of the schools in the county. He must have spent every working day visiting the different schools in the county. Rhome certainly was one of his favorite places to visit; hence his many and varied reports on the Rhome school.

By 1921 affiliation was one of the main concerns of the Rhome school and its patrons. High optimism was shown in the report of the opening of school in 1921.

> Rhome high school opens Monday, September 12th, and a full attendance is expected. The coming term promises to be one of the most successful years we have had yet. The faculty for the high school has been selected: S. D. Handley, superintendent; Miss Gabie Sue Carpenter, principal; Miss Cora Hicks, Miss Glenn Barker. The intermediate grades and primary departments will be under the following teachers: Misses Velma Carpenter, Lillian Rickman, and Glenn Barker. Miss Lena Rickman will teach piano. Very few changes have been made in the faculty since Mr. Handley has been here and for that reason better results have

been obtained. The school has the highest classification it has ever had, and we have no doubt that the school will be affiliated the coming term.[30]

This affiliation was not achieved quite so soon as the community expected. It took quite a few years and much hard work to secure all the units needed for full affiliation as a high school.

For many years it was a custom for the Rhome school to hold a picnic usually near April 1st, or "April Fool's Day." A first account of one of these picnics was found in the year 1923.

> The school picnic was held Thursday at Shaw Springs was well attended. The day was a perfect picnic day. After the bountiful lunch had been eaten, Mr. Gribble volunteered to escort the crowd to the famous old Indian cave and spring. There the young folks found names and dates written years ago. A number of the names were those of our most prominent men, together with their sweetheart's names.[31]

Martin Simmons recalls that Shaw Springs was about one half mile southwest of the old C. C. Leonard place, while he remembers that the cave was about a half mile north east of the springs.

Mr. Gribble was superintendent of Rhome schools at this time. The next year brought another superintendent for Rhome. This time it was a gentleman named C. W. Williamson. At that time the school board for Rhome school was President, L. W. Renshaw; Trustees, Messrs. J. L. Stone, C. Q. Woody, Earl Van Meter, Mack Holt, J. H. McGlothlin, and Mrs. J. H. McGlothlin, secretary.

With the school's help a literary society was organized for Rhome. It was planned that the organization should meet every two weeks. The public was invited to attend. "Officers of the literary society were as follows: President, Millard Horton; Vice-President, Sam Roberts; Secretary, Sue Ella Van Meter; Critic, Mr. Williamson; Tellers, Irvin Watkins and Okie Sparks."[32]

Another of the innovations planned for Rhome school was the introduction of hot lunches for the students. With the aid of Miss Jewell Taylor, the mothers of the town and country met to discuss a way to give the children better lunches. Since the school was not prepared to offer the entire lunch, a demonstration on preparing hot chocolate was given for the mothers. "Soups and other nourishing foods may be used to give variety, but only one dish is served each day."[33] The mothers also discussed how to prepare a sanitary lunch bucket, and it was suggested that the common every-day syrup bucket would be the most economical and sanitary type of lunch container. The order in

ASSEMBLY PROGRAM STYLE Show.

which the bucket should be packed was also discussed. "... the above lunch can be brought to school by those who walk, ride, motor, or ride a galloping horse without being turned upside down."[34]

The Parent Teachers Association was becoming a larger part of the school in 1923. The meetings were well-attended, and the purposes of the organization were being outlined. "The club voted to affiliate with the Texas Congress of Parents-Teachers' Association, which will enable the local club, among other privileges, to work up some splendid programs with the materials furnished by the affiliation . . . ."[35]

Probably the first yearbook for any Rhome school was done during 1926. The following material gives the list of those chosen for special honors for the yearbook sponsored by Mrs. Amellia Thurmond.

In the popularity contest the following were elected:
High school—Most handsome boy, James Ward; Most beautiful girl, Miss Marie Ferguson; Most popular boy, Arnold Shaw; Most popular girl, Miss Syble Terry.

212

Seventh grade—Most beautiful girl, Miss Lois Thompson; Most handsome boy, Leroy Smitherman; Most popular girl, Miss Lois Thurmond; Most popular boy, Charles Sparks.

Fifth grade—Most popular boy, Jack Terry; Most popular girl, Miss Helen Bost; Most beautiful girl, Miss Pateray Ward; Most handsome boy, Gussie Mondrick.

Fourth grade—Most beautiful girl, Miss Eugenia Terry; Most handsome boy, Albert Lisby; Most popular girl, Miss Lorene Smitherman; Most popular boy, Manson Bost.

Third grade—Most beautiful girl, Miss Imogene Richardson; Most handsome boy, Burnice Brilton; Most popular girl, Miss Blanche Evelyn Thompson; Most popular boy, Leon Terry.

Second grade—Most beautiful girl, Miss Helen Stewart; Most handsome boy, Billie Sparks; Most popular girl, Miss Isla McGlothlin; Most popular boy, Mr. John Will Finlayson.

First grade—Most beautiful girl, Miss Marie Chambers; Most handsome boy, Paul Logan; Most popular girl, Miss Wynama Williams; Most popular boy, G. H. Ward.[36]

It was in 1926 that the senior class bought new stage scenery. They met with a representative from the Fort Worth Scenic company to select the type of scenery for their class gift.

It was in the spring of 1926 that Rhome won honors in the declamation contest for District X. "Arnold Shaw of Rhome won the beautiful Neiman-Marcus cup, which was offered as a first prize in the Junior Boys High School Declamation Contest, in District X, which is composed of Dallas, Denton, Tarrant, Parker, and Wise counties . . . Arnold is the son of Mr. and Mrs. C. E. Shaw."[37]

Rhome public school opened on Monday, September 20, 1926, with a good attendance. The faculty for the year was as follows: C. A. Nichols, Superintendent; Miss Dewberry, Principal; Miss Viola Fowler, sixth and seventh grades; Mrs. C. A. Nichols, fourth and fifth grades; Miss Verda Logan, second and third grades; and Miss Pauline Mason, primary.

The Parent-Teachers Association made a special study of the problem of hot lunches for the school children, in 1926. They realized the need for warm lunches and a committee was appointed to make plans for serving a hot dish at school during the winter months that might be a supplement to the lunches brought from home.

> Parent-Teachers Association hope to have everything in readiness by the middle of November to begin serving the supplementary hot dish. The work will be under the management of Mrs. Nichols.
>
> Four II girls will plan the weekly menu and write it on the board each Firday morning so that every child will know what is to be served each day. Everyone will bring the required dish from home to get his soup, cocoa, chili, or whatever is being served. The Parent-Teachers Association will finance the project and the foods will sold to the pupils at the minimum cost possible.[38]

Apparently this was the forerunner of the modern school cafeteria for the Rhome school.

The Rhome school was still striving for affiliation in 1927. Much time and effort by both students and teachers was devoted to this effort.

> Mr. C. A. Nichols, superintendent of Rhome school, has received from the state department of education an acknowledgement of the receipt of his report and application for classification. The department assures him that no difficulty will be experienced in securing this necessary prerequisite to affiliation. Rhome had 46 in high school on the day of the visit, 12 of whom are seniors. Mrs. C. A. Nichols, primary teacher, has a bright group of 20 first graders who are doing unusually good work. . . Rhome scored the highest of any school yet visited and might easily reach the requirements for standardization.[39]

In 1927 Rhome was given an excellent recommendation on the standard of work that it was doing. The county superintendent Wallace Gregg, highly approved of the efforts being made in Rhome.

> Rhome has the distinction of being the only one of the small high schools of the county that maintains a nine months' term. The area of the district is 12,687 acres, on which a school tax of seventy-five cent tax, fifty-five cents goes to maintenance and twenty cents goes to bonds and interest. Rhome employs six teachers and maintains ten grades of school work . . .[40]

Rhome continued to strive for affiliation with the State Department of Education. In 1927 the Rhome P.T.A. purchased for the high school library the reference books in English and history necessary to meet affiliation requirements. The state at that time required at least $400 worth of books in the library.

A report came to Rhome in 1928 of the recognition that it had

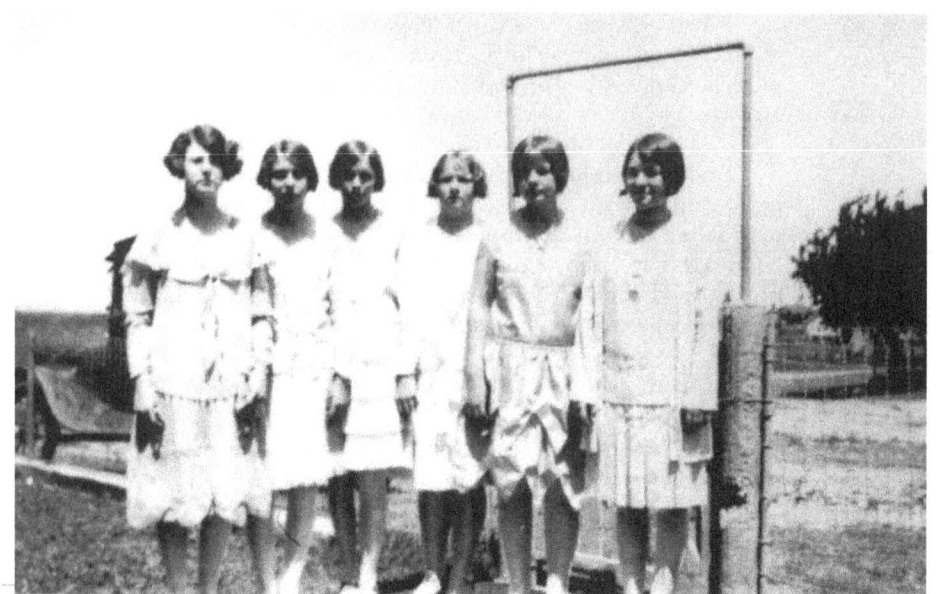

(L to R) LANA MACON BYROM, Sara Byrom, Beatrice Ward, Dora Dean Logan, Marguerite Green, Alice McGlothlin. Rhome High School—Class of 1928.

been seeking. If the story of affiliation seems unduly long drawn, it is deliberately told so that younger generations can understand the long, hard task that it was for the school personnel. When full affiliation came with 18½ credits, the news was welcomed with great happiness and gratitude for the chore that had been accomplished. Final affiliation did not come until 1935. The following report is only the beginning of the struggle.

> The Rhome school has been awarded classification as a three-year high school by the High School Division of the State Department of Education, and has won five units of affiliation. The subjects accredited are Ancient History, American History, Plane Geometry, Algebra, 2 units.[41]

The faculty for 1928 was as follows: Superintendent, Mr. C. A. Nichols; Principal, Miss Ella Faye Kendell; Sixth and seventh grades, J. T. Watson of Chico; Fourth and fifth grades, Miss Jane Hoyle; Second and third grades, Miss Katie Ruth Anderson; Primary, Mrs. C. A. Nichols; Music and Expression, Miss Janette Scott of Olney.

The Parent-Teachers Association thrilled the students at Rhome by a purchase they had installed on the school grounds at the southeast corner of the old red brick school building.

ISLA MC GLOTHLIN AND Billy Sparks on the playground at school.

VIEW LOOKING NORTHWEST, showing the red brick school building. The two-story house was owned by the Brammers and the one-story was the Sparks' home.

> The Merry Whirl, super playground apparatus, which has recently been installed on the campus of the Rhome High school by the P.T.A. is proving very popular with the children. So eager are they to ride the merry whirl that teachers have to supervise the play by lining the children up in shifts and taking turns of one minute each at riding.[42]

Tragedy struck the Rhome school in March, 1929. Reports came from all the nearby papers on the holocaust that destroyed the magnificent two-story red brick building of which Rhome had been so proud since its construction in 1912.

> The Rhome high school building was destroyed by fire Tuesday night about 10 o'clock. When the fire was discovered, the auditorium in the building was a mass of flames, and without fire protection, the citizens of the little town has to stand by and see their magnificent school building wiped up by the flames. The building was insured for $15,000, in a report coming to the *Messenger*. The original cost was $45,000. Work of rebuilding will start immediately.[43]

The churches of Rhome immediately provided space for the school to continue its work during the time of rebuilding. The citizens of Rhome also came to the aid of the school. By May there was a report of a new bond issue and also an increase in the school taxes. "Big majorities carried the bond and tax elections at Rhome . . . on April 27. Rhome voted $30,000 bonds by a 72 to 3 count and increased the school tax from $.75 to $1.00 by a vote of 71 to 4 . . . Rhome will build a splendid new structure to house both the grammar grades and the high school."[44]

Rhome was determined to build a school building that would be virtually indestructible. Perhaps evidence of that resolve may be found in the fact that today (1978) the Rhome building is the only one still standing in the Northwest Independent School District. The following report gives many particulars of this deliberately careful planning for the school by its trustees and the citizens who were involved:

RHOME TO HAVE FIRE PROOF SCHOOL BUILDING

> Mr. E. E. Richardson, president of the school board at Rhome, is enthusiastic over the new school building now under construction at Rhome. Commenting on the progress being made recently, Mr. Richardson said: "We are making our building as nearly fire-proof as possible. The whole structure will be of brick, steel, and concrete . . .[45]

CLASS OF 1935 when they were in the 3rd Grade. Miss Verda Logan, teacher.

Probably this building was the first structure to be laid on a concrete slab in Rhome. The floors over the slab were wood and the door frames were wood, but the remainder of the building was completely fireproof.

> ". . . The floors will be laid on concrete. The partitions are of steel and concrete. The roof is supported by steel joists over-laid with two inches of concrete. The ceilings are made of steel lath and plaster. The window frames are of steel construction. We are trying to erect a building that will make impossible a repetition of our fire experience last spring. We hope to have a building that will not require any fire insurance.
>
> "We gave the order just the other day for our program clock. It embodies the very latest ideas in program clock making. Our stage scenery will be complete in every detail. We have ordered our laboratory furniture and will have a well-equipped room for teaching the high school sciences. Water will be piped directly to and on the playground. The heating system will be the new gas-steam arrangement. The building throughout will be lighted with electricity. All wiring and plumbing fixtures are being installed as the building goes up."[46]

All during the time this construction was going on, the school was still working toward affiliation. In the same issue of the *Messenger* that carried the story of the fire, there was a story of application for seven more units of affiliation. This time they were applying for seven units in Modern History, General Science, Spanish I and II, English I, II, and III. "Mr. Nichols and his school board are considering the matter of adding next year the seventh teacher and the eleventh grade."[47]

The Rhome shcool was also becoming very proficient in the sport of basketball as evidence in a game with Paradise high school. "Edward Bost led both teams in scoring with 14 points . . . Aside from winning high point scoring honors, Bost probably played the best game of his career, as least the best of this season. His generalship was unusually good for a high school boy and together with his floor work, displayed a brand of ball to be remembered always. Sparks, Rhome forward, showed more fight than any other Rhome player on the floor . . ."[48]

Because of the terrific interest in basketball engendered by games like this one, the school board and administration were eager for the boys to have a proper place to play. On October 10th of that year there was a notice about plans for a new gymnasium for Rhome. "Members of the Rhome School Board were in Springtown Sunday afternoon inspecting the Gymnasium in that place."[49] The next week's edition of

A GROUP OF Rhome school teachers, circa 1933. Left to Right: Sue Ella VanMeter, Mrs. Mable Nichols, Daisy Russell, R. C. Elrod.

RHOME SCHOOL SUPERINTENDENT Mr. C. A. Nichols.

the same paper announced that Rhome was to get the county-wide basketball tournament.

> The Wise county basketball tournament will be held at Rhome next February. This was the decision of the basket ball coaches at a meeting held during the Institute last week. Rhome is to build a splendid new brick gymnasium in the near future and will accommodate the tournament in it.[50]

While the gymnasium was under construction, other big plans were in progress for Rhome. Work on the new school building was fast being completed, and the school personnel were working on plans for a formal dedication of the new structure.

> A notable occasion was that at Rhome last Friday night, October 18, when formal exercises were held dedicating Rhome's new $40,000 school plant. A great throng of keenly interested people thronged the auditorium of the new building to hear the excellent program arranged for the occasion. Dr. J. L. Ledlow of Denton Teachers College was the principal speaker. Members of the board who appeared on the program were E. E. Richardson, president, and J. H. McGlothlin, secretary.
>
> The Rhome building is the most completely equipped school structure in Wise county. In elegance of appointments, it is the last word in school architecture. An air of refinement pervades the whole building. The auditorium is fitted with opera chairs, complete and beautiful stage scenery, and graced with the finest baby grand piano...[51]

A note of nostalgia for the writer enters here because the writer's mother, Mrs. J. R. Troxell, was on the committee to select the piano, an Ivers and Pond baby grand. The condition of the once lovely piano will wring a sigh from the hearts of those who chance to see its condition today.

There was yet another innovation to be added to the Rhome high school auditorium. The planners had their hearts in the right place, but the architect, unfortunately, did not know enough, apparently, about planning for the project.

> The splendid auditorium in the new school building at Rhome is being equipped for motion pictures. A fireproof booth is being provided for the motion picture machine which will be installed soon. Superintendent Nichols states that the educational pictures issued by the University of Texas will be used in teaching various subjects. Miss Ella Faye Kendell, English

teacher, is looking forward with much interest to the use of the
machine in her classes.[52]

The idea was fine, but unfortunately the projection angle and the height of the room would not work. It was certainly a loss to the students and teachers who had looked forward to using it.

Within a month there was another dedication program for Rhome school. This time it was the new gymnasium which was notable particularly for the fact that it was the only such structure in the entire county.

> Coach J. T. Watson of the Rhome High School announces the formal opening of the new Rhome High School Gymnasium on the night of November 15th. Mr. Watson is arranging a suitable program in connection with the opening and hopes to have representatives from all parts of Wise county in attendance. Immediately following the exercises of the evening, there will be played three games of basketball: Boyd vs. Paradise, Chico vs. Ponder, and Rhome vs. Newark.
>
> The Rhome Gym is unique in that it is the only high school gymnasium in Wise county. The structure is built of tile and brick, and its architecture is in harmony with that of the new school building. A playing floor thirty-five by seventy feet gives ample room for games. Tiers of seats rising on either side of the playing floor will accommodate some 500 spectators. Two dressing rooms with baths are built into the far corners from the entrance. High-powered electric lights will make playing at night even better than in daylight . . .[53]

For a comparison of these playing conditions with those of previous years, see the picture of an outdoor court shown in an earlier chapter of this book. The excitement Rhome was feeling at this time was certainly justified, and certainly a great deal of credit goes to these pioneers who foresaw the need for good schools.

However, all this glowing elation was to be dampened by the events of the coming years of depression and war. The Rhome school was not closed for lack of funds at any time during these hard years as fell the lot of many other schools at this time. Even Decatur fell under the burden of supporting a school during such hard times. In 1933 the Decatur school was closed for half a term for lack of sufficient funds to run the school. Rhome certainly suffered with the others, but at least we were spared closing the school. In 1932 Rhome was notified by the State Department of Education that it was then fully accredited with a total of 16½ credits. By 1934-35 Rhome had added vocational

ELLIS TROXELL'S WORK shop at Rhome High School (L to R) C. C. Calvert, Paul Troxell, Truitt Wilson, Ellis C. Troxell, Joe Thurmond.

LOIS WALKER, SOCIAL studies teacher, and Golda Rie Brown, music teacher, two of Rhome High School's favorites.

agriculture and home economics departments to its curriculum. At this time Rhome had achieved 18½ credits.

The school at Fairview continued its work during these years under good teachers. A report from the *Decatur News* gave a good description of the Fairview school.

> Mr. Morgan and Mrs. Jesse Carpenter, teachers of the Fairview school, 4 miles northeast of Rhome, believe in putting in full time at their school work. They have their pupils go to work immediately upon reaching school, and on the morning of the visit, practically the entire group of 39 sutdents were present and at work by 8:30 o'clock. Fairview has a good two-room modern building, pleasantly situated in a rich farming district. The taxable valuation of the district makes it one of the richest districts in the county being almost equal to that of the Slidell district which now maintains 7 teachers. Mr. Layfield is having his pupils doing some excellent map work in geography.[54]

In 1934, Fairview began its plans for a new school building. "There is quite a lot of excitement in Fairview, work has begun on the new school building and we expect to see a new brick building in the near future. The church is also being painted white."[55] There was also a report of a picnic in Mr. T. M. Yant's pasture. The children also enjoyed an egg hunt and a baseball game.

The new Fairview school building was erected in 1934. "It was a modern brick structure with two class rooms, two cloak rooms, and a small porch. The patrons are very proud of this achievement. A school bus was also owned by the patrons to take the children to and from school."[56]

Among the teachers of the Fairview schools during these years were Mrs. Hunt, Ben Garnder, Mr. McKinnon, Eileen Rowan, Ina Yant, Morgan Layfield, and Lois Thurmond. Some of these teachers were pupils who returned later to teach in the school. The last teacher was Bertye Lue Wilson, who taught there nine years.

> In 1948 the patrons were faced with the question to consolidate their school. They were to consolidate with schools at Rhome, Justin, Roanoke, Haslet, and surrounding areas. A meeting was called and everyone agreed on the situation. On February 22, 1950, the new school was started. It was named Northwest School in the Northwest School District. It was located on Highway 114 between the towns of Rhome, Justin, Roanoke, and Haslet. The district covers 216 square miles.[57]

(L to R) MRS. LULA SUMMERS, Mrs. Kate Troxell, Mrs. Lucy Looney, Mrs. Alice Brammer.

Churches

By the beginning of these two decades the churches of Rhome were well-established. Their activities were very much the same as they had been during the past decades. However, the end of this period and the beginning of the 1940's saw some changes in the church community. The Presbyterian church sold its church building to the Methodists and ceased to exist as a church organization. The Assembly of God church began about the end of the 1940's. So that once again Rhome had four churches within its city limits.

The First Baptist Church continued one of its annual entertainments. There were reports of the Thanksgiving banquet in both 1920 and 1921.

> The ladies of the Baptist Church will serve public dinner on Thanksgiving Day. This is an annual feast, with a history of many years back. The proceeds always to to Buckner's Orphans Home. Everybody is cordially invited to cooperate. On the night of Thanksgiving a program composed of addresses and special music will be rendered at the Baptist Church. All denominations and all people have a part in this union service.[1]

The B.Y.P.U., the Ladies Aid Society, and the Sunbeam Bands were all very active during this time. In 1923 W. F. Willis was superintendent of the Sunday school; Mrs. W. E. McGhee was president of the Ladies Auxiliary; and Mrs. C. E. Shaw was leader of the Juniors and Sunbeam Band with Miss Flora Leach as her assistant. A. J. Leach was the pastor of the church.[2]

During 1925 the Baptist Church had an outstanding musical program planned for the community:

> The musical program conducted by Professor John Sparks at the Rhome Baptist Church last Sunday afternoon was one of the best ever held in the county. Every number which had been arranged for was present with additional quartets. Professor I. R. Reynolds and his party from the Baptist Seminary, Fort Worth, gave a pleasing variety of solos, duets, quartets, and instrumental music. Taken as a whole, the afternoon program contained such variety that everyone present might enjoy his special kind of music. Mr. Sparks is commended for his untiring effort in and capable direction of this pleasing program. A record-breaking crowd was present.[3]

The Baptist Church's birthday celebration was an occasion of great joy for the church members.

THE BAPTIST PARSONAGE at Rhome, designed after a house which Mr. Zack Bobo had admired in his travel on the interurban to Dallas.

W. F. WILLIS, Sr., Sunday School Superintendent in the First Baptist Church.

> Last Sunday was the forty-seventh anniversary of the establishment of the First Baptist Church at Rhome, and a big celebration was had. Attorney General McGraw was present and delivered an address, which was appreciated very much by the big crowd. Mr. Zack Bobo was present, and he carried the distinction of having been clerk of the church for forty-two years. Mrs. Bobo was the only charter member at the meeting . . .[4]

The Baptist Church remained in its first red brick building until sometime in 1966. It was in that year that plans were made and carried out for the new church building which it occupies on the same location today. During the time that the building was under construction, the church body attended services in the school auditorium. The pastor during this time of rebuilding was Jerry Watson, an active young man who was very helpful with all of the church programs.

The Church of Christ grew extremely fast during these years, and in order to accommodate its growing congregation, the church decided to build a new building. Sometime before 1937 the old white church building was razed. Since at that time the Presbyterian church was not in use, the Church of Christ "borrowed" the building for their own church meetings. The cream-colored brick church was completed for the Church of Christ congregation sometime in the latter part of 1937 or early part of 1938. They continued to meet in this building until about 1960 when they began construction of the air-conditioned, red brick church building which they occupy today.[5]

Mrs. Juanita Chambers and Mrs. Ruth Slay were kind enough to supply a list of the pastors who have served their church. Although the dates of service were not available, the following pastors have served the church: J. K. Bentley, W. N. Carter, G. A. Dunn, Foy Wallace, Horace W. Busby, J. W. McCall, Tillet S. Tedlie, John C. Cash, Jessie Powell, Bro. Stubblefield, Willard Morrow, Morris Moore, Joe Rhoten, Carl Brachen, Foy Kickpatrick, Dwain Davenport, Albert Trent, Roy Deaver, and Joe Malone.

Today the church also owns a handsome brick parsonage, which had been built by Mrs. Thurman Hudnall as her residence until she moved from Rhome to be with her daughter and son-in-law.

The Cumberland Presbyterian Church suffered a period of lack of growth during these decades. The church directory published in the *Messenger* in 1923 listed the following information: "Preaching every fourth Sunday in each month, morning and evening, Sunday school at ten a. m. L. R. Randolph, superintendent; Ladies Aid Society, Monday at three p.m., Mrs. J. D. Burch, president; W. A. Binyon, pastor."⁶

On the same date as the preceding notice, the Ladies Aid took part in the monthly trades day for Rhome citizens.

> Sunday school at this usual hour last Sunday with fair attendance and good interest. Ladies' Aid was well attended on Monday afternoon. Several visitors present on last program day and the invitation is still extended for our next, which will be held Monday afternoon at three o'clock. The Ladies Aid will serve sandwiches, cake, and drinks on the square on next trades day, the first Saturday in July.⁷

The Cumberland Presbyterian Church of Aurora held a large revival service in August of 1923. The Reverend W. A. Binyon who was part-time pastor of the Rhome church, was the preacher for this revival.

> ... Brother Binyon needs no words of commendation from the people of Aurora community. He has been preaching at Rhome for several years and has brought that congregation from a state of spiritual lethargy into a flourishing condition that speaks volumes for his work as a preacher. The Aurora people feel that they were to be congratulated on securing the services of this man.

> Some of the services were held in the specially constructed arbor and others in the school building.... The meeting closed with an all-day get-together on the grounds. A large crowd carried the dinners with them and visitors from Rhome, Newark, Boyd, and other adjoining communities enjoyed the good things provided ... The day was one of the most enjoyable and profitable in the history of the community, and Brother Binyon's work has left a lasting impression for good ...⁸

Brother Binyon was still the pastor in 1926 because there was a notice in the *Decatur News* about a pounding given to him on December 3, 1926. Other pastors following Brother Binyon were the following: J. F. Foster, Lockett Adair, W. J. Johnson, and N. B. Baker.

There was very little news of the church in the following years, but according to information from James Drummond Burch the church membership was growing smaller and they were finding it difficult to meet the presbytery dues. The Presbytery officially closed the church at Rhome in 1937. During these last few years the Presbyterians and the Methodists shared their church services, meeting in one church on one Sunday and in the other on the next Sunday. Mr. C. A.

THE PRESENT-DAY building which houses the United Methodist Church of Rhome. This building was remodeled from the older Cumberland Presbyterian Church building.

Nichols was superintendent of the Methodist church, and Shaw Ford had a similar responsibility in the Presbyterian church. After the closing of the Presbyterian church, the congregation still owned the church property. It was used in 1939 as a W.O.W. meeting hall for some time, and also the Boy Scouts organization held meetings there. It was about 1940-41 when the Methodist church finally purchased the property from the Presbyterian congregation.

Before they decided to raze their old building, the Methodists began a drive to enlarge their congregation. A rally was held in May of 1921 for representatives from all churches in the county.

> An all-day Sunday school rally of the Methodist Church last Sunday was very enjoyable, as well as a profitable occasion. Representatives from the Methodist Sunday schools of Alvord, Chico, Decatur, and Boyd were present. An excellent address at the eleven o'clock hour by Reverend Oliver, pastor of Alvord, was much enjoyed. Mrs. Baldridge of Chico delivered a tender and appealing message on the training of the young life, followed by an able and effective talk on teacher training work by Supt. Outler Gose of Decatur. Brother Oliver conducted the round table discussion. Music for the day was in charge of Prof. John Sparks. Lunch was served at the church.[9]

The church directory of 1923 read as follows: Preaching each second and fourth Sunday, morning and evening. Sunday school at ten a.m. S. A. Lowance, superintendent. Missionary society, Monday at three p.m. Mrs. P. T. Gribble, president. Prayer-meeting, Wednesday evenings. E. G. Roberts, pastor.[10]

In those days when the small churches could not afford to keep a full-time pastor, they had a pastor on one or two Sundays of each month. Usually they attended one of the other church's services on the Sunday when they did not have a pastor.

On October 5, 1939, the announcement was made that the Methodists were to demolish their old building. Several factors entered into the decision. The new highway would take part of the church property, and the building was also old and worn. They proceeded to make other arrangements for a church building by purchasing the Presbyterian building.

> According to a statement by Rev. R. E. Porter, pastor of the Rhome Methodist Church, the church building will be demolished next Monday, and the farewell sermon will be preached in the church next Sunday, October 8th at 11 o'clock a.m. All members and friends are invited to be present. Special service and music. Rev. Forrester of Decatur will deliver the sermon.[11]

One of the final notes taken on the Methodist Church's activities was one of a union service of the churches in Rhome. "The clear Easter morning sun was received by an Easter Sunrise service staged by members of the three churches combined. A group of thirty gathered on Renshaw Hill to sing and receive a short Easter message delivered by Reverend Porter, the Methodist minister."[12] Since that first Easter Sunrise service, a traditional Easter Service has been held in the Aurora Cemetery, on the hillside facing Rhome. Watching the sun rise over the little town of Rhome provides the participant with a special feeling of awe and reverence.

During these two decades the following pastors served the Methodist Church: J. T. Bludworth, George R. Slagle, E. G. Roberts, J. R. Jordan, J. Thomas Brown, R. E. Porter, N. L. Glasco, O. A. McBrayer, James E. Carter, Roy Montgomery, Leon Turner, Kenneth Johnstone, J. G. Forrester, Kenneth Watson, and Robert Hall. Many of these pastors served the church for one of two terms and then returned to Rhome to serve a second time. Both Reverend Porter and Reverend Montgomery have served many years in the Rhome pastorate, and have been very much loved by their congregations as well as the town in general.

The Assembly of God Church was started in a gospel tent in 1949. The church building was erected in 1950-1951 in the north area of Rhome. The first service was held in the building on July 17, 1951. Reverend M. R. Barrons was the first pastor, followed by C. R. Barnett, W. L. Hopper, and G. L. Howard in 1960. The charter members of the church were Mrs. Floyd (Audie) Young, Mrs. P. C. Moore, Mr. and Mrs. Wendell M. Splawn, Clyde Idell, Mrs. Clyde Idell, Mr. and Mrs. Hershell Brawley, Mr. and Mrs. Curtis Judge, Mr. James M. Hyatt, Leona Hyatt, Pauline E. Idell, Rosa Idell, Mrs. Ross Arrington, and Mrs. M. M. Ford.

While the Rhome churches were changing, so was the church at Fairview. "The church has had its trials, but for several years, it has had full time pastors, services every Sunday."[13]

In 1947 the Baptist church at Fairview began construction of a small parsonage for its pastors. It has been enlarged since it was built, and now the pastors either live on the field grounds or stay there on the weekends. The church and parsonage are located on grounds donated for the school by Mr. John F. Thurmond. "Today the church is going strong and is growing."[14]

The Thurmond-Fairview Cemetery is also receiving good care by the citizens of Fairview. "When Fed Thurmond, the brother of the late J. F. Thurmond, died in 1921, he willed $1,600 to the Fairview Cemetery, and this money with money from trust funds that others have set up, is loaned out and the interest is used for maintenance of the cemetery."[15]

By 1951 an organization was formed to set up perpetual care for the cemetery. The association was incorporated under the name Thurmond Fairview Cemetery Association. It was about this same time that they provided a fence for the cemetery and planted grass.

Fairview Community Center

When the Fairview rural school consolidated with the Northwest School District, a deed for the Fairview school building was given to the people of the community.

At that time the Fairview Community Club was organized with Mrs. Jack Layfield, chairman; Mrs. Joe Thurmond, Vice-chairman; Mrs. Truett Wilson, Secretary; Wayne Tribbble, boy chairman; and Peggy Griffith, girl chairman.

The first work that the club did to renovate the new community center was plastering, plumbing, and painting, along with carpentry work. A kitchen was made with builtin cabinets, a linoleum was laid on the kitchen floor, running water was installed, and a gas stove was bought.

The Fairview Community Club bought dishes to serve 50 people, and an electric coffee urn was purchased. Each lady in the community made and donated two cup towels. They also purchased card tables and folding chairs. They old piano was repaired and tuned. In 1950 there were 20 families in the community, and all were members of the Fairview Community Club.[16]

MISS VIRGINIA BOBO'S 3rd and 4th grade class at Rhome School about 1920.

NEW ASSEMBLY OF God Church

APARTMENT COMPLEX

NEW CHURCH OF Christ Building

STAR TANK AND Trailer Mfg. Company.

NEW BUILDING FOR the First National Bank in Rhome.

BARKER — CROW

Oscar Hunt Barker was the tenth of the twelve children of Hugh B. Barker and Kiziah Alice Randel Barker. He was born March 15, 1868, in Prentiss County, Mississippi. He enjoyed joking, telling "tall tales" and the consumption of good food.

Oscar and Exsa Crow were married in Boyd, Texas, on July 18, 1900. They established their first home in Rhome, but moved the following year to the Barker home place northeast of Boyd, where they lived until 1905.

The family moved about considerably, living in Marlow, Oklahoma, from 1907 to 1913, while engaged in farming. They returned to Rhome for a year or so and then moved to Burkburnett, Texas, where they remained until 1916, when they again returned to Rhome, remaining there until 1922. It was during this time that they must have owned and operated a grocery store and filling station on the Meridian highway, near the E. L. Smitherman home. In 1922 they moved to Fort Worth, Texas. Horace, a son, secured employment in the Santa Fe Railroad Shops at Cleburne, Texas, on November 16, 1922, where he was employed until his retirement on August 1, 1964.

Oscar and Exsa Barker had two sons: Horace Barker and Roelene Crow Barker. Horace Barker married Etta Mae Hutchison, and Roelene married Geraldine Hartman.

Roelene Barker worked for the Gulf Oil Corporation in Fort Worth for a number of years prior to going to Cleburne in 1936. In 1937 he entered the service of the Santa Fe Railroad Company from which employment he retired in 1964.

Following a stay in Fort Worth, Oscar and Exsa moved back to Rhome about 1928, remaining there until 1936, when they moved to a farm east of Cleburne, where they lived until 1945, at which time they moved to a home purchased closer to Cleburne. Here Exsa died on September 7, 1954. Oscar continued to live in the home until his failing health forced his removal to a nursing home in 1958, where his death occurred on November 29, 1959.

BARKER — CALDWELL — TROXELL

Lynn Boyd Barker was born on February 3, 1859, in Kentucky, the sixth child of Hugh Brown Barker and Kiziah Alice Randal Barker. As a young man in his teens, Lynn Boyd Barker accompanied his widowed mother and her children to Texas. Boyd lived with his mother and the other children until he was twenty-one years old; he

THIS IS LYNN Boyd Barker and his wife, Maggie Troxell Barker; his children: Opal Barker, Gordon Barker, and Glenn Barker.

was then married to Margaret Caldwell and they made their home in the Deep Creek Community near his mother's home. To this union were born three children: Willie Pearl, often called Pearlie, who married "Bud" Logan and bore him eight children, seven of whom reached adulthood whose descendants now number twelve grandchildren, twenty-one great grandchildren, and one great-great grandchild; Hubert B. Barker, who died in early childhood; and Maggie Barker, who married Clarence Hudnall.

Margaret Caldwell Barker died at the age of twenty-three years; six years later Mother Kiziah Barker, who had assisted in rearing the children, died. Some ten years later, Boyd Barker moved to the prairie near Rhome, Texas, where he was married for a second time.

Lynn Boyd Barker married Margaret (Maggie) Emma Troxell, daughter of John Troxell and Mary Mosshart Troxell, on January 3, 1897, in Rhome, Texas. A brother, Hugh Banks Barker, also married one of the Troxell daughters, Clara Alice Troxell, thus making the children of these families double cousins. Margaret Emma was born near Hiawatha, Kansas, on February 27, 1872, where the Troxells lived for several years.

Having managed to make a down payment on 160 acres of land at the Rhome location, Boyd settled on this as the site of their home. With a will to work and save, they began to farm—a milk cow and a mare, blind in one eye, were the livestock they had to begin what became a successful operation. The home, having been a bachelor's domain for a while, required a thorough cleaning, which along with the "woman's touch" and the beautiful rag rugs made by the bride, all added to a pleasant and comfortable place to live.

Maggie was typical of the farm wives who always prepared well in advance for feeding the harvest and threshing crews; it was a heavy responsibility and a busy time indeed. During grain harvest she would seat sixteen men at the huge dining table for breakfast, noon, and evening meals. That was in addition to the family and anyone else who "dropped by." In addition to the three "square meals," she packed a lunch or afternoon snack which was taken to the field about 4:30 p.m. This was far more than a coffee break, for it helped the men hold their strength until the late evening meal, for they worked as long as they could see what they were doing, and it was indeed a long day.

The threshing was considerably easier for the homemaker, as the cook shack with a hired cook was a part of the group that went from farm to farm threshing the shocks of grain until all was completed. About 1928 the combines came into use, which cut the labor problem down to about four men who cut and threshed the grain at the same time.

The children learned early that their father demanded obedience and respect. This was motivated in large part by his concern for their welfare in the future.

Another phase of his relationship with his children was evidenced by the following incident: The mother reported to Boyd that two of the children had been disrespectful to the hired hand. After a scolding, they were sent to bring a switch to be applied where it would do the most good. After selecting the smallest broom-weed available, they returned to "face the music." A pitiful sight they were! Boyd's tenderness for this children and his sense of humor overcame his intentions of stern discipline. He had to smile, and of course there was no switching.

Another memory of their childhood was being gathered together in the living room on Sunday afternoons while their father read from the Bible.

Maggie taught her daughters to cook and to sew, and she saw to it that each received a college education. She herself kept books for Boyd and discussed business affairs with him and knew enough of his extensive land holdings to be able to carry on the family business affairs capably after his death.

Four children were born to this marriage: Alice Glenn Barker, who did not marry; Mary Opal Barker, who married Chester January; John Gordon Barker, who did not marry; and Ella Burch Barker, who married Dale Maeyers.

L. Boyd Barker died of a stroke on January 8, 1929, in Rhome, Texas. His widow, Margaret Emma Barker, lived on in the family home on the farm about a mile north of Rhome until her death on October 27, 1946. They are buried in the Deep Creek Cemetery.

BARKER — RANDEL

Hugh Brown Barker, the eldest child of Asbury Edmund Barker, was born in 1836 in Pulaski County, Kentucky. He married Kiziah Randel, daughter of Alexander Randel. She was born August 14, 1833, in Alabama. Hugh Brown Barker died on September 2, 1874.

Shortly after his death, probably in 1876, Kiziah moved with her family to Aurora, Texas. Horace describes the events of this trip as his father, Oscar Barker, related it to him when reminiscing. He says: "These conversations pointed up to me the courage that our grandmother must have had to face the problems of widowhood with a family of nine to provide for at a time when the economy of the South was at an all time low following the War between the States. Some of the neighbors from Prentiss County had made the trip to Texas and cien Barker, who died in early childhood; Hugh Banks Barker, who married Clara Alice Troxell; Bascom Randel Barker, who married Bertha Samuels; Oscar Hunt Barker, who married Exsa Crow; Samuel Edgar Barker, who married Abagail Crowder; and Virgil DeWitt Barker, who died at one year of age.

Kiziah Barker died on January 26, 1892, and is buried in the Barker plot in Deep Creek Cemetery, near Aurora and Rhome, Wise County, Texas, along with several of her children and grandchildren. Gordon Barker, son of Lynn and Margaret Emma Troxell, requested in his will that a trust fund be set up for the perpetual care of Deep Creek Cemetery and this was done with the interest on the principal amount set aside being used for this purpose.

BARKER — SAMUELS

Bascom Randel Barker was born on February 6, 1866, in Prentiss County, Mississippi. He was given his mother's name of Randel, her name having been Kiziah Randel before her marriage. Bascom was only ten years old when they made the trek to Texas, and it must have been an exciting time for him. He was one of the four younger children that lived in the family home during their mother's lifetime and for a number of years after her death.

Bascom Barker was married to Bertha Samuels, but she lived only a short time after their marriage. She died in childbirth and so did the baby born to them. She is buried in a cemetery south west of Bridgeport, Texas. Bascom had a small place near Boyd, Texas, where they lived. After her death, he became ill and finally in 1909 he rented his place out, and Boyd Barker brought him to his and Maggie's (Margaret Emma) home where he lived the greater portion of the time thereafter. Until Boyd's death in 1929, he lived with and was cared for by the Boyd Barker family. After Boyd's death he was entered in Wichita Falls Sanatarium, where he died in 1934. He is buried in the Barker family plot in Deep Creek Cemetery.

BARKER — TROXELL

Hugh Banks Barker, son of Hugh Brown Barker and Kiziah Rendel Barker, was born on February 4, 1863, in Albertville, Alabama. He married Clara Alice Troxell, daughter of John Troxell and Mary Mosshart Troxell, on November 23, 1902, in Rhome, Texas. Clara Alice Troxell was born on November 17, 1879, in Rhome, Texas.

Christine Barker Donald spoke lovingly of her father:

cien Barker, who died in early childhood; Hugh Banks Barker, who married Clara Alice Troxell; Bascom Randel Barker, who married Bertha Samuels; Oscar Hunt Barker, who married Exsa Crow; Samuel Edgar Barker, who married Abagail Crowder; and Virgil DeWitt Barker, who died at one year of age.

Kiziah Barker died on January 26, 1892, and is buried in the Barker plot in Deep Creek Cemetery, near Aurora and Rhome, Wise County, Texas, along with several of her children and grandchildren. Gordon Barker, son of Lynn and Margaret Emma Troxell, requested in his will that a trust fund be set up for the perpetual care of Deep Creek Cemetery and this was done with the interest on the principal amount set aside being used for this purpose.

BARKER — SAMUELS

Bascom Randel Barker was born on February 6, 1866, in Prentiss County, Mississippi. He was given his mother's name of Randel, her name having been Kiziah Randel before her marriage. Bascom was only ten years old when they made the trek to Texas, and it must have been an exciting time for him. He was one of the four younger children that lived in the family home during their mother's lifetime and for a number of years after her death.

Bascom Barker was married to Bertha Samuels, but she lived only a short time after their marriage. She died in childbirth and so did the baby born to them. She is buried in a cemetery south west of Bridgeport, Texas. Bascom had a small place near Boyd, Texas, where they lived. After her death, he became ill and finally in 1909 he rented his place out, and Boyd Barker brought him to his and Maggie's (Margaret Emma) home where he lived the greater portion of the time thereafter. Until Boyd's death in 1929, he lived with and was cared for by the Boyd Barker family. After Boyd's death he was entered in Wichita Falls Sanatarium, where he died in 1934. He is buried in the Barker family plot in Deep Creek Cemetery.

BARKER — TROXELL

Hugh Banks Barker, son of Hugh Brown Barker and Kiziah Rendel Barker, was born on February 4, 1863, in Albertville, Alabama. He married Clara Alice Troxell, daughter of John Troxell and Mary Mosshart Troxell, on November 23, 1902, in Rhome, Texas. Clara Alice Troxell was born on November 17, 1879, in Rhome, Texas.

Christine Barker Donald spoke lovingly of her father:

I cannot think of my father's young manhood without recalling how vivid to him was his conversion experience. He said it was the happiest moment of his life and he never doubted that he had received salvation, and he loved to testify to it... He was an ardent Methodist, and my mother (who also had a striking conversion experience) joined the Methodist Church with him in Mineral Wells when I was a very small child and the church was "my second home."

He was a bachelor for a number of years, being 39 years old when he married my mother, and in the course of the years, he must have "squired" quite a few girls, for as a child I remember when we were looking at our box of pictures and would ask our mother who certain girls were, she would reply, "Oh, that is one of your dad's old girl friends." My sister was almost five years older than I, and I recall that in a fit of jealousy she took a fist full of these pictures one day and we destroyed them! When my mother learned what we had done, she laughed heartily about it. I was a very little girl and I did not understand any of it, either my sister's jealousy or my mother's mirth.

When they first married, Clara and Banks lived several miles south of Rhome until about 1907. They had no close neighbors, and Clara was afraid to be alone especially when "hoboes" would drop off the train out of town and walk up the long path from the tracks to their home to ask for a handout. She would watch and when she saw one coming, she would hurriedly pack a lunch and with sack in hand and a butcher knife grasped firmly in the other hand behind her back, she would hand out food to the hobo. Once the door was closed behind her, she would lean against the wall trembling with relief that she was safe once more.

Several months preceding the birth of Christine, Banks, had a severe case of typhoid fever, from which he almost died. The doctor suggested that he move to Mineral Wells to have the benefit of the water; so he went ahead and stayed at a boarding house. They bought eight acres of land about a mile west of Mineral Wells for a house site and several hundred acres of pasture land adjoining. Clara's younger sister, Kate Troxell, stayed with her until she could go to Mineral Wells. Her brother, Jim Troxell, unmarried at the time, went on to supervise the building of the house west of town, where Clara remained the rest of her life.

Hugh Banks Barker died in Mineral Wells on July 20, 1929. Clara Alice Barker died on January 11, 1950, also in Mineral Wells at the family home. They were both buried in the Elmwood Cemetery in Mineral Wells, Texas.

Two children were born of this marriage: Pearl LaRue Barker, who died of multiple schlerosis when she was twenty-two; and Christine Alice Barker, who married (1) Homer Alvin Wood, killed in the Air Force, (2) D. R. Blackerby, who died in 1955, and (3) J. M. Donald, an attorney from Bowie, Texas, who died in 1977.

BEAUCHAMP — CASH

William B. (Bill) Beauchamp, the son of Dorne Beauchamp and Josephine Slimp Beauchamp, was born on May 20, 1891, in Greenwood, Wise County, Texas. On October 8, 1910, William B. Beauchamp married Icey Belle Cash, daughter of William John Cash and Lucy D. Wheeler Cash, of Boyd, Texas. Icey Belle Cash was born on October 8, 1890, in Vernon, Alabama, before the Cash family moved to Texas around 1895.

Six children were born to this union: LeeRoy Beauchamp, who married (1) Juanita Stephens and (2) Jewel Payne; Beatrice Beauchamp, who married John William McKee; Kathryn Beauchamp, who married Leon Atkerson; Anna Lois Beauchamp, who married Dr. James Paul Heberle; Billy Beauchamp, who married Eula Pearl Williams; and Travis Beauchamp, who married Yvonne Griffeth.

William B. Beauchamp died on December 10, 1958, in Wise County, Texas. He is buried in the Aurora Cemetery. His widow, Icey Belle Cash Beauchamp, died a year latter on December 25, 1959. She is also buried in the Aurora Cemetery.

BEAUCHAMP — PUTTON

Captain Finis Dudley Beauchamp, one of Aurora's oldest residents, came to Texas in 1872. He was born in Lawrence County, Alabama, on November 15, 1825. He served in the United States Army while he was living in Mississippi. Two of his sons, Dorn and Hugh preceded the family to Texas.

Finis Dudley Beauchamp married Mary Caroline Putton, who was born on February 10, 1829, in Fayette County, Alabama. The couple moved to Mississippi after their marriage. It was there that their eight children were born. These children were as follows: Dorn Beauchamp, who married Josephine Slimp; Hugh Beauchamp; Eugene Beauchamp, who died in Mississippi before 1872; John Beauchamp, who died in Mississippi before 1872; Sallie Ann Beauchamp, who married J. D. Reynolds; William Burges Beauchamp, who was not married; Jefferson Davis Beauchamp, who was not married; and Finis Dudley Beauchamp, Jr., who married Dollie Norvell.

Captain Finis Dudley Beauchamp died in Aurora, Texas, on June 12, 1893. He was buried in the Aurora Cemetery with Masonic honors. His widow, Mary Caroline Putton Beauchamp, followed him in death on April 10, 1915. She is also buried in the Aurora Cemetery.

BEAUCHAMP — SLIMP

Dorme, (or Dorn as he was known), Beauchamp was born in March of 1851 in Mississippi. His parents were Dudley and Caroline Beauchamp. He married Mary Ann Josephine Slimp, and daughter of Landon C. and Nancy Lloyd Slimp. Josephine Slimp was born on May 16, 1860, in Mississippi.

Three children were born to this union: Lula May Beauchamp, who married James Byrom; Ed Beauchamp, who married Mollie E. Wheelock; and Will Beauchamp, who married Icey Belle Cash.

Josephine Slimp Beauchamp died on January 31, 1893, in Wise County, Texas. She is buried in the Slimp Cemetery northwest of Aurora, Texas. After the death of Josephine Beauchamp, Dorn married Minnie Balch.

Dorme Beauchamp died in Wise County, Texas, during the winter of 1921, and he is buried in the Slimp Cemetery at Aurora, Texas.

BOBO — COWARD

Simpson Bobo was born July 29, 1828, in Spartenburg, South Carolina. He was married to Sarah Jane Coward of Tuscaloosa, Alabama, on August 5, 1847. She was born on August 15, 1824.

Seven children were born to this union: Doratha Quentille Bobo, who married Tom H. Alexander; John L. Bobo, who died when he was about sixteen; Delia A. Bobo, who married a Mr. Turner, from whom she was later divorced; Charley Sharp Bobo, M.D., who married Katie Crow; Zachariah Blount Bobo, who married Elizabeth Tabitha Morris; Simpson W. Bobo, who married Zelon Watson; and Sallie Virginia (Jennie) Bobo.

The Simpson Bobo family came to Texas in 1873 with their six children, settled on Hog Branch near Boyd, Texas. Later they moved to Aurora, Texas. Simpson Bobo, with two of his daughters, Delia and Jennie, moved from Aurora back to Boyd, and then later they moved to Fort Worth, Texas, where they lived until their deaths.

MR. AND MRS. Zack Bobo, shown leaving their beloved Baptist church.

BOBO — MORRIS

Zachriah Blount Bobo was born February 20, 1858, in Panola, Choctaw County, Mississippi. He came to Texas in November of 1873, in a covered wagon drawn by a four-mule team. He settled at Aurora with his family.

He married Elizabeth Tabitha Morris on June 9, 1885, at the home of her parents, Colonel Benjamin and Roxana Blair Morris, in Rhome, Texas. The June wedding was a social event of such proportions that Colonel Morris had an extension built to the family home to accommodate the wedding party. Elizabeth Tabitha Morris was born in Eufaula, Alabama, on July 11, 1867.

In 1885, the same year as his marriage, he passed the Texas pharmacy examination and began his practice with the license number 281, which meant that he was the 281st man to be registered in the State of Texas to practice pharmacy.

Zack Bobo also became an undertaker. In Rhome, Texas, he opened a furniture and drug store, which he operated until old age and ill health caused his retirement from business. He was active in the business of the town. At one time he was a stockholder and a director of the First National Bank of Rhome. He was intensely devoted to his church and its affairs, helping to plan and build the second church building for the Missionary Baptist Church of Rhome. He was also responsible for the design and building of the parsonage for Baptist ministers. He served as a deacon in the church, and he was secretary and treasurer for more than forty years. Mrs. Bobo was equally active as a Sunday school teacher and a worker in the church.

Twelve children were born to this happy union: Bennie Ruth Bobo, who married J. B. Castleberry; Salle Louise Bobo, who married Carl L. Christian; John Simpson Bobo, who died as a young man of nineteen; Early Virginia Bobo, who married Lafayette William Renshaw; Elizabeth (Bess) Bobo, who married Dewey Gibbs Ellis; Dr. Zack Blount Bobo, who married Ruth Marrs; Dr. Thomas Carroll Bobo, who married Estelle Alene McKaig; Mary Roxana (Ann) Bobo, who married Dr. Clifton Earl High; Paul Revere (Pat) Bobo, who married Inez Farrell; Clara Barton Bobo, who died as a young child; Florence Naomi Bobo, who married Robert Byron Huddleston; and Cora Margaret Bobo, who died as a baby.

Zachriah Blount Bobo died on August 27, 1942, in Rhome, Texas. He is buried in the Aurora Cemetery. His widow, Elizabeth Tabitha (Betty) Bobo continued to live in the family home until shortly before her death on December 6, 1962, in Decatur, Texas. She is also buried in the Aurora Cemetery.

BOST — NIX

Philip Safrit Bost and Jessie Marie Nix were married at Alton, Oklahoma, on January 11, 1908. They were descendants of German immigrants to Pennsylvania. The Bosts were ardent Lutherans who migrated south to North Carolina. The Nix family were ardent Quakers who migrated to new lands in Georgia.

The Bost family migrated to Micklenberg County, North Carolina, in 1754 and engaged in farming and milling. They supported the American cause during the Revolution as patriots and soldiers, and later they would serve the Confederacy during the Civil War.

PHILIP S. BOST circa 1910.

FORMER JESSIE MARIE NIX—MRS. PHILLIP S. BOST

The Nix family are known to have arrived in Georgia by 1810. They were cotton farmers and despite their Quaker heritage held slaves. Their migration to Texas in 1866 was made by wagon and required three months to reach the land they had leased twelve miles south of Dallas. They would migrate to obtain free homestead land in Greer County, Oklahoma, in the spring of 1878. At this point they were ardent Baptists.

By 1908 Philip and Jessie Bost had established their first home in Blair, Oklahoma. On November 15, 1908, they welcomed their first child, Nell Marie. In 1911 they were making their home at Megargel, Texas, where Philip tended a herd of horses and worked on oil drilling rigs. Their first son, Edward Lawson, was born in October, 1911. In 1913 the enlarged family moved to Fate, Texas, and Philip returned to barbering. On September 9, 1913, Helen Lucille was born. They would remain at Fate for the next three years and experience the tragic loss of their Nell Marie on November 15, 1914, and the joy of a second son with the birth of Manson Philip on October 3, 1915. Mary Jane was born on August 31, 1917. In 1918 Philip moved his family to Paris, Texas, where they were among the fortunate few families that did not lose a member during the flu epidemic of that year.

In the summer of 1918, Philip's father, Lawson P. Bost, purchased land in the Fairview community and made plans to expand his farming and horse production. These plans did not materalize due to his unexpected death. His obituary stated in part that Mr. Bost had gone to Rhome in Wise County on December 31, 1918, to transact some business and was expected to return to Rockwall, Texas, on the 2nd of January. Repeated phone calls to Rhome by his wife alarmed the townspeople. They went to the house, where he was found dead in his bed. At the autopsy in Rhome, the two physicians pronounced the cause of death as heart failure.

A letter addressed to Mrs. L. P. Bost, Rockwall, Texas, on a letter head of the W. W. Morris General Merchandise, dated 1/9/19 reads as follows:

Dear Mrs. Bost,

> Please permit me to extend to you my most sincere and deepest sympathies in this the saddest time of your life. Sympathies and tears however cannot drive away this great loss you have sustained. Only the love and promises of Our Maker can alleviate this great bereavement.
>
> I can truthfully state in my short acquaintance with Mr. Bost I never have found a man that was more congenial, truthful, and

reliable. Our natures seemed to blend, and I was fairly in love with him. May God's richest blessings be yours.

I am most sincerely,
(signed) W. W. Morris

Philip and Jessie Bost arrived in Rhome on a cold and rainy day in February, 1920. Their household furnishings were loaded into two wagons directly from the train, while Jessie and the four children warmed themselves in the railway station. As they headed north on the gravel road, an extra team had been hitched to each wagon. Upon reaching Illinois Lane, where they were to travel east, the mud became a real challenge. It was necessary at times to hitch all the teams to one wagon in order to cross three low lying stretches of the road. When they finally reached the Fairview Church and School, where they were to turn north, the road narrowed and it seemed that each time the wagons had to make a slight turn, they would surely slide into the ditch. A trip that would ordinarily have been made in an hour took five. Their nearest neighbor was John and Mary Petras, with whom they became friends for life.

By the fall of 1921, it was apparent that Philip was not a farmer and did not share or choose to develop his father's interest in farming and stock animals. He moved his family to the town of Rhome and opened a barbarshop. The next six years would always be recalled as the time "we lived at the Bobo place." During these years Frances Myrta was born on January 22, 1923, and Harold R. followed on January 15, 1926.

On the night of July 4, 1924, a fire destroyed several business establishments on the south side of "Main Street." Among those destroyed were Philip's barbershop, Sam Leonard's butchershop, and Jonas Ward's Feed and Seed Store. The barbershop and feed store were relocated on the highway just north of Fate Renshaw's residence. In 1925 Philip Bost and Ray Reynolds joined in building the first solid concrete walled building just north of Ed Smitherman's residence. This building would house the Bost barbershop and the White House Cafe operated by Roy Reynolds. In these larger quarters hot bath facilities with soap and towel furnished were offered for $1.00 per month. One could order a tailor-measured suit and get it cleaned and pressed on the premises. Edward Bost alternately served as shine boy, pressman, and bath cleaner.

In early 1927 Philip and Jessie made plans to build their home. A corner lot on the west of Main Street was purchased and excavation was begun for the foundation and basement. At the same time the barn was started on the back of a lot. What was planned and began as a

WHITE HOUSE CAFE

barn was to become a "temporary" home for the Bost family in 1928. The excavation in the front yard was to remain a viable dream for Philip and one tolerated by Jessie until 1952. They agreed that it was time that the front yard needed to be leveled.

In 1929 a persistent "lumbago" that physicians related to barbering was all the reason Philip needed to try his hand in the building business. This would be the trade he would follow for the remainder of his life. Jessie turned her talents to sewing. She proved equally adept at sewing up simple cotton frocks and creating a Vogue Fashion by cutting her own pattern from a picture. In later years she turned her talents to furniture upholstry.

In 1939 the decision was made to re-open the White House Cafe. Travel was increasing and the Texas Centennial to be celebrated the next year offered hope of a profitable operation. The family moved into living quarters in the rear of the Cafe; Jessie's home-cooked meals were offered as 25¢ plate lunches, hamburgers for 10¢, and all the coffee one could drink for 5¢. Jane and Frances served, Harold washed dishes when he could be found. By 1938 when the highway was re-routed one block west, the "home place" had been renovated, the restaurant closed, and the Bost family moved back home.

In 1958 Philip and Jessie celebrated their 50th wedding anniversary. Their children and grandchildren and friends filled their home. They enjoyed and appreciated all.

Philip died at home Decemeber 8, 1963, leaving to others the completion of his last dream the house he had begun some months earlier. Jessie maintained the family home and managed the other property they had accumulated until her death on October 28, 1973. They are both buried in the Aurora Cemetery.

Philip and Jessie Bost were representative of a generation dedicated to self reliance, their children, Christian ethics, and formal education. They gave to each, all that they had to give.

For Dad

All things are new under the sun
The newness of every morning rises and gleams in the sun.
No remembrance of a thousand previous days can foretell
    the surprise that the new day will bring.
To gather and sift through the beloved rubbish of our memories
    is to retire from our ongoing involvement in the
    streaming world.
To prolong the nostalgic rehearsal of the dead will leave us
    as wilting grass; leave us floundering in the stagnant
    puddle of our backward dreams.
He would not have it so, he who sharpened his interest on new
    things. He who loved to go and see.
Yesterday, with his last breath, that newness was his, that
    surprise was his to enjoy in company more divine
    than any he left behind.
Then shall we mourn? Part of him lives on; his seed lives
on in his children and his grandchildren.
Shall we tend that seed with tears and morbid backward glances?
The measure of a man is in what he dreams not in what he
    finally accomplishes.
Our greatest tribute to him will be the living out of his
    intent to build, to serve, to seek the truth.
To love one another and our God who makes all newness possible.
Flesh is a stubborn retainer long after the joys are gone,
    and thought has forsaken in dwelling place,
    and pain has made the body its home.
Who would wish the journey prolonged?
In MY house, said the Lord, are many rooms.
Can we not be joyful that an invitation has been issued?
Who would hold the door against the final healing
    of one we love?
Friends have gone before and friends will follow after

Each having lived in his weakness and strength,
In his homeliness or beauty,
Each loved for what he was.
Let us bind ourselves in homage to them all
And gratefully bow to our Lord and creator
Who makes all things new under the sun.

FRANCES BOST BARNEY

For Phillip Bost, Dec. 9, 1963

BRAMMER — BRAMMER

Samuel Jefferson Brammer was born October 16, 1861, in Virginia. He married Elzora Brammer in Virginia, in approximately 1882. She was born May 26, 1866, in Virginia.

None of their ten children were born in Virginia before the family moved to Texas. These children were as follows: William Clabe Brammer, who did not marry; Calvin J. Brammer; Euna V. Brammer; Chester Jackson Brammer, who married Dessie Duke; Mark Hannah Brammer; Dollie S. Brammer, who married O. Z. Thorell; Samuel Richard Brammer; Dewey Donald Brammer, who married Lois Roberts; and Katie Mae Brammer. The last child was Bessie Bell Brammer, who was born in Texas in 1908.

Samuel Jefferson Brammer died March 22, 1916, in Rhome, Texas, and is buried in the Aurora Cemetery, Aurora, Texas. His widow, Elzora Brammer, died May 14, 1929, in Rhome, and she is also buried in the Aurora Cemetery.

One of the sons, Dewey Brammer, recalls the move to Texas. Two of the younger children had died while the family was still in Virginia: Calvin, six years old, who was accidentally shot while hunting with his brother Clabe; and Euna, who died from membrane croup when she was nine years old.

"This family lived in Woolwine, Virginia, a small town with only a post office. The Brammer family caught the train in Roanoke, Virginia, bringing all their belongings in trunks. The train was a passenger train that went by the way of the northern route through Cincinnati, Ohio, then down to Texas. The trip took three days and nights. The best I can remember, our river crossing was by ferry—some narrow place in the Mississippi.

Chester contracted typhoid fever during the trip from a blanket brought with us from Virginia. Each and every one had the fever very bad. My father went eight days and nights without pulling off his shoes."

WALTER CURTIS BRAMMER, working as a Pinkerton guard at the Texas Electric plant at Eagle Mountain Lake.

The Brammers had purchased the Wess Greer place about two miles southwest of Rhome. Dr. Burch was the doctor who attended the family during the bouts with typhoid fever.

BRAMMER — NESMITH

Walter Curtis Brammer, son of James Matthew Brammer and Mary Brammer, came to Texas as a young child from Stewart Township, Virginia, where he was born. As a young man around fifteen years of age, he left home to go on the rodeo circuit with the "Wild West Show." He received the nickname of "Humpy" by the other cowboys because of the way he rode the wild broncs. He came back to Rhome, and while he was riding in a rodeo, a young girl, Alice Gertrude NeSmith saw him and told her sister, "I'll marry that boy someday." Two years later she did just that. Alice had come to Texas on the train from Leighton, Alabama, where she was born. Her parents were John Leigh NeSmith and Georgia Ann Goodwin NeSmith.

Walter and Alice were married for thirty years. Alice died at the age of forty-nine, and Walter died at the age of sixty-seven. They were the parents of five children: Ruth Harlen Brammer, Alvin Kenneth Brammer, Curtis Harold Brammer, Gloria Ann Brammer, and Billy Ray Brammer.

Walter was a man of many trades, but his first love was ranching. He wore western clothes and cowboy boots all his life. Some of the jobs Walter had were as follows: ranching, truck driving, hotel manager, school bus driver, carpenter, cotton gin operator, drug store manager, restaurant owner. He was a Pinkerton guard for Texas Electric Service Company and also he worked for the Lone Star Gas Company.

BROWN — DAVIS — HILL

Joseph Hamilton Brown was born August 3, 1811 in Tennessee. His parents were William Brown and Lydia Holman Brown, both of whom were born in Tennessee of Scotch-Irish ancestors.

Joseph Hamilton Brown married Mary Ann Davis on January 10, 1838. Seven children were born to this union: William H. Brown, Hanna H. Brown, Thomas Elijah Brown, Albert Brown, Tommie Brown, Rob Brown, and Lydia Brown.

Mary Ann Davis Brown died in 1874 in Aurora, Texas. She is buried in the Deep Creek Cemetery.

Joseph Hamilton Brown was a Civil War veteran. He served as a gun smith. His second marriage was to Mary Ann Elizabeth Hill, who was born in Mississippi. Mary Ann Elizabeth Brown had come from Mississippi to Nacogdoches, Texas, thence to Aurora, Texas. Her father was a school teacher, who brought some slaves with his family to Texas.

Ten children were born to this second union: George W. Brown; Henry C. Brown; Joseph H. Brown, Jr., who married Ruth Pope Brown; Annie Bell Brown; Mattie Lillie Brown; Nancy Brown, who married Lon Randolph; Sarah Brown, Nancy's twin sister; Grover C. Brown; Martin Brown; and Rachel Brown, who married Charley Payne.

The family lived in Aurora until they purchased the old Brown home place. Besides having been a gunsmith, Joseph Hamilton Brown sold pictures, rub boards, black boards, and washing machines. He also raised goats and rented out some of the over 700 acres which he owned.

When Joseph Hamilton Brown and Mary Ann Elizabeth Brown

JOSEPH HAMILTON BROWN, and his wife, Mary Ann Elizabeth Hill Brown.

decided to move from Aurora, they built a ten-room house on the old home place. Joseph Hamilton, Jr., was the first child born in the new two-story house. The Brown farm between Boyd and Newark has been in the Brown name for over 100 years.

Joseph Hamilton Brown built the ten-room house with lumber hauled by mules from Dallas, Texas. Also, their furniture came from Dallas by covered wagon. Mouverneen Brown Gaston has a wardrobe and a table of this furniture. "My Grandma has told me stories of their hardships. They carried water from the creek, while carefully looking around to see whether the Indians were near."

Mary Ann Elizabeth Brown died on January 9, 1940. Joseph Hamilton Brown died on October 13, 1909. They are both buried at Deep Creek Cemetery in Wise County, Texas.

BROWN — POPE

Joseph Hamilton Brown, Jr., was born March 18, 1882, in Aurora, Texas, in the new ten-room house which his parents, Joseph Hamilton Brown, Sr., and Mary Ann Elizabeth Hill Brown, had built between Boyd and Newark.

Joe Brown and Ruth Pope were married in Rhome, sitting in their buggy in front of the Hambright Hotel, on September 7, 1907. Joe Brown was a barber in Rhome when he married Ruth Pope. He continued barbering until his untimely death at the hands of the Hunsucker gang on January 27, 1933. Mr. Brown was Constable in Rhome for about twenty years. Mr. Brown is buried at Deep Creek, a few miles north of Aurora.

Two children were born to this union: Lady Mouverneen Brown, who married Silas H. Gaston; and Carl Oswald Brown, who married Gladys Baker. Joe Brown was very proud of these two children. Mouverneen lives in Justin, while Carl lives on the farm which he inherited from Joe Brown's father and mother.

Ruth Pope Brown continued to live in Rhome the rest of her life except for the last five years which she spent with her daughter, Mourverneen Gaston. She died on September 11, 1975, and is buried at Deep Creek Cemetery beside her husband. They were both members of the Church of Christ in Rhome, Texas.

BROWN — THURMOND

Martha Elizabeth Thurmond, daughter of J. F. and Amanda Thurmond, was born December 18, 1889, in Rhome, Texas. She married Robert J. Brown, who was born May 18, 1876. They lived in Henrietta, Clay County, Texas, where their children were born. These were as follows: Don Brown, Rachel Brown Shaffer, and Robert J. Brown, Jr.

Martha Elizabeth Thurmond died February 12, 1961, in Rhome, Texas. Robert J. Brown died May 15, 1972, in Henrietta, Texas. Both are buried in the Bellevue Cemetery in Bellevue, Texas.

BROWN — TULLEY

Thomas Elijah Brown was born August 3, 1884, in Aurora, Texas. His parents were Joseph Hamilton Brown and Mary Ann Davis Brown.

Thomas Elijah Brown married Amanda S. Tulley, whose parents were citizens of the first Prairie Point, Texas, Marshall D. Tulley and

JOSEPH HAMILTON BROWN, JR., and his wife, Ruth Pope Brown, being married in their buggy before the Hambright Hotel.

JOSEPH HAMILTON BROWN, JR., Deputy Sheriff of Rhome, Texas.

Mary Matilda Tulley. Amanda S. Tulley was born on September 13, 1862. Marshall D. Tulley was listed in the 1860 U.S. Census records as a teamster in Prairie Point.

Three children were born to this union: James Albert Brown, who married Josephine Harris; Thomas Gilbert, who married Ella Harris; and Robert Lee Brown, who married Maude Bowman.

Amanda S. Tulley Brown died in 1888 and is buried in East Texas.

BURCH — DRUMMOND

Dr. James Kerr Burch was a Presbyterian clergyman, a Doctor of Divinity. He was born in Kentucky. His wife was Maria Drummond Burch, who had been born in Alloa, Scotland. She and her sister, Jacobina Drummond, had come to America. The two sisters were very devoted to each other. Jacobina Drummond first married a man named Thompson; then later she was married to Dickerson B. Wayland, a direct descendent of the first Justice of the Supreme Court of the United States. The family lived in Yazoo City, Mississippi. Dr. James Kerr Burch had asked Jacobina for the hand of her sister in marriage in June, 1839.

Dr. James Kerr Burch died seven months after the marriage, two months before the birth of their son, James Drummond Burch. After the death of Dr. Burch, Maria married a man named Miller. This man had grown sons. The marriage was an unhappy one. Maria left and came to Aurora to live with her son, Dr. James D. Burch, until her death in 1895. She is buried by her son, Dr. Burch.

After the death of Jacobina Drummond Wayland, Uncle Wayland went to live with his sister-in-law, Maria Burch, in Aurora, where he resided until his death.

Jacobina Drummond Wayland had been a very thrifty person. She was the one who preserved all the family heirlooms. Also, she was the one who saw to it that her nephew, Dr. James Drummond Burch, received the very best education possible.

BURCH — McAFEE

James Drummond Burch was born February 12, 1840, in Georgetown, Kentucky. His parents were Dr. James Kerr Burch and Maria Drummond Burch. James Drummond Burch married Florence McAfee on October 6, 1874, in Salvisa, Kentucky. Florence McAfee Burch was called by the endearing name of "Grand Dear" by her grandchildren. She was born on December 13, 1854, in Kentucky.

FLORA MC AFEE BURCH   DR. JAMES DRUMMOND Burch

    Dr. James Drummond Burch was graduated from Centre College, in Danville, Kentucky, in 1860; he attended medical lectures at Jefferson Medical College, Philadelphia, 1862-63; and at the Kentucky School of Medicine, 1863-64, and was graduated M.D. in 1864 with highest honors. Later he was a dean at the Louisville Medical College in Kentucky. He was a Latin and Greek scholar and contributed many papers to medical journals.

    Florence McAfee Burch's grandfather was a Mr. James McAfee who had come with his six brothers into Kentucky, along with Daniel Boone to Boonesboro Fort. After the town of Harrodsburg, Kentucky, was established, the McAfee family built their homes at a location which later became known as McAfee, Kentucky. Florence's father was John McAfee, who married a widow by the name of Mrs. Brawless. John McAfee had owned a race track in Kentucky and bred some of the finest horses in the state of Kentucky.

    Florence "Grand Dear" Burch had two brothers, William

Hamilton McAfee and Caldwell McAfee. Caldwell McAfee's wife was the person who preserved much of the McAfee family history. John McAfee had placed a clause in his will that read that his daughter, Florence McAfee, was not to marry any men of whom Caldwell McAfee did not approve. Florence's marriage came before the death of John McAfee; so it was that Dr. James Drummond Burch wrote to John McAfee to ask the hand in marriage of Florence McAfee.

Dr. James Drummond Burch and Florence McAfee Burch had three children: Charles Drummond Burch, born in Kentucky on November 10, 1878; McAfee Wayland Burch, born August 14, 1883, in Kentucky; and James Drummond Burch II, born February 12, 1892, in Texas. The family lost two young daughters, who were born and died in Yazoo City, Mississippi: Anna Mary Burch, who was born January 23, 1876 and died December 1, 1876; and Florence Stuart Burch, who was born November 21, 1881, and died September 1, 1882. During the siege of yellow fever, Dr. Burch had moved his family back to Kentucky, where the two elder boys were born.

After Dr. Burch left Kentucky for the second time, he came to Texas, where he was offered a medical partnership with a Dr. Beall, a good friend. His other doctor friend, Dr. Capps, Dr. Irons, and Dr. Saunders, urged him to specialize, but he preferred to go to a frontier town.

Dr. Burch was located in Aurora by 1880, where he found some other fine aristocratic Kentuckians, such as Dr. Roark, Dr. Bobo, Dr. Barr, the Haydens, and numerous others. Dr. Burch lived in Aurora three years before he sent for his wife and children. Florence Burch left Kentucky about the time that McAfee Wayland Burch was born. She came by train to Fort Worth. "Grand Dear" was unhappy about leaving her family and friends in Kentucky. She yearned for the "blue grass" of Kentucky.

Dr. Burch had a great interest in farming. He had been known throughout Kentucky as a raiser of blooded and fancier of the finest blooded sheep. In Aurora Dr. Burch urged vegetables and fruits for his patients. Dr. Burch practiced medicine and surgery, riding horseback to his patients. He was recognized by the medical societies in Texas, making addresses at Fort Worth, Dallas, and Houston.

On February 23, 1890, Charles Drummond Burch died of spinal meningitis. By 1894, after the railroads had come and moved to both sides of Aurora, virtually abandoning the old town, Dr. Burch sought a better place for his family to live. He chose LaPorte, Texas, where he had built a model home, designed after the "Twin Hearts" home that he had seen at the Chicago World's Fair. The home was placed on land near the Sylvan Beach Pavillion in La Porte. The home burned in

1900, and Dr. Burch decided to move back to Aurora, where he remained in practice until his death on June 25, 1905. He is buried in the Aurora Cemetery. Florence McAfee Burch died in June, 1933, and she is also buried in the Aurora Cemetery.

Several interesting stories are told by the family of Dr. Burch. One concerned the children, delivered by Dr. Burch, who had been named after him. He always remembered his namesakes with birthday gifts. Another story concerns the telephone line which Dr. Burch had installed from his office in Rhome to his home in Aurora. It was built of three-inch metal poles. The residents of Fairview also constructed a line along the fences to hook into Dr. Burch's line to Aurora. The line to Aurora was still in service when James Drummond Burch was a teen-ager. Drummond Burch leased the line to Mr. Charlie Hudnall, for which the Burches got free telephone service. Later the poles were taken up and used on the Drummond Burch's farm. Dr. Burch used a pair of horses with his buggy. When the mud in Illinois Lane became impassable, he unhitched "Old Bess" and rode her horseback to his patient. Because of his love for his horses, the two horses were used in Dr. Burch's funeral procession. Just behind the hearse were the two horses hitched to his wagon with his medicine kit on the empty seat of the buggy.

BURCH — SHAW

McAfee Wayland Burch was born on August 14, 1883, in Bardstown, Kentucky, the second son of Dr. James Drummond Burch and Florence McAfee Burch. He married Dora Belle Shaw, the daughter of Drury Pressley Shaw and his wife, Susan Joanna Weems Shaw, on June 5, 1904. Dora Belle Shaw was born on January 17, 1880, in Aurora, Texas.

"Mac," as McAfee Wayland Burch was known, graduated at Aurora, probably from the ninth grade. Then he attended Coles Military Academy in Dallas. From there he went to Texas A. and M. College. Professor Cornell of the department of agriculture told "Mac" that he should study law or some literary courses. McAfee Burch left Aurora after two and one-half years at A. and M. and went to Kentucky. There he engaged in business with his uncle, Caldwell McAfee, in a crossroads general store. He also served as railroad agent at Van Arsdale, Kentucky, for the Southern Railroad. He served as express agent and post master at Van Arsdale. While in Kentucky, he became interested in famous race horses.

McAfee Wayland Burch returned to Wise County, engaged in farming, and bought cattle and operated the Burch farm for one year.

BELLE SHAW BURCH   MC AFEE WAYLAND BURCH.

In addition, he carried the mail from the postoffice at Rhome, Texas. While carrying the mail, he studied for a degree in law. Belle Shaw Burch helped her husband in his studying for law to gain his admission to the Bar of Texas. Belle, in helping her husband in his studies, developed quite an unusual understanding herself and was very helpful to Mac in his career. At one point she worked as his legal secretary.

Belle Shaw Burch was very energetic in political and social circles and held auspicious offices in the women's clubs in Decatur. Both she and Mac traveled over the state in support of the Democratic Party and its candidates. McAfee Burch was County Attorney for Wise County in 1922-23. After that service, he carried on his private practice in law.

Belle Shaw Burch died on January 18, 1932. She is buried in the Oaklawn Cemetery in Decatur, Texas.

After the death of his first wife, McAfee Burch became a right-of-way legal attorney for the State of Texas. It was then that he married a second time, a union which was unhappy and the couple divorced. Mac returned to Decatur where he lived until his death on May 25, 1955.

McAfee Wayland Burch and Belle Shaw Burch had two daughters: Jacobina Stuart Burch, born March 6, 1906, and Katherine Drummond Burch, born March 20, 1907. Both girls attended college and later taught school. Jacobina Burch married Charles Harding of Decatur, Texas, and Katherine Burch married (1) Neilson Young and (2) Richard P. Berkley. Katherine D. Burch Berkley died August 4, 1971.

BURCH — THORELL

James Drummond Burch III was born June 25, 1916, in Fairview. His parents were James Drummond Burch II and Nell Mount Troxell Burch. He married Geneva Thorell on August 25, 1945, at the First Methodist Church in Rhome, Texas. Geneva Thorell was born to O. Z. Thorell and Dollie Brammer Thorell in Rhome, Texas.

Three children were born to this union: Sharon Nell Burch, born August 23, 1946; Sheila Ozelle Burch, born November 29, 1947; and James D. Burch IV, born January 29, 1960.

BURCH — TROXELL

James Drummond Burch II was born February 10, 1892, in Aurora, Texas. He was the son of Dr. James Drummond Burch and Florence McAfee Burch. He married Nell Mount Troxell, the daughter of Jacob Henry Troxell and Serena Mount Troxell, on July 25, 1915. Nell Mount Troxell was born March 3, 1894, in Fairview, Texas.

James Drummond Burch attended school in Aurora. When Drummond was thirteen, his father died. He went to Kentucky with his mother, Florence McAfee Burch, where he attended the Lindsey Wilson Training School near Cumberland, Kentucky. When he was eighteen, Drummond returned to Rhome. He was interested in farming and cattle; for awhile he worked for W. J. Logan, and later he worked for the Rhome Milling Company.

Nell Troxell Burch attended school in Fairview, Decatur Baptist College, and Denton Normal (N.T.S.U.), where she received a teaching certificate.

After Drummond and Nell were married, they lived for a time on Henry Troxell's farm in a house north of the Henry Troxell home place. James was born while the family lived here on June 25, 1916.

JAMES DRUMMOND BURCH   NELL MOUNT TROXELL

Then the family bought land in Aurora, near Blue Creek, across the creek from the Slimp Cemetery. Henry Troxell Burch was born in this home on March 25, 1919.

The boys started to the Aurora school, where their teachers were Sarah Wren and Gladys Troxell, a sister of Nell Burch. In 1925 the family moved to Amarillo for a venture at farming, but they stayed there only one year. Then they moved back to Rhome, Texas. Here they lived in town in a house which they rented from the Logans. Again Drummond Burch worked at the Rhome Milling Company. Sometime later the Burches moved again, this time to a farm north of Rhome. It was during this time that Henry Troxell Burch became seriously ill.

Nell and Drummond moved from the place north of Rhome to a house on Elizabeth Creek near the Day home. It was at this time that little Henry Troxell Burch died on June 25, 1929. He was a little boy who did not have much liking for school. After attending an impressive ceremony held for the graduation of the Rhome sixth graders into high school, he said, "Well, I'll tell you one thing, I'll never have to go through anything like that." He liked the school's burning very much because he thought that meant he wouldn't have to go back to school.

This Burch family moved again just before World War II, to a ranch near Haslet, which was leased by Joe Day. Drummond subleased a part of the ranch between Justin and Haslet. They lived there until the spring of 1943.

By 1945 they had moved into Saginaw and bought a place where they lived eighteen years. Then after Drummond died, Nell went to live with her son James Drummond. While in Saginaw, Drummond had worked for Consolidated Vultee, now General Dynamics; then later he worked for the Federal Aviation Authority after the war.

Drummond was a very dedicated and hard-working man. The family had many visitors; they were especially interested in the youth of the community. As early as the time they had lived in Aurora, Drummond made a wagon school bus and took the local youngsters, George Hines, Martin Simmons, Jimmy Neel, the Taft Slimp children, and others, to a county-wide stock judging contest at the Short ranch. The party went through blind gates and pastures. They took all morning getting to their destination. Terracing was another of the new progressive subjects for the 4-H Club boys to study. They got home late in the afternoon.

Durmmond's last job was as a maintenance man for the outer facilities for the F.A.A. He was held in high esteem, and he received the Sustained Superior Performance Award at the end of his career. He worked on the last day of his life.

Nell Burch was interested in poultry raising, encouraging people to keep up-to-date housing for the birds and to provide balanced rations. Nell raised poultry until about 1950 in Saginaw.

Nell was a very outstanding woman of great depth, intellectually, morally, and culturally. She was a leader in the church, community, and the school. She inspired those around her, especially the young people. After losing her son Henry, she fought off being engulfed in grief by being involved in areas outside the home. She became Worthy Matron in the Eastern Star; she was a charter member of the Thursday Study Club; and she was a member and worker in the Presbyterian Church.

James Drummond Burch and Nell Mount Troxell had two children: James Drummond Burch, who married Geneva Thorell; and Henry Troxell Burch, who died in childhood at the age of ten.

James Drummond Burch died on February 6, 1961. He is buried in the Aurora Cemetery. Nell Troxell Burch died on December 2, 1966. She is buried beside her husband.

CALDWELL — BROWN

Tol L. Caldwell was born in Kentucky about 1874. His parents were Dan C. Caldwell and Winnie Jane Gidens Caldwell. He married Nova B. Bowman Caldwell, a niece of Sallie Bowman, for whom the historical marker was erected at Deep Creek. Tol Lindsey Caldwell and Nova B. Bowman Caldwell had five children: Homer J. Caldwell, who married Burnie Lee Mason; Warren G. Caldwell; Joe Ferguson Caldwell, who married Elfrieda Muller; Foy Sue Caldwell, who married Cecil C. Patton; and B. Joyce Caldwell, who married B. J. Walker.

Tol Lindsey Caldwell died on September 27, 1937.

CALDWELL — GIDENS

Dan C. Caldwell was born in Butler County, Kentucky, about 1840. His parents were James Caldwell and Martha Cunningan Caldwell. Dan C. Caldwell married Winnie Jane Gidens, also born about 1846 in Kentucky. Her parents are not known to the writer.

The Caldwell family came to Texas in a covered wagon, which probably indicates that they were one of the earlier families to arrive in the area. Dan C. Caldwell owned and operated a large ranch in the area west of Fairview.

There were eight children born to the Caldwell family: Margaret Caldwell, who married Boyd Barker; Mae Caldwell, who married Jot Rogers; Bertha Caldwell, who married Bill Bryan; Sarah Caldwell, who married Henry Byrom; Laura Caldwell, who married James Wilson; Lizzie Love Caldwell, who married Tom Leonard; Rhoda Caldwell, who married Bob Dacus; and Tol Lindsey Caldwell, who married Nora B. Bowman.

Both Dan C. Caldwell and Winnie Jane Gidens Caldwell died in Rhome, Texas, and they are buried in the Deep Creek Cemetery near Aurora.

CALDWELL — MASON

Homer J. Caldwell, son of Nora B. Bowman Caldwell and Tol Lindsey Caldwell, was born in Rhome, Texas, on December 28, 1918. On February 4, 1939, he married Burnie Lee Mason, daughter of Nathan Burnie Mason and Katie Lee Neal Mason. Burnie Lee Mason was born in Wise County, on February 8, 1920. Her parents had come to Wise County in 1918 from East Texas. Her grandfather, Charley

Perry Mason, a descendant of Scottish emigrants, had settled between Boyd and Decatur. Her mother and father moved to Rhome from Aurora about 1932.

Homer J. Caldwell and Burnie Lee Caldwell have one daughter, Carolyn J. Williams, and two grandsons, Sean and Shane.

CARPENTER — FORD

Dr. David Alcorn Carpenter was born May 2, 1872, in Hustonville, Kentucky. His parents were Jacob C. Carpenter and Susan Hannah Riffe. Dr. Carpenter moved to Texas with his family at an early age, settling in Bosque County, Texas, where he was reared. Clifton was considered home for the family who resided in a smaller rural community.

A doctor gave young Carpenter a medical kit while he was still a boy and from that time he knew he would enter the medical profession. He was admitted to practice in 1896 and chose Hamilton, Texas, as his first location. He was married on August 2, 1896, to Mary Dorca Ford, also of Clifton. She was born on August 26, 1874, to James Tyson Ford and Gabrella Helm Ford.

After practicing medicine in Hamilton and later in Clifton, Dr. Carpenter moved to Rhome, Wise County, in 1900, to open his medical practice in this section of the state. He was the only doctor in Rhome at this time. Citizens of a neighboring community, Fairview, built a telephone line directly to Dr. Carpenter's office so that he could be called on in an emergency.

So prompt was Dr. Carpenter in answering calls, it was said that he would be at the bedside of the sick before the caller could cool a cup of coffee after paging the doctor.

Dr. Carpenter moved his practice to Denton in 1910 and continued there until 1927 when he moved back to Clifton, where he practiced until 1947. In this year he retired due to the illness of Mrs. Carpenter and moved back to Decatur. Mrs. Carpenter died on February 6, 1956. She is buried in Oaklawn Cemetery in Decatur, Texas.

Three children were born to this union: Gabie Sue Carpenter, who married George E. McCaleb; David Carl Carpenter, who married Bertie Mae Underwood; and Mary Velma Carpenter, who married Fred Arnold Davenport.

Dr. Carpenter kept several teams of fine horses in the early days of his practice—in the days when doctors went to the home of the sick. Also, he was one of the first people in Wise County to buy an automobile. It was said that he was the kind of doctor who would visit his patients several times a day or night until his condition was improved and would charge for only one call.

At the time of his death on July 26, 1968, Dr. Carpenter made his home with his daughter, Gabie Sue Carpenter. He is also buried in the Oaklawn Cemetery, Decatur, Texas.

CARPENTER — WEST — Mc CLAIN

Edmond Powell Carpenter, who was born March 14, 1866, in Lincoln County, Kentucky, came to Texas with his father's family in 1880. The family first lived in McLennon County, Texas, moving to Wise County sometime after 1895. Edmond Powell Carpenter's parents were Jacob Young Carpenter and Susan Hannah Riffe Carpenter.

Eda West became the first wife of Edmond Powell Carpenter, on the 15th of June, 1890, in Dallas, Texas. She was born June 15, 1860.

Five children were born to this union: Willie David (Bill) Carpenter, who married Frankie Henderson; Sol West Carpenter, who never married; Mary Elizabeth Carpenter, who married James M. McKinnon; Lillie B. Carpenter, who married Cletie Brammer; and Jesse Hall Carpenter, who married Mitron Crowder.

Eda West Carpenter died on April 6, 1910. She is buried in the Thurmond Fairview Cemetery.

Edmond Powell Carpenter married his second wife, Mima Elizabeth McClain, on September 14, 1911. Mima Elizabeth McClain was born November 8, 1884, near Boyd, Texas. Her parents were Alfred T. McClain and Mary Edna Caldwell McClain. This union was blessed with two children: Maggie Emma Carpenter, who married Wilbur F. Spain; and E. P. Carpenter, Jr., who married Jessie McCluney.

Edmond Powell Carpenter died March 20, 1956, in Dallas, Texas. He is buried in the Thurmond Fairview Cemetery. Mima Elizabeth McClain Carpenter died April 24, 1970, in Decatur, Texas. She is also buried in the Thurmond Fairview Cemetery.

CATE — CROWLEY — (DAVIS)

William Arthur Cate was born March 23, 1850, in Grapevine, Tarrant County, Texas. His parents were James Cate and Elvira Minter Cate. William A. Cate married Mary Frances Crowley on September 9, 1869, in Grapevine. Mary Frances Crowley, whose parents were Elijah Crowley and Louisa Jane Younger Crowley, was born January 8, 1952.

ALLIE CATE BUERBAUM, wife of Carl Buerbaum.

William A. Cate died sometime after 1879, when Mary Frances Cate moved to Rhome, Texas, where she became a milliner and later managed the Davis Hotel. William Arthur Cate is buried in Minter's Chapel Cemetery on the edge of the present Dallas-Fort Worth Airport. Minter's Chapel was named for William's grandfather, the Reverend Green Washington Minter, founder of the church.

Four children were born to this first union: Anna Louise Cate, who married William Wade Morris; James Cate, who married Audrey

_____; Allie Cate, who married Carl Buerbaum; and Robert Ernest Cate, who married Julia Reaves, a daughter of Noah Reaves, one of Rhome's old-time citizens.

After moving to Rhome, Mary Farnces Cate married John Davis, on November 7, 1887, who served as a deputy sheriff for the new town. There were no children born to this union. Mary Farnces Cate Davis died in Rhome, Texas, on November 2, 1930, at the hotel, which she was still managing at her death. Mary Frances Cate Davis is buried in the Aurora Cemetery.

CHAMBERS — PRUNTY

Joel R. Chambers was born December 24, 1887, in Denton, Texas. His parents were Jim W. Chambers and Laura Porter Chambers. He married Juanita Prunty on June 3, 1917. Juanita Prunty was born May 6, 1896, in Rhome. Her parents were Tom W. Prunty and D'Etta Fullerton Prunty.

Joel and Juanita Chambers moved to Rhome in 1924. Joel began work at the First National Bank on February 15, 1924, where he worked for the next thirty-five years. He retired from the bank on January 15, 1959. He had served in the Armed Forces during World War I.

Two children were born to this union: D'Etta Marie Chambers, who married Bryan A. Chrisman; and Joel Chambers, Jr., who married Carolyn Shugart. Joel Chambers, Jr., served in the Armed Forces during World War II.

Joel R. Chambers died on November 3, 1970, in Rhome, Texas. He is buried in Denton, Texas. His widow, Juanita Chambers, still lives in the family home in Rhome, Texas.

CRISWELL — RUSSELL

Lemuel David Criswell was born September 9, 1913, in Wichita Falls, Texas. His parents were Franklin Lafayette Criswell and Elma Sarah Hampton Criswell. Lemuel David Criswell married Nell Russell on May 25, 1939, in Lovington, Oklahoma.

Nell Russell was born March 31, 1914, in Rhome, Texas. Her parents were Dr. W. L. Russell and Clifford Henderson Russell.

Three children were born to the Criswells: David Russell Criswell, who married Bennie Sue Cook; Tommy Lemuel Criswell; and Claudia Criswell, who married William Jacob Hatchel.

Nell and L. D. Criswell taught in the Northwest Public School system until their retirement in 1976. Today they live at the family home in Rhome and spend much time in traveling to further their interest in gem stones.

DAY — DOUGLASS

John Fletcher Day, a native of Rhea County, Tennessee, came to Texas in the late 1850's, searching for good grass land for a string of horses he had brought with him, and for more space for his growing family. The first year or two he took up land near Comanche Peak in Johnson County. But his wife had relatives already settled at Lewisville, and knowing life would be more pleasant for her, he searched for acreage sufficient for his needs in the vicinity. He finally located his ranch in an area centered in Denton, Tarrant, and Wise Counties. He chose a location near a spring fed stream in Denton County on which to build their first log cabin home.

Since they were bringing along a stock of Tennessee bred horses and cattle as well as two small children and a third on the way, together with a family of black people (slaves) and several young neighbors who wanted to come to Texas, prospecting, the journey over well marked roads required at least six weeks. His young wife, the babies attended by a black nurse, rode in a carriage, hoping in that way to make the journey less arduous. The distance covered each day was of necessity short, because the cattle and horses stopped to graze along the way.

John F. Day, born February 10, 1829, in Rhea County, Tennessee, the son of John Day and Sarah Jane Henry, both natives of Tennessee and both descended from men who fought in the American Revolution.

John F. Day's wife was Mary Eliza Douglass, born March 4, 1835, in Monroe County, Tennessee. Her parents were Jonathan Douglass and Jane Crockett Young, both natives of Washington County, Tennessee.

The young couple were married February 14, 1854. Their children were as follows: John Carrick Day, born January 11, 1855; James Thomas Day, born October 29, 1857, both of Monroe County, Tennessee; Fannie Crockett Day, born October 28, 1860; Mary Hannah Day, born December 16, 1864; and Emma Tennessee Day, born December 31, 1874; the latter children were native Texans.

During the Civil War, Captain John Day with a detachment of troops, was assigned to gather and deliver food and supplies to the Confederate troops training and fighting in the Northern District of Texas and Louisiana.

Since he was away from home for long intervals, Captain Day's wife and children were left protected only by their black people. As the war wore on, the Indian raiders visited their pioneer cabin with increasing frequency, carrying off cattle, horses, and poultry. During the trip home, Captain Day moved his family to Lewisville so that they could be near relatives, leaving the black men to protect the cabin and the stock.

John Day and his wife, after the trying years of reconstruction, built a comfortable two-story country house, architecturally typical of the homes with which they were familiar in Tennessee. The children grew up, educated by a series of governesses and teachers who were always a part of the household while in their employment. Then the children were sent to academies and military schools in North Texas.

They lived to see a town and post office within three miles of their home, a part of the Fort Worth and Denver City railroad route, which served them to ship cattle and bring in supplies. Both of the sons, John C. and James T. became ranchers and horsemen, spending the remainder of their lives on the ranch which their father had established.

John C. Day married Mary Henderson of Grapevine; James T. Day married Margaret Tilley of Cherokee County; Fannie C. Day married Byron C. Rhome, Wise County; Mary H. Day married Dr. James Monroe Mullins, Fort Worth; Emma T. Day married Dr. Frank Marion Mullins, Fort Worth.

John Fletcher Day died March 6, 1892, and was buried in Oakwood Cemetery, Fort Worth; his wife, Mary E. Day, died July 4, 1900, and is buried in Oakwood Cemetery, Fort Worth; John C. Day died in 1909, and is buried beside his parents in Oakwood Cemetery; James T. Day died in 1932, and is buried in Aurora Cemetery; Fannie Day Rhome died in 1930, and is buried in Oakwood Cemetery, Fort Worth; Mary Day Mullins died in 1928, and is buried in Greenwood Cemetery, Fort Worth.

John C. Day, Fannie C. Day, and Emma T. Day each had only one child. Mary H. had no children; James T. had four children, but only two lived to maturity: Joseph Fletcher Day and Nellie Roscoe Day.

by Marion Day Mullins

DAY — TILLEY

James Thomas Day was born October 29, 1857, in Monroe County, Tennessee. His parents were John Fletcher Day and Mary Eliza Douglass Day. James T. Day came to Texas with his parents when he was one year old.

Although his might have been a more glamorous story if the family had moved west in an ox-drawn covered wagon, they came, as a matter of fact, in a fine surrey, drawn by high-stepping blueblood Tennessee horses.

James T. Day learned to rope calves and ride the range when other boys his age were mastering their ABC's and the multiplication tables. For more than a half century he moved in that aristocracy of cattlemen who doted on fine animals. The Days, father and uncle of James T. Day, had brought the first registered Shorthorns into Texas.

Denton County at that time had practically no schools, so that when the boys were toddling, they went into the saddle. It was not until he had passed the ordinary age for quitting school that James T. Day listened to his mother's urging and enrolled in old Tehucana University. He was one of the first to enroll there.

In 1881, James Thomas Day married Margaret Tilley, who was born in 1855 in Cherokee County, Texas. She was the daughter of Captain and Mrs. Brittain Tilley. When she was sixteen, she graduated from the first girls' school in East Texas, the Tyler Seminary.

Four children were born to the James T. Day family; however, only tow of these children lived to maturity: Joseph Fletcher Day, who married Blanche Hutchison, and Nellie Roscoe Day, who married Dr. Henry B. Trigg.

In 1885, James T. Day left his father's ranch to embark on a cattle venture of his own. Equipped with vast knowledge of cattle, quick powers of observation, and keen trading instincts, he amassed large herds and a large ranch. For more than forty years he lived on the ranch four miles east of Rhome.

James T. Day died at his home on the ranch in October, 1932. Margaret Tilley Day died at the ranch house near Rhome in April, 1936. A little over two years later the ranch house in which they had both died burned to the ground. The *Wise County Messenger* carried the story on October 6, 1938:

> Priceless heirlooms were destroyed recently in a fire at the Jim T. Day ranch house on the intersecting Tarrant, Wise, and Denton County lines near here.
>
> The ranch house was built 50 years ago of ship timbers hauled by ox teams from east Texas. It was owned by Jim T. Day, and the family had collected many valuable old guns and heirlooms which were lost in the fire.

MR. AND MRS. Loyd Douglas and daughter, Jackie.

DOUGLAS — MATHESON

Loyd Robert Douglas was born on September 12, 1891, in Rhome, Texas. His parents were James C. Douglas and Betty Smith Douglas. On June 14, 1922, he married Ora Mae Matheson. Ora Mae Matheson was born on August 11, 1901, in Cottondale, Texas.

One child was born to this union: Jackie Louise Douglas, who is married to Paul Barker (Pat) Logan.

Loyd Robert Douglas was cashier of the First National Bank of Rhome for many years. He was a member of the Masonic Lodge of Rhome.

Loyd Robert Douglas died on March 30, 1970, in Rhome, Texas. He is buried in the Aurora Cemetery. His widow, Ora Matheson Douglas, still lives in the family home in Rhome.

DOUGLAS — SMITH

James C. Douglas was born in Love, Mississippi, on February 14, 1852. He married Betty Smith Robertson, a widow who had first married Samuel A. Robertson. Betty Smith was born May 21, 1869, in Aurora, Texas. Her parents were James and Elizabeth Smith.

Betty Smith Robertson had one child by her first marriage: Odie Robertson, who married Shaw Ford. James C. Douglas and Betty Smith Robertson Douglas had six children by their marriage: Erwin L. Douglas, who married Ella Oates; Loyd Robert Douglas, who married Ora Matheson; Allie L. Douglas, who married Bert DeArmand; Gladys A. Douglas, who married Opal Sparks; Edna Grace Douglas, who died as a child; and Beryl A. Douglas, who married Mamie Douglas.

James C. Douglas died on March 10, 1914, in Rhome, Texas. He is buried in the Aurora Cemetery. Betty Smith Douglas died on February 4, 1940, in Forth Worth, Texas. She is also buried in the Aurora Cemetery.

FINLAYSON — DAY

W. J. Finlayson, one of Rhome's early citizens, was born on April 24, 1843, in Alabama. His father was John Finlayson.

William J. Finlayson married Margaret Day, whose parents were Elbert Day and Zerena Hutchison Day. Margaret Day Finlayson was born may 1, 1861, in Denton County. Four children were born to this family: Alberta (Bertie) Finlayson, who married J. Pugh Morris on June 23, 1907; Lee R. Finlayson, who was not married; Lanie B. Finlayson, who married Ada Terrell in May, 1908; and Ones T. Finlayson, who married Ruth Scott on September 1, 1917.

William J. Finlayson died in Rhome on May 18, 1924, and is buried in the Aurora Cemetery. His widow, Margaret Day Finlayson, died January 14, 1931, in Decatur, Texas. She is also buried in the Aurora Cemetery.

FINLAYSON — SCOTT

Ones Tomas Finlayson, son of W. J. Finlayson and Margaret Day Finlayson, was born on January 10, 1898, in Rhome, Texas. Ruth Scott was born on March 13, 1898, in Aurora, Texas. Her parents were John M. Scott and Mary Ann Van Meter Scott.

Today Ruth and Ones Finlayson live on their home place east of

THE FARM HOME of Ones and Ruth Scott Finlayson.

Rhome. Two children were born to this union: John Will Finlayson, who married Isla Finlayson on April 9, 1938; and Dorothy Finlayson, who married John Estill.

FORD — DIGBY

Mannon M. Ford was born October 10, 1878, in Alabama. His parents were Lewis Ford and Alice Neighbors Ford. He was married to Ruberta Digby Ford, whose parents were Zimmariah Digby and Jim Cora Horn Digby. She was born in Mississippi on October 21, 1883. She came to Aurora, Texas, with her mother and little sister when she was a very small child. Her father had died before that time. They lived in Aurora vicinity until she was seventeen years of age.

In 1900 she married Mannon M. Ford. They moved to a farm about four miles west of Rhome. There they lived as farmers until Mr. Ford died in April of 1941. He is buried in the Dido Cemetery.

After Mr. Ford's death, she moved to Rhome where she lived until her death on November 16, 1961. She is also buried in the Dido Cemetery. Ruberta Digby Ford was a charter member of the Assembly of God Church in Rhome, Texas.

Fourteen children were born to this union: Carlton Ford, who died in infancy; Little Baby Ford, who died in infancy; Alton W. Ford, who married Mary Lou Childs; Ima I. Ford, who married Prentice L. Harvey; Forest Ford, who died in infancy; Earl J. Ford, who married Jessie Mae Tucker; Digby M. Ford, who married Allah V. Layfield; Victor L. Ford, who married Oleta Jolley; Cora A. Ford, who married O.K. Anderson; Arlene Ford, who died in infancy; Lynndine Ford, who married George Nunn; Belfa Ford, who married B.K. Montgomery; Mannon M. Ford, Jr., who married Elwanda Dotson; and Little Baby Ford, who died in infancy.

FORD — HARPER

Jasper Morrell Ford was born on April 2, 1858. His parents were Benjamin Ford and Sarah Taylor Ford. He married Sarah Vashti Harper on November 23, 1876. She was the daughter of William F. Harper and Elizabeth Fogleman. She was born on March 26, 1861.

> Jasper Morrell Ford and Sonora Vashti Harper . . . eloped on horseback. She was 15; he was 18. Both had lived in Wise County, but she had to go to live with an aunt and uncle who lived in Kaufman County. I'm not sure where the elopement took place, but I know it is true because my grandfather told me about it. They were married 64 years.
> The children of Jasper and Sonora were born in Wise County, with the exception of Lydia Ann (Lena) born in Montague County, and Stella born in Oklahoma. The family must have gone to Oklahoma when the rush for land took place. The family lived in the Fairview community which was called the Illinois settlement in the early days. My grandfather was a farmer and was very interested in the activities of the community.
> In 1917 Lena Nelson and family moved to Floyd County. Within the next 5 or 6 years Jasper and Sonora and their children and families moved to Floyd County, except for May Smith who lived around Wellington and Shamrock and Homer who lived at McAdoo in Dickens County.
> At present only two children are living. Dennis is in a convalescent home in Amarillo and Homer lives in Lubbock, Texas.
> The parents of Jasper are buried in a field northeast of Rhome, on the north side of the old Illinois Lane. The graves have a fence around them. It is the remains of an old cemetery. William F. Harper and Mary Elizabeth Harper are buried in a field south of the Aurora Cemetery in Wise County.

Eight children were born to this marriage: Ida May Ford, who married Malcomb E. Smith; Sarah Elizabeth Ford, who married Phill M. Smitherman; Nettie J. Ford, who died as an infant; Lydia Ann

(Lena) Ford who married Hugh J. Nelson; Stella LeOna Ford, who married Ford Albert Smith; Dennis B. Ford, who married (1) Bertie Mullenax and (2) Bertha Wheelock; Homer Nugent Ford, who married (1) Velma Robertson and (2) Celia ____; and an infant daughter who died at birth.

Jasper Morrell Ford died on December 2, 1940, in Floydada, Floyd County, Texas, and is buried at the Lakeview Cemetery. Sonora Vashti Ford died on December 28, 1940, in Floydada, Floyd County, Texas. She is buried beside her husband.

—Opal J. Higgins

FUQUA — MAYS

Henry Temple Fuqua was born January 31, 1901, in Red Oak, Texas. His parents were John Henry Fuqua and Nora Belle Hamm Fuqua. He married Allene Mays, who parents were Walter Earnest Mays and Millie Ann Blankenship Mays. Allene was born June 12, 1904, in Somerville, Alabama.

Five children were born to this union: Leon Mays Fuqua, who married Billie Evelyn Moore; Henry Temple Fuqua, Jr., who married Barbara Ann Muck; Geneva Belle Fuqua, who married J. W. Bratton; Robert Vance Fuqua, who married Eva Jean Nelson; and Mary Helen Fuqua, who married DeWitt Gadberry.

Henry Temple Fuqua died on March 13, 1979 in Rhome, Texas. He is buried in Rose Lawn Memorial Cemetery at Denton, Texas. Allene Mays Fuqua live on the family place near Rhome, Texas.

GREER — McGLOTHLIN

Clarence Thomas Greer was born on August 27, 1906, in Decatur, Texas. His parents were Thomas Hollis Greer and Sally Reiger Greer. He married Alice Katherine McGlothlin on January 10, 1932, in Marietta, Oklahoma. Alice McGlothlin was the daughter of John Henry McGlothlin and Maude Sampson McGlothlin. She was born on July 20, 1912, in Jayton, Texas, before her parents moved to Rhome, Texas, about 1917. Her young girlhood was spent in Rhome, where she graduated from Rhome High School.

One child was born to this union: John Thomas Greer, who married Sue Riley on June 18, 1965. At present, Clarence and Alice Greer live in Midland, Texas.

GREGG — TROXELL

Marshall Gregg was born August 2, 1856. His family, the John Robert Greggs, had come to Texas at the same time that the John Troxells came. He married Mary Ellen Troxell on February 11, 1883, in Fairview. Mary Ellen Troxell, daughter of John and Mary Mosshart Troxell, was born in Ragersville, Ohio, on July 14, 1864.

Seven children were born to Marshall and Ellen Gregg: Wallace Maxwell Gregg, who married Ella Gentry; Earl Burch Gregg, who married Juliet Pope; Marion Ollie Gregg, who married John Lanham Gentry; John Ernest Gregg, who married Mary Elizabeth Williams; Robert Nolen Gregg, who married Kara Cates; Ruth Troxell Gregg, who married Murdock Embry Young; Esther Mae Gregg, who married Hale Belew.

The following story is taken from the Troxell family history as told by Ellen Gregg's eldest son, Wallace Maxwell Gregg:

> In the early 1880's a tall, jaunty, black-headed, black-bearded young Marshall Gregg came courting Mary Ellen, the eldest daughter of John and Mary Mosshart Troxell. They were married in February, 1883, and made a striking couple in their wedding garb as shown in a tin-type photograph. Marshall took his bride to a log house in the Cross Timbers village of Anneville on the banks of Walnut Creek.
>
> Here Marshall had already established the business of gathering surplus chickens, eggs, and butter from the farmers of a wide area—he hauled by wagon these products to Fort Worth and returned with supplies of calico, ginghams, sugar, coffee, spices, chewing and smoking tobacco and many other items which he sold or traded to his customers . . . This business served the needs of the day for it provided an outlet for surplus produce and gave the farmers a source of supply for their staples . . .
>
> Words are inadequate to express the priceless heritage bestowed on the children of Ellen and Marshall. They were faithful members of the Anneville Methodist Church . . . It was about 1899 that all six transferred to the Sand Hill Methodist Church, the first church of any denomination to be organized in Wise County back in 1854. Still later the three remaining children became members of the Methodist Church . . . .
>
> Marshall and Ellen soon realized that village life was no place to rear their brood . . . Then, too, Aurora and its saloons were too

near . . . So in 1891 they bought and moved to the 112 acres on which Nolen and Kara later lived . . .

The country schools were ungraded and fitted to cotton picking and spring field work. At best they attained the equivalent of grade six or seven, and those fortunate enough to go to college spent three years attaining freshman status. Wallace spent one year at D.B.C. and two years in Polytechnic (Fort Worth) before he was admitted as a freshman. Marshall and Ellen gave all their children one or more years at college.

Marshall Gregg died April 30, 1925, in the family home in Decatur, Texas. Mary Ellen Gregg took care of her mother, Mary Mosshart Troxell, who died at Ellen's home one month after the death of Marshall Gregg. Mary Ellen Gregg died on July 24, 1951, in Decatur, Texas.

HALL — NORMAN

Lee Hall was born on February 20, 1906, in Springtown, Texas, in Parker County. His parents were J. W. Hall and Mae Lavender Hall. Lee Hall married Ruth Norman of Rhome, Texas. Ruth Norman, daughter of James Norman and Letha Lisby Norman, was born on November 18, 1909, at Boyd, Texas.

Ruth and Lee Hall have lived in Rhome all of their married life. They had one daughter, Dorothy Hall, who was born November 21, 1933, in Rhome. Ruth Hall has worked for the Rhome Telephone Company for many years, and Lee Hall has been a farmer in the area.

HAMBRIGHT —

H. H. H. Hambright, whose parents were natives of Tennessee, was born in 1836 in Tennessee. He married Sarah L. "Sallie" Hambright, whose parents were also native of Tennessee. She was born in Tennessee in 1836. They came to the southwestern part of Wise County from Atwood, Georgia, in 1877. At that time the area was sparsely settled. It was wide open range land.

The Hambright family moved to the Rhome area before 1880, where they opened the Cottage Hotel. H. H. H. Hambright was very active in the development of Rhome. At times he served as a justice of the peace, in addition to his duties in managing his hotel business. He was a very prolific writer, contributing many articles and news reports to both the *Wise County Messenger* and the *Decatur News*. Judge

(R to L) HIRAM RICE HAMBRIGHT, Hiram Hingston Howe Hambright, Ben T. Hambright.

Hambright and his wife Sallie were very interested in the young people of the community, giving many parties and entertainments for their children and friends.

Six children were born to this union: Jennie W. Hambright; Edgar E. Hambright; Addie Hambright; Katherine Wells Hambright, who married William Arthur Helm; Benjamin T. Hambright; and Hiram Rice Hambright.

H. H. H. Hambright died in 1918. Sallie Hambright died in 1919. They are both buried in the Aurora Cemetery.

HARVEY — FORD

Prentice L. Harvey was born on May 29, 1908, in Newark, Texas. His parents were Thomas D. Harvey and Bulah Pegues Harvey. P. L. Harvey married Ima Ford who was born July 14, 1906. Her parents were Mannon M. Ford and Ruberta Digby Ford, who lived on Route 1, Rhome, Texas.

Four children were born to this union: Norma Jean Harvey, who married Ivan Matthews; Harold H. Harvey, who married Peggy Ewing;

Jerry D. Harvey, who married Greta G. Smith; and Ronnie G. Harvey, who married Sandra Smith.

The P. L. Harvey family, who have lived in Rhome since the early 1940's, have been very active in the civic affairs of Rhome, as well as in their church, the Church of Christ. P. L. Harvey and his sons own and manage the only grocery store left in Rhome today. They also own and manage a restaurant in the town.

HOLT — RAY — FRITZ

Nathan Green Holt was born on November 25, 1836, in Tennessee. He was the son of Moses Holt and Elizabeth Bradshaw Holt. The Holt family moved to Illinois when Nathan was two years of age. His mother died when he was four years old. His older brother kept him until he was thirteen years old. It was then that Nathan went to work for a family by the name of Tilford. He saved enough money to buy a place of his own. When he was twenty-two years old, he married a girl by the name of Sarah R. Ray in 1858.

Five children were born to this union: Emily E. Holt, Margret E. Holt, Thomas S. Holt, Nettie J. Holt, and Noah G. Holt.

In 1872 five or six families in Illinois decided they wanted to come to Texas. They started out following the Katy Railroad to Dennison, Texas, which was the end of the railroad at that time. So they started across the bald prairie land and came to Indian Creek in the Dido community in the northwest part of Tarrant County. The Holts and their first three children arrived here on May 6, 1872. They bought 160 acres of land. The last two children were born here. The Holts lived on this place six years when they bought land in the Aurora community. Here they built a new house and barn. They cleared the land with saw and axe. In 1892 Sarah R. Holt and two of their children died.

Adjoining the Aurora farm was the farm of a neighbor by the name of Richard Fritz. After Mr. Fritz died in 1895, Nathan G. Holt married the widow, Mrs. Laura Fritz. One child, Marvin Holt, was born to this union. The Holt family lived on the farm until Marvin was six years old. Then they moved to Rhome, Texas, in 1902, where they lived until their deaths.

Marvin Holt graduated from high school and then went into the garage business in 1914. In 1916, he married Jewel Looney. He remained in the garage business until 1936, when the building was burned in one of Rhome's destructive fires. He went into the farming and ranching business until he retired in 1960.

Marvin and Jewel Holt have been members of the United

NATHAN G. AND Laura Holt with their infant son, Marvin, in his christening gown.

Methodist Church of Rhome for many years and are very devoted to their work in the church. Nathan G. Holt, Marvin's father, was one of the earliest members of the church and was one of the committee selected to plan the building of the church house for the Rhome Methodist Church.

HUDNALL — APPLING

Charlie Hudnall married Bell Appling in Kentucky. They moved with their three sons, Guy, Thurman, and Rhea, from Lee Town, Kentucky, to Wise County, Texas in 1904.

The family first moved to the Deep Creek community and lived on the Tom Prunty place. Later they moved to the Aurora community and lived on the Nathan Holt place.

In 1912 the family moved to Rhome, where Mr. Hudnall bought the Rhome Telephone Company from Tom B. Stephens. Mr. Hudnall operated the telephone company for many years.

HUDNALL — RUSSELL

Thurman Hudnall, the son of Charlie B. Hudnall and Bell Appling Hudnall, was born in Lee Town, Kentucky. He married Cassie Fry Russell, the daughter of J. Wood Russell and Flora Atwood Russell.

Thurman Hudnall served in World War I, entering the service on July 5, 1917. He served overseas from June 26, 1918 to December 9, 1918. After returning to Rhome from his service in the United States Army, he went to work for W. W. Morris Lumber Company, which he later owned.

One daughter was born to this union: Sandra Hudnall, who married Frank Jones.

HUDSON — BENNETT

James Jasper Hudson was born on November 14, 1824, in Madison County, Kentucky. His father was born in Virginia and his mother was born in Kentucky. James Jasper Hudson married Nancy A. Bennett in 1855. Nancy A. Bennett was born in 1839, in Kentucky. Her father, Hamilton Bennett, had brought his family to Texas with the Peters' Colony that settled near Dallas.

Seven children were born to this union: Johnnie Hudson and Willie Hudson, both of whom died in childhood and were buried at Indian Creek Cemetery; Mary Frances (Molly) Hudson, who married George Washington Whittington; Laura Josephine Hudson, who died in her early twenties; Robert Alexander Hudson, who married Ora Earp; Dora Ella Hudson, who married W. J. Logan; and Leslie Luther Hudson, who married Willie Heath.

Uncle Jimmy Hudson never claimed to be the first settler in Wise County, but he used to tell how he and his brother Will built their log cabin and then rode up in the north part of the section that later became Wise County and found Sam Woody just cutting the logs for his cabin, but Mr. Woody later claimed to be the first settler in Wise County.

Uncle Jimmy, as most of the folks who knew him called him, lived in Kentucky until he was about twenty-five years old. The land was poor around the Hudson's home, and Jimmy wasn't quite satisfied. In 1849 the news of gold in California proved too great a temptation and he started west. He traveled across the continent, sometimes walking and sometimes riding. He used to tell how thirsty they would get crossing the desert and when his party would find a stream of water, they would just wade out into it and start drinking.

Uncle Jimmy came back from California by boat by the way of Panama. He returned to his home in Kentucky with his $4000 that he had made in California. That much money made a man rich in those days. His father showed him around the country, trying to help him find a place to buy and settle down. But Uncle Jimmy had seen too much of the country and he knew that he would never be satisfied at home.

In 1853, he came to Shreveport by boat, accompanied by his brother, Will. At Shreveport they bought an old horse and saddle and started out across Texas. The boys took turns riding the horse and walking. The next year they settled west of Dallas about fifty miles in what was later named Wise County. Jim and Will built a log cabin with clap-board doors and a stick chimney. They went to East Texas to buy cattle.

Near the Hudson's home was a family named Bennett, who had a daughter named Nancy. Jimmy and Nancy were married in 1855. They lived in Uncle Jimmy's log cabin for eight years. Because their family was growing larger, they built a newer and more modern house.

During the Civil War, the men in Wise County were exempt from the Army for frontier protection. When the men in the county heard of Indians near by, they banded together to run the Indians out of the country. Uncle Jimmy narrowly escaped being killed and scalped at a small spring. Jimmy's friend, Jacob Moffett crossed the spring a few minutes later where he was accosted by Indians, killed and scalped.

Uncle Jimmy was a very good horseman and usually had about 400 horses in his herd. He also ran approximately 1500 head of cattle, plus many hogs, too. Every winter he would kill about twenty-five hogs just for his family to eat. One day he had been helping his old friend Tony Day work some horses. Tony wanted to pay him, but Jimmy said he never took pay for helping a friend; so Tony gave him a fine registered Berkshire hog. Uncle Jimmy took the pig home and his family was almost as pleased with it as Jimmy was. They named the pig "Kate," and they fed her constantly. They even bathed her in suds from the wash water. After they had "Kate" for several weeks, Uncle Jimmy began making plans for a visit to Kentucky. He remarked one day, "I'm afraid you will let my pig starve while I'm gone." This was all the challenge his children needed. While he was gone, they fed Kate continuously. When he left, Kate weighed thirty pounds; when he returned thirty days later, the pig weighed ninety pounds.

Uncle Jimmy was a stern father, but he gave his children few spankings. Bob, one of his sons, said he only remembered getting three spankings from his father in his whole life. Uncle Jimmy didn't believe in telling his children not to do anything because he thought that just helped them to think up things to do.

They ate well at Uncle Jimmy's house and there was usually company there. It was not at all unusual for Nancy to go to the general store and buy a $300 bill of goods. About the only groceries they bought were barrels of syrup and sugar. They ate lots of meat, but few vegetables.

On the way to church in Rhome one Sunday, Jimmy and Nancy were overtaken by a neighbor who told them that their house was on fire. After their home was destroyed, they decided to move to town. They built a large frame house in Rhome.

Nancy A. Bennett Hudson died in 1911 in Rhome, Texas. She is buried in the ____ Cemetery. After her death, Uncle Jimmy went to live with his daughter, Mrs. W. J. Logan. She lived just one block south of her parents' home in Rhome. Uncle Jimmy lived there until his death on his 90th birthday in 1914. He is buried in the ____ Cemetery. The Hudsons were active members of the Church of Christ in Rhome until their deaths.

Uncle Jimmy Hudson was a generous, good-hearted, hardworking pioneer, truly typical of the spirit of the Southwest.

HUSE — SIMMONS

Richard Lee Huse was born in Eustace, Texas, on January 5, 1906. His parents were Issac Jefferson Huse and Frances Judson Norris Huse, both of whom are buried in Callisberg, Texas.

Richard Huse came to Rhome where he met and married Estelle Simmons, whose parents were Ezra and Addie Marshall Simmons. Her parents are both buried at Aurora Cemetery.

Two children were born to this union: Jackie Marcella Huse and Roy Allen Huse. Today Richard and Estelle Huse reside in Rhome in the home which was the birthplace of this writer.

LAYFIELD — TROXELL

Clifford Columbus Layfield was born August 9, 1873, near Columbus, Georgia. He came to Texas as a young man, settling in the vicinity of Rhome, where he met and married Minnie Dora Troxell on April 30, 1899, in the Troxell home at Fairview. Minnie Dora Troxell, daughter of John Troxell and Mary Mosshart Troxell, was born on January 31, 1878, in Rhome, Texas. Minnie Dora was the first of the Troxell children to be born in the Fairview Community near Rhome, Texas.

For a time after their marriage, they lived on the Troxell place, near the family home; then they moved to Marlow, Oklahoma, where they lived for about a year. They returned to Texas and settled near the Fairview Community. In 1917 the family purchased a place in the Oliver Creek Community, where they lived until the death of Clifford C. Layfield on March 10, 1946.

Minnie was considered perhaps the jolliest of the Troxell sisters; she was always hospitable, enjoyed preparing meals, and welcomed company as long as she was able to keep house. She especially enjoyed the times when the sisters got together for a day's visit and gab fest; on one occasion six of the sisters (all but Eliza) met at the Layfield home with Christine chauffering the group and Ruth acting chef—the girls were in their early twenties—and when all had arrived, Minnie announced that this was *their* day, and the girls were to take over. The sisters deposited themselves in comfortable chairs and such laughter and noise rang out that surely even the distant neighbors knew that something unusual was happening at the Layfields.

Upon the insistence of her children after "Click's" death, Minnie sold the farm and purchased a home in Decatur. She lived happily there until ill health forced her to move to Stephenville, Texas, to be near her daughter Ruth, where she lived in the Sunset Rest home until her death. She died on May 21, 1967, in Stephenville. Minnie Dora Troxell Layfield and Clifford Columbus Layfield are both buried in the Thurmond-Fairview Cemetery.

LAYFIELD — WRIGHT — WHITTEN

John Willie (Will) Layfield was born May 9, 1871, in Harris County, Georgia. He was the second son of a Civil War veteran, M. C. (Richard) Layfield, and Tarzey Blackmon Layfield. He came to Texas at the age of 18. He joined his older brother, Jefferson Davis (Jeff) Layfield, who had come to Allen, Collin County, Texas, two years earlier. In Collin County, Will lived with and worked for a Mr. Gilbert.

In 1893 the Gilbert family and Will Layfield, along with other families, went by wagon train to the Indian Territory (now southwest Oklahoma, near Hollis) and staked claims on lands being offered by the United States government for settlement. After two and one-half years of near starvation and other frontier hardships, Will saddled his horse and headed back to Texas, abandoning his claim. He slept under the stars with his saddle for a pillow, stopping at farm houses during the day, where he worked for food.

After five days, Will arrived in the Fairview community where his brother Jeff had settled after he had married and left Collin County. It was in this community in 1896 that Will became one of the charter members of the Fairview Baptist Church. He lived in the Fairview community until his death at the age of 87 in 1958, with the exception of two years when he moved to Montague County. He was the only charter member of the Fairview Baptist Church surviving until 1958.

After Will's return from the Indian Territory, he worked for his brother Jeff and for Mr. Eugene A. Wright, one of the early settlers of the community. It was Ella Nettie Wright who became Will Layfield's first wife. She was born on February 4, 1878, and died on January 8, 1903. She left one son, Otis Eugene Layfield, who now resides in New York City, with his wife Ella Seiler.

In late 1905 Will returned to Georgia briefly and married Jakie Ozella Whitten on December 27, 1905. Jakie Ozella Whitten's parents were Alfred (Bud) Whitten and Lydia I. Dunnigin Whittin. Five children were born to this union: Willie Florence Layfield, who did not marry; Sanford Morgan Layfield, who married Yolanda Tyler; Harold Walton Layfield, who did not marry; Norine Palmer Layfield, who did not marry; and John William (Jack) Layfield, who married Sibyl Novis Eaves. At this writing (1977) only two, Sanford Morgan and John William (Jack) are living. Both reside in the Fairview community and attend the Fairview Baptist Church. Jack has been a lifetime resident of the community, and Morgan returned to the farm where he was born upon his retirement from a career in the field of aviation. Both Morgan and Jack served with the Armed Forces during World War II.

Will Layfield had two brothers, C. C. (Click) Layfield, W. W. (Woods) Layfield, and one sister, Mrs. Lula Belle McKinney, who came to Texas after he arrived. C. C. (Click) Layfield married Minnie Troxell, and W. W. (Woods) Layfield married Myrtle Wright, a sister of Will's first wife. At one time they all lived in Rhome and Fairview communities. All are now deceased.

John Willie Layfield died May 12, 1958, in Fairview and is buried in the Thurmond Fairview Cemetery. Jakie Ozella Layfield died January 22, 1942, and she is also buried in the Thurmond-Fairview Cemetery.

LEONARD — RAGSDALE — TRINKLE (LEWIS)

Collin Campbell Leonard was born in old Tishomingo County, Mississippi on June 24, 1837. His parents moved to Marshall County, Tennessee, where he spent the early years. When Mr. Leonard was fifteen years of age, his parents again moved to Jackson County, Arkansas, where Collin Campbell Leonard was married to Mary A. Ragsdale.

In the spring of 1860, Mr. Leonard moved to Wise County, Texas, where he settled in the area of present-day Boyd, Texas. Mary A. Ragsdale died on July 7, 1861. Mr. Leonard entered the Confederate Army after this time, where he remained for three years and one month.

Upon his return to Wise County, Mr. Leonard was married to Mary J. Trinkle-Lewis of Wise County, on August 12, 1866. In 1868 he settled on the Leonard home place two miles northwest of Rhome, Texas. At various times during the next fifteen years, he served as Justice of the Peace, as tax assessor, and as a county commissioner, in Precinct 5, Wise County, Texas.

The parents of Mary Jane Trinkle were Peter Trinkle and Rebecca Golden Trinkle. Mary Jane Trinkle was born on November 4, 1844, in Cairo, Illinois.

Eleven children were born to this union: Alpha Wayne Leonard, who died when he was only five years old; William Thomas Leonard, who was married to Lizzie Caldwell; Samuel Lee Leonard, who was married to Lucy Lee Holden; Annie Laura Leonard, who married Harry Moore; Susie Rebecca Leonard, who married Homer Ivey Watkins; Allie Mae Leonard, who was married to Joe Gordon Robertson; Emma Alto Leonard, who was married to Asbury Nicholas Rives; Ophelia Kate Leonard, who was married to Robert Lee Smith; Ella Bam Leonard, who was married to Luther Thomas Green; Ora Ellen Leonard, who was married to Robert Leigh NeSmith; and Robert Edgar Leonard, who was married to Lola Gertrude Hardy.

"Squire" Leonard, as he was affectionally known by his friends and neighbors in Rhome, died in November 17, 1924, in Rhome, Texas. He is buried in the Deep Creek Cemetery. His wife, Mary Jane Leonard, followed him in death on March 28, 1929. She is also buried in the Deep Creek Cemetery.

LISBY — CAGLE

Walter Lisby was born on February 23, 1862, in Lawrence County, Alabama. His parents were William Lisby and Mary Jane Morrow Lisby. He married Martha Cagle Lisby of Lawrence County, Alabama, about 1880 in Moulton, Lawrence County, Alabama. Her parents were John Cagle and Elvina Stokes Cagle.

Five children were born of this marriage: I. S. Lisby, who married Jennie Barnes; Lula Lisby, who married R. A. Bayne; Beulah Lisby, who married Ned Richardson; Letha Lisby, who married James Norman; and Hazel Lisby, who married Floyd Byrom. The family moved to Rhome in 1903, where Walter Lisby was a farmer for the rest of his life.

Walter Lisby died February 23, 1934, in Rhome, Texas. Martha Cagle Lisby died October 26, 1950, in Rhome, Texas. They are both buried in the Aurora Cemetery.

LIVENGOOD — COFFMAN

John Thomas Livengood was born February 5, 1887, in Weatherford, Texas. His parents were James Madison Livengood and Mary Elizabeth Irwin Livengood. John Thomas married Leola Jean Coffman, daughter of Alexander Clingman Coffman and Vandalia Provence Coffman, on September 19, 1909, at Lucky Ridge, near Keeter, Texas. Leola Jean Coffman was born on May 7, 1894, in Cottondale, Texas.

John Thomas and Ola Coffman Livengood, with their family, moved from the Cottondale Community in January of 1929. They bought a three-room house from Claude Shaw and added three rooms to it. Mr. Livengood purchased an icehouse in Newark, Texas, which he moved to Rhome. The walls of this building were insulated with cottonseed hulls. This insulation made it warm in winter and cool in the summer. He then set up his shoe repair shop, which he conintued to operate until his death in 1943. With Mrs. Livengood's help, they did upholstering, furniture refinishing, harness and binder canvas repair work. Both Mr. and Mrs. Livengood were members of the Church of Christ at Rhome, Texas.

Four children were born to this marriage: James Zollie Livengood, who married Zela Cogburn; Juanite Thelma Livengood, who married George A. Young; Peggy Joyce Livengood, who married (1) William Wade McCurdy and (2) Joe S. Baker; and John Thomas Livengood, Jr., who married Mary Lou Slay.

SHOE REPAIR SHOP owned by John Livengood.

John Thomas Livengood died on June 22, 1943, in Rhome, Texas. He is buried at the Fairview Cemetery. His widow, Leola Jean Livengood now lives at the Golden Years Haven in Decatur, Texas.

LIVENGOOD — COGBURN

James Zollie Livengood, son of John Thomas Livengood and Leola Jean Coffman Livengood, was born May 12, 1915, in Wise County, Texas. He was married to Zela Cogburn, the daughter of George A. Cogburn and Maude L. Smith Cogburn, at Los Angeles, California, on October 4, 1941. Zela Cogburn was born June 30, 1916, in Cooke County, Texas.

Zollie Livengood attended school at Rhome, Texas, where he graduated with the Class of 1935. His occupation today is that of a plaster pattern maker at Grand Prairie, Texas.

Two children were born to this union: James Zollie, Jr., born November 3, 1942; and Charolotte Louise, born June 18, 1944.

LIVENGOOD — SLAY

John Thomas Livengood, Jr., was born in Cottondale, Texas, on December 21, 1926. He is the son of John Thomas Livengood and Leola Jean Coffman Livengood. He married Mary Lou Slay, daughter of Ruth Bennett Slay and Carl Weir Slay, on August 28, 1954, at

Rhome, Texas. Mary Lou Slay was born September 13, 1925, at Decatur, Texas.

Both Mary Lou and John Thomas Livengood attended public school at Rhome, Texas, where they graduated from high school. John Thomas Livengood graduated from Texas Christian University in Fort Worth, Texas, in June, 1955. He served in the United States Navy from 1944 to 1946. His occupation is aircraft engineering. Today the Livengoods live on their ranch near Rhome, Texas.

Two daughters were born to this marriage: Mary Ann Livengood, born August 5, 1956; and Molly Sue Livengood, born July 6, 1961.

LOGAN — BARKER

LOGAN — HUDSON

Broner Washington (Bud) Logan was born in 1865. He and his three brothers, Will, Lee, and Dallas, moved to the southwest part of Wise County in the late 1800's. Bud and Will started farming and ranching operations near Rhome. Will Logan married Dora Hudson, the daughter of a forty-niner, Jim Hudson, who had struck it rich and returned to buy the southwest corner of Wise County. Through the financing of Will's father-in-law, Jim Hudson, the two Logan brothers began to expand. They opened a general store in Rhome. They also began to buy and lease large tracts of land around Rhome with the financing of Jim Hudson. The Logan brothers were business men and made a good living from profits of the store and the farming operations. Bud and several other business men speculated in oil business in Wichita and Archer Counties. After the oil boom hit in that area, Bud owned several producing wells.

Bud Logan married Willie Pearl Barker in 1901. Willie Pearl Barker was born September 24, 1881. Her parents were Lynn Boyd Barker and Margaret Caldwell Barker.

The Bud Logan family continued to increase the size of its farms. At the time of Bud Logan's death in 1934, the farms had grown to around 2100 acres. In 1925, a tornado swept through the Rhome area, destroying the Logan homestead house on the Denton-Wise County line. The house was rebuilt later.

Bud and Pearl worked hard rearing their children, sending them through public school, and on to Abilene Christian College. Two girls made teachers and wives. The boys were in farming and ranching business. Jim and Pat Logan served in the United States Army. Soon after returning home, Jim passed away from wounds received in Normandy. Pat is the only member of the original family living at this time, 1978.

Bud was a very stern, domineering type man. He gave orders to several hired hands and sons. They worked from sun up to dark. Pearl also worked hard, moving to the farm in summer, where she cleaned chickens by the dozen to be cooked and served to the hired men and the family. She did her washing on the rub board. The big event of the year was the end of harvest. Pearl (Granny) would pack a big picnic lunch, including water-melons, and the family was off to Forest Park Zoo in Fort Worth for the day.

The family moved back to town in the fall so that the children could go to school. Pearl was a charitable woman; neighbor children were always at her house, even after they were grown. Hoboes also had her house marked for a soft touch.

Bud and Pearl were faithful members of the Rhome Church of Christ. Pearl kept preachers for meetings. Bud served as a board trustee for Abilene Christian College; his name appears on a plaque in front of the administration building.

Broner Washington (Bud) Logan died July 5, 1934. He is buried in Aurora Cemetery. Willie Pearl Barker Logan lived in the family home until her death in a Fort Worth hospital on April 13, 1956. She is also buried in the Aurora Cemetery.

LOGAN — RICHARDSON

William Boyd Logan, son of Bud and Pearl Logan, started to school in Rhome in 1910 and graduated from high school in 1921. After graduation, Boyd attended Abilene Christian College. He made the college football team without any previous high school experience. In 1925, Boyd, a senior at A.C.C. with only six weeks to go before graduation, was called home, never to return to college.

In 1926 Boyd was introduced to Lucille Richardson. They were married October 23, 1926. To this union four children were born: June LaRue Logan, who married Claud Edward Griffeth; Billy Boyd Logan, who married Jeanine (Jen) Furrow; Peggy Jean Logan, who married Floyd Thomas McCurdy; and Bobby Max Logan, who married (1) Shirley Ann Green and (2) Lorrene Zenkner.

This marriage was supposedly the perfect match in southwest Wise County. Both families were solid financially. Boyd was the only young man to own his own automobile. Boyd and Lucille moved into a newly constructed house, rebuilt on the old Logan homeplace.

Lucille was the only bride in this part of the county to start housekeeping with a new set of furniture. The Logan family, especially

Boyd, were hard-working people. The Boyd Logan family survived the years of the great depression with the help of his parents. Boyd and Lucille were separated in 1943, after seventeen years of marriage. Because of religious beliefs, the couple were never divorced. June went to Pearl (Granny) Logan's home to live; the other children, to their grandfather Richardson's home.

Lucille went to work for The Fair, a department store in Fort Worth, as a saleslady. When this store closed, she worked at Monnigs. After this she kept the children of two Birdville school teachers, John Spicer and Jim Harden. In 1960 Lucille moved back to her parents' home to help care for them till their deaths. Since that time, Lucille has lived with her older daughter, June Logan Griffeth.

Boyd worked at several different jobs. He was a welder's helper at Star Tank Company in Rhome, and also at Baker's Built Feeder Company. Later he worked for Garbet Brothers in Fort Worth. Soon after his retirement, he suffered a stroke and died on February 17, 1970.

McCURDY — LIVENGOOD (BAKER)

Peggy Joyce Livengood, daughter of John Thomas Livengood and Leola Jean Coffman Livengood, was born November 15, 1924, at Cottondale, Texas. She was married to William Wade McCurdy, son of Charles Everett McCurdy and Winnie Mae Morris McCurdy, on November 25, 1942. William Wade McCurdy was born March 15, 1925, at Idalou, Texas.

Peggy Livengood attended public school in Rhome, Texas, where she graduated from Rhome High School in the Class of 1942. William Wade McCurdy also graduated from Rhome High School in 1942. He served in the navy from 1943 to 1945. He was discharged with the rating of Quartermaster 2/c. He graduated from Texas Christian University in Fort Worth, Texas. His occupation is that of contract negotiator. Peggy McCurdy and William Wade McCurdy were divorced on October 25, 1964.

Three children were born to this union: Jacqueline Wade McCurdy, born September 8, 1944; Stephen Riley McCurdy, born September 14, 1951; and William Blake McCurdy, born March 31, 1957.

Peggy Joyce Livengood McCurdy was married in Hillsboro, Texas, on June 19, 1970, to Joe Baker of Rhome, Texas. Today they reside near the Baker-Built Feeder Shop, a business which Joe Baker built and managed until recently.

McCURDY — MORRIS

The family of William Thomas McCurdy and Cordelia Jane Hathaway lived in the community of Lebanon in Collin County, Texas, on October 9, 1908, when a son, Charles Everette McCurdy, was born to them. He was the second son in a family that finally numbered nine—five girls and four boys. Sometime around the turn of the century, they purchased a farm in Denton County, just northeast of the little town of Ponder.

They remained here for a number of years while the older children grew up, went to college in Denton, and at last the two older ones were wed into local families, and one, Ollie McCurdy, began her teaching career there.

When Everette was about twelve years of age, about 1909, the family moved again—this time to another farm just northeast of Rhome. Here they remained for several years, and most of them finished their high school educations, and the older children settled down to raise their families. But the war in Europe, combined with the oil boom and land speculation called. William Thomas McCurdy and Cordelia Jane answered again. They sold their crops in 1917 and went West.

But not before Everette, who was now a young man, was married on his twentieth birthday, October 9, 1917, to the daughter of a local merchant, W. W. Morris. Winnie Mae Morris was the daughter of William Wade Morris and Anna Louise Cate Morris. Winnie Mae Morris was born in Rhome on October 15, 1895, and had lived there until her marriage on October 9, 1917, at the Weatherford Street Methodist Church in Fort Worth, Texas.

Later in the fall Everette and Winnie Mae went with the rest of the McCurdy family to buy another farm and settle down on what was then called the East Plains of West Texas, about twenty miles from the town of Crosbyton. They eventually moved closer to town, and although they kept very close ties with the people of Rhome, they did not come back there to live until the dust bowl and depression of the 1930's forced them back to Rhome in 1935. They finally left the farm in 1941 to seek defense work during World War II. Two of their children, Billy and Mary Lee McCurdy, entered the service in the United States Navy.

Charles Everette McCurdy was accidentally killed by a fall from a ladder while painting on July 21, 1955. Winnie Mae McCurdy remained a widow in Rhome until she finally was laid to rest on October 9, 1978, at Aurora Cemetery beside her husband's grave.

—Ruth McCurdy Tolan

VIEW OF RHOME looking west from the top of the Rhome Milling Company.

MC CURDY

Although Floyd and his wife, the former Peggy Logan, and their family are the only McCurdys presently living in the Rhome community, Allan and Elton and their families continue to live in the Blewett community where our immediate family has lived since 1915. Dorothy McCurdy Blessing has a country home there and her oldest son Tommy teaches vocational agriculture in Boyd. Calva and Beatrice, the other two sisters, live in Breckenridge. Both are teachers although Beatrice has now retired.

Our families' coming to Wise County first dates back, however, to our maternal grandparents, William Hicks and Laura Rogers Chambers. They came to Wise County about the turn of the century and settled in what later became the Blewett Community. When the rural families desired a school for their children, a Mr. Blewett gave the corner of land and our grandfather, W. B. Chambers, gave the cash money for the first Blewett School. That original building still stands on the land now owned by Allan McCurdy. Blewett School was the Rhome Rural Route 2, and form many years was served by J. R. Whitehead, a most faithful rural mail carrier.

When Grandpa Chambers died in 1914, his surviving four children inherited his land surrounding this school. These children were Edwin Chambers, Ava McCurdy, Allie B. Van Meter, and Erma Lou Douglass. Mrs. Van Meter's son, Archie Van Meter, and wife, nee Patsy Thurmon of Fairview Community, are teachers in Fort Worth.

For many years Floyd's great uncle, Tom McCurdy, lived east of Rhome. Children of this family were Clyde, Bertha, Ollie, Nora, Russell, Dave, Clara, and Everett.

McGLOTHLIN — SAMPSON

John Henry McGlothlin was born on February 4, 1879, in Missouri. His parents were Alfred Herd McGlothlin and Alice Wright McGlothlin. He met and married Maude Sampson in Clairmont, Texas, on August 25, 1911. They moved to Rhome about 1917, where he became a depot agent for the Fort Worth and Denver City Railway Company.

Maude Sampson McGlothlin was born on June 14, 1892, in Clairemont, Texas. Her parents were John J. Sampson and Permelia Katherine Morris Sampson.

J. H. and Maude McGlothlin were influential members of their community. They were active in both church and civic work. Mr. McGlothlin served on the public school board of trustees and took an active part in the Masonic work. He managed the Aurora Masonic Cemetery for years and was extremely devoted to his work. The McGlothlins were members of the First Baptist Church and served there in many different capacities. Mrs. McGlothlin was active in the Thursday Study Club and its work.

Three children were born to this union: Alice Katherine McGlothlin, who married Clarence Thomas Greer; Inez McGlothlin, who married William Beal Cheatham; and Isla McGlothlin, who married John Will Finlayson.

Maude Sampson McGlothlin preceded her husband in death on July 12, 1940, and is buried in the Aurora Cemetery. John Henry McGlothlin died on April 24, 1955, and he is also buried in the Aurora Cemetery.

MASON — TEAL

Nathan Burnie Mason came to Wise County with his family, Mr. and Mrs. Charles Perry Mason about 1918, from East Texas. He married Katie Lee Teal.

Three children were born to this union: Burnie Lee Mason, who married Homer J. Caldwell; Iva Oleta Mason, who married Herbert Swiney; and Norma Jean Mason, who married Lonnie Brown.

MATHESON — LAIRD

George M. D. Matheson was born in Talledega, Alabama, in 1872. He came to Texas with his parents when he was five years old. He was married on December 26, 1892, in Cottondale, Texas, to

Margaret Rebecca Laird.

Margaret Rebecca Laird was born on October 1, 1872, in Cottondale, Texas. She was the daughter of Francis W. Laird and Sarah Ruth Mann. George M. D. Matheson served as Wise County tax assessor-collector in the late 1920's.

There were eight children born to this union: Ruth Matheson, who died in childhood; Lela Matheson, who married Lewis A. Womack; Velma Matheson, who married Calvin Faulkner; Ora Mae Matheson, who married Loyd Douglas; Alva Ray Matheson, who married Glenn A. Reiger; Veda Lou Matheson, who married Carl Meeks; J. P. Matheson, who married Ruth Shores; and Donald Matheson, who married Jimmie Lee Knight.

George M. D. Matheson died on August 11, 1933, in Clarendon, Texas. His widow, Margaret Rebecca Laird Matheson, died in February 5, 1945, in Decatur, Texas.

MOBLEY — TROXELL

Reese L. Mobley was born April 4, 1871, in Georgia. He married Elizabeth Ann Troxell, daughter of John and Mary Mosshart Troxell. Elizabeth Ann Troxell was born July 22, 1868, in Ragersville, Ohio.

Elizabeth Ann Troxell picked cotton to earn enough money to attend Decatur Baptist College. After she earned her teaching certificate, she taught at the Fairview School. The school was in session for three months in those days and she got the huge salary of $25.00 per month.

It was at one of Eliza's school programs that she met young Reese Mobley, who had moved from Georgia to Texas to make his fortune. He first settled in Grayson County, later moving with his mother to Wise County, where he rented a house and acreage from Colonel B. C. Rhome. It was to this home that be brought Elizabeth Troxell after their marriage, on December 7, 1898, in Rhome, Texas.

Three of the children were born while they lived on the land rented from Colonel B. C. Rhome: Jennie Ethel Mobley, who married Louis Christopher Walters; Rhome Elmo Mobley, who married Marian Grace Hines; and Walden Lloyd Mobley, who married Sarah Mansfield.

In June of 1903, a cyclone struck, carrying the house with five people in it, out into the nearby wheat field, completely demolishing the house. There were minor injuries, and the family certainly believed that the Lord took care of them that night. Mr. Rhome built a new house, where they lived until moving to Amarillo in 1905.

Three more children were born to the family after the move to

Amarillo: Margaret Mable Mobley, who married Ernest S. Ames; Robert Noble (Bob) Mobley, who married Alma Sue Brooks; and Woodrow Wilson Mobley, who married Cleo Neva Utley.

Reese L. Mobley was killed in a tragic automobile accident just at the time he was intending to retire from the dairy business and take life easy. He died July 6, 1927, in Amarillo, Texas. His widow, Eliza Mobley, lived with her children during the remainder of her life. She died on April 11, 1944.

MONDRICK — VACKER

Charles H. Mondrick was born November 4, 1883, in Schulenberg, Texas. His parents were Peter Mondrick, born in Germany, and Annie Kother Mondrick. He married Laura Vacker in 1904 at Gonzales, Texas. Laura was born to Martin Luther Vacker and Mary Stipa Vacker, on February 24, 1887.

Charles and Laura Mondrick moved to Rhome in the fall of 1919. He was a blacksmith, and they did farm work. They raised chickens and guineas. Laura told her daughter Virginia that she dressed and sold guineas for twenty-five cents apiece. Laura spoke only Czech when she moved to Rhome. Gus was her interpreter. She had had only a small amount of schooling and could not write or read English; yet she managed to build two cafes and pay for them. Charley built two filling stations and both of them were paid for with hard labor. He still did some blacksmithing, even after tractors began to take over the farm work.

Charles H. and Laura Vacker Mondrick had five children: Joe Mondrick; Roman Mondrick; Ella Mondrick, who married Grady Morris; Gus Mondrick, who married Marcella Scroggins; and Rachel Virginia Mondrick, who married Woodrow W. Wylie, on July 20, 1940.

Charles H. Mondrick died September 11, 1971, in Decatur, Texas. He is buried in the Aurora Cemetery. Laura Vacker Mondrick preceded him in death on July 1, 1968, in Fort Worth. She is also buried at Aurora Cemetery, Aurora, Texas.

MORRIS — BLAIR

Colonel Benjamin Morris was born in 1829 in Martinsville, Henry County, Virginia. His parents were William Morris and Tabitha Cheatham Morris. His father's parents were Samuel Coleman Morris and Susannah Wade Morris. Susannah's parents were William Wade and Ann Cawthorn Wade. The Morris family is one that perpetuates

THE FAMILY OF Mrs. Roxanna Blair Morris, seated in the center of the picture. Back row: Winnie Mae McCurdy, Iota Morris, Betty Bobo, Early Morris, Bob Morris, W. W. Morris, Pugh Morris, Berta Morris, a cousin, Mrs. Lightner, from St. Louis, Ann High, ____, Nell Rowland. Front row: ____, Roxie Morris, Roe Morris, Morris Rowland.

family names in the names of its children; thus it is that the eldest son of Colonel Benjamin Morris was named William Wade Morris.

Benjamin Morris was a tobacco buyer who traveled from New York to Alabama, conducting his business in tobacco and cotton. He traveled the beautiful Dan river from Martinsville to Danville, Virginia. Later trips carried him south down the Chattahoochie river to Eufaula, Alabama. There he met and married Roxana Blair, the daughter of Elizabeth Bishop Blair and William Blair, a plantation owner who lived near Clayton, Alabama. Roxana Blair Morris was born July 14, 1838.

Roxana and Benjamin were married in Clayton, Barbour County, Alabama, on March 4, 1856. They lived in Clayton during the Civil War, which Benjamin advanced to the rank of Lieutenant Colonel with the 29th Alabama Infantry Regiment, C.S.A.

Five of their children were born while they lived in Clayton: William Wade Morris, who married Anna Louise Cate; Edward Mitchell Morris, who married Mary L. Neel; Benjamin Logan Morris, who never married; Noley Morris, who died in childhood; and Robert (Bob) Sidney Morris, who never married.

After the family moved to Eufaula, Alabama, Benjamin operated a general merchandise store. It was in Eufaula that the remainder of their family were born: Elizabeth Tabitha Morris, who married Zachariah Blount Bobo; Richard Briggs Morris, who married Loretta Geneva Salles; Mattie Roxana Morris, who married Dr. William Dossey; Mary Early Morris, who married Charles Rowland; and James Pugh Morris, who married Alberta Finlayson; and Maggie Mae Morris, who never married.

In August, 1879, Benjamin Morris moved with his family to Wise County, Texas, settling on 1500 acres of land in the southeast part of the county near the old village of Prairie Point. He purchased the land from Whit T. Fain for $4500.00. Whit Fain had obtained the land from Samuel Sheets. This purchase included the original building called the "Crossroads Tavern" that was built in the area before Samuel Sheets drew up the town plat for Prairie Point.

In 1881 Benjamin was approached by the agents of the Fort Worth and Denver City Railroad Company with the proposal that he dedicate 100 acres of his land for the railroad right-of-way and a townsite. An agent for the townsite company drew up a plat for a town which was finally named *Rhome* for Colonel B. C. Rhome, a prominent businessman and a close friend of Colonel Morris.

Colonel B. Morris went into the farming business on the land which he had purchased. His sons became successful merchants, businessmen, and farmers, like their father before them. Because of a bitter quarrel and lawsuits for twenty years involving the townsite agent, life was not so pleasant and serene as it should have been for Colonel Benjamin and Roxana Morris.

Although he was beset by problems with the townsite question, Colonel Morris found time to exercise great interest in the growth and development of the town of Rhome, in the politics of the county and state, and also in national affairs through numerous friends in Austin and Washington, D. C. He served on numerous occasions as a delegate to the State Democratic Conventions, such as the one in Galveston in 1886. He was also intensely interested in the Farmer's Alliance, and at one time he provided land for the organization to build headquarters in Rhome.

From his land he donated lots for a school, a cemetery, the various churches, and a mill to be built by Bradford and Stephens.

Roxana Morris, besides her interest in the welfare of Rhome and her family, was devoted to the Methodist Church of Rhome, where today the names, Colonel B. and Roxana Morris, are found in their memory in the stained glass window of the little church. Roxana became a charter member of the Methodist Church; later the Colonel and many of their children joined the same church.

Colonel Benjamin Morris died in Rhome, Texas, on March 21, 1913. He is buried in the Aurora Cemetery. Roxana lived on in the original family home that had been started many years before by Samuel Sheets. Her youngest daughter, Maggie Mae, lived with her. Roxana Morris died in 1920 and is buried in the Aurora Cemetery beside her beloved Colonel. The house which was later owned by a grandson Comer Dossey, was torn down in the 1970's.

MORRIS — CATE

William Wade Morris was born on June 4, 1857, in Clayton, Barbour County, Alabama. His parents were Colonel Benjamin Morris and Roxana Blair Morris. He preceded his father's family to Texas to select the land upon which the family was to settle. According to stories told by his eldest daughter, Rena Morris Troxell, he rode out on horseback as far as Sam Woody's home on Deep Creek. Then he returned to the Prairie Point area, which he recommended to his father. The family located in this area, purchasing land from Whit Fain and others.

William Wade Morris married Anna Louise Cate, the daughter of William A. Cate and Mary Frances Crowley Cate. William A. Cate was born June 4, 1871, near Minters Chapel, in Tarrant County, Texas. He

WILLIAM WADE MORRIS   **ANNA LOUISE CATE Morris.**

died on September 9, 1869. His widow, Mary Frances Cate then moved to Rhome, Texas. It was in Rhome, Texas, that William Wade Morris met and married Anna Louise (Lou) Cate on March 28, 1886, where the Justice of the Peace, T. G. Gardner, officiated. Mary Frances Cate, Lou Morris' mother, later married John Davis on April 20, 1917, in Rhome, Texas.

William Wade Morris and his brother Edward ran the Morris Brothers Mercantile and Hardware Store. Later W. W. bought out his brother's interest and also purchased the lumber yard in Rhome.

Eight children were born to this union: William R. (Son) Morris, who died as a teen-ager; Serena Frances (Rena) Morris, who married James Robert Troxell; Roxana Morris, who married Caleb Earl Van Meter; DeWitt Talmadge Morris, who married Ada Sullivan; Winnie Mae Morris, who married Everitt McCurdy; Charles Blair Morris, who married Ella Faye Kendall; Grady Morris, who married Ella Mondrick; and Allie Morris, who died in early childhood.

In June 1935, W. W. Morris was honored by a large group of friends and relatives, who gathered at Harmon Field in Decatur,

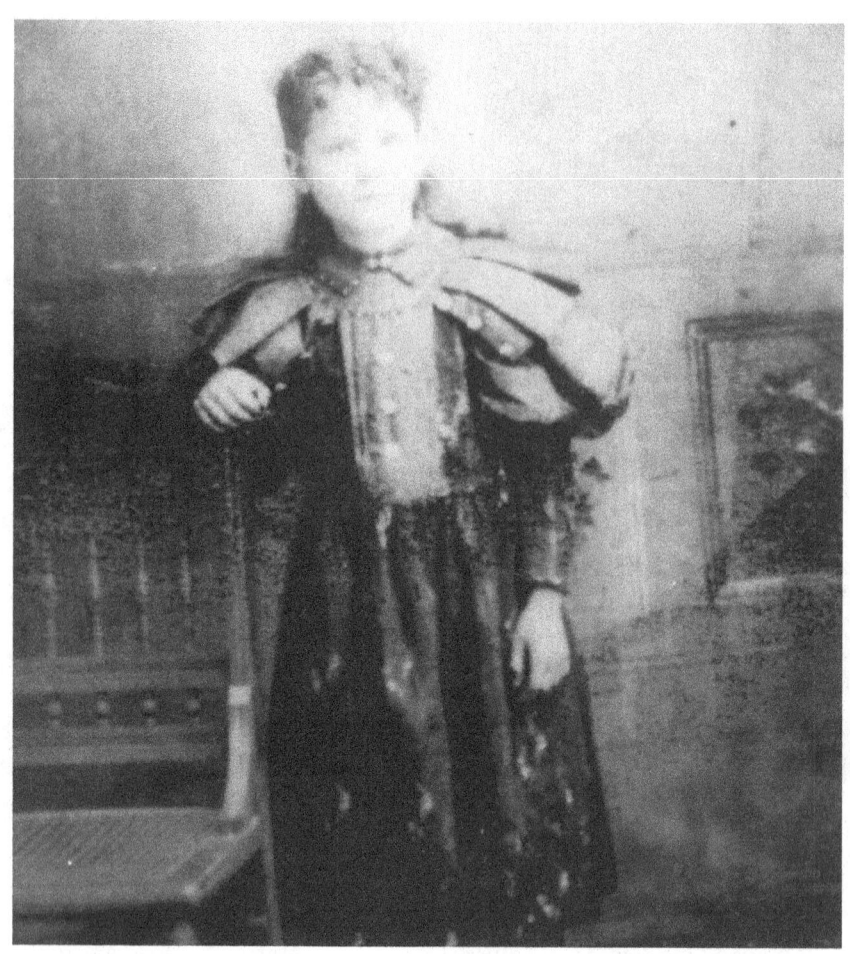

RENA FRANCES MORRIS, Age 11, eldest granddaughter of Colonel B. Morris.

honoring him on his 75th birthday. At this time he had retired from active business pursuits and spent most of his time with his son, Grady Morris. Before partaking of the food, a beautiful and impressive prayer was offered by Mrs. Z. B. Bobo, a sister of Mr. Morris. Following the supper, Mr. Morris made a brief speech, expressing in sincere, heartfelt words his deep appreciation of the love and friendship that prompted the celebration. The response was made by Mrs. Chas. Rowland of Fort Worth, another sister of the honored guest.

William Wade Morris died on March 23, 1938, at the home of his daughter, Rena Morris Troxell, in Decatur, Texas. He is buried in the Aurora Cemetery. Anna Louise (Lou) Cate Morris died in Fort Worth, Texas, on May 4, 1943. She is also buried in the Aurora Cemetery.

J. PUGH MORRIS, and his wife, Alberta Finlayson Morris.

MORRIS — FINLAYSON

James Pugh Morris was born on August 13, 1875, in Eufaula, Alabama. His parents were Colonel Benjamin Morris and Roxana Blair Morris. He married Alberta (Bertie) Finlayson, the daughter of W. J. Finlayson and Margaret Day Finlayson, on June 23, 1907, in Rhome, Texas. There were no children born to this union.

Pugh Morris, a retired farmer and stockman, came to Fort Worth from Eufaula, Alabama, with his parents in 1879, when he was only four years. The family lived in Fort Worth several months until the Morris family home was completed on the 1700 acre site which they had purchased where Rhome now stands. Pugh and Bertie Morris lived all of their lives in a home that was built on the site of the original schoolhouse in old Prairie Point.

Bertie Morris was a member of a pioneer Wise County family and lived all of her life within five miles of her birthplace. Both Pugh and Bertie Morris were members of the First Methodist Church of Rhome.

Pugh Morris died in Rhome, Texas. He is buried in the Aurora Cemetery. His widow, Bertie Morris, lived on in the family home until ill health forced her to go to the hospital in Decatur, Texas, where she died. She is also buried in the Aurora Cemetery.

MORRIS — KENDALL

Charles Blair Morris, son of William Wade Morris and Anna Louise Cate Morris, was born in Rhome, Texas. He married Ella Faye Kendell, daughter of Dolph and Desda Kendell of Bridgeport, Texas. Ella Faye Kendell was born May 13, 1906.

Charles Blair Morris worked for his father in the Morris Mercantile Company and also for the Morris Lumber Yard. He served for some time as postmaster of the Rhome Postoffice. Ella Faye Kendell Morris came to Rhome before their marriage as an English and Spanish teacher in Rhome High School.

Two children were born to this union: William Wade (Bill) Morris, who has not married; and Mary Kendell Morris, who married Lawrence Troni on March 10, 1973.

Charles Blair Morris died in Fort Worth, Texas, on September 25, 1977. Before his death he arranged for his body to be donated to medical science. Ella Faye Kendell Morris lives with her son Bill in San Antonio, Texas.

MORRIS — MONDRICK

Grady Morris was born in Rhome, Texas, about 1895. His parents were William Wade Morris and Anna Louise (Lou) Cate. Grady Morris married Ella Mondrick, the daughter of Charles H. Mondrick and Laura Vacker Mondrick of Rhome, Texas.

Three children were born to this union: Jo Ann Morris, who married Roland Weaver; Robert (Bobby) Morris, who has not married; and Brooks Morris.

After studying watch making in Elgin, Illinois, Grady Morris was a jeweler in Decatur, Texas, for many years. He collected rare coins and antique clocks. Besides repairing antique clocks, he spent many hours working on the clock in the courthouse at Decatur.

Grady Morris died in Decatur, Texas, on September 5, 1976. He is buried in the Aurora Cemetery beside his father and brother.

Ella Mondrick Morris has had a very successful career in banking in Dallas, Texas, until her retirement recently. Today she makes her home in Dallas.

MORRIS — SULLIVAN

DeWitt Talmadge Morris, son of William Wade Morris and Anna Louise Cate Morris, was born April 7, 1892, in Rhome, Texas. He married Ada Sullivan, the daughter of George Sullivan and Sally Glenn Sullivan. Ada Sullivan was born April 17, 1892, in Rhome.

DeWitt Talmadge Morris managed the W. W. Morris Mercantile and Hardware stores in Rhome. He also ran the Morris Lumber Yard in Rhome. In addition to these duties, he was a rancher, owning a large tract of land about two and one-half miles north of Rhome.

There were no children born to this union. DeWitt Talmadge Morris died on February 10, 1942, of a heart attack on a ranch near his own land north of Rhome. He is buried in the Aurora Cemetery. His widow still lives in the family home in Rhome.

MOUNT — BROWNING

Seymour Houston Mount was born on March 17, 1871, in Centralia, Illinois. His parents were Joshua Houston Mount and Kizzie Frances Ward Mount. He married Katie Elizabeth Browning on November 4, 1894, at Copperas Cove, Texas. Katie Elizabeth Browning, daughter of John Rutherford Browning and Julia Ballard Browning, was born July 19, 1875, in Copperas Cove, Texas.

Apparently they came to Rhome, Texas, about one year after they were married. The Mount family biography states that they moved to the Indian Territory about 1900, but since there was a child born in Rhome about 1904, it is probable that they did not move until after that time. There were nine children born to this union: Pearl Mount, Mable Mount, Clara Mount, Houston Browning Mount, Alma Mount, Ruth Mount, Velma Lee Mount, Verda Mount, and Raymond Leslie "Mike" Mount.

Katie Elizabeth Browning was a sister of the husband of Emily Frances Mount, who married William Lafayette Browning.

Seymour Houston Mount died on February 16, 1952, in Ada, Oklahoma, and is buried in the Memborial Park Cemetery of Ada, Oklahoma. His widow, Katie Elizabeth Mount, died on October 2, 1963, in Ada, Oklahoma. She is buried beside her husband in the Memorial Park Cemetery.

MOUNT — VAN METER

Timothy Silas Mount, one of Rhome's early businessmen, was the son of Joshua Houston Mount and Kizzie Frances Ward Mount. He was born on January 6, 1872. He married Martha Alcinda Van Meter on August 25, 1895, in Rhome, Texas.

Martha Alcinda Van Meter, daughter of Caleb Jackson Van Meter and Mary Ann Standifer Van Meter, was born February 21, 1875, in Rhome, Wise County, Texas.

Timothy Silas Mount and Martha Van Meter Mount moved to the Indian Territory about 1904. Four of their children were born before they left Rhome: Marguerite Yanzi Mount, who married Marvin E. Nimmo; Conrad Caleb Mount, who married Louise Renegar; Victor Timothy Mount, who married (1) Virginia Walker, (2) Mayme Shockley, and (3) Trenna ____; Maymie Grace Mount, who married (1) Ellis Jones and (2) Robert McIntosh. The Timothy Silas Mount children who were born after the move to Indian Territory were as follows: Zelma Hope Mount, who married Joseph Preston Yadon; Coral Virginia Mount, who married John Malcom Hutchinson; and Norma Earle Mount, who married James Edwin Smith.

Timothy Silas Mount died on July 2, 1954, in Oklahoma City, Oklahoma, where he is buried in the Memorial Park Cemetery. His widow, Martha Alcinda Van Meter Mount, followed her husband in death on December 8, 1966, and is buried beside her husband in the Memorial Park Cemetery.

MOUNT — WARD — WARD

Joshua Houston Mount was born May 26, 1833, in Tennessee. He was the son of William Mount and Frances Williams Mount. His first marriage was to Elizabeth Jane Ward, daughter of Artemis and Priscilla Ward, on April 7, 1959. Elizabeth Jane Ward was born in 1837 in Indiana. They had one child, Isabelle Ellen Mount, who was born January 5, 1860. Elizabeth Ward Mount died on December 12, 1864, in Kell, Marion County, Illinois. She is buried in the Pleasant Hill Baptist Cemetery in Jefferson County, Illinois.

While he was still living in Illinois, Joshua Houston Mount married a second time. This marriage on March 21, 1867, was to Kizzie Frances Ward, who was the daughter of Hosea and Emily Johnson Ward. Six children were born to this union: Serena Jane Mount, who married Jacob Henry Troxell; Seymour Houston Mount, who married Katie Elizabeth Browning; Timothy Silas Mount, who married Martha Alcinda Van Meter; Emily Frances Mount, who married William Lafayette Browning, a brother of Seymour Mount's wife; Emmett Elijah Mount, who married (1) Blanche Wells and (2) Blanche Bailey Giles; and Harriet Florence Mount, who married the Reverend Henry H. Bain.

The family moved to Rhome, Texas, about 1885. With a group of friends they had decided to move south. Near Rhome, Texas, they found land to their liking and settled there. In addition to his immediate family, Joshua Houston Mount brought his daughter by his first marriage, Ellen Mount Byars, and her three sons, Evan, Earl, and Edgar. With his three sons, Joshua Mount operated a mercantile store, Mount and Sons. He also operated a freight service by horse and wagon to Fort Worth from Rhome. By 1900 the Mount Brothers had purchased the old mill site and were rebuilding the roller mill in Rhome. They operated the mill until it was sold to a group of three buyers, Lafayette Renshaw, Steve Lillard, and a Mr. Malone.

The Mount family built the house which is standing today just south of the Baptist parsonage. It is one of the loveliest examples of early architecture in the area. Today the house belongs to the Logan family.

Joshua Houston Mount died on March 28, 1900, in Rhome, Texas. He is buried in the Fairview Cemetery at Fairview, Texas. His wife, Kizzie Ward Mount followed him in death on April 22, 1913, and is buried beside her husband at Fairview.

The *Decatur News* printed the following obituary on April 6, 1900, for Joshua Mount:

Uncle Josh Mount of Rhome died Wednesday and was followed by a large concourse of friends Thursday. Mr. Mount was one of the oldest and most substantial citizens of this end of Wise County, and his death removes a prominent figure from our midst.

MOUNT — WELLS — GILES

Emmett Elijah Mount was born April 18, 1880, in Decatur, Marion County, Illinois. He was the youngest son of Joshua Houston Mount and Kizzie Ward Mount. His first marriage was to Blanche Irene Wells, daughter of David Wells and Amy Morrison Wells, who was born on April 20, 1886.

Emmett started school at Fairview and then attended school in Rhome. As a youth he helped his father, Joshua Mount, with the freight wagon service that the elder Mount operated from Rhome to Fort Worth. When Emmett was eighteen, his elder brothers included him in their plans to rebuild the old roller mill at Rhome, Texas. Their operation of the roller mill was successful and was finally sold to a group of three men, Steve Lillard, Lafayette Renshaw, and a Mr. Malone.

Four children were born to Emmett Elijah Mount and his first wife, Blanche Irene Mount. The children were as follows: Lawrence Mount, Okla Irene Mount, Stanley Arthur Mount, and Orin Emmett Mount. The Mount family history states that this Mount family moved to Indian Territory in 1902. Blanche Wells Mount died on July 2, 1954, and is buried in the Oaklawn Cemetery in Bristow, Oklahoma.

On February 23, 1956, Emmett E. Mount married Blanche Rebecca Bailey Giles, the widow of a family friend, William R. Giles. She was the daughter of William A. and Julia A. Bailey. There were no children born to this union.

Emmett Elijah Mount died April 5, 1960, in Okmulgee, Oklahoma. He is buried beside his first wife in Oaklawn Cemetery in Bristow, Oklahoma.

NELSON — FORD

Hugh J. Nelson was born March 17, 1884, in Atwood, Moultrie County, Illinois. His parents were William Nelson and Mary Rardin/Reardin Nelson. He married Lydia Ann (Lena) Ford on January 18, 1906, in Decatur, Wise County, Texas. She was the daughter of Jasper Morell Ford and Sonora Vashti Harper Ford. She was born on September 24, 1883.

Hugh J. Nelson and Lydia Ann (Lena) Ford were married January 18, 1906, and lived about one mile west of the Fairview school in the original J. H. Troxell house. Six of their oldest children were born in that house. Our doctors were from Rhome or Decatur. We traveled by buggy, wagon, or horseback. We bought our first car, a Studebaker, about 1912. Most of our trading was done in Rhome—some in Decatur and once or twice a year my father would go in a wagon to Fort Worth to get other needed supplies. That took two or three days. He took our wheat to the mill in Rhome to be ground into flour. Our Fairview school was a one-room building. It was also our church meeting place. A Baptist church was built near the Fairview Cemetery about 1915. I remember having a "dinner on the ground" at the north end of the church. That occasion must have been to celebrate the finished church building. I had to take care of my brother Lloyd, who was walking real good and biting every child he would get near. A sad experience for me was the death of Naomi Layfield. A happy experience was to attend my first wedding when my uncle Dennis Ford was married.

The family moved to the plains in June, 1917 and settled in the Lakeview Community about 10 miles south east of Floydada, Texas. Two daughters were born to this family in Floydada. At the present time in early 1979 the 8 of us are still living at the following places:

Opal (Nelson) Higgins	LaMesa, California
H. Raymond Nelson	Plainview, Texas
Carl F. Nelson	Floydada, Texas
Herman Nelson	Lubbock, Texas
William Lloyd Nelson	Borger, Texas
Elmo (D.E.) Deane Nelson	Bellflower, California
Alma Ruth Nelson	Floydada, Texas
Lena Mae (Nelson) Ooley	Plainview, Texas

Opal Josephine married Bernie Monroe Higgins; Hubert Raymond married Ora Estrella Harris; Carl Ford married Audrey (Burgett) Johnson; Herman Jasper married Ethel Viola Warren; William Loyd married Fannie Ruth E. Patton; Elmo Dean married Clovelle Gregory; Alma Ruth, who was never married; Lena May who married R. Klyce Ooley.

Hugh J. Nelson died on February 23, 1961, in Floydada, Texas. He is buried in the Lakeview Cemetery. Lydia Ann (Lena) Nelson died on February 7, 1957, in Floydada, Texas. She is buried beside her husband.

—Opal J. Higgins

NESMITH — CHILDS

William Wallace NeSmith was born January 20, 1860, in Wolf Spring, Lawrence County, Alabama. His parents were John Rhea NeSmith and Pamelia Greenhill NeSmith. He married Laura Jane Childs in Lawrence County, Alabama. Her parents were Russell Ander Childs and Polly Fry Childs. Laura Jane Childs was born September 25, 1859, in Lawrence County, Alabama.

Five children were born to this union: Lieu Etta NeSmith, who first married Jim Counts in 1900 and later married Walter Dunlap, in 1945; John Rhea NeSmith, who married Zula Gentry; Emmett R. NeSmith, who married Sue Dickey; Ora NeSmith, who married Jim Lynch; and Robert Leigh NeSmith, who married Ora Ellen Leonard.

William Wallace NeSmith was a deacon in the Baptist Church at the age of eighteen. In 1908 he became the pastor of the Baptist Church in Rhome and was pastor there for eight years. His father and three of his brothers were also Baptist ministers. Before he came to Rhome, he was in politics in Alabama, where he served as a state representative and as state senator.

After he left the Rhome community, William Wallace NeSmith was pastor in several other Wise County towns. Bridgeport, Texas, was his last home, where he served as pastor until he retired. He died on December 11, 1949, in Dallas, Texas, and is buried in Bridgeport Cemetery in Bridgeport, Texas.

Laura Jane Childs NeSmith preceded him in death on March 2, 1944, in Bridgeport, Texas. She is buried beside her husband in the Bridgeport Cemetery.

NESMITH — LEONARD

Robert Leigh NeSmith was born October 3, 1891, in Lawrence County, Alabama. His parents were William Wallace NeSmith and Laura Jane Childs NeSmith. He moved to Rhome, Texas, in 1908, with his parents. He was married to Ora Ellen Leonard on October 28, 1910, in Fort Worth, Texas. Ora Ellen Leonard was born October 24, 1887, in Rhome, Texas. Her parents were Collin Campbell Leonard and Mary Jane Trinkle Leonard.

Two daughters were born to this union: Mary Laura NeSmith, who is married to Agee Ray; and Nancy Roberta NeSmith, who is married to James George Willis.

In 1921, Robert Lee NeSmith was the youngest student, in the shortest length of time, with the highest honors, to graduate from

Cumberland University. He furthered his career as a lawyer in Sedgwick County, Kansas, and served as a district judge there for four terms. He resigned during his last term and returned to private practice and continued in this capacity unil his death June 13, 1964. He is buried in Wichita, Kansas.

Ora Ellen Leonard lived on the old Leonard place north of Rhome until she moved to Fort Worth, where she died in December 20,1975. She is buried in Rosehill Cemetery in Fort Worth, Texas.

NORMAN — LISBY

James Norman was born May 9, 1888, at Cottondale, Texas, in Wise County. His parents were Elijah Norman and Manervia Hamilton Norman. He married Letha Lisby of Boyd, Texas. Letha Lisby was born April 17, 1893, in Moulton, Alabama. Her parents were Walter Lisby and Martha Cagle Lisby.

Five children were born to this union: Ruth Norman, who married Lee Hall; Iva Mae Norman, who died in childhood; J. E. Norman, who has not married; Beryl Norman, who married Dorotha Thornton; and Billy Norman, who married Barbara Hild.

The Norman family lived for forty years on the place which Marcus Taylor Oates had built for his family. Then their son, J. E. Norman, built a new home for them on the old Luther Benton place north of Rhome, just a short distance from their beloved home on the Oates place. They reside there with their son today. During the fall of 1978, vandals set fire to and burned the old Oates home, a landmark in the town, having been located there since the Prairie Point days.

OATES — HOYL

John Edward Oates, son of William Sloan Oates and Mary Ann Whitworth Oates, was born May 28, 1862, on the old home place south of Aurora, Texas. He married Mary Jane Hoyl, who was born March 6, 1863.

Six children were born to this family: Mary Oates, who married J. G. Stroud of Rhome; William Robert Oates; Otie F. Oates, who married Stella Willis; Flossie Oates, who married James Wilson, a grandson of Dan Caldwell; Cora Oates, who married Robert Willis; and Brawley H. Oates. The Brawley Oates family lives today in the Rhome-Aurora community. Part of the old family place is still in the family name.

John Edward Oates died on April 11, 1939. His widow, Mary Jane Hoyl Oates, died on November 7, 1941. They are both buried in the Aurora Cemetery.

THE OATES FAMILY: (L-R) John Oates, Jim Oates, Brawley Oates, Rob Oates, Marcus Taylor Oates.

OATES — WARD

Marcus Taylor Oates was born on January 7, 1847, in North Carolina. His parents, William Sloan Oates and Mary Ann Whitworth Oates, were also born in North Carolina. M. T. Oates came to Texas in 1858 with his parents.

Marcus Taylor Oates married Mary Ann Ward, who was a sister of the late Reverend Lawrence Ward of Decatur. The Oates family lived most of their lives on the wheat and stock farm one-half mile north of Rhome.

The Oates family was in the Rhome area by 1858 during the time of the establishment of the old village of Prairie Point. During that time, Indians quite often were seen near Prairie Point. A grandson, Ray Ellars, tells one of the favorite stories about Mark Oates and the Indians: "This time Grandpa (M. T. Oates) was breaking in a new saddle pony. It happened in the area of Oates Branch, where the woods and prairie meet. All of a sudden, he found himself surrounded by a group of Indians, about eight or ten. He kicked the spurs into the horse's ribs. Instead of running, the pony started bucking and pitching. By this time the Indians had formed an arena, just waiting for Grandpa to hit the ground, as he was just hanging on, half way out of the saddle on the pony's neck. The next jerk threw him back into the saddle. He put spurs to the horse again. This time she started running and Grandpa got away. Hurrah!"

Nine children were born to the marriage of Marcus Taylor Oates and Mary Ann Oates: Laura J. Oates, who was not married; Joseph H. Oates; Lucy Margaret Oates; Benjamin F. Oates, who married Lillian Van Meter; Grover Oates; Willie Oates, who married Walter Ellars; Ella Oates, who married Irwin Douglas; Faye Oates, who married a Mr. Etheridge; and Lawrence Oates.

Mary Ann Ward Oates died on April 27, 1920. She is buried in the Aurora Cemetery. Marcus Taylor Oates died on August 13, 1926. He is also buried in Aurora Cemetery.

The following paragraph was taken from M. T. Oates' obituary in the *Wise County Messenger* on April 27, 1926. "In the passing of this good man, the county loses a good and honorable citizen; one who did his part in its advancement, and he lived to witness the transforming of a sparsely settled county to a thriving, busy and progressive section. He was honorable in all his dealings, and the universal regrets over his departure attest the man's worth and usefulness to his town, community, and county."

MR. AND MRS. M. T. Oates, Rhome pioneers.

MARCUS TAYLOR OATES, a Rhome pioneer.

OATES — WHITWORTH

William Sloan Oates, one of the first settlers of the Prairie Point area, was born June 29, 1824, in North Carolina. His parents were James Sloan Oates and Lucy Hartshorne Oates. He married Mary Ann Whitworth in 1845 in Waco, North Carolina.

Mary Ann Whitworth was born in North Carolina in 1825. Mary Ann Whitworth Oates and her husband William Sloan Oates moved to Bond County, Illinois, after their marriage. Then in 1858, the family moved to Texas. They settled about two miles south of Aurora. Five of their children were born before the move to Texas: Marcus Taylor Oates, who married Mary Ann Ward; Cynthia Oates, who married a Mr. Mullis; Lucy Oates, who was not married; Margaret Oats, who married Roe Helm, a son of William Helm; and James White Oates, who married Jennie Harlan. Three more children were born in Texas: William Brawley Oates, who married Mrs. Clara Barr; Robert Sloan Oates, who married Mary Alice Bigelow; and John Edward Oates, who married Mary Jane Hoyl.

One of the earliest deeds to a lot in the town of Prairie Point was made out to William S. Oats. He owned a lot in the block that was in the northeast corner of the town.

William Sloan Oates entered the Confederate Army and died on March 10, 1854, while in service. He is buried in a Confederate Cemetery at Boggy Depot, Oklahoma. Mary Ann Whitworth Oates died on May 16, 1873. She is buried in the old Teague Cemetery, which is one mile south of the Aurora Cemetery.

PAYNE — BROWN

Charles Payne married Rachel Brown, daughter of Joseph Hamilton Brown and Mary Ann Elizabeth Hill Brown. In 1916 Charles and Rachel Payne moved to Rhome from Newark, Texas, where they were born and reared. They lived in Rhome for about three years before moving to the Logan farm four and one-half miles east of Rhome. The family lived there until 1930, when they moved across the creek to the B. C. Rhome ranch.

Charles Payne was a member of the school board the year that the old red brick schoolhouse burned. He was also a member of the Masonic Lodge, and both he and Rachel were members of the Rhome Church of Christ. They left the Rhome area about 1937, moving to Arlington, Texas.

They had three children: Aaron, Gilbert, and Helen. Rachel now lives with her daughter Helen in Haltom City. Gilbert is retired and lives in Arlington. Aaron is retired and lives on Eagle Mountain Lake near Azle.

RENSHAW — NEEL — BOBO

Lafayette William Renshaw was born November 9, 1876, in Decatur, Texas. His parents were Lucius (Lute) Renshaw and Melinda Belle Terrell Renshaw. He married Jennie Bess Neel on October 14, 1900, in Boyd, Texas. Her father was Thomas Neel. She was born in Morgantown, Kentucky, on February 4, 1878.

William Lafayette Renshaw and Jennie Bess Renshaw had three children: L. Wayne Renshaw, who married Merle Van Meter; Eula Mae Renshaw, who married Foy Wallace Byrd; and Lawrence Eugene Renshaw, who was not married.

L. W. Renshaw was owner and manager of the flour mill in Rhome for many years, having purchased it from the Mount family. He originated the name "Light Crust Flour," which Burris Mills purchased from him, when it was discovered that a small Texas flour mill owned the patent on the name that they were advertising nationally.

Jennie Bess Noel died in 1923, and is buried in Oaklawn Cemetery in Decatur, Texas.

Lafayette William Renshaw married Early Virginia Bobo on July 1, 1929. She is the daughter of Zachariah Blount Bobo and Elizabeth Morris Bobo. She was born December 8, 1893. "Virgie" taught school in Fort Worth until her marriage, having earned her degrees from Baylor and Columbia Universities.

One daughter, Anna Bess Renshaw, was born to this union. Anna Bess Renshaw is married to Wesley Mowery.

Lafayette William Renshaw died on January 1, 1965, and is buried in Oaklawn Cemetery in Decatur, Texas. Virginia Bobo Renshaw is still living in the family home.

RENSHAW — VAN METER

L. Wayne Renshaw was born April 13, 1901, in Rhome, Texas. His parents were Lafayette William Renshaw and Jennie Bess Neel Renshaw. Wayne married Merle Marguerite Van Meter on May 23, 1926, at her home in Decatur, Texas. Merle Van Meter was born on March 28, 1904, in Rhome, Texas. Her parents were Abishi Archibald Van Meter and Mary Ellen Bryan Van Meter.

Two children were born of this marriage: L. Wayne Renshaw, who married (1) Patsy Jean McGinnis and (2) Greta Woods; and Larry Alan Renshaw, who married Catherine Sue Witmer.

Today Wayne and Merle Renshaw are both retired and live in the family home in Rhome, Texas. Wayne Renshaw managed the Renshaw mill and ginning company for many years, taking over after his father's retirement. Merle Renshaw taught in the Rhome Public School and in Northwest Public School for many years before her retirement.

RHOME — LOFTIN — DAY

Byron Crandall Rhome, son of Peter G. and Nancy Almira Crandall Rhome, both of New York State, was born November 22, 1837, in Richmond County, Georgia. The Peter G. Rhomes came to Georgia in 1836 and to Jacksonville, Texas, in 1854. Peter G. Rhome was a member of the Texas State Convention in 1861.

Byron Crandall Rhome married first on August 31, 1864, to Ella Elizabeth Loftin of Cherokee County, Texas. To them were born six children, only three of whom lived to maturity. They were Byron Crandall Rhome, Jr., born February 2, 1871; Joseph Otto Rhome, born May 8, 1874; and Ella Rhome, born November 14, 1876. From 1867 to 1879 the Rhome family made their home in Etna, Smith County, Texas.

B. C. Rhome, Sr., enlisted in 1862 in the 18th Texas Infantry, serving in General Walker's division, in the Trans. Miss. Department, General E. Kirby Smith, commanding. He was in the battles of Opelousis, Mansfield, and Pleasant Hill, Louisiana, and the battle of Jenkins Ferry, Arkansas. He was wounded at Opelousis. He entered service as First Sergeant, afterward elected to 2nd Lieutenant, was promoted to 1st Lieutenant and later to Captain. He continued in active service until Lee's surrender.

He and his father had been engineers and merchants in East Texas, but at the death of his first wife in 1879, B. C. Rhome moved to Wise County, Texas, and became a rancher and cattleman.

In March, 1880, he married Fannie Crockett Day of Denton County. They had one son, Romulus John Rhome, born on the Wise County ranch on February 15, 1881.

B. C. Rhome's ranch became known as Hereford Park because of the hundreds of Hereford cattle grazing on it, a breed which he introduced into Texas in 1887. Some of the finest stock in this country was raised by Mr. Rhome, among which was *Harkaway*, a fine Hereford bull which captured the blue ribbon at the Texas State Fair in 1890. At a later show in Chicago, one of the Rhome Herefords won the silver cup and grand prize for best in his class. Colonel Rhome, as he was known to his friends and associates, was one of the founders of the Fort Worth Fat Stock Show.

The Rhome family moved from the ranch to a home on Penn Street in Fort Worth in 1906. The Colonel and his family immediately became prominent members of the Central Christian Church. Both he and his son, Rom, were members of the Board of Trustees of Texas Christian University.

Colonel B. C. Rhome died November 10, 1919, and is buried in Oakwood Cemetery, Fort Worth, Texas. After Colonel Rhome's death the Hereford herd which he had built up was sold to many cattlemen who needed the animals with which to upgrade their stock.

His sons continued to reside in Texas. Byron C. Rhome, Jr., married Minnie Ryder of Weatherford, Texas. Joseph O. Rhome married Daisey Cogdell of Granbury, Texas. Rom Rhome married Eugenia Wellborn of Fort Worth. Ella Rhome married Charles Woody of Weatherford, Texas. They moved to New York. Byron and his wife had no children. Joe and his wife had three sons: Byron, Otto, and Dan, and a daughter, Marion. Rom had one son, Rom J. Rhome, Jr. Ella Rhome Woody had two children Rhoma and Charles, Jr.

—by Marion Day Mullins

RICHARDSON — HAMMACK

Edward E. Richardson left his home in Bellevue, Clay County, Texas, as a young man. He moved to Jack County to seek employment as a ranch hand. Upon reaching Jack County, he hired out for the Halsell Ranch. After working a short time on the ranch, he moved to Decatur, Wise County, Texas, and enrolled in Decatur Baptist College. It was at the college that he met Aurora Flossy Hammack of Stoney, Denton County, Texas. They were married on February 4, 1906, at Aurora's brother's home in Stoney.

The new couple made their home in Rhome. Ed was employed by Z.B. Bobo of Rhome, where he served as a druggist, undertaker, funeral home director, and furniture retailer, making twenty-five dollars a month. Soon after this time, Ed left the drug business, and sought employment for the Rhome Milling Company, as a traveling salesman. During his year as a salesman, Ed began taking some business courses at Fort Worth Business College.

In 1907 the first daughter, Lucille, was born. Later that year the Richardson family moved to Bridgeport, Texas, where Ed worked in the brick plant. While the family lived in Bridgeport, their first son, Earl Brent Richardson, was born.

Ed then got a job as manager of the Steve Lillard Mill in Decatur in 1910, and the family moved again. While in Decatur, Ed saw his chance to go into business for himself. He and J. W. Malone went together as partners and bought a cotton gin located in Alvord. The family once again packed and moved to Alvord. While the family was located in Alvord, their son J. T. Richardson was born in 1913 and their daughter Imogene was born in 1916.

The year 1919 brought still another move for the family. Ed packed his wife and children and moved south to the blackland prairie at Newark. In Newark the family built a new home across from the Baptist Church. Ed ran the Newark cotton gin. During 1924 their daughter Lucille graduated from Newark High School. Later in that same year the family made its last move up the hill to Rhome. Ed, now a successful and prominent businessman, built the Farmer's Gin, which he owned and operated until his retirement in 1946. The gin was located on the main street of Rhome, where the Star Tank and Trailer Manufacturing Company is located. In 1925 the last daughter Betty Joe was born.

In 1925 the family built a new brick house in Rhome, which today is the third house east of Rhome Elementary School. In this house the Richardsons lived until their deaths in 1968 and 1972.

The children born to this union were as follows: Lucille Douglas

Richardson, who married William Boyd Logan; Earl Brent Richardson, who married Sue Ella Van Meter; James Travis Richardson, who married Pauline (Sally) Gill; Imogene Richardson, who married Homer Irvine (Pete) Watkins; and Bettie Joe Richardson, who never married.

ROWAN — THURMOND

James F. Rowan was born in Dallas, Texas, in 1870. He moved to Rhome, Texas, where he later married Catherine Greenwood Thurmond. Catherine Thurmond was born in Dallas, Texas, on November 3, 1876. Catherine Thurmond's parents were John Favor Thurmond and Amanda Merryfield Thrumond.

For many years Mr. Rowan was president and a director of the Rhome National Bank before he retired and moved to Decatur, where he lived until his death.

From this union were born five children: Myrtle Eileen Rowan, who married William H. Burge; Allen Thurmond Rowan, who married Ruth Marie Shook; John Houston Rowan, who married Josie Wilson; Edward Floyd Rowan, who married Elizabeth Harper; and Alma Pearl Rowan, who married Walter Cox.

James F. Rowan died in 1955, and Catherine Greenwood Thurmond Rowan died February 27, 1960. Both are buried in the Thurmond Fairview Cemetery.

RUSSELL — ATWOOD

J. Wood Russell, son of Caleb J. Russell and Julia Sugg Russell, was born in the Pleasant Grove community in Wise County, Texas. He moved to Rhome in 1905. He married Flora Atwood, daughter of Captain Davis Chase Atwood and Josephine Genelle Atwood. She was born at Koscuisko, Mississippi. She moved to Rhome in 1907. J. Wood Russell and Flora Atwood Russell were married on November 25, 1909.

J. Wood Russell ran the Rhome Telephone Company for a number of years. He was an employee of the Lone Star Gas Company from the time it was brought to Rhome until his death on October 20, 1946.

Flora Atwood Russell lived in Rhome until her death on January 14, 1955. They are both buried in the Aurora Cemetery.

One daughter was born to this union: Cassie Fry Russell, who married Thurman Hudnall.

WHITFIELD LEGGETT RUSSELL   CLIFFORD HENDERSON RUSSELL

RUSSELL — HENDERSON

Whitfield Legget Russell, a physician who came to Rhome during the early days of the century, was born near Cason, Texas, on December 25, 1882. His parents were Whit L. Russell and Jennie Wall Lowe. He was married in Cason, Texas, on January 11, 1908, to Clifford Henderson. Clifford Henderson was born August 31, 1891, in Cason, Texas. Her parents were Humphrey Henderson and Nancy Catherine Littlefield Henderson.

In his youth Whitfield L. Russell united with the Methodist Church in his community of Cason. He entered the College of Medicine at the University of Tennessee in 1901. By 1905, he had completed his medical training, and he went to Cason, Texas, to practice medicine. With his new bride he moved to Waterman, Texas, where he practiced until 1911.

Little did William J. Logan know when he placed an advertisement in the May, 1911, *Dallas Morning News* that his search for a physician for the town of Rhome would bring a gentleman who would serve the community for the next fifty years. In 1954 Dr. Russell received a certificate from the University of Tennessee, commenorating his fifty years of service in the field of medicine.

On October 17, 1959, Dr. Russell received a moving tribute from the people whom he had helped for so many years. He was the guest of honor at the annual Rhome Homecoming, where he was presented with a plaque that read as follows: "In appreciation for the unselfish service rendered the families of this community since 1911 and for a life of devotion and loyalty to his profession." From his meticulously kept records it was found that he had delivered four hundred and eight babies in the homes of Rhome citizens. The last child that he delivered was for the J. R. Hines family on November 10, 1948. His fees for delivering babies had ranged from $7.50 to $34.00 during the years. However, some of his payments came in the form of yard work, insurance premiums, barbering, watermelons, sausage, shop work on buggies and cars, carpenter work, and washing and ironing.

When Dr. Whitfield L. Russell, his wife Clifford, and his daughter Daisy, moved to Rhome, they moved into a house which had been built in Aurora for a Mr. Balch and later moved to the Rhome location for a former doctor, Dr. Cherry. It was from this house that Dr. Russell carried on his practice until 1920, when he built his first office.

Dr. Russell was considered one of the best-read men of his day. He kept an extensive library containing both literature and medical books. He was very proud of his library. Another interest that he pursued was his collection of birds. One wall of his office was occupied by a glass case containing many of his birds. His knowledge on this subject was exceptionally wide.

Sometime after the death of Dr. Russell, Mrs. W. L. Russell received a request from the publishers of the *Encyclopedia of American Biography* for data concerning the life and work of Dr. Russell.

Whitfield Leggett Russell and Clifford Henderson Russell had three children: Daisy Russell, who married Harold Van Meter; Nell Russell, who married Lemuel David Criswell; and Claude Hudson Russell, who married Vivian Hunter.

Dr. Whitfield L. Russell died on July 16, 1963, in a Fort Worth hospital. He is buried in the Aurora Cemetery. His widow, Clifford H. Russell, still resides in the family home at Rhome, Texas.

RUSSELL — HUNTER

Claude Hudson Russell was born February 28, 1917, in Rhome, Texas. His parents were Dr. W. L. Russell and Clifford Henderson Russell.

Claude Russell married Vivian L. Hunter Russell on October 12, 1949, in California. Vivian L. Hunter was born on February 11, 1922, in Oklahoma.

Two children had been born to this union: Gary Whitfield Russell and Rodney Karl Russell.

SCOTT — VAN METER

John Michael Scott, one of Rhome's earliest citizens, was born in Danville, Virginia, on January 8, 1867. His father was Samuel Scott, and his mother was Nancy Prunty Scott.

Mary Ann Van Meter, a daughter of Caleb Jacob Van Meter and Mary Ann Standifer Van Meter, was born in Rhome, Texas, on November 8, 1872. Her parents had lived in the area long before Rhome became a town. The family had moved here during the end of the Prairie Point years. Mary Ann Van Meter married John M. Scott on December 24, 1893.

John M. and Mary Ann Scott had six children: Paul B. Scott, who married Ruby Mae Rush in May, 1922; Ruth N. Scott, who married Ones Tomas Finlayson on September 1, 1917; Mary Naomi Scott, who married Paul E. Harding in June, 1921; Madge L. Scott, who married Tom L. Terrell in November, 1929; Blanche L. Scott, who married Herbert N. Ferguson in November, 1929; and Oswald V. Scott, who married Elizabeth Ward, in October, 1927.

John M. Scott died February 12, 1945, in Decatur, Texas. He is buried in Oaklawn Cemetery in Decatur. Mary Ann Van Meter Scott died June 24, 1970, in Decatur. She is buried beside her husband in Oaklawn Cemetery.

SIMMONS — BROWN

Martin Ezra Simmons was born January 17, 1904, in Rhome, Texas. He was the son of Ezra Simmons and Addie Griffin Simmons. He married Emma Jean Brown on October 23, 1927. Her parents were Thomas G. Brown and Ella Hand Harris Brown.

Four children were born to the Simmons family: Imagine Simmons, who married Charles Mecashug; Martin Brown Simmons, who married Joyce Aiken; Virginia Ann Simmons, who married Jack Read; and Emily Jane Simmons, who married Bobby Hubbell.

Martin and Emma Simmons live in Rhome today, where Martin deals in art supplies and picture framing. Martin and Emma have carried on an active life in the First Baptist Church, where he has served in many different capacities. Another of their interests is the Wise County Art Association, where Martin has served as treasurer for several years.

SIMMONS — GRIFFIN

Ezra Simmons, son of Martin E. and Mary Keel Simmons, was born August 26, 1883, in Centralia, Illinois. He married Addie M. Griffin, whose parents were J. M. Griffin and Jenny Byrd Griffin.

Sometime before the marriage, Ezra Simmons had moved to Rhome, Texas. All of their nine children were born in Rhome: Martin Ezra Simmons, who married Emma Jean Brown; Jennie Bell Simmons, who married Dewey Utley; Myrtle M. Simmons, who married (1) Boyce Stewart and (2) ____ Pittman; Allie Estelle Simmons, who married Richard Huse; Ettie May Simmons, who married O.B. Jeffries; Oscar John Simmons, who married Hazel Thomas; Esther Simmons, who married Everett Roper; Bonnie Jean Simmons, who married Nelson Keen; and Cecil Russell Simmons, who married Loraine Johnson.

Addie Griffin Simmons preceded her husband in death in 1941. She is buried in the Aurora Cemetery, Aurora, Texas. Ezra Simmons was married a second time to Kate Burton. He died in 1966, and he was also buried in the Aurora Cemetery.

SIMMONS — KEEL

Martin Elihu Simmons, nicknamed "Doc", was born on November 22, 1955, in Tennessee. His father was Henderson Simmons. Martin Simmons married Mary Ann Keel in May, 1856.

The family lived for a time in Centralia, Illinois, where four of their children were born. These were as follows: Alfred Simmons, who married Ruth Taylor; Nora Simmons, who married Richard Wilkerson; Ezra Simmons, who married Addie M. Griffin; and Allie Simmons, who married Curtis Wilkerson. Three more children were born after the family had moved to Era, Cook County, Texas: Oscar Simmons, who did not marry; Arthur Simmons, who married Meda Browning; and Ettie Simmons, who married W. N. George.

Mary Ann Keel Simmons preceded her husband in death in 1895.

MRS. KATE TROXELL Shaw, holding her nephew, William Morris Troxell, and sitting beside her, her son Arnold Shaw.

She is buried in the Thurmond Fairview Cemetery.

Following Mary Ann Simmon's death, Martin Elihu Simmons was married a second and a third time; first, to Jenny Bird Griffin Simmons, and later, to Hattie Hall Simmons.

Martin Elihu Simmons died on June 6, 1946, and is also buried in the Fairview Cemetery.

SHAW — TROXELL

Claude E. Shaw was born November 14, 1878, in Aurora, Texas. His parents were Drury Pressley Shaw and Susan Joanna Weems Shaw. He married Katherine D. Troxell, daughter of John Troxell and Mary Mosshart Troxell, on February 28, 1911, in Rhome, Texas. Katherine (Kate) D. Troxell was born October 12, 1887, in the Fairview Community near Rhome, Texas.

Claude Shaw worked at farming and various other jobs, including as a miller at the Rhome Milling Company. Later he served as postmaster for the Rhome postoffice from 1914 to 1921. Katherine (Kate) Shaw also served as postmaster for Rhome from 1940 until her retirement in 1957.

Kate Shaw was very active in the affairs of her beloved Missionary Baptist Church where she was a charter member. She served as Sunday school teacher for over forty years, directed the "Sunbeams" for thirty-five years, and was given the "Master Workman" diploma, awarded in 1964 from the Southern Baptist Convention.

One child was born to this union: Arnold Shaw, who married Lucile Jane Craig. Two children were born to Arnold and Jane Shaw: Sandra Sue Shaw and Sally Jane Shaw, both adored by their "Granny Kate," along with three equally adorable great-granddaughters.

Claude Shaw died on February 28, 1944, and is buried in the Aurora Cemetery. Katherine (Kate) Shaw went to live with her son in 1978 in Lufkin, Texas, where she died on September 22, 1978. She is also buried in the Aurora Cemetery.

SHAW — WEEMS

Drury Pressley Shaw was born on December 12, 1849, in Indianapolis, Indiana. By the time he was twenty-five years of age, he had migrated to Aurora, Wise County, Texas. There he met Susan Joanna Weems, whom he married on January 19, 1876, with C. C. Leonard officiating as the Justice of the Peace.

Susan Joanna Weems had been born in Little Rock, Arkansas, on March 17, 1849. Susan had at one time lived in the Rhome area with the Whit T. Fain family. The Shaw family called her "Mama-Shaw." The Whit T. Fain family lived in the first home built in the Prairie Point area, the original Crossroads Tavern building, which was probably erected by the first land owner, Samuel Sheets.

The Shaw family had six children, all of whom were born in Aurora, Texas. They were as follows: Jessie Lea Shaw, who married John Dalton; Claude Erwin Shaw, who married Katherine Troxell; Belle Shaw, who married McAfee Burch; Frank Shaw, who died as an infant; Susie Shaw, who never married; and Stella Shaw, who married A. B. Van Meter.

SLAY — BENNETT

Carl Weir Slay was born on September 15, 1899, in Frost, Texas. His parents were John Robert Slay and Linnie Mae Weir Slay. Carl Weir Slay married Ruth Irene Bennett on June 16, 1920, in Fort Worth, Texas. Ruth Irene Bennett's parents were Arthur Clifford Bennett and Delia Gertrude Whittington Bennett.

Two children were born to this union: Mary Lou Slay, who married John Thomas Livengood, Jr.; and Carl Weir Slay, Jr., who died as a child.

Carl and Ruth Slay moved to a farm five miles south of Rhome, Texas, in November of 1921, where they built their home, and they have lived there ever since. Mr. and Mrs. Slay are members of the Church of Christ in Rhome, Texas, where he serves as an elder. Mr. Slay has been a farmer and rancher since the move to Rhome. Mrs. Slay was a charter member of the Thursday Study Club of Rhome and remained an active member until it disbanded in 1956.

SLIMP — LLOYD

Landon C. Slimp, a well-known figure in Aurora's past history, was born February 18, 1829, in Butler, Tennessee. His parents were also born in Tennessee. He married Nancy Lloyd on October 25, 1855, in Butler, Tennessee. Nancy Lloyd was also born in Tennessee on August 1, 1836.

All of his six children were born in Aurora, Texas: John L. Slimp; Mary Ann Josephine Slimp, who married Dorme Beauchamp; Emmy Jane Slimp; Lafayette Slimp; William Slimp; and Minnie Slimp.

Landon C. Slimp died on June 20, 1912, in Aurora, Texas. His wife, Nancy Lloyd Slimp, preceded him in death on September 25, 1876. They are both buried in the Slimp Cemetery, which is located just northwest of the center of the old town of Aurora.

SMITH

Emma Smith was born in Rhome, Texas, the child of former slaves, who came to Texas with the Colonel Benjamin Morris family. Her grandmother and mother worked for Colonel Morris and his family. Her grandmother was named Susan, and her mother was Sallie. Emma was probably the only Negro child ever born in the town of Rhome. Her own story follows:

I was born in Rhome in your great grandfather's yard in a log house, one room and sat right where your Aunt Mag lived in her last days. My Grandma was named Susan. Everybody called her "Aunt Susan." My Mother's name was Sallie. Grandma came to Rhome to cook for Colonel Morris, and my mama was the maid. No Negroes ever did live in that town you call Rhome. We were the only ones that ever did live in Rhome, and my playmates were all white. Grandma's Baby son found out where we was and that was when he moved us to Fort Worth so that I could get to go to school. Yes, your grandfather, W. W. Morris, had a lumber yard, the only place for miles where you could buy lumber. Bennie, Sallie, and Sister was the ones I played with, and Roxana. I was at your grandma Lou Morris's house every day.

There was only one hotel for drummers to come stay to sell and take orders for the Stores and that was the Hambright Hotel until later Mrs. Davis, your great grandma came and built her a hotel. Only one drug store in Rhome. Mr. Zack Bobo. Two groceries. Mr. Perkins. His wife was the dressmaker. One Baptist Church, one school right where Uncle Pugh Morris lived before he died . . . Oh, I loved Rhome. After I moved here, I went back to see the folks I knew. We kids got run out of Pa's grainery where he kept his wheat.

My Grandma Susan's Son taken me up to your Grandpa W. W. Morris and ask him for some help for me, and he said he would build me a house, and Mrs. Bettie Bobo said she would give me the lot, but there was nothing I could do to make a living in Rhome. So that is why I am here.

Oh, yes, they was a family living east of Rhome about ½ mile, maybe not that far, however, that made syrup out of sugar cane, and I would go there to play with their kids. They would give me a jug of syrup to help ride on the horses and make them walk around and round to grind the cane. Don't guess you ever seen that. Their name was Fultons. Wasn't too many people in Rhome. Oh, yes, I knew the Logans that had dry goods.

I remember I went back to Rhome when I was about eight years old. I told my grandma I wanted to go to Rhome, and she let me go. So I stayed a week with Mag. One day I told Mag I wanted to come home. So she said tell Pa when he comes to dinner to give you some money and you can catch the evening train. Only two trains a day. So I asked him for the money. He said, "Oh, shucks, you ain't worth a chaw of tobacco." I said, "Yes I am." So he gave me the money to come home and Mag combed my hair in two long plaits, and I said, "Mag, I want some ribbon on my hair." She said, "Emma, I don't have no ribbon. Here, take this note down to Logan's store and get you some." So I did and got about five different kinds of ribbon. I told the lady, "Give me some of this kind and some of that kind" until I had a bunch of ribbon to wear home. Mag just laughed at me. She didn't care . . .

I hope you can find something out of this to help you with your book. I don't see too good. Only got to the 4th grade. My mother died when I was nine years old. I had to go to work helping a lady with her little baby for 50 cents a week . . .

In later years after Emma moved to Fort Worth, she worked for the Frank Korth family as a nursemaid for their children.

I lived with them 40 years, not in the back yard, but right in the house. My room was next to the baby's room. The only thing I did was nurse the three children. They had a cook, wash woman, and maid, so I just reared the children. I went to Washington and stayed one year while Mr. Korth was Secretary of the Army under Frank Pace; then we come home because the Republicans won and he was a Democrat. Then he went back when President Kennedy got in. Then Mr. Conley got Mr. Korth to come take his job as Secretary of the Navy so that he could come to Texas and be Governor of Texas . . .

This information has been taken from personal letters from Emma Smith to the writer.

SMITHERMAN — ROBERTS — HUTCHESON

Edward LeRoy Smitherman was born in Florence, Alabama. He came to Rhome, Texas, when a young man in his early twenties and worked on a farm for a few years. He was employed by the W. W. Morris Grocery where he worked several years before opening his own grocery business, which he operated about twenty years. He retired about two years before his death.

Mr. Smitherman was first married to Miss Mattie Roberts of Rhome in 1905. Two children were born to this union: one son, LeRoy Smitherman; and one daughter, Lorene Smith, who married Manson Bost. Mrs. Mattie Roberts Smitherman died in 1918.

In April, 1921, Mr. Smitherman was married to Mrs. Frankie Hutcheson of Fort Worth. No children were born to this union.

Mr. Smitherman became a member of the Methodist Church in Alabama before coming to Texas. He united with the Rhome

E. L. SMITHERMAN, Rhome grocer.

Methodist Church, where he held membership at the time of his death. He served the church as church clerk for many years; also he was a member of the Board of Stewards for several years. He was always actively interested in all church, school, and civic work in his town and community. He also owned and managed a grocery store next door to the Rhome National Bank for many years.

SPARKS

Charles Sparks was born in Alabama and came to Texas in 1895. He was converted at the age of seventeen and was baptized into the Baptist Church of Rhome by Dr. J. B. Tidwell about 1901. He remained a member of the church until his death. He was a gospel singer for thirty years. His father and mother were Mr. and Mrs. A. J. Sparks. Charles Sparks had six brothers: Will, Jake, John, Jim, Burge, and Tom. He also had two sisters: Omadell and Mrs. Simpler.

Mr. Sparks was active in his religious work until his death. On many occasions he conducted choirs for churches all over the state. He was known everywhere as a great choir director and singer. His services were greatly missed after his death.

Charles Sparks died in San Angelo, Texas, on May 30, 1936. He is buried in the Deep Creek Cemetery, north of Aurora.

SULLIVAN — GLENN

George Sullivan and Sally Glenn Sullivan first lived in Bosque County, Texas. From there they moved to the Illinois Lane community at Fairview. Later Mr. Sullivan farmed about five miles out of Rhome, near the Day place. When it was necessary to send their children to school, they moved to town and occupied the house which had been built by the John Scott family. The Sullivan children were Mattie Sullivan, Alice Sullivan, Kate Sullivan, Ada Sullivan, and Ed Sullivan.

TAYLOR — VAN METER

William A. L. Taylor was born November 2, 1859, in Indiana. His parents were Henry J. Taylor and Mary Elizabeth Nelson Taylor. He married Isabelle Jane Van Meter, born December 31, 1863. She was the daughter of Caleb Jackson Van Meter and Mary Ann Standefer Van Meter.

There were ten children born to this union: Mary Elizabeth Taylor, who married Fred C. Brouer; Ruth Gertrude Taylor, who married A. A. Simmons; William Arthur Taylor, who died as an infant; Lorena Ellen Taylor, who married E. G. Bryan; Muade Christine Taylor, who married Andrew J. Taylor; Joseph Raymond Taylor, who married (1) Mary Shankle and (2) Belva Bridges; Edith Vera Taylor, who married Jessie L. Sparks; Kate Lillian Taylor, who married Ellis Clyde Troxell; and Isabelle J. Taylor, who did not marry.

W. A. Taylor came to Wise County from Indiana in a covered wagon pulled by six oxen. The wagon was filled with everything they could get on it. W. A. and his father, Uncle Henry Taylor, better known to all as "Granddad Taylor," ran a wagon express from Fort Worth to West Texas. Sometimes the roads would be very muddy. Mr. Taylor told about one man who ran a wagon express. they met on the road and the man with the empty wagon did not want to give any of the road. Mr. Taylor was loaded with supplies. He said that he stopped and got out his lunch basket and let the oxen rest until he decided to go around and give the man the road to go on his journey.

Mrs. Taylor came to Texas in a wagon train. There were several families who came together. She told about crossing the Mississippi

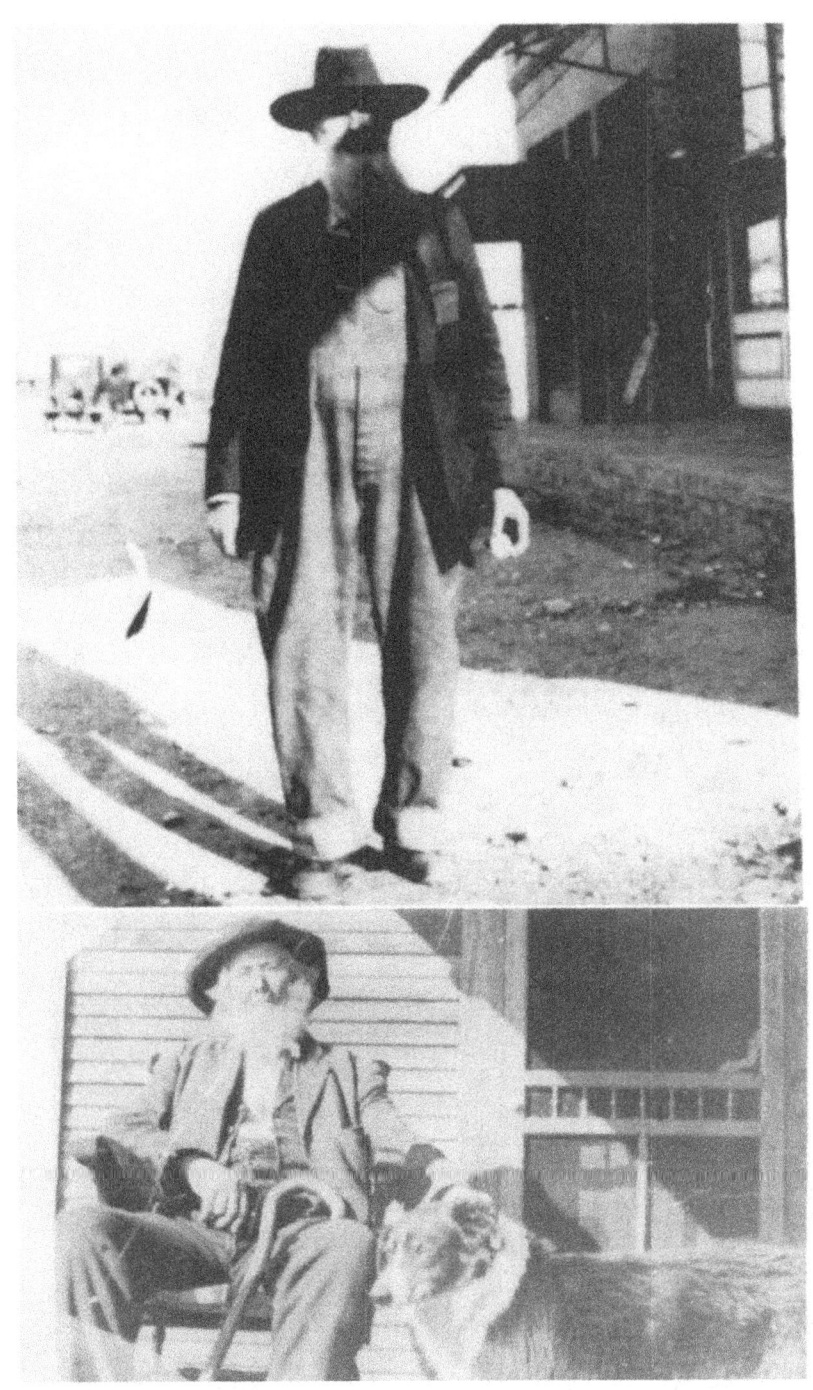

HENRY TAYLOR, RHOME pioneer.

MEN'S SUNDAY SCHOOL Class of the Missionary Baptist Church.

river and the water came up to the wagon beds. She told about her grandmother, who fell and broke her back. The family was delayed over a month for her to recover so that she could ride in the wagon. Grandpa Van Meter brought all his money with them on the wagons. One wagon was loaded with corn, and Mr. Van Meter buried the money in the corn in order to protect it.

They settled on some land which is now owned by Harold Van Meter. That land was originally bought for one dollar per acre.

THORELL — BRAMMER

O. Z. Thorell was born in Rhome, Texas on November 14, 1891. His parents were Augustus Thorell and Emma Mary Mansfield Thorell. He married Dollie S. Brammer on May 27, 1917. Dollie Brammer was born in Patrick County, Virginia, on April 10, 1898. Her parents were Samuel Jefferson Brammer and Elzora Brammer.

Four children were born to this union: Juanell Thorell, Carl Thorell, Geneva Thorell, and Maxine Thorell.

O. Z. Thorell died June 7, 1941, and is buried in the Aurora Cemetery. His widow, Dollie Brammer Thorell, resides with her daughter, Juanell Thorell, in the family home just east of Rhome.

THORELL — MANSFIELD

Augustus Thorell was born on May 29, 1840, in Sweden. He came to America approximately the year 1858. Upon arriving in the United States, he had a difficult time communicating with people—he could not speak English. However, he was able to communicate well enough with one young lady, Emma Mary Mansfield, whom he married on February 12, 1891. She was born June 8, 1868, in Kentucky. Augustus Thorell lived in Rhome until his death on November 25, 1927. His widow, Mary Emma, lived until November 15, 1939. They are both buried in the Aurora Cemetery.

One child, O. Z. Thorell, was born to this union on November 14, 1891. He married Dollie S. Brammer.

THURMOND — MERRYFIELD

John Favor Thurmond was born in Georgia on October 14, 1853, and later moved to Alabama with his parents, who were William Thomas Thurmond and Elizabeth Amanda Morton Thurmond. When John was fifteen, he came with his parents to Dallas County, Texas. He was married in 1875 to Amanda Elizabeth Merryfield.

John F. Thurmond moved to Wise County, Texas, in 1875, with his wife and his first born child, Catherine Greenwood Thurmond, who married James F. Rowan. He had previously buried his second born child, William Thomas Thurmond, in Dallas County, Texas. Ten more children were born to this union. Six of their twelve children died in infancy. Five of these children, Jennie Lee Thurmond, Millard H. Thurmond, an infant daughter, Joel Morton Thurmond, and Marcus Wise Thurmond are buried in the Thurmond-Fairview Cemetery. The other five children were as follows: Martha Elizabeth Thurmond, who married Robert J. Brown; Mary Alice Thurmond, who never married; James Forrest Thurmond, who married (1) Ruth Morgan and (2) A. Atchison; Forrest Thurmond; Milam Frank Thurmond, who married Margaret Ann Vance; and Joe Thurmond, who married Ina Yant. Joe and Ina Thurmond lived until 1978 on the Thurmond homestead in Fairview, when they moved to Saginaw, Texas. Joe is the only child still living in the large family.

John F. Thurmond was very active in the civic life of Fairview and Rhome. Although he was not a Baptist, he was very much interested in the Fairview Baptist Church and helped to support it.

John F. Thurmond was a benevolent benefactor to many people. Many knew nothing about this. He supported many widows and their families. He was also a large contributor to Radio Church Ministries. He donated land for the Fairview Cemetery, Fairview Baptist Church, and the Fairview public school.

John F. Thurmond's name occurs often in the history of Rhome simply because he took such a great interest in the welfare of the town and its people.

Mrs. J. F. Thurmond was a charter member of the Fairview Baptist church, which was organized in 1895.

MR. AND MRS. John Thurmond.

THURMOND — MORGAN

James Forrest Thurmond, son of John Favor and Amanda Elizabeth Thurmond, was born in Rhome on August 5, 1890. He married Ruth Morgan on September 20, 1911. The children born to this marriage were as follows: Lois Merle Thurmond, John Morgan Thurmond, and James Forrest Thurmond, Jr. James Forrest Thurmond died in January, 1954, in Fort Worth, Texas. He is buried in the Thurmond-Fairview Cemetery. Ruth Morgan Thurmond died March

2, 1920. She is also buried in the Thurmond-Fairview Cemetery.

Lois Merle Thurmond married Elbert H. Martin on November 26, 1936. John Morgan Thurmond was married to Ovay Louise Winfrey on June 29, 1951. James Forrest Thurmond, Jr., married Joyce Beyer on June 28, 1947.

THURMOND — VANCE

Milam Frank Thurmond was born on June 10, 1894, in Rhome, Texas. He married Margaret Ann Vance on October 28, 1915. Margaret Vance was born April 21, 1894. Three children were born to this union: Ruth Arnette Thurmond, Robert Vance Thurmond, and Milam Frank Thurmond, Jr.

Milam Frank Thurmond, Sr., died in Austin, Texas, on December 7, 1950. He is buried in Memorial Garden in Austin, Texas. Margaret, whose father was Charles Vance, was also born in Wise County.

Ruth Arnette Thurmond was married to Harold E. Nicholson, Jr., on October 23, 1948. Robert Vance Thurmond married Nina Rawles on December 15, 1944. Milam Frank Thurmond, Jr., married Bettie Bledso on June 5, 1951.

THURMOND — YANT

Joe Thurmond was born October 10, 1899, in Wise County, Texas. He is the son of John Favor Thurmond and Amanda Thurmond. He married Ina Yant, whose parents were W. H. Yant and Ettie Lou Estep Yant.

Joe and Ina Thurmond lived for many years on the old Thurmond homestead in Fairview. Today they live in Saginaw, Texas.

The children of Joe and Ina Thurmond are as follows: Betty Joe Thurmond, who married (1) A. R. Nichols and (2) Jack W. Roach; and Patsy Ann Thurmond, who married Archie Winston Van Meter.

TROXELL — GARDNER — PITTMAN

Joseph Albert Troxell was born in Ragersville, Ohio, on February 16, 1867. His parents were John Troxell and Mary Mosshart Troxell. He married Lena Gardner on August 17, 1897, at the Fairview Church. Lena Gardner's parents were Thomas S. Gardner and Sarah F. Brown Gardner. Lena Gardner was born April 1, 1878.

Joseph Albert Troxell went to Amarillo in 1887, before it was a town. He didn't go to Amarillo among the first settlers—he was there waiting for them in a half-dugout, near "Wild Horse" lake. He filed on several sections of land which is now a thickly populated area in Amarillo. When there was an Indian scare, for protection he would go to Canyon, which at that time was a Fort.

Somewhere along the line, while in Rhome, where his parents resided, he met and fell in love with Lena Gardner. One day, while living in his dugout in Amarillo, he decided that he had to see Lena; so he traded his claim for a pair of pants and a pair of boots, and went back to Rhome to marry Lena Gardner.

Two children were born while they were living in Rhome: Trula Troxell, who married Keith Taylor; and Sara Elizabeth Troxell, who married W. A. "Tex" Thornton.

Joe Troxell then moved his little family back to Amarillo where two more children were born: Mary Jo Troxell, who married Lee R. Stroud; and Lena Troxell, who married John Slater.

Joe Troxell's wife Lena died when the baby Lena was two weeks old. After her death the children lived with their grandmother Troxell in Rhome, and with other relatives until Joe Troxell married a second time to Ruth Pittman. She mothered the little girls, with the exception of Mary Jo who remained with her grandmother, Mary Mosshart Troxell, until Mary Jo married and moved away from Rhome.

Joseph Albert Troxell died on January 27, 1942, in Amarillo, Texas.

TROXELL — MORRIS

James Robert Troxell was born November 1, 1881, in Rhome, Texas. His parents were John Troxell and Mary Mosshart Troxell. He married Serena "Rena" Frances Morris, daughter of William Wade Morris and Lula Cate Morris, on July 3, 1910. Rena Morris was born August 24, 1888.

James "Jim" Robert Troxell grew up on the Troxell farm in the Fairview Community. As the youngest son, he naturally spent much time helping both his father and his mother. He attended Tyler Commercial College in Tyler, Texas. After his father died, he took over his mother's business affairs, for which he kept a very strict and accurate account. He also served as bookkeeper for the Morris Mercantile Company, until his appointment as rural mail carrier on Route One, Rhome, Texas, in 1913. He remained on this route until he was transferred to Decatur, Texas, in 1934. There he served as a rural mail carrier until his retirement in the late 1950's. In 1959 the family decided to move back to the Rhome community, where they built a new

JAMES ROBERT TROXELL

RENA MORRIS TROXELL

home on the family farm southeast of Rhome, Texas.

Rena Morris Troxell graduated from high school in Rhome. She studied music in Dallas, while living with the Carl Buerbaum family, her uncle and aunt. Both before and after she married, she taught music to many students in Rhome.

Two children were born to this union: William Morris Troxell, who was an invalid most of his life; and Catherine Alice Troxell, who married (1) Jack Hastings and (2) Gerando David Gonzalez, from whom she was divorced in 1973. The Troxells had one grandson, James David Hastings, whom they both adored and petted as long as they lived.

The Troxells remained in the home on the farm as long as their health permitted with Jim gardening and playing his favorite games, checkers and dominoes, in the little domino hall which he had helped to build and maintain in Rhome. James Robert Troxell died in Decatur, Texas, on August 11, 1966.

Rena Morris Troxell lived on in the family home until ill health forced her to move with her invalid son, Morris Troxell, to the Fireside Lodge in Fort Worth, Texas, where Morris died on September 25, 1972. Rena Morris Troxell died on December 26, 1973, in Fort Worth, Texas. They are buried in the Aurora Cemetery.

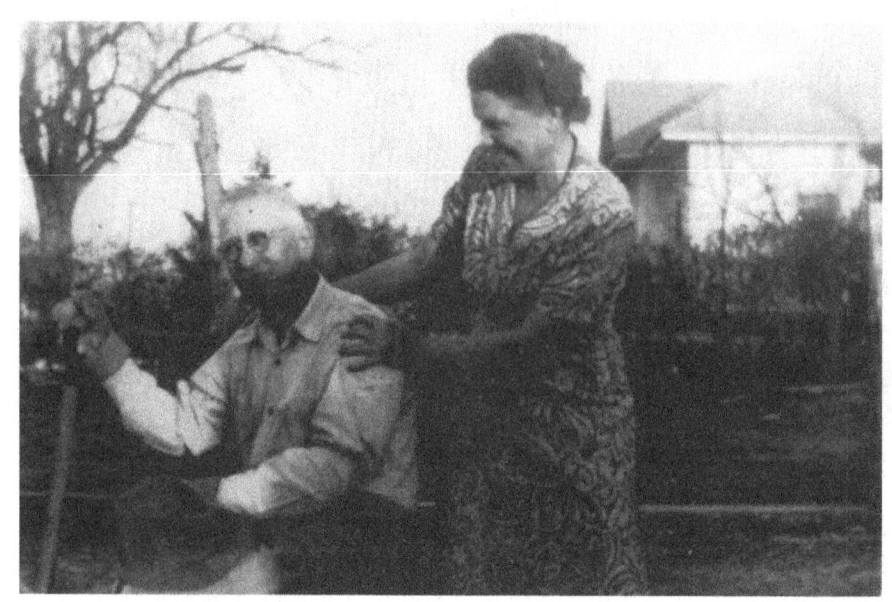

JIM AND RENA Troxell.

JIM TROXELL AND his grandson, James David Hastings.

TROXELL — MOSSHART

Johannes (John) Troxell was born on November 1, 1834, near Frutigen, Switzerland. His parents were Johannes Trachsel and Susanna Zurbrugg. The family with John, two sisters, Margrith and Katherina, and one brother, Jacob, came to the United States in 1842 or 1843, settling in Auburn Township, Tuscasawas County, Ohio. The family name was changed by John and Jacob from Trachsel to Troxell; however, the exact date of the name change is not known.

John Troxell married Mary Mosshart on November 22, 1863, in Ragersville, Ohio. Her parents, Christian Mosshart and Magdalene Chappler Mosshart, had come from the same area near Thun, Switzerland. Mary Mosshart was born April 27, 1844, in Ragersville, Ohio.

Thirteen children were born to this union: Mary Ellen Troxell, who married Marshall Gregg; Jacob Henry Troxell, who married Serena Jane Mount; Joseph Albert Troxell, who married Lena Gardner; Elizabeth Ann Troxell, who married Reese L. Mobley; George William Troxell, who married Charlie Jones; Margaret Emma Troxell, who married L. Boyd Barker; John Elmer Troxell, who died as an infant; Ida Mae Troxell, who married Samuel Wilson; Minnie Dora Troxell, who married Clifford C. Layfield; Clara Alice Troxell, who married Hugh Banks Barker; James Robert Troxell, who married Rena Frances Morris; Grover Cleveland Troxell, who was killed in a fall from a horse during his fourteenth year; Katharine D. Troxell, who married Claude E. Shaw.

The first four children of this family were born in Ragersville, Ohio. The next four children were born while the family lived in Hiawatha, Kansas. The last five children were born in the Fairview community, Wise County, Texas. It was from Hiawatha, Kansas, that the John Troxell family traveled with another family, the John Robert Greggs, to Texas. They moved by wagon train through the wilds of Indian territory to the prairie grass lands of southeastern Wise County. They were heading for West Texas, but they stopped at Deep Creek to camp for the night. Upon learning of their destination, Uncle Sam Woody urged them to delay their trip just one day so that he could show them prairie country to the east. When they viewed what is now the Fairview community, they were so very much impressed that they decided to stay in the area. They settled down near the other settlers who had named the area "Illinois Lane" because of the large number who had come there from Illinois. The Troxells were a busy, relatively happy household with all the children learning how to work and being expected to do their share of the work. As the family increased in size,

MARY MOSSHART TROXELL

JOHN TROXELL

the older girls took over much of the care of the house and the smaller children.

A huge Christmas tree was put up each year and had to be hauled in from "cedar country," probably from Deep Creek. Christmas was an event to look forward to each year. Weddings were the social event of the year, and since six daughters were married at the farm home, the parlor became known as "The Wedding Room." Along with the bridegroom's dinners given for the sons, the Troxells contributed their share to the community social life.

After the youngest son, Jim, left the farm and went into business for himself, his father, being in poor health, sold the farm as he could not run it alone. He bought a comfortable home in Rhome where they moved with the youngest child Katherine, and where John Troxell died on October 30, 1908. This home was the house which Joshua Mount had built when he first came to Rhome. It is still standing today, although unoccupied. It has been variously known as the Mount house, the Troxell house, and today the Logan house.

"GRANDMA" MARY TROXELL, Rhome pioneer, on the porch of her home.

Mary Jo Troxell, a daughter of Joe Troxell, made her home with her grandmothr during her school years, and always during these last years, their mother had the watchful care of Jim and Rena Troxell, who lived next door, and Kate and Claude Shaw, a few houses away. When she was unable to stay alone, Mary Mosshart Troxell sorrowfully bade her home goodbye, and without complaint, she went to make her home with her eldest child, Ellen Gregg, in Decatur, Texas. Ellen's husband, Marshall Gregg, died on April 30, 1925, followed a month later by the death of Mary Mosshart Troxell on May 23, 1925. Grandsons were pall bearers for the well-loved grandmother, who was laid to rest in Fairview Cemetery beside her husband, John Troxell.

TROXELL — MOUNT

Jacob Henry Troxell, son of John and Mary Mosshart Troxell, was born in Ragersville, Ohio, on July 29, 1865. He married Serena Jane Mount, daughter of Joshua Houston Mount and Kizzie Frances Ward Mount. She was born on August 18, 1868, in Foxville, Illinois. Jacob Henry Troxell and Serena Jane Mount were married on January 27, 1889, in the Joshua Mount home in Rhome, Texas.

Jacob Henry Troxell, as the oldest son in the Troxell family, was heir to the family heirloom, the Powder Horn dated 1692 and initialed

JACOB HENRY TROXELL and his wife, Serena Mount Troxell.

A. T. It goes in turn to the older son of the oldest son, thence down the line. Today it is in the possession of E. C. Troxell, Jr., son of Ellis Clyde Troxell.

Jacob Henry Troxell was a farmer who loved the land and tilled it with care, teaching his sons to do the same. They lived on the old home place near the John Troxell farm home in the Fairview community.

Nine children were born to this marriage: Ellis Clyde Troxell, who married Katherine Lillian Taylor; Nell Mount Troxell, who married James Drummond Burch; Clarence William Troxell, who married Mary Roe Morris; Paul Kruger Troxell, who married Daisy Wilson; Charles Cecil Troxell, who married Beatrice Beasley; Gladys Serena Troxell, who married Homer L. Merritt; Jacob Henry (Bill) Troxell, Jr., who married Virginia Ferguson; Houston Wayne Troxell, who died as a child; and one infant, born and died on March 31, 1907.

The daughter of Henry Troxell, Gladys Troxell Merritt, gives this resume of her father's life:

> This sandy-haired man named Troxell, the oldest son of John and Mary, was a kind, humanitarian man. Even though the Lord saw fit to take away Serena, the mother of his seven living children, he was always a considerate and faithful husband, mak-

ing every effort in her behalf. During her extended illness, he never complained even though he was at times maintaining two households. Bill, aged three, and Gladys, just older, were privileged to get to stay with Serena when she had to go to warmer climates, but how they looked forward to the periodic visits of their father, who always managed to make them feel that he could hardly wait to get there.

Serena's brother, Seymour Mount, and Henry were closer than most brothers. They had many hilarious experiences when they traveled by wagon, selling lightning rods. This closeness lasted throughout their life time; and many years later, they recalled those days when they met. After Henry and Serena married, Seymour continued to spend much time at their house . . .

As the years went by, Henry became concerned that the Negro children of the community had no place to go to school. Consequently, he fixed up a one-room house on the farm, added homemade benches, and found a Negro teacher. At all the programs that these children had, it was his pleasure that they moved over so that the "Mr. Troxell" could sit and listen. He was very proud of them.

James Drummond Burch, son of Nell and Drummond Burch, and oldest grandson of Henry Troxell, remembers his grandfather in this way:

He made an impression on the people of the community for he was one of the most successful farmers in that community and was a man held in high esteem and whose opinion was sought after for he was an authority on growing wheat and other crops. But to stop there would sell him short, for he was a fine craftsman and very versatile. He built his own house and barns, had a fireplace that lasted half a century; he had a blacksmith ship well-equipped, and he did his own work; he was a good welder and knew how to drill water wells . . .

He showed his German Swiss background in his food, liking cheese, buying salt mackerel by the keg, etc.; his speech had an accent only when he was agitated, and the youngest son, Bill, would purposely get him aggravated just to catch the accent.

Serena Jane Mount, who was ill for a great part of her life, died on October 14, 1916, in Rhome, Texas. She was buried in the Thurmond-Fairview Cemetery. Jacob Henry Troxell died on June 16, 1930, in Rhome, Texas. He is also buried in the Fairview Cemetery beside his beloved Serena Troxell.

TROXELL — TAYLOR

Ellis Clyde Troxell, son of Jacob Henry Troxell and Serena Mount Troxell, was born November 10, 1889, in Rhome, Texas. He was married on August 27, 1916, to Katherine Lillian Taylor, the daughter of William L. Taylor and Isabelle Jane Van Meter Taylor. Katherine Lillian Taylor was born in Rhome, Texas, on October 11, 1897.

Four children were born to this union: Nelma Eloise Troxell, who married Jerome Chester Wylie; Vivian Juanita Troxell, who married William Emmett Middleton; Ellis Clyde Troxell, Jr., who married Mary Ruth Henderson; and William Henry Troxell.

In 1916, E. C. Troxell, Sr., owned and operated a garage and worked on automobiles. He moved to Fort Worth in 1917, where he worked for a Cadillac dealership as head mechanic and supervisor. He invented the main oil ring which is used in cars today. In 1918, he moved back to Rhome when his daughter Nelma was only six weeks old.

He was the first person to own and operate a silent motion picture show in Rhome, where he also owned the first player piano. He invented a steam engine which turned the popcorn machine. The picture show was later sold to his uncle, Mr. Jim Troxell. After the picture show was closed, Jim Troxell sold the player piano to Mrs. O. Z. Thorell, who still owns the piano.

In 1919 Ellis Troxell owned the first tin shop and a stone feed mill. He ground flour, meal, graham flour, grits, and a small amount of cow and hog feed. In 1921 he made the first wireless radio in the county and sold the more expensive sets for $125.00 each. Some eighty-three persons purchased these radio sets.

By 1922 Ellis Troxell owned and operated the first International Farm Implement company in Wise County. He sold tractors, plows, threshers, etc. Also, he farmed and used this product to demonstrate the superiority of the machine over the horse. During this period, he invented the first cotton and pecan picker. This machine would also suck boll weevils off the cotton plants.

In 1938, he worked as wiring inspector for the R.E.A., inspecting all the farm houses when electricity was installed in the rural houses. In 1945, he worked for the federal government, teaching vocational welding, mechanics, and wood work to the farmers in the area. The farmers would pay a small amount for each hour they would be on the job training to learn this trade. The work was done in cooperation with the Rhome High School. The program was disbanded in 1949, when the high school was consolidated with three other schools into Northwest High School.

In 1949, he owned and operated his own Farm Repair Shop. He invented the first cotton and maize stalk knocker and made nearly two hundred before a salesman for a reliable firm visited him and saw the invention. The following year it was patented by a reliable farm implement company. Of all the things he invented, Ellis Troxell received only $300.00 and the patent lawyers got the patent and the money. Ellis Troxell operated his farm repair shop until his death on August 11, 1967. He is buried in the Aurora Cemetery. His widow, Kate Troxell, lives in the family home with her son William Troxell.

TULLY (TULLEY)

Marshall D. Tulley, who was listed as a butcher in the 1860 United States Census for the Prairie Point precinct, was one of the very first citizens of the little town. He was born on January 16, 1832. On March 11, 1860, he married Mary Matilda ____. Four children were born to this union: Amanda S. Tulley, Marshalle Dee Tulley, Mark Arthur Tulley, and Mary Elizabeth Tulley.

Marshall D. Tulley died August 24, 1871. His widow, Mary Matilda Tulley, then married a Mr. Rankin. From this union were born two children: Louis R. Rankin and Millie Stacy Rankin.

VACKER — STIPA

Martin Luther Vacker was born November 7, 1854, in Czechoslovakia. He was married to Mary Stipa. They lived on a farm near Gonzales, Texas, when she died in 1897.

Mary Stipa Vacker had asthma and was not well many days of her life. Their daughter Laura was only thirteen when her mother passed away. Annie Vacker Urban, another daughter, was ill like her mother.

Sometime before 1919 Martin Vacker moved to Rhome, Texas, to live with Mary and John Petras on a farm northeast of Rhome. He did shoe repair work. Later he owned a shoe repair shop in Rhome. Martin Luther Vacker died April 3, 1936, in the home of his daughter, Mrs. Charles Mondrick of Rhome.

Mary Stipe Vacker and Martin Luther Vacker had a family of seven: Katie Vacker, who married Tom Hobizal; Mary Vacker, who married John Petras; Laura Vacker, who married Charlie H. Mondrick; Annie Vacker, who married John Urban; Carrie Vacker, who married G. W. Sledge; Charles Henry Vacker, who married Frances Catherine Dorinack; and Lottie Vacker, who married Bessie Kosarek. Several of the descendants of Martin Luther Vacker have lived in Rhome at different times, including the Petras, Mondrick, and Sledge families.

VAN METER — BRYAN

Abishi Archibald Van Meter was the eldest son of Caleb Jackson Van Meter and Mary Ann Stendefer Van Meter. He was born February 6, 1860, in Douglas County, Illinois. He came with his parents to Texas when he was twelve years of age.

He married Mary Ellen Bryan on September 24, 1879, in Fairview. Mary Ellen Bryan's parents were Mr. and Mrs. R. K. Bryan. She was born in September, 1862, in Hillsboro, Illinois. The Bryan family moved to the Illinois Lane settlement of Fairview.

Six children were born to this union: Archibald B. Van Meter, who married (1) Stella B. Shaw and (2) Allie B. Chambers; Mamie Estelle Van Meter, who married (1) James B. Gill and (2) Charley W. Buckner; Jennie Belle Van Meter, who married James Preston Bowlin; Caleb Earl Van Meter, who married Roxana Morris; Mary Mellisa Van Meter, who married Robert L. Fergason; and Ruth Bryan Van Meter.

Abishi Archibald Van Meter died on March 26, 1915, in Rhome, Texas. His widow, Mary Ellen Bryan, died on May 29, 1925, in Rhome. They are both buried in the Fairview Cemetery.

VAN METER — MORRIS

Caleb Earl Van Meter was born November 24, 1889, at Rhome, Texas. His parents were Abishia Archibald Van Meter and Mary Ellen Bryan Van Meter. He married Roxana Morris on September 29, 1912, in Fort Worth, Texas.

Roxana Morris Van Meter's parents were William Wade Morris and Anna Louise Cate Morris. Roxana Morris was born October 15, 1890, at Rhome, Texas.

Caleb Earl Van Meter lived for the first part of their marriage on the old C. J. Van Meter home place east of Rhome. Their three children were born there: Marjorie Earl Van Meter, who married Harold Hardy; Mary Frances Van Meter, who married T. J. Taylor; and Caleb Earl Van Meter, Jr., who married Doris Brownlow.

Caleb Earl Van Meter and his family moved to West Texas in 1925, where most of the children and grand children still reside. There they farmed a section of land which is still owned by members of the family.

Caleb Earl Van Meter died on June 7, 1947, at Lubbock, Texas. Roxana Morris Van Meter died in Crosbyton, Texas, on November 18, 1975. They are both buried in the Crosbyton Cemetery.

VAN METER — RUSSELL

Harold Belmont Van Meter was born December 16, 1906, in Rhome, Texas. His parents were Archibald Belmont Van Meter and Stella B. Shaw Van Meter. Harold Van Meter married Daisy Russell on July 18, 1930. Daisy Russell was born October 15, 1909, in Cason, Morris County, Texas. Her parents were Dr. Whitfield Legget Russell and Clifford Henderson Russell.

One child was born to this union: Harold Michael Van Meter, who married Rose Bentley on August 8, 1964, in Rhome, Texas.

Today Harold and Daisy Van Meter live on the old Caleb Jackson Van Meter home place, which has been owned by the Van Meter family since 1872. Much of the original land purchsed still belongs to members of the Van Meter family.

VAN METER — SHAW — CHAMBERS

Archibald Belmont Van Meter was born January 29, 1882, in the log house east of Rhome. His parents were Abishi Archibald Van Meter and Mary Ellen Bryan Van Meter. On June 11, 1903, he married Stella B. Shaw, whose parents were Drury Pressley Shaw and Susan Joanna Weems Shaw, in Rhome, Texas. Stella Shaw was born in Aurora, Texas, on February 23, 1887.

To this union were born four children: Merle Van Meter, who married Wayne Renshaw; Harold Van Meter, who married Daisy Van Meter; Sue Ella Renshaw, who married (1) Earl Richardson and (2) Maurice Johannes; Maurine Van Meter, who married Cleo Rann.

Stella B. Shaw died June 5, 1915. She was buried in the Thurmond-Fairview Cemetery.

Archibald B. Van Meter was married a second time to Alice Beatrice Chambers on May 22, 1918. Alice Beatrice (Allie B.) Chambers was born April 20, 1891, in Allen, Collin County, Texas. From this marriage was born one son: Archie Winston Van Meter, who married Patsy Ann Thurmond.

Archibald B. Van Meter, who was active in farming and ranching circles, retired in 1961. He held interests in Wichita, Archer, Young, and Wise Counties.

Archibald B. Van Meter died on September 6, 1973, in Decatur, Texas. He is buried in the Thurmond-Fairview Cemetery.

MR. AND MRS. Caleb Jackson Van Meter.

VAN METER — STANDEFER

Caleb Jackson Van Meter was born in 1837, in Coles County, Illinois. His parents were Jacob Van Meter and Sarah Taylor Ven Meter. On February 18, 1868, C. J. Van Meter married Mary Ann Standefer in Coles County, Illinois.

Mary Ann Standefer was born on April 21, 1841, in Moultree County, Illinois. In 1871 the family moved to Texas. The first year was spent in Johnson County, near Alvarado. The following year 1872 the Van Meter family moved to Wise County.

The earliest deed, bearing the signature of C. J. Van Meter and recorded in the Wise County Clerk's office, is dated August 10, 1872. This deed shows the purchase of four hundred seventy-five acres located east of Rhome on Elizabeth Creek, a branch of the Denton fork of the Trinity River.

There were two houses already built on the newly purchased land. C. J. Van Meter chose to live in a one-room log house which stood near the present day home of Harold Van Meter. About one half of the room was ceiled to make an attic which served as sleeping quarters for the children.

When it became evident that this house was too far from the water needed from Elizabeth Creek, he moved his family into the other house to which rooms were added to accommodate the growing family.

Four children were born to this union before the family moved to Texas: Abishi Archibald Van Meter, who married Mary Ellen Bryan; Caleb Jackson Van Meter, Jr., who married Laura Ellen Auvenshine; Sarah Margaret Van Meter, who was not married; and Isabella Jane Van Meter, who married William A. Taylor. After the family arrived in Texas, five more children were born to Caleb Jackson and Mary Ann Van Meter: Mary Ann Van Meter, who married John Michael Scott; Martha Alcinda Van Meter, who married Timothy Silas Mount; Lilla Van Meter, who married (1) Benjamin Franklin Oates and (2) Barney M. Shoemaker; Jacob Van Meter, who married Ella Wilson; and Chester Arthur Van Meter, who married Marie Beauchamp.

Following the tradition that Hollanders know a good thing when they see it, C. J. Van Meter purchased more than one thousand acres of land, most of which joined the home place. Much of this land still belongs to grandchildren and great grandchildren.

C. J. Van Meter was County Commissioner, Precinct No. 2, on February 14, 1876. He was on the County School Board from 1873 to 1876. C. J. Van Meter dedicated his life to the ministry in 1883. Mary Ann Van Meter, after coming to Rhome in 1872, became affiliated with the Methodist Church in 1890. The elder Van Meters lived the rest of their lives in the house on Elizabeth Creek.

Caleb Jackson Van Meter died on June 12, 1928, in Decatur, Texas. He is buried in the Thurmond-Fairview Cemetery. Mrs. Mary Ann Van Meter died on Wednesday, January 10, 1917, at her home two miles east of Rhome, as a result of a stroke of paralysis, which she had suffered some time before.

WARD — WARD

Jonas L. Ward, son of George Ward and Anna Ward, was born on November 9, 1859, in Statesville, Tennessee. He was married to Sintha Ward in January, 1879, in Statesville, Tennessee. Sintha Ward was born on February 18, 1862, in Missouri. Her parents were Joseph Ward and Susie Gray Ward.

Jonas L. Ward and Sintha Ward had four children: Lassie Susanna Ward, who married Walter Smith; George Hershel Ward, who married Allie Summars; Eathel Ward, who married Reedy Williams; and Dessie May Ward, who married John Byrom. All of their children were born in Statesville, Tennessee.

Jonas and Sintha Ward moved from Tennessee to Rhome, Texas, in September, 1903, bringing with them two daughters, Lassie and Dessie, and some household goods. They settled east of the railroad, near the depot.

Their son, Hershal, was married and living in Tennessee. Their other daughter, Eathel, was also living in Tennessee. The son and daughter moved to the Rhome community three years later in 1906.

After living in Rhome for about a year, Jonas and Sintha bought a tract of land and movd to it near the Aurora Cemetery. They resided there until 1917; then they purchased a house in Rhome at the corner of West 2nd and D Street, where they resided the rest of their years. Jonas Ward was a former constable and public weigher.

Jonas Ward died on December 6, 1945, in Rhome, Texas. He is buried in the Aurora Cemetery. Sintha Ward died November 16, 1939, in Rhome, Texas. She is buried beside her husband in the Aurora Cemetery.

WHITEHEAD — MOORE

John Russell Whitehead was born August 14, 1881, in Medina, Texas. His parents were Richard Lynn Whitehead and Ella Sanders Whitehead. Myrtle Moore was born in Cuero, Texas, on May 12, 1891. Myrtle and John Russell Whitehead were married in Gonzales, Texas. Her parents were Richard Moore and Dora Finley Moore.

J. R. Whitehead came to Rhome in 1906. He worked for W. W. Morris in the dry goods store. Later he opened his own dry goods store in Rhome and then in Saginaw, Texas. He became a rural mail carrier for Rhome, Texas, on Route 2. He held this same job for thirty-two years. By the time he retired, the two Rhome routes had been combined, and he took over both jobs.

The Whitehead family consisted of nine children: Dora Faye Whitehead, who married S. A. Howell; Bessie Mildred Whitehead, who married Bert Smith; Alberta Margarite Whitehead, who married Joe Wilkerson; John Russell Whitehead, Jr., who married Doris McCage; Virginia Whitehead, who married Ben F. Forgy; Ada Mae Whitehead, who married Bob Johnson; James Calvin Whitehead, who married Jackie Wacasey; Billie Joe Whitehead; and Bobby Whitehead.

John Russell Whitehead, Sr., died on March 30, 1951, in Rhome, Texas. He is buried in the Aurora Cemetery at Aurora, Texas. His widow, Myrtle Moore Whitehead, lives at the family home in Rhome, Texas.

WHITTINGTON — BARKER

Unfortunately no one remembers any specific facts as related by the family members concerning the only Barker daughter, Tabitha Alice; however, Christine Barker Donald recalls that her father always spoke lovingly of his sister and seemingly she was very special to him, so much so, in fact, that he named Christine *Alice* for his sister.

She was born on March 28, 1857 in Kentucky. She was married to George Washington Whittington, whose first wife was a Hudson girl who died at an early age leaving two small children. The Hudson family took the children and were so attached to them that they did not want to give them up when their father married Tabitha Alice Barker on September 8, 1882. Alice and G. W. Whittington were married in Wise County, Texas.

It would seem to indicate a great deal about Alice's generous spirit and unselfishness when she told the grandparents that she would not think of hurting the children or of upsetting their lives; however, she would like to help with the children by sewing for them and doing anything that would be helpful. This story was related to Burch Maeyers by Ruth Bennett Slay whose grandmother was one of the Hudson children. Alice, herself, lived only about a year after her marriage, and she is buried in Indian Creek Cemetery, located near Newark, Texas, which is the Hudson family cemetery.

George Washington Whittington was a school teacher at one time and from 1884 to 1885, he was the first post master at the new post office established in Rhome, Texas.

WILSON — TROXELL

William Samuel Wilson was born June 11, 1876. He married Ida Mae Troxell, daughter of John Troxell and Mary Mosshart Troxell, on July 23, 1899, in Rhome, Texas. Ida Mae Troxell was born August 21, 1875, about two months before the Troxell family made the move from Kansas to Texas. She told her children that a man who accompanied the family to Texas suggested that they throw her into the river because of her crying when the wagon stopped for the team to drink. The suggestion was made to tease her brothers and sisters, but she was later teased by them about the incident.

In her accounts of her early life, Ida showed a deep love and appreciation for her family. She told of working in the fields with the older children and of their sharing the responsibilities of the home. Her oldest brother, Henry, was especially dear to her.

Singing schools and a penmanship school at Fairview were highlights in her youth. In singing schools she mastered the "do, re, mi's" and from that learned to play the organ, as well as learning to sing the alto part of the hymns. She enjoyed singing and continued to sing in her beautiful, clear, and rich voice until almost the end of her life.

The social activities of the Troxell young people during Ida's life at home consisted largely of singings at their home and other homes in the community, ice cream suppers, and church meetings. It was in the process of the Troxell girls' arranging for his sisters to attend a singing that William Samuel Wilson first saw Ida Mae Troxell. Several years later on July 23, 1899, they were married in the Troxell family's parlor and began more than fifty-three years of a life together that was closely united in ideals, interests, and efforts.

Three children were born to this union: Raymond Wilson, who married Imola Faye Young; Gilbert Wayne Wilson, who married Mary Lou Brown; and Katherine Bibb Wilson, who married Jarrett Hudnall.

Ida Mae Troxell Wilson died August 29, 1952. William Samuel Wilson died on April 17, 1956. They are both buried in the Thurmond-Fairview Cemetery.

YOUNG — LIVENGOOD

Juanita Thelma Livengood, daughter of John Thomas Livengood and Leola Jean Livengood, was born on November 17, 1917, at Cottondale, Texas. She was married to George A. Young, son of Robert Hardy Young and Florence Belle Young, at Las Vegas, Nevada, on May 29, 1940. George Young was born March 5, 1916. The Youngs were divorced on November 9, 1976.

Juanita Thelma Livengood attended Rhome schools and graduated in 1935, a member of the largest class that ever graduated from Rhome High School.

Four children were born to this marriage: Juanita Louise Young, born March 14, 1942; Margaret Ann Young, born September 9, 1943; George A. Young, Jr., born July 21, 1945; and Kathryn Jean Young, born January 20, 1951.

(L to R) JIM HALL, J. D. Johnson, E. M. Rogers, J. R. Troxell, W. W. Gilbert, W. W. Woods, J. H. House (Houssel ?).

MEMORIES OF RHOME

It is my hope that through my own childhood memories, I can recall for the reader long forgotten memories of his own. It is almost an after thought that I have added this section, although the sketches were written at the very beginning of the book. I sat down one night and tried to recall the Rhome that I had known.

As a child I remember the barber shop and confectionery that were owned and operated by Mr. Joe Brown, the town constable. The building was directly west of Dr. Childress' office, a building which had at one time served as a millinery shop. The confectionery part of Mr. Brown's business was cool and dark. Wrought iron chairs and tables will always remind me of pleasant times in the old confectionery, eating Eskimo Pies. Somehow today, Eskimo Pies just aren't the same. Those old ones had a foil type paper, and they were icy cold, but the chocolate always had a smooth, good taste, never reminding one of the waxy chocolate on today's version. I suppose that I sometimes drank soda pop there, but the only food I can almost taste today is the ice cream. The long counter was on the west wall of the room, and there must have been a mirror behind the bar. Near the back of the room a door opened into the barber shop.

I suppose I must have had my hair cut there. In those days, beauticians were unknown to our little village; so I must have sat in the high barber's chair facing the north wall mirror. Today my memory of that room is clouded by the terrible tragedy that took place there when outlaws shot Mr. Brown to death. His son Carl was my friend, and I still remember the pain of knowing that someone close to me had suffered a tragic loss.

William Wade Morris, my grandfather, owned the General Merchandise and Hardware Store in the old stone building. It was a place of special fascination to me. I remember the cracker barrel and the big round of cheese on the wheel, with a knife blade that sliced off lovely thin slices of longhorn cheese which tasted wonderful with a stolen cracker from the barrel.

Directly in front of the cheese counter was the candy case. With so many grandchildren around to swipe a handful of candy, "Uncle D," DeWitt Morris, must have arranged the best candy in the front of the case on purpose. Short, pudgy, childish arms couldn't reach that far without one's having almost to crawl into the case. He put a hard, brownish candy near the sliding door to the case. It had a rather bitter sweet taste.

Under the next case which smelled of tobacco, he had a nail keg in which he placed tin-foil rolled into balls. I do not remember why we liked to steal the tin foil, except that it was fun to have a roll of it to wrap around rocks, in order to pretend that we had great wealth in our silver rocks.

Papa's desk was at the back of the merchantile store near the door that opened into the hardware section. It had a huge roll top, and Papa used a check writer. The safe was in the corner behind his desk. Across the hallway that led to the back door, was the wire-enclosed cage where bacon, lard, and other perishable items were kept. There was a barrel of mackeral, and also a barrel of pickles.

On the west wall of the store was located the drygoods section. If we children could catch Uncle D away from the store, we knew that Charlie Morris and Grady Morris wouldn't say a word if we played on the ladder that reached almost to the ceiling of the store. It rolled along the wall so that one could reach the boxes of shoes and other items that were placed on the high shelves behind the glass counters. Inside the glass cases there were all kinds of fascinating items. Ribbons, laces, flowers, and toys were there, as were bolts of piece goods. The old country store was indeed an exciting place.

The hardware section was not quite so thrilling to a youngster because there one found tools, nails, bolts, harness, china, pans, skillets, and glasses. We generally stayed away from the east part of the store.

I recall standing by the telephone pole that remained at the west corner of the building after the fire which destroyed the four businesses. I cried, with smut from the fire mingling with my tears. It seemed as though someone had taken away great big chunks of my childhood.

Z. B. Bobo owned the red brick building on the northeast corner of Block 16, fronting on 1st Street. In contained The Drug Store, a building which both fascinated and frightened me. It was always dark and cool, even on hot summer days. One entered through a double set of doors, first a screen door, then a short hallway, and a heavy glass door. The wide passageway provided deep window cases for displays of merchandise, especially Cara Nome cosmetics.

Inside the store one found along the west wall glass counters and high shelves arranged on the back wall. I recall that there were always pictures, framed prints that one bought as gifts for birthdays. I remember particularly one case that contained toys, especially tiny celluloid dolls. Another case contained a box of birthstone rings.

On the east wall toward the back was an enclosed area in which

Uncle Zack mixed the medicines that we didn't like and the rose water and glycerine that I thought would make me beautiful.

The back of the store was taboo for me. I knew that there were sometimes caskets there, and on occasion I knew that bodies had been embalmed there. That fact was enough to insure that I wouldn't see that part of the building until much later when I went back to Rhome to teach. At that time in the 1940's the Post Office was located in that room, but I never quite lost my feeling of anxiety upon entering the Post Office. Because of the east entrance to the Post Office, I pretended that it was not the same building.

Uncle Zack was a tall, stately gentleman whom I felt would grow angry if I spoke too loudly in the drugstore. Miss Nona George always waited on me, unless I was there to get medicine.

Across 1st Street to the north in the 1920's was located the United States Post Office. Claude Shaw was the postmaster, and my father, J. R. Troxell, and "Pap" J. R. Whitehead were the rural mail carriers. One entered double doors from the south side of the building, which also housed up the stairs, the Masonic Lodge. In fact, the post office department rented its part of the building from the Masons, who still own and use the building today. But, to me, it was The Post Office.

I was granted many special privileges here also because not only was my father a rural mail carrier, but also Uncle Claude's wife, Kate Shaw, was my father's sister. I remember long afternoons sitting with Aunt Kate when she was assistant to Uncle Claude, long before she became the post master herself. We talked about everything! She told me stories that I wish I could remember today. I'm sure that my history would be very greatly enriched if I could remember the stories. In her last years she graciously recorded stories as she remembered them, but I shudder to think of all the rich memories I could have recorded then.

We planned parties. I wonder if those who were youngsters then realize how much fun we had because of her imaginative plans for very super parties. She knew all kinds of games. I remember especially a "hobo" party when they gave us paper bags, and we went from door to door to collect the goodies for our party refreshments. The food was good, but what fun it was to walk all over town in the dark with that special fellow. Rhome didn't have street lights. We put up strings of electric lights in the front yard for our parties.

The post office had approximately one hundred boxes. I believe our box number was 92 then, as it was later when we moved back to Rhome. It was the third box up from the botton right beside the window where Uncle Claude waited on the customers. Along the east wall of the post office near the front window were two desks where Dad and Pap "put up" the mail every day before going out on the route.

Upstairs in the Masonic Building we sometimes had training from our teacher in declamation, Mrs. Golda Rie Brown of Boyd. I always felt strange going up the narrow stairway at the back of the building because I knew that the Masons were a secret organization with secret rites, and I felt like an interloper in the atmosphere that was foreign to me. It was a great, big room with tall windows that made me wonder what kind of secrets they could possibly have. But nevertheless, we did go there for our lessons. I always wanted to win the five dollar gold piece that was given in declamation, but somehow I never could manage to pull it off.

Next door to the post office was another building that possessed a whole world of thrilling memories for me. I know that I some times slept on a shelf under the ticket window. Mother, Rena Morris Troxell, sold tickets, and Dad, J. R. Troxell, ran the projector and kept the delco batteries going. After I grew older, I was allowed to peddle the player piano. I especially liked one number called "Lucky Lindy".

Ellis Troxell, my cousin, built the movie theater, and my father, Jim Troxell, bought it some time in the early 1920's. There were hard wooden benches arranged in front of the silver screen. They were graduated in height back to the projection booth. At the very back were some bleacher type seats where the Negroes were allowed to sit. Once in a great while, I was allowed to go into the projection booth with my dad. I even got to move the glass slides in and out of the projector. These were prepared advertising slides which the merchants provided.

I recall seeing *The Birth of a Nation*, some William S. Hart westerns, and one special thriller called *The Cat and the Canary*. Isla McGlothlin and I sat with our arms around each other and shivered as the hairy hands reached out from a trap door in the headboard of the bed to grasp the girl's lovely white throat!

On my eighth birthday, in 1925 my father and mother gave me a party at the picture show. Dad ordered a number of cartoons, and Mother made ice cream and cake. Every youngster in town was invited, and it was a birthday party to end all parties! I have hanging in my livingroom today a picture, "Blue Boy" from Z. B. Bobo's drug store that my cousin Arnold gave me at that party.

Still another building which I recall with fond memories is the old red brick two-story building that was located on the hill to the west over-looking the town of Aurora. I did not attend school here until the third grade when I had Miss Verda Logan for my teacher. I recall an incident when one little girl brought an orange to school. Some of the boys took it away from her and tossed it around until it broke. She cried, and Miss Verda required all of us to bring oranges to the girl because none of us would tell who broke the orange.

The wide steep center stairway leading to the second floor auditorium was an especial terror to me. I could manage it if I could hold to the rail, but if I had to negotiate the center, I was petrified.

In the fourth grade I think we had Miss Hazel Alexander for our teacher. I will always recall the stove in the northwest corner of the room. It was huge; I think it must have been six feet in diameter, and it warmed whichever side one presented to it, while the other side froze! It was while we were attending this class that the school presented a play for the community, "Mammy's Lil' Wild Rose," I recall vividly the cabin built across one corner of the stage. We spent days making crepe paper roses to decorate the cabin and the fence.

It must have been about this time that the building caught fire and burned to the ground. I was in my upstairs bedroom on the north side of the Richard Huse' home, which was a house that Jim Troxell built and in which I was born. I saw shadows crossing the ceiling of my room when I finally got up to investigate. It was the school building on fire, and my immediate reaction was the remembrance of a day or two before when one of the boys had said as we filed out of the north entrance to the school, "I wish this old place would burn down!"

I called my mother and dad. Dad immediately got "Uncle Ed" Richardson on the phone. He called "Mr. Mac" (McGlothlin) to tell him. We gathered in the cool March air to watch helplessly as the building crackled and burned to the ground. I can still hear the flames and feel the heat on my body. I stood just by the old giant stride.

The following essay by Frances Bost Barney is included in the Memories of Rhome because "Granny" Russell (Flora Atwood Russell) was indeed one of the dear memories of Rhome. This writer can remember with delight the many occasions when "Granny" kept her entertained with her stories and well-fed with her luscious cinnamon rolls. Many a stormy night was spent in "Granny's" cellar, waiting for the fury to abate. What great fun it was to be allowed to sleep in her feather bed!

GOODBYE TO GRANNIE

The day was too lovely for a funeral. Late spring rains and a warm June sun had called forth every dormant seed from the fertile slopes outside the little town. All the beauty that Grannie cherished was evident in the green-bearded pastures splotched with rusty-red Indian paint brushes. A yellow sea of sunny broomweed blooms billowed away and away down the draw.

In the little square church, in a satin-lined casket, Grannie lay a corpse. Thinking of it, I couldn't resist a smile. Grannie never liked the artificial, and she hated to be cramped. She would hate being stared at by the mourners—neighbors and friends filing past with red eyes and sober faces. She who loved to grow things would think the huge wreathes of gladiolus wired together so unnaturally a waste of money. The expensive blanket of roses with "Mother" on it would have embarrassed her.

But I didn't have to worry about Grannie. Her spirit had discarded a worn-out body day before yesterday. For all I knew, she was swinging through that very patch of broomweed bloom on her way early after the cows, and walking just for the joy of it.

I could imagine something in the apron she always wore—a scared baby cottontail bunny too little to make its way; or, it could be a wounded sparrow or a baby lark nestled in her apron pocket.

With some twist of irony, I felt sure Grannie had walked out on her own funeral. My sadness on the occasion was not for Grannie.

NOTE: This was written by Frances Bost Barney for Grannie Russell, a long time resident of Rhome and closest neighbor to the Bost family from 1928 until her death. It was published in a small private edition of Frances' writings presented to members of the Bost family at Christmas 1972.

FOOTNOTES

CHAPTER 1

1. Elliott, Claude, *"Union Sentiment in Texas 1861-1865"*, The Southwestern Historical Quarterly, Vol. L, July, 1946 to Arpil, 1947, p. 452.
2. *Texas Republican*, November 1, 1862.
3. *The Southwestern Historical Quarterly*, Vol. L, July, 1946 to April, 1947, p. 455.

CHAPTER 2

1. From research done by Joe Max Wilson.
2. Ibid.
3. From the Troxell Family History.
4. From research done by Joe Max Wilson.
5. Ibid.
6. Ibid.
7. Ibid.

CHAPTER 3

1. Personal papers of Colonel Benjamin Morris.

CHAPTER 4

The Early Years

1. *Wise County Messenger*, September 14, 1883.
2. *Ibid*.
3. Wise County Courthouse Records, Deeds Book 23, p. 515.
4. *Texas State Gazeteer and Business Directory, 1890-1891*, Chicago, R. L. Polk and Company, 1890.
5. *Wise County Messenger*, February 7, 1885.
6. *Ibid*., January 9, 1886.
7. *Ibid*., January 12, 1886.
8. *Ibid*., January 16, 1886.
9. *Ibid*., February 28, 1886.
10. *Ibid*., April 27, 1890.
11. Letter from the personal files of Colonel B. Morris.
12. *Wise County Messenger*, June 20, 1891.
13. *Ibid*., September 14, 1891.
14. *Ibid*.
15. *Ibid*., October 4, 1891.
16. *Ibid*., October 29, 1891.
17. *Ibid*., May 13, 1892.
18. *Ibid*., May 31, 1893.
19. *Decatur News*, January 9, 1893.
20. *Ibid*.
21. *Ibid*., May 31, 1901.
22. *Ibid*., January 20, 1901.
23. *Ibid*., November 15, 1894.

24. *Decatur News*, July 6, 1896.
25. *Wise County Messenger*, July 2, 1897.
26. *Ibid.*, September 3, 1898.
27. *Ibid.*, February 25, 1899.
28. *Ibid.*, December 8, 1898.

Manufacturing Interests

1. *Wise County Messenger*, September 5, 1885.
2. *Ibid.*, January 8, 1889.
3. *Ibid.*, April 2, 1890.
4. *Ibid.*, July 2, 1890.
5. *Ibid.*, June 20, 1891.
6. *Ibid.*, October 25, 1891.
7. *Decatur News*, March 16, 1893.
8. *Wise County Messenger*, November 16, 1894.
9. *Ibid.*, April 5, 1895.
10. *Ibid.*, April 12, 1895.
11. *Ibid.*
12. *Ibid.*, April 26, 1895.
13. *Ibid.*, February 19, 1897.
14. *Ibid.*
15. *The Decatur News*, May 15, 1895.
16. *Ibid.*, June 11, 1895.
17. *The Wise County Messenger*, April 6, 1900.
18. *Ibid.*, May 19, 1896.
19. *The Decatur News*, May 19, 1896.
20. *Ibid.*, July 6, 1896.
21. *Ibid.*, August 24, 1896.
22. *Ibid.*, October 22, 1900.

Farmers and Their Farms

1. *The Wise County Messenger*, July 17, 1885.
2. *Ibid.*, July 25, 1885.
3. *Ibid.*, October 24, 1885.
4. *Ibid.*, November 28, 1885.
5. Personal letter from James B. Hogg to Colonel Benjamin Morris, January 21, 1899.
6. *The Wise County Messenger*, January 9, 1888.
7. *Ibid.*, January 27, 1888.
8. *Ibid.*
9. *Ibid.*, March 24, 1888.
10. *Ibid.*, March 24, 1891.
11. *Ibid.*, March 28, 1891.
12. *Ibid.*, May 12, 1891.
13. *The Decatur News*, September 29, 1894.
14. *Ibid.*, August 22, 1895.
15. *Ibid.*, November 23, 1895.
16. *Ibid.*, September 10, 1896.
17. *Ibid.*, October 27, 1896.
18. *The Wise County Messenger*, July 8, 1897.

19. *The Decatur News,* December 15, 1899.
20. *The Wise County Messenger,* June 8, 1900.

Natural Resources

21. *Ibid.,* December 19, 1885.
22. *Ibid.,* June 5, 1886.
23. *Ibid.,* November 27, 1886.

Transportation and Communication

1. *Ibid.,* March 6, 1896.
2. *Ibid.,* April 30, 1897.
3. Excerpt from the personal papers of Colonel B. Morris.
4. *The Decatur News,* April 24, 1895.
5. Postmasters of Rhome, Texas (submitted by the U. S. Postal Department, 1964).
6. From a speech given by James D. Burch on May 20, 1962, as Master of Ceremonies at the dedication of the new Rhome Post Office.
7. Letter from the files of Mrs. Kate Shaw, Rhome, Texas.

Rhome's Churches

1. *Wise County Messenger,* March 24, 1891.
2. *The Decatur News,* August 24, 1896.
3. Methodist Quarterly Conference records, 1900.
4. From the personal records of Mrs. Kate Shaw.
5. *The Wise County Messenger,* June 5, 1886.
6. From the personal records of Mrs. Kate Shaw.
7. *Ibid.*
8. *Wise County Messenger,* August 29, 1893.
9. *Ibid.,* January 5, 1894.
10. From the personal records of Mrs. Kate Shaw, submitted by Joel Chambers in 1927.
11. *Wise County Messenger,* May 11, 1900.
12. *The Decatur News,* October 11, 1894.
13. *Wise County Messenger,* August 30, 1886.
14. *Decatur News,* December 2, 1899.
15. *Ibid.,* October 5, 1900.
16. Information contributed by James Drummond Burch.

Education

1. *The Wise County Messenger,* October 31, 1883.
2. *Ibid.,* November 7, 1885.
3. *Ibid.,* December 12, 1885.
4. *Ibid.,* January 1, 1886.
5. *Ibid.,* September 26, 1886.
6. *Ibid.,* November 6, 1886.
7. *Ibid.,* September 1, 1887.
8. *Ibid.,* January 5, 1888.
9. *Ibid.,* April 4, 1891.
10. *Ibid.,* April 22, 1891.

11. *The Decatur News*, February 4, 1895.
12. *Ibid.*, February 25, 1895.
13. *Ibid.*, June 11, 1895.
14. *Ibid.*, January 6, 1896.
15. *Ibid.*, December 14, 1897.
16. *The Wise County Messenger*, October 21, 1898.

Medicine: Doctors and Druggists

1. *The Wise County Messenger*, February 27, 1886.
2. *Ibid.*, February 28, 1886.
3. *Ibid.*, March 27, 1886.
4. *Ibid.*, February 11, 1890.
5. *Ibid.*, February 20, 1890.
6. *Ibid.*, February 26, 1890.
7. *Ibid.*, March 1, 1890.
8. *Ibid.*, March 8, 1890.
9. *Ibid.*, March 12, 1890.
10. *Ibid.*, March 26, 1890.
11. *Ibid.*, April 4, 1890.
12. *Ibid.*, February 6, 1891.
13. *The Decatur News*, June 11, 1895.
14. *Ibid.*, June 25, 1895.
15. *Ibid.*, January 6, 1896.
16. *Ibid.*, April 16, 1896.

Social Life, Amusements, and Recreation

1. *The Wise County Messenger*, January 12, 1886.
2. *Ibid.*, February 28, 1886.
3. *The Decatur News*, February 4, 1895.
4. *Ibid.*, February 4, 1895.
5. *Ibid.*
6. *Ibid.*, March 20, 1895.
7. *Ibid.*, July 6, 1896.
8. *Ibid.*, July 14, 1896.
9. *The Wise County Messenger*, February 16, 1899.
10. *Ibid.*, February 28, 1886.
11. *Ibid.*, April 12, 1886.
12. *Ibid.*, September 17, 1892.
13. *Ibid.*, August 9, 1894.
14. *The Decatur News*, November 15, 1894.
15. *The Wise County Messenger*, January 19, 1894.
16. *Ibid.*, February 9, 1899.
17. *The Decatur News*, November 5, 1895.
18. *The Wise County Messenger*, April 27, 1900.

Rhome and Politics

1. *The Decatur News*, July 18, 1893.
2. *The Wise County Messenger*, June 26, 1886.
3. *Ibid.*, August 14, 1886.

4. *Ibid.*, April, 1892.
5. *Ibid.*, June 25, 1892.
6. *Ibid.*, October 25, 1892.
7. *The Decatur News*, May 2, 1893.
8. *Ibid.*, August 22, 1893.
9. *Ibid.*, August 29, 1893.
10. *Ibid.*, February 12, 1895.
11. *Ibid.*, August 24, 1896.
12. *The Wise County Messenger*, March 12, 1887.
13. *Ibid.*, March 15, 1887.
14. *Ibid.*, April 28, 1887.

Military Organizations

1. *The Wise County Messenger*, July 24, 1886.
2. *Ibid.*, July 28, 1886.
3. *Ibid.*, August 14, 1886.
4. *Ibid.*, December 9, 1898.

Law and Order in Rhome

1. *The Wise County Messenger*, November 14, 1885.
2. *Ibid.*, October 13, 1892.
3. *Ibid.*, January 15, 1893.
4. *Ibid.*, May 30, 1893.
5. *Ibid.*, April 6, 1900.

Chapter 5

1. *The Decatur News*, November 2, 1902.
2. *The Wise County Messenger*, October 25, 1901.
3. *The Decatur News*, December 3, 1915.
4. *Ibid.*, November 22, 1902.
5. *Ibid.*
6. *Ibid.*
7. *The Wise County Messenger*, November 1, 1904.
8. *The Decatur News*, February 3, 1908.
9. *The Wise County Messenger*, February 11, 1910.
10. *Ibid.*, December 1, 1915.
11. *Ibid.*, November 29, 1901.
12. *Ibid.*, April 4, 1904.
13. *Ibid.*, January 30, 1905.
14. *Ibid.*, March 10, 1905.
15. *Ibid.*, September 28, 1906.
16. *The Decatur News*, November 21, 1902.
17. *The Wise County Messenger*, October 15, 1906.
18. *Ibid.*, January 18, 1918.
19. *The Decatur News*, November 22, 1902.
20. *The Wise County Messenger*, November 3, 1905.
21. *Ibid.*, January 15, 1902.
22. *The Decatur News*, May 31, 1901.

23. *Ibid.*, February 4, 1909.
24. *Ibid.*, November 22, 1902.
25. *Ibid.*, October 27, 1915.
26. *Ibid.*, October 1, 1915.
27. *Ibid.*, October 1, 1915.
28. *The Wise County Messenger*, August 28, 1908.
29. *Ibid.*, February 19, 1915.
30. *Ibid.*, January 12, 1906.
31. *Ibid.*, April 20, 1906.
32. *Ibid.*, August 25, 1906.
33. *Ibid.*, November 22, 1909.

Manufacturing Interests

1. *Wise County Messenger*, April 6, 1900.
2. *The Decatur News*, October 22, 1900.
3. *The Wise County Messenger*, May 20, 1901.
4. *The Decatur News*, November 22, 1902.
5. *Ibid.*, March 2, 1904.
6. *Ibid.*, May 31, 1904.
7. *Ibid.*, February 5, 1912.
8. *Ibid.*, October 1, 1915.
9. *The Wise County Messenger*, August 18, 1901.
10. *Ibid.*, September 27, 1901.
11. *The Decatur News*, November 22, 1902.
12. *The Wise County Messenger*, May 24, 1905.
13. *The Decatur News*, January 12, 1906.
14. *The Wise County Messenger*, April 27, 1906.
15. *The Decatur News*, March 30, 1909.
16. *Ibid.*, September 23, 1909.
17. *Ibid.*, March 10, 1911.
18. *Ibid.*, December 26, 1911.

Agricultural Interests

1. *Wise County Messenger*, March 6, 1903.
2. *The Decatur News*, March 2, 1904.
3. *The Wise County Messenger*, March 2, 1906.
4. *Ibid.*, March 9, 1906.
5. *Ibid.*, July 16, 1909.
6. *Ibid.*, May 9, 1917.
7. *Ibid.*, April 28, 1914.
8. *The Decatur News*, October 29, 1915.
9. *The Wise County Messenger*, January 23, 1904.
10. *The Decatur News*, October 29, 1915.
11. *The Wise County Messenger*, December 15, 1905.
12. *Ibid.*, July 13, 1906.
13. *Ibid.*, April 11, 1910.
14. *The Decatur News*, July 30, 1915.
15. *Ibid.*, June 23, 1916.
16. *Ibid.*, May 31, 1918.
17. *The Wise County Messenger*, October 22, 1915.

Natural Resources

1. *The Wise County Messenger*, July 8, 1908.
2. *Ibid.*, July 31, 1908.
3. *Ibid.*, August 31, 1909.
4. *Ibid.*, August 3, 1908.
5. *Ibid.*, July 6, 1906.
6. *Ibid.*, September 17, 1915.
7. *Ibid.*, January 14, 1916.

Transportation and Communication

1. *The Decatur News*, January 26, 1906.
2. *The Wise County Messenger*, March 2, 1906.
3. *Ibid.*, May 25, 1906.
4. *The Decatur News*, July 9, 1906.
5. *The Wise County Messenger*, June 22, 1906.
6. *Ibid.*, July 13, 1906.
7. *Ibid.*, February 21, 1908.
8. *The Decatur News*, June 28, 1901.
9. *Ibid.*, November 7, 1919.
10. *The Wise County Messenger*, March 27, 1903.
11. *Ibid.*, May 4, 1906.
12. *Ibid.*, May 18, 1906.
13. *The Decatur News*, September 8, 1908.
14. *The Wise County Messenger*, June 23, 1909.
15. *The Decatur News*, December 10, 1915.
16. *Ibid.*, Decemb 17, 1915.
17. *The Wise County Messenger*, December 8, 1916.
18. *Ibid.*, February 16, 1917.
19. *Ibid.*, August 7, 1917.
20. *Ibid.*, November 23, 1917.
21. *The Decatur News*, December 15, 1916.
22. *The Wise County Messenger*, March 29, 1918.
23. *The Decatur News*, July 20, 1917.
24. *The Wise County Messenger*, February 7, 1919.
25. *Ibid.*, October 8, 1915.
26. *The Decatur News*, March 2, 1904.
27. *Ibid.*, August 2, 1906.
28. *The Decatur News*, October 1, 1915.
29. *The Wise County Messenger*, September 1, 1905.
30. *Ibid.*, October 27, 1905.
31. *Ibid.*, November 24, 1905.
32. *Ibid.*, February 23, 1906.
33. *The Decatur News*, July 6, 1906.
34. *The Wise County Messenger*, June 25, 1909.
35. *Ibid.*, January 25, 1915.
36. *The Decatur News*, 1919.
37. *The Wise County Messenger*, September 25, 1920.
38. *The Decatur News*, December 13, 1901.
39. *The Wise County Messenger*, May 1, 1903.
40. From a speech given by James Drummond Burch at the dedication ceremony

for the new Rhome post office, May 20, 1962.
41. *The Decatur News*, November 17, 1905.
42. James D. Burch speech, May 20, 1962.
43. *The Wise County Messenger*, December 18, 1914.
44. *The Decatur News*, February 11, 1916.
45. *Ibid.*, October 26, 1917.

Law Enforcement

1. *The Decatur News*, November 17, 1905.
2. *The Wise County Messenger*, January 1, 1907.
3. *Ibid.*, April 30, 1909.
4. *Ibid.*, June 12, 1909.
5. *Ibid.*, June 14, 1912.
6. *Ibid.*, February 22, 1904.

Banking Affairs

1. *The Decatur News*, March 2, 1904.
2. *The Wise County Messenger*, June 15, 1906.
3. *Ibid.*, February 13, 1914.
4. *Ibid.*, April 17, 1914.

Medicine and Drugs

1. *The Decatur News*, February 22, 1901.
2. *Ibid.*
3. *Ibid.*, August 12, 1904.
4. *Ibid.*, November 22, 1902.
5. *Ibid.*, August 12, 1904.
6. *Ibid.*, November 21, 1902.
7. *Ibid.*, October 6, 1905.
8. *Ibid.*, February 23, 1906.
9. *Ibid.*, November 22, 1902.
10. *The Wise County Messenger*, May 17, 1907.
11. *Ibid.*, August 19, 1910.
12. *Ibid.*, January 4, 1916.
13. *Ibid.*, January 4, 1916.
14. *The Decatur News*, February 25, 1916.
15. *Ibid.*, September 16, 1917.
16. *Ibid.*, October 11, 1918.
17. *Ibid.*, October 25, 1918.
18. *Ibid.*, June 4, 1907.

Politics and Government

1. *The Wise County Messenger*, April 6, 1902.
2. *The Decatur News*, November 22, 1902.
3. *Ibid.*, April 12, 1908.
4. *The Wise County Messenger*, March 7, 1902.
5. *Ibid.*, June 23, 1908.
6. *Ibid.*, January 9, 1914.

7. *Ibid.*, June 27, 1913.
8. *Ibid.*, January 16, 1914.
9. *Ibid.*, March 20, 1914.
10. *Ibid.*, June 21, 1918.
11. *The Decatur News*, July 5, 1918.

Rhomes's Churches

1. *The Decatur News*, November 21, 1902.
2. *The Wise County Messenger*, May 25, 1900.
3. From the personal records of Mrs. Kate Shaw.
4. *The Decatur News*, November 22, 1909.
5. *The Wise County Messenger*, April 11, 1913.
6. From the personal records of Mrs. Kate Shaw.
7. *The Wise County Messenger*, Decembr 24, 1915.
8. *The Decatur News*, January 7, 1916.
9. *Ibid.*, August 2, 1900.
10. *The Wise County Messenger*, November 8, 1901.
11. *Ibid.*, November 29, 1901.
12. *Ibid.*, April 18, 1902.
13. *Ibid.*, May 23, 1902.
14. *Ibid.*, March 31, 1903.
15. *The Decatur News*, August 29, 1905.
16. *Methodist Church Quarterly Conference Record*, December, 1910.
17. *The Decatur News*, October 15, 1915.
18. *The Wise County Messenger*, April 20, 1906.
19. *Ibid.*, April 30, 1912.
20. *The Decatur News*, January 22, 1904.
21. *Ibid.*, May 31, 1904.
22. *The Wise County Messenger*, October 21, 1912.
23. *The Decatur News*, June 16, 1916.
24. *The Wise County Messenger*, February 18, 1918.
25. *Ibid.*
26. *Ibid.*, August 13, 1902.
27. *Ibid.*, August 29, 1904.
28. *Ibid.*, 1908.
29. *Ibid.*, February 2, 1916.
30. *Ibid.*, June 21, 1901.

Education and Educators

1. *The Wise County Messenger*, June 21, 1901.
2. *Ibid.*, November 8, 1901.
3. *Ibid.*, March 13, 1902.
4. *Ibid.*, September 19, 1904.
5. *The Decatur News*, March 2, 1904.
6. *Ibid.*, September 8, 1905.
7. *Ibid.*, September 29, 1905.
8. *The Wise County Messenger*, June 1, 1906.
9. *Ibid.*, August 7, 1907.
10. *Ibid.*, September, 1908.
11. *Ibid.*, October 12, 1909.

12. *Ibid.*, February 11, 1910.
13. *Ibid.*, August 19, 1910.
14. *Ibid.*, September 9, 1910.
15. *The Decatur News*, September 17, 1917.
16. *Ibid.*, October 1, 1915.
17. *Ibid.*, October 22, 1915.
18. *Ibid.*
19. *Ibid.*, November 5, 1915.
20. *Ibid.*, December 17, 1915.
21. *Ibid.*, February 22, 1916.
22. *Ibid.*, September 21, 1917.
23. *The Wise County Messenger*, May 17, 1918.
24. From the personal records of Mrs. Kate Shaw.

Amusements, Recreation, and Social Life

1. *The Wise County Messenger*, September 20, 1901.
2. *Ibid.*, July 28, 1902.
3. *Ibid.*, March 25, 1906.
4. *Ibid.*, November 3, 1905.
5. *Ibid.*, November 10, 1905.
6. *Ibid.*, April 20, 1906.
7. Interview with Mrs. Ellis C. (Kate) Troxell.
8. *The Wise County Messenger*, June 23, 1913.
9. *The Decatur News*, January 14, 1916.
10. *The Wise County Messenger*, March 27, 1914.
11. *The Decatur News*, October 3, 1915.
12. *Ibid.*, October 2, 1908.
13. *Ibid.*, September 24, 1915.
14. *Ibid.*, October 1, 1915.
15. *The Wise County Messenger*, October 15, 1915.
16. *The Decatur News*, August 31, 1917.
17. *The Wise County Messenger*, October 21, 1912.
18. *The Decatur News*, February 18, 1916.
19. *The Wise County Messenger*, February 5, 1912.
20. *Ibid.*, February 18, 1918.

Military Obligations

1. *The Wise County Messenger*, June 1, 1917.
2. *Ibid.*, July 20, 1917.
3. *Ibid.*, July 26, 1918.
4. *Ibid.*
5. *Ibid.*, August 30, 1918.
6. *The Decatur News*, November 17, 1918.
7. *Ibid.*, November 9, 1917.
8. *Ibid.*, December 3, 1917.
9. *Ibid.*, September 27, 1918.
10. *The Wise County Messenger*, October 18, 1918.
11. *Ibid.*, December 13, 1918.
12. *Ibid.*, April 25, 1919.

Chapter 6

Boom and Depression Years — 1920 to 1945

1. *The Wise County Messenger*, February 22, 1921.
2. *Ibid.*, November 1, 1921.
3. *Ibid.*, May 18, 1923.
4. *Wise County Messenger*, April 27, 1923.
5. *Ibid.*, June 1, 1923.
6. *Wise County Messenger*, June 8, 1923.
7. *Ibid.*, June 29, 1923.
8. *Wise County Messenger*, July 13, 1923.
9. *Ibid.*
10. *Ibid.*, July 27, 1923.
11. *Wise County Messenger*, August 10, 1923.
12. *Ibid.*, May 18, 1923.
13. *Ibid.*, July 20, 1923.
14. *Ibid.*, November 23, 1923.
15. *Ibid.*, March 6, 1925.
16. *Wise County Messenger*, September 25, 1925.
17. *Ibid.*, March 30, 1933.
18. From the files of Mrs. Kate Troxell Shaw.
19. *Wise County Messenger*, November 8, 1934.
20. *Ibid.*, June 15, 1939.
21. *Ibid.*, July 20, 1939.
22. *Ibid.*, May 18, 1923.
23. *Ibid.*, June 15, 1923.
24. *Ibid.*, June 22, 1923.
25. *Ibid.*, May, 1924.
26. *Ibid.*, March 30, 1933.
27. *Ibid.*, August 27, 1926.
28. *Ibid.*, September 10, 1926.
29. *Decatur News*, September 13, 1923.
30. *Ibid.*, October 1, 1926.
31. *Wise County Messenger*, May 4, 1923.
32. *Ibid.*
33. *Ibid.*, May 4, 1923.
34. *Ibid.*, May 18, 1923.
35. *Ibid.*, May 26, 1923.
36. *Ibid.*, June 12, 1925.
37. *Ibid.*, May 17, 1929.
38. *Decatur News*, May 24, 1929.

Transportation

39. *Wise County Messenger*, May 25, 1923.
40. *Ibid.*, September 7, 1923.
41. *Decatur News*, March 24, 1921.
42. *Ibid.*, April 12, 1923.
43. *Ibid.*, June 21, 1923.
44. *Wise County Messenger*, August 10, 1923.
45. *Decatur News*, February 13, 1925.

46. *Wise County Messenger*, March 6, 1926.
47. *Decatur News*, April 26, 1926.
48. *Wise County Messenger*, May 14, 1926.
49. *Ibid.*, October 26, 1926.
50. *Ibid.*, November 18, 1927.
51. *Ibid.*, May 12, 1932.
52. *Decatur News*, January 4, 1923.
53. *Wise County Messenger*, October 8, 1926.
54. *Ibid.*, August 1, 1935.
55. *Ibid.*, April 7, 1938.
56. Interview with Mr. P. L. Harvey.
57. *Wise County Messenger*, December 21, 1939.
58. *Ibid.*, October 26, 1923.
59. *Ibid.*, March 6, 1925.
60. *Ibid.*, April 15, 1927.
61. *Ibid.*, August 10, 1923.
62. *Ibid.*, February 1, 1924.
63. *Decatur News*, July 13, 1928.
64. *Wise County Messenger*, March 1, 1929.
65. *Ibid.*, March 9, 1933.
66. *Ibid.*, March 30, 1933.
66b. Material submitted by Mrs. John Naugle.
67. *Decatur News*, July 7, 1932.
68. From a speech made by James D. Burch, 1961.
69. *Wise County Messenger*, May 11, 1923.
70. *Ibid.*
71. *Ibid.*, May 18, 1923.
72. *Ibid.*, June 22, 1923.
73. *Ibid.*, August 3, 1923.
74. *Ibid.*, September 14, 1923.
75. *Decatur News*, January 4, 1923.
76. *Ibid.*, April, 1923.
77. *Wise County Messenger*, March 25, 1925.
78. *Wise County Messenger*, October 10, 1929.
79. *Ibid.*, February 2, 1933.
80. *Decatur News*, February 2, 1933.
81. *Wise County Messenger*, February 2, 1933.
82. *Decatur News*, July 13, 1933.
83. *Ibid.*, July 20, 1933.
84. *Wise County Messenger*, July 20, 1933.
85. *Decatur News*, January 20, 1921.
86. *Wise County Messenger*, June 8, 1923.
87. *Decatur News*, November 20, 1923.
88. *Wise County Messenger*, September 28, 1928.

Social Affairs and Other Activities

1. *Wise County Messenger*, November 1, 1921.
2. *Ibid.*, July 13, 1923.
3. *Ibid.*, August 31, 1923.
4. *Ibid.*, February 19, 1926.
5. *Decatur News*, March 1, 1929.

6. *Wise County Messenger,* June 22, 1923.
7. *Ibid.,* March 2, 1933.
8. *Ibid.,* May 14, 1936.
9. *Ibid.,* March 18, 1937.
10. *Ibid.,* December 15, 1938.
11. *Ibid.,* January 5, 1939.
12. *Ibid.,* April 6, 1939.
13. *Ibid.,* July 20, 1939.
14. *Ibid.,* March 30, 1939.
15. *Ibid.,* April 27, 1939.
16. *Ibid.*
17. *Ibid.,* June 22, 1939.
18. *Ibid.*
19. *Ibid.,* June 1, 1939.
20. *Decatur News,* November 11, 1927.
21. *Ibid.,* July 13, 1928.
22. *Ibid.,* December 12, 1929.
23. *Wise County Messenger,* August 24, 1939.
24. *Ibid.,* November 6, 1952.
25. From a speech given by Mrs. J. Pugh Morris, 1951.
26. *Fort Worth Star Telegram,* April 1955.
27. *Wise County Messenger,* January 23, 1936.

Education

28. *Ibid.,* October 22, 1920.
29. *Ibid.,* September 13, 1921.
30. *Ibid.,* August 12, 1921.
31. *Ibid.,* April 27, 1923.
32. *Ibid.,* October 12, 1923.
33. *Ibid.,* October 19, 1923.
34. *Ibid.,* October 19, 1923.
35. *Ibid.,* October 12, 1923.
36. *Ibid.,* February 12, 1926.
37. *Decatur News,* April 23, 1926.
38. *Wise County Messenger,* October 22, 1926.
39. *Decatur News,* November 11, 1927.
40. *Wise County Messenger,* July 8, 1927.
41. *Decatur News,* August 10, 1928.
42. *Ibid.,* December 21, 1928.
43. *Wise County Messenger,* March 8, 1929.
44. *Decatur News,* May 10, 1929.
45. *Ibid.,* July 25, 1929.
46. *Ibid.,* July 25, 1929.
47. *Wise County Messenger,* March 8, 1929.
48. *Ibid.,* March 1, 1929.
49. *Decatur News,* October 10, 1929.
50. *Ibid.,* October 17, 1929.
51. *Ibid.,* October 24, 1929.
52. *Wise County Messenger,* October 10, 1929.
53. *Decatur News,* November 14, 1929.
54. *Wise County Messenger,* November 11, 1927.

55. *Decatur News*, April 5, 1934.
56. From material submitted by Joe Max Wilson.
57. *Ibid.*

Churches

1. *Wise County Messenger*, November 10, 1921.
2. *Ibid.*, May 11, 1923.
3. *Ibid.*, March 13, 1925.
4. *Decatur News*, August 19, 1937.
5. Interview with Mary Lou Slay Livengood.
6. *Wise County Messenger*, May 11, 1923.
7. *Ibid.*
8. *Ibid.*, August 17, 1923.
9. *Ibid.*, December 12, 1921.
10. *Ibid.*, May 11, 1923.
11. *Ibid.*, October 5, 1939.
12. *Ibid.*, April 13, 1939.
13. *From material submitted by Joe Max Wilson.*
14. *Ibid.*
15. *Ibid.*
16. *Ibid.*

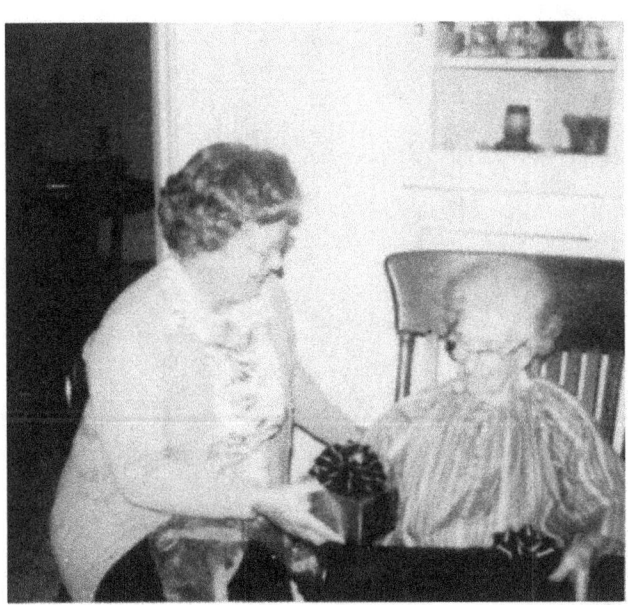

CATHERINE GONZALEZ WITH her aunt, Kate Shaw, celebrating Christmas, 1977.

INDEX

ADAMS, Solomon W., 5
ALDERSON, Charley, 55, 67
ALDERSON, J. E., 55
ALDERSON, Minnie, 55
ALDERSON, Rudy, 55
ALDERSON, W. S., 55, 79, 81
ALEXANDER, A. Charles, 86, 95, 117, 155, 183
ALLEN, A. E., 5
ANDERSON, Alma, 55
ANDERSON, Katy Ruth, 205, 215
ASH, Adran, 132, 153
ASH, Wayne, 168
ASKEY, John A., 11
ASSEMBLY OF GOD, Charter Members and Pastors, 232
AUSTIN, Bessie, 153

BAILEY, Amon, 5
BAILEY, J. Wesley, 140
BAIN, Prof. H.H., 139
BAKER, Green W., 54
BAKER, Joe, 183
BAKER, S. A., 54
BALCH, J. F., 154
BALL, S. L., 54-55
BARKER, Glenn, 144, 146, 197, 210
BARKER, Horace, 197
BARKER, John Gordon, 147-148
BARKER, Kate, 135, 151, 153
BARKER, Lynn Boyd, 127
BARKER, Opal, 144, 146
BARKER, Oscar H., 95
BARKER, Mrs. O. H., 135, 204
BARTON, Zack, 146
BAUGH, Luther, 154-155
BEARD, Georgia, 59
BEARD, John W., 59
BEARD, Mrs. J. W., 59, 137
BEARD, Jonny, 59
BEARDEN, J. P., 182
BEARDEN, Tom P., 182
BEAUCHAMP, Dorn, 175
BEAUCHAMP, W., 159
BECKER, Annie, 62
BECKER, D. R., 58, 60, 61, 63, 74
BECKER, Mamie, 62

BEDECARRAX, Annie, 63
BELLAH, Walter, 19, 99
BENNETT, Mrs. Robert, 207-208
BENTLEY, Rev. W. A., 138
BENTON, A. L., 58
BENTON, Ellen, 58
BENTON, Eli, 11, 58
BENTON, Luther, 157, 161, 186
BENTON, M. P., 58
BENTON, O. P., 58
BINYON, Rev. W. A., 137, 229
BLACKMON, G. S., 85
BLAYLOCK, Bill, 187
BOBO, Elizabeth Morris, 14, 56, 130, 154
BOBO, John, 140, 149
BOBO, Paul "Pat", 145, 198-199
BOBO, Simpson, 22, 60, 72
BOBO, Dr. Tom, 144, 171
BOBO, Zachariah Blount, 28-29, 34, 36, 57, 67, 117-122, 127, 152, 153, 171-172, 227-228
BOBO, Dr. Zach, Jr., 144, 197-198
BOST, Edward, 219
BOST, Frances, 203
BOST, Harold, 169
BOST, Lizzie, 69
BOST, Philip S., 160, 164, 185, 188
BOURLAND, Davidson, 5
BOWEN, R. C., 180
BOWERS, Mary, 59
BRADFORD, James, 37
BRAMMER, Alice, 225
BRAMMER, H. T., 154
BRAMMER, Hannah, 146
BRAMMER, Homer F., 154
BRAMMER, Mrs. J. M., 205
BRAMMER, Lena, 109
BRAMMER, Sam A., 108
BRAMMER, Mrs. S. A., 160
BRIDGES, John, 155
BROCK, Perry G., 5
BROCK, W. C. P., 5
BROOKS, W. A., 1, 161
BROWN, Bill, 150
BROWN, Golda Rie, 223
BROWN, Grover C., 154

BROWN, Joseph H., Jr., 53, 86, 165, 191-194
BROWN, Tom, 85
BROWNING, Kate, 70
BROWNING, Loyd, 207
BRYAN, Robert, 11, 52, 127
BRYANT, Gillian D., 154
BRYANT, Mrs. G. D., 131
BURCH, Drummond, 153
BURCH, Dr. J. D., 36, 60, 66. 68, 75, 118
BURCH, James D., III, 230
BURCH, McAfee W., 110-111, 127-128, 149, 153
BURCH, Mrs. M. W., 148-149, 153, 205
BURCH, Nell Troxell, 150-151, 203, 206-207, 229
BURDICK, Benjamin, 5
BURDICK, Ira, 5, 7
BUTLER, Blanche, 159
BYARS, Edgar W., 85, 90, 91
BYRD, Mrs. Foy, 205
BYROM, Mrs. Floyd, 159
BYROM, Jim, 159
BYROM, Lana Macon, 215
BYROM, Richard, 159
BYROM, Sara, 215
BYROM, Sarah, 159
BYROM, Tom, 160

CAGLE, A. J., 159
CALDWELL, Dan C., 11, 94
CALDWELL, Lizzie, 100
CALDWELL, Tol, 95
CALL, Mable, 140
CALVERT, C. C., 223
CAMERON and Company, 38, 42
CARPENTER, Dr. David A., 108, 118, 120
CARPENTER, E. P., 127, 161
CARPENTER, Gabie Sue, 210
CARPENTER, Jacob Young, 10
CARPENTER, Mrs. Jesse, 224
CARPENTER, Solomon, 154
CARPENTER, Timothy, 6
CARPENTER, Willie "Bill", 62, 188
CARPENTER, Velma, 197, 210
CASEY, Bud, 19

CASEY, Mrs. Bud, 19, 34, 131
CAST of "The Laff Round-Up" 1938, 200
CASTLEBERRY, Bennie Bobo, 149
CATES, Allice, 55
CATES, Cliff, 7
CATES, James P., 55
CATES, Robert E., 55
CENTRE, L. E., 50
CHAMBERS, Joel R., 117, 183-185, 198
CHAMBERS, Mrs. J. R., 58, 198, 203, 207
CHAMBERS, Joel R., Jr., 201
CHANCE, Joseph C., 5
CHANCE, Newton, 7
CHERRY, Dr. G. P., 84, 118-119, 171
CHILDRESS, Dr. J. M., 160, 171
CHILDRESS, Mrs. J. M., 205
CHRISTIAN, Sallie Bobo, 53, 140, 152
CHURCH OF CHRIST, List of Ministers, 228
CITIZENS COMMITTEE for Good Roads, 103-105
CITIZENS PETITION FOR PROHIBITION, 125
CLARK, Mrs. O. C., 205
COATES, Gypsy, 197
COATES, Leslie, 159
COBB, Allan, 202
COLEMAN, Claude, 149
COLLINS, R. C., 5
COLVILLE, John, 32
CONN, John, 5, 7
COTTAGE HOTEL, 86
CROCKETT, Annie L., 55
CROCKETT, J. F., 54
CROCKETT, Lizzie, 54, 61
CROCKETT, M. E., 54
CROCKETT, W. B., 54
CROCKETT, Willie E., 54
CUNDIFF, W. C., 7

DANIEL, Ruth, 111
DAVIS, John H., 26, 114
DAVIS, Laura, 70
DAVIS, Mary Cates, 32, 34, 54-55, 86, 88, 131

DAY, A. J., 14
DAY, Blanche Hutcherson, 152, 206
DAY, Eb, 21
DAY, F. M. S., 14
DAY, James T., 48, 70, 94, 117, 127
DAY, Joe, 94, 152
DAY, Margaret Tilley "Bunnie", 56
DEWEES, Bill, 62
DILL, Drummond, 146
DILL, G. C., 150
DISON, John, 81
DODGE, Gen. Granville, 16
DODSON, Mrs. Tom, 206
DOHNAN, Lucile, 135
DOLMAN, Vida, 150
DONALD, Christine Barker, Preface
DOSSEY, Comer, Preface, 144, 146
DOSSEY, Dr. William J., 34, 36, 66, 118
DOTTERER, J. D., 19
DOUGLAS, J. D., 19
DOUGLAS, Gladys, 153
DOUGLAS, Jackie, 201
DOUGLAS, Loyd R., 117, 153, 155, 183, 189, 197-198
DOUGLAS, Mrs. L. R., 198, 203, 207
DUNCAN, Greenberry, 5
DUNN, Mrs. John R., 207
DYSON, John, 83

EAGAN, J. J., 80, 154
EATON, Roy, Preface
EDWARDS, Roy B., 118, 120
EDWARDS, Rev. S. M., 34, 57, 129
ELDER, J. A., 21
ELLARS, Grant G., 76, 84
ELLARS, John, 21
ELLARS, Ray, 146
ELLIS, Bess Bobo, 151-152, 156, 198
ELROD, R. C., 220
EVANS, Rev. F. V., 54, 69
EVANS, Mrs. J. A., 160
EVERIDGE, Mr., 29
EWING, J. C., 145, 153
EWING, Orville, 165, 201-202

FAGAN BROTHERS, 34
FAIN, Whit T., 9, 14
FAIRCHILD, Abishi A., 50, 80

FAIRCHILD, Elizabeth J., 55
FAIRCHILD, Ervay Lee, 151
FAIRCHILD, Ollie Mae, 140, 153
FERGUSON, B. F., 182
FINLAYSON, Dorothy, 206
FINLAYSON, Isla McGlothlin, 203, 206-208, 216
FINLAYSON, John Will, 186
FINLAYSON, Ones T., 151-152, 158, 198
FINLAYSON, Ruth Scott, 151-152, 198, 203-204, 207
FINLAYSON, William J., 52
FINLAYSON, Mrs. W. J., 131
FLEMING, Jeremiah, 5
FLEMING, Thomas J., 5
FLOYD, C. B., 56
FLOYD, Lula, 56
FLYNN, Tom, 67
FORD, Benjamin, 11, 71
FORD, Jasper, 11
FORD, Willie, 153
FOSTER, Mrs. F. E., 59
FOWLER, Meredith, 2, 5
FOWLER, Vida, 213
FRITZ, George, 5
FRITZ, George W., 5
FRITZ, John, 5
FULTON, Minnie, 61
FUQUA, May, 201

GALLASPY, W. E., 19, 34, 67
GARDNER, Katie, 56, 62
GARDNER, Lena, 62
GASTON, Mavourneen Brown, 205, 207
GEORGE, Clarence, 146
GEORGE, Jeff, 145-146, 153
GEORGE, Nona, 85, 132, 151, 153, 197-198
GILL, Jim, 84
GILL AND SMITH, 36
GILL, John P., 55
GOODENOUGH, A. D., 39, 40, 41
GREGG, Rosalie Mann, Preface
GREGG, Wallace, 210, 214
GREEN, Gussie, 56
GREEN, Lillie, 56
GREEN, Mrs. L. T., 160

GREEN, I. T., 95
GREEN, Mary T., 56
GREEN, Marguerite, 215
GREEN, S. H., 37
GREEN, Mrs. Tom, 135, 153
GREEN, W. T., 56
GREER, Alice McGlothlin, 205
GRIFFETH, June, 232
GRINER, Frank, 97

HALE, John, 7
HALL, D. R., 58
HALL, Lettie, 58
HAMBRIGHT, Addie, 59, 150-151, 153
HAMBRIGHT, Ben T., 59, 63
HAMBRIGHT, Edgar, 65
HAMBRIGHT, H. H. H., 11, 29, 32, 34, 44, 59, 63, 86, 87, 106, 116, 124, 137
HAMBRIGHT, Mrs. H. H. H., 59
HAMBRIGHT, Hiram Rice, 59, 71, 76, 151
HAMMACK, Ozelle, 197
HANDLEY, S. D., 210
HANEY, Ben B., 2, 5
HARBIN, L. D., 184
HARDIN, Will, 92
HARGRAVE, A. E., 38
HARMON, Bill, 82
HARPER, J. L., 75
HARRIS, Sam, 48
HARRISON, Charles P., 25, 26, 28, 36, 49, 56, 60
HARRISON, Polly, 153
HARRISON, Zeddie, 56
HARVEY, P. L., 87, 163-165, 171, 181
HATLER, Francis M., 25-27, 53, 56, 57, 130
HATLER, Mrs. Jane, 56, 129, 131
HAWKINS, Mattie, 56
HAWKINS, W. H., 26
HAZEN, H. C., 63, 85
HAZEN, Mrs. H. C., 130
HELM, Ivie, 62
HELM, Joe, 94
HELM, Ruth, 55, 62, 70
HELM, Sallie, 55, 70
HELM, Virgil, 62

HELM, William A., 55
HELM, W. Monroe "Roe", 28, 44, 48, 49, 70
HICKS, Cora, 210
HICKS, Lois, 203
HIGH, Ann Bobo, 14, 121, 123, 144, 197, Preface
HILDRETH, Amanda, 140
HILL, G. C., 150
HILL, Marco, 85
HOCKETT, Ada, 60
HOGAN, Tom, 20
HOGE, Will, 146
HOGG, James B., 46
HOLMES, Addison, 5
HOLT, Jewel Looney, 197, 203, 207
HOLT, Mack, 211
HOLT, Marvin, 103, 162-163, 180, 197, 198
HOLT, Nathan G., 55, 147
HOLT, Mrs. Laura, 131, 154
HORTON, Ethel, 197
HORTON, Gertrude, 197
HORTON, Millard, 211
HORTON, W. E., 160
HORTON, Mrs. W. E., 131
HOYLE, Jane, 205, 215
HUDDLESTON, Florence Bobo, 164, 197-198
HUDDLESTON, Ralph, 201
HUDNALL, Cassie Russell, 187, 196-197, 203, 207, 228
HUDNALL, Charles C., 131, 155, 182
HUDNALL, Mrs. C. C., 131, 153
HUDNALL, Guy, 154
HUDNALL, Jarrett, 132, 153, 155, 169, 176, 197-198
HUDNALL, Thurman, 109, 155-156, 161, 197, 198
HUDSON, Bob, 94
HUDSON, J. J., 5, 127
HUDSON, William J., 7
HUFF, Alice, 62
HUTCHISON, Etta Mae, 147, 198
HUTCHISON, Knox, 189-190

INMAN, J. W., 201
ISBELL, James, 5

JENKINS, Lela, 132
JENKINS, Lula, 132
JOHNSON, C. M., 54
JONES, Dr. B. M., 118, 121
JONES, Mrs. B. M., 131
JONES, Mrs. B. P., 59
JONES, Lula, 59
JUNIOR WOMEN'S CLUB 1935, 209
JUNIOR WOMEN'S CLUB 1957, 209

KEELE, Elizabeth P., 56
KEELE, Mattie, 26, 28, 50, 56
KEELE, Isaac H., 67
KEELE, Sarah, 56
KEELE, William, 56, 57, 130
KEELE, William Jr., 56-57
KEETER, A. L., 29
KENNEDY, John, 86
KINDER, Amos, 5
KING, Joshua G., 5
KNIGHT, A. S., 58
KNIGHT, G. W., 58
KNIGHT, May, 61

LANDERS, Rev. E. D., 56
LARSON, S. F., 90
LAWLEY, Josiah, 5
LAWSON, Prof. A. A., 62
LAYFIELD, Mrs. Jack, 232
LAYFIELD, Jeff D., 10
LAYFIELD, John Will, 10, 13
LAYFIELD, Mrs. J. W., 12
LAYFIELD, Morgan, 224
LEACH, Rev. A. J., 226
LEACH, Flora, 132, 197, 226
LEONARD, C. C., 10, 21, 81, 108, 127, 189, 210
LEONARD, Kate, 151
LEONARD, Lizzie Caldwell, 129, 135, 154, 156
LEONARD, Robert E., 107, 131, 140, 144, 145
LEONARD, Mrs. R. E., 131
LEONARD, S. L., 118, 121, 160
LEONARD, Wm. T., 82, 90, 101
LEUTY, Abraham A., 2, 5
LEWIS, William, 5
LILLARD, Mrs. Terrill, 153
LILLEY, J. T., 54

LISBY, Jack, 146
LOCKRIDGE, Eliza, 55
LOGAN, Boyd, 146, 198
LOGAN, B. W., 105, 127, 186
LOGAN, Dallas, 82
LOGAN, Dora Dean, 215
LOGAN, Harry, 146
LOGAN, Mrs. Harry, 207
LOGAN, Lucille Richardson, 198, 203-204
LOGAN, Mrs. Rachel, 59
LOGAN, William, 70
LOGAN, William J., 29, 74, 94, 127
LOGAN, Mrs. W. J., 165
LOGAN, Verda, 198, 203, 213, 218
LOGAN BROTHERS, 36, 42, 84, 85, 94, 114
LONG, Fannie, 59
LONG, Sarah, 131
LOONEY, Lucy, 225
LOONEY, Walter "Budd", 190, 192-194
LOWANCE, Dottie Daye, 147
LOWANCE, S. A., 172-173
LOVELL, Frank, 5
LYLE, Annie, 140

MAEYERS, Dale, 197-198
MAEYERS, Burch Barker, 198, 203, 207
MALONE, Mrs. H. F., 206
MALONE, Jim, 90
MAPLE, Henry R., 5, 7
MARSHALL, Mamie, 61
MARTIN, C. E., 103, 116-117
MARTIN, Rev. G. W., 130
MASON, Pauline, 213
MAY, Louisa, 55
MAY, Rev. W. S., 50, 55, 133
MAYS, Leroy, 171
MELLON, Andy, 164
MERRITT, Gladys Troxell, Preface
METHODIST CHURCH Pastors, 231
MILES, W. H., 159
MOFFAT, Jacob, 5
MONDRICK, Charlie, 181
MONDRICK, Ella, 184
MONDRICK, Gussie, 181
MONTGOMERY, R. E., 16-18, 23

MONTGOMERY, Rev. Roy, 231
MONTGOMERY, Mrs. Roy, 207
MOORE, Garland, 170
MORRIS, Alberta Finlayson, 203-207
MORRIS, Allie, 140
MORRIS, Col. Benjamin, 13-18, 21, 23-24, 26, 37, 40, 45-47, 49, 51-52, 54, 55, 57-59, 71, 74, 79, 88, 100, 118, 123
MORRIS, Ben L., 14, 48, 54, 150
MORRIS, Brooks, 161
MORRIS, Charles Blair, 186, 197, 199
MORRIS, Mrs. C. P., 132
MORRIS, DeWitt T., 161, 165, 202
MORRIS, Edward M., 14
MORRIS, Ella Fae Kendall, 205, 215, 221
MORRIS, Grady, 161
MORRIS, James Pugh, 3, 14, 55, 152
MORRIS, John S., 5
MORRIS, Lou Cate, 54, 60, 131, 135, 154
MORRIS, Maggie Mae, 14, 55, 62
MORRIS, Mattie R., 14, 54
MORRIS, Mary Early, 14, 54, 131
MORRIS, Maude, 146, 197
MORRIS, Richard B., 14
MORRIS, Robert S., 14
MORRIS, Roe, 146, 197
MORRIS, Roxana Blair, 13-15, 54, 57, 59, 127
MORRIS, Roxie, 197
MORRIS, Wendall, 146
MORRIS, William Wade, 14, 29, 30, 32, 34-36, 55, 75, 79, 83, 84, 97, 105, 108, 115, 117, 127, 140, 147, 164-165
MORRIS, Zaeta, 146, 197-198
MORROW, Jennie, 59
MORTON, Chas., 151
MORTON, Frank, 151
MOUNT, Emmet Elijah, 84
MOUNT, Joshua Houston, 10, 25, 27-28, 34, 42, 48, 56-57, 76, 89
MOUNT, Seymour H., 70, 84
MOUNT, Timothy S., 33-35, 67, 84
MULHOLLAND, Joe, 19
MULLINAX, Beulah, 135, 144
MULLINAX, Mrs. W. J., 154

McCARTY, Alfred, 1, 5-7
McCARTY, Mattie, 56
McCRARY, Mrs. Glen, 167
McCURDY, Mrs. Clyde, 135
McCURDY, Dave, 146
McCURDY, Everett, 152-153
McCURDY, Nora, 85, 135
McCURDY, Pearl, 135, 151, 153
McCURDY, Russell, 146
McCURDY, Tom, 105
McCURDY, Winnie M. Morris, 135, 152-153
McEACHIN, Neel, 81
McGALUGHIR, Wm. B., 5
McGARRAH, S. G. S., 5
McGHEE, Prof. W. E., 62
McGHEE, Mrs. W. E., 226
McGHEE, Loretta, 197
McGLOTHLIN, Alice, 215
McGLOTHLIN, Maude Sampson, 197, 203-204, 207, 211
McGLOTHLIN, John H. "Mac", 19, 159, 175-176, 197-198, 210-211, 221
McGOODWIN, Sidney, 154-155, 158
McKEE, Lonnie, 181
McKINN, Jim, 5, 7
McKINNON, Jim, 167
McKINNON, John, 167
McKINNON BROTHERS, 161, 167
McMURRAY, Hon. J. T., 124-125
McLAIN, S., 26

NASH, Jacob, 5
NAUGLE, John, 197-198
NAUGLE, Glennice Looney, 109, 197-198, 203, 207
NEEL, James E., 32, 76
NEAL, Mattie, 132, 150, 151
NEAL, Velma, 150
NeSMITH, J. L., 174
NeSMITH, Robert, 140
NICHOLS, Alfred, 201
NICHOLS, C. A., 198, 204, 213-215, 220, 230
NICHOLS, Mrs. C. A., 198, 204, 207, 213, 215, 220
NORMAN, Mrs. J. E., 159

OATES, Brawley, 5

OATES, Elizabeth, 5
OATES, Maggie, 62
OATES, Marcus Taylor, 9, 26, 45, 50, 51, 96, 102, 174
OATES, Mrs. M. T., 131
OATES, Otis F., 3, 15, 146, 155
OATES, Willie R., 146, 154
OATES, W. S., 2, 5, 14
OVVER, Janey, 58
OWENS, C. P., 182
OWENS, Robert, 182

PALMER, George O., 86
PALMER BROTHERS, 85
PAMPLIN, Henry J., 5
PARSONS, Nancy A., 55
PATTERSON, B. P., 67
PATTON, Horace, 5
PATTON, W. H., 2, 5
PAYNE, Aaron, 169
PAYNE, Charles E., 198
PAYNE, Mrs. C. E., 198, 204
PEAK, John C., 3, 5
PEGUES, Etta, 20
PENNINGTON, G. B., 5
PERKINS, E. D., 5
PERKINS, John P., 25, 26, 29, 34, 36, 55, 66
PERKINS, Nannie M., 54
PERRY, D. H., 105
PETROS, John, 164
PHILLIPS, Alley, 56
PHILLIPS, Henry L., 5
PICKETT, G. B., 60
PLUMBLY, Jess, 70
PORTER, Rev. R. E., 231
POTEET, Cora S., 55
POTEET, Marvin, 130, 144, 146
POTEET, Thomas M., 55
PRUNTY, John W., 54, 55
PRUNTY, Mrs. J. W., 131
PRUNTY, Mertie, 58
PUGH, Senator James L., 52

RAMSEY, C. C., 150
RANDOLPH, L. R., 228
REECE, N. S., 56
REED, Rev. O. J., 135
REESE, Cresidus, 140

REEVES, John E., 55
REEVES, Julia, 55
REEVES, Lizzie, 55, 100
REEVES, Nannie, 55
REEVES, Major, 49, 55
REEVES, Ollie, 55
REEVES, S. Henderson, 71
REID, Mildred Madeline, 147
RENSHAW, Allie, 140
RENSHAW, Eula Mae, 197
RENSHAW, Jennie Neel, 154
RENSHAW, Merle Van Meter, 197, 204, 206-207
RENSHAW, Lafayette W., 90, 91, 94, 127, 149, 161, 173, 178, 211
RENSHAW, L. Wayne, 144, 148, 199, 204
RENSHAW, Sam, 94
RENSHAW, Virginia Bobo, Preface, 90, 156, 197, 205, 207, 233
RHODE, Fred, 75
RHOME, Col. Byron C., 25-27, 29, 35, 48, 84, 94, 131, 164
RHOME, B. C., Jr., 69
RHOME MILLING Company, 38, 127
RHOME'S FIRST Year Book 1926, 212-213
RHOME SCHOOL Class Pictures 1905, 141-142
RHOME TELEPHONE Operators and Linemen, 182
RHOME AND WARD, 76
RICHARDSON, E. E., 168, 173, 199, 217, 221
RICHARDSON, Ike, 94
RICHARDSON, J. T., 171
RICKMAN, Lena, 197, 210
RICKMAN, Lillian, 197, 210
RIDER, Minnie, 69
ROBERTS, J. F., 54
ROBERTS, Mattie, 55
ROBERTS, Sam, 211
ROBERTSON, Chas. 146
ROBERTSON, Jack, 145
ROGERS, Alvey, 84
ROGERS, Ella, 56
ROGERS, Waymon, 146
ROGERS, W. J., 25, 29, 32, 34, 54
ROWAN, Aleen (Eileen), 156, 224

ROWAN, James H., 11, 117, 185
ROWAN, John H., 11, 156
RUDE, Martin, 5
RUSSELL, Claude, 171
RUSSELL, J. Wood, 107, 108, 153, 196-197
RUSSELL, Dr. W. L., 118-119, 121, 154, 171, 181
RUSSELL, Mrs. W. L., 131
ROWE, A. J., 85
RUTLEDGE, Rev. W. C., 58, 59

SAMPSON, Dannie, 197
SANDIFER, I. T., 32, 86
SAWYER, Grace Aiken, Preface
SCHLUTER, Mrs. Hans, 207
SCHRODER, Emma, 55
SCOTT, Janette, 215
SCOTT, John M., 56, 94, 98, 100
SCOTT, Louise, 205
SEELY, M. E., 56
SENTER, Elmer L., 35, 63
SHANKLE, Edward E., 80
SHANKS, F. E., 55, 56, 90
SHANKS, Grace, 56
SHANKS, Ida, 56
SHANKS, Mrs. F. E. (Josie), 56, 136
SHANKS, Ruth, 56
SHAW, Arnold, 213
SHAW, Claude E., 83, 111, 113-115, 149-150, 153, 161, 197-198, 204, 213
SHAW, Mrs. D. P., 70, 131
SHAW, Kate Troxell, 52, 53, 59, 129, 131-132, 135, 140, 149, 186, 197-198, 204, 206-217, 226, Preface
SHEETS, Samuel, 1, 5, 6, 9, 14
SHERWOOD, Bettie A., 55
SHERWOOD, Bink, 85
SHERWOOD, Rev. F. M., 135
SHERWOOD, Lola M., 55
SHORT, Mrs. Gladney, 62
SHRADER, Rev. H. P., 57
SIMMONS, Arthur, 153
SIMMONS, Mrs. Earl, 205
SIMMONS, Elzey E., 154
SIMMONS, Martin, 211
SIMMONS, Martin E., 154

SIMMONS, Mrs. M. E., 154
SIMMS, M. E., 105, 130
SIMS, Nannie, 55
SIMPSON, W. H., 5
SLAY, Carl, 198, 204
SLAY, Mrs. Carl, 198, 203-204, 206-207
SLEDGE, Claude, 164
SLEDGE, G., 166
SLIMP, L. C., 147, 163, 198, 204
SLIMP, Mrs. L. C., 198, 204
SLIMP, Mrs. W. M., 160
SMITH, Henry W., 36
SMITH, John, 54
SMITH, Kate Beard, 59
SMITH, Leta Janice, 147
SMITH, Ollie, 182
SMITHERMAN, Edward L., 82, 83
SMITHERMAN, Mrs. Ed. L., 135
SNEED, Samuel C., 52
SPARKS, Billy, 216
SPARKS, Burge, 153
SPARKS, Charles, 198
SPARKS, Jim, 153, 160
SPARKS, Joe, 146
SPARKS, John, 226
SPARKS, Louis, 153
SPARKS, Omadell, 197
SPARKS, Okie, 211
SPARKS, Tom, 88, 153
STANFIELD, Rev. R. W., 34, 59, 75, 130
STANFIELD, Robert, 60
STANLEY, S. D., 54
STEPHENS, Basil Wells, 18, 26, 27, 77, 164
STEPHENS, Mrs. B. W., 160
STEPHENS, Henry A., 5
STEPHENS, J. M., 25-27
STEPHENS, Robert, 154
STEPHENS, Tom, 94, 108, 182
STEPHENS, Thomas, 5
STEPHENS, W. M., 91
STEPHENSON, J. W., 37
STEVENS, H. E., 2, 5
STEVENSON, Mrs. Emma, 59
STEVENSON, F. T., 183
STEVENSON, R. L., 75
STONE, J. L., 90, 160, 211

STRUNK, E., 58
STURGES, Rev. T. W., 56
SUMMERS, Mrs. Lulu, 225
SVENSON, Aleeta May, 144, 146, 197
SVENSON, Margaret, 144, 197
SVENSON, C. J., 24
SWEET, Nathan, 5

TADLOCK, Jane E., 5
TANNER, R. B., 109, 111
TARKENTON, James W., 5
TAYLOR, Henry, 11
TAYLOR, Joe R., 112, 153, 185, 198
TAYLOR, Mary Shankle, 153, 198, 207
TAYLOR, William A., 11
TEAGUE, E. A., 5
TERRELL, Acia A., 54
TERRY, Marco, 159
THOMAS, Rev. I. A., 135
THOMAS, O. L., 18
THOMPSON, Rev. E. J., 131
THORELL, August, 55
THORELL, Dollie Brammer, 152
THORELL, Ocie, 152
THURMOND, Fed, 232
THURMOND, Forrest, 156, 204
THURMOND, Mrs. Forrest, 204
THURMOND, Joe, 186, 286
THURMOND, Mrs. Joe (Ina), 93, 207, 232
THURMOND, John Favor, 10, 12, 48, 102, 155, 232
THURMOND, Mrs. J. F., 12
THURMOND, Lois, 224
THURMOND, Mary, 155
THURMOND, Milan Frank, 154
THURMOND, William T., 10
TIDWELL, Rev. J. W., 130
TILLEY, Louis, 81
TOMLINSON, W. A., 204
TOMLINSON, Mrs., 204
TRIBBLE, Wayne, 232
TRIGG, Dr. Henry, 94
TROXELL, Catherine, 203
TROXELL, Charles, 197-198
TROXELL, Clarence, 156
TROXELL, Ellis C., 103, 148, 152, 157, 223

TROXELL, Gladys, 197-198
TROXELL, Henry, 10, 11, 156
TROXELL, James Robert, 83, 85, 111-112, 148, 150, 152-153, 197
TROXELL, John, 10
TROXELL, Katherine Taylor, 151-153, 225
TROXELL, Mary Mosshart, 131
TROXELL, Mary Jo, 197-198
TROXELL, Paul, 223
TROXELL, Rena Morris, 135, 150, 204, 206, 210, 221
TROXELL, William, 157
TRUAX, M. E., 56
TRUAX, Ollie, 56
TRUSSELL, Mamie, 198
TULLY, Marshall D., 5
TULLY, Mark A., 5
TULLY, Stacy, 5

UNITED STATES Census 1900, 78-79

VANDIVER, R. M., 165
VAN METER, Abishi A., 63, 127
VAN METER, Archie B., 94
VAN METER, Mrs. A. B., 206-207
VAN METER, Basil, 153
VAN METER, Rev. Caleb J., 10, 27, 61, 95
VAN METER, Caleb, J., Jr., 140
VAN METER, Earl, 140, 146, 211
VAN METER, Daisy Russell, 205, 206-207, 219
VAN METER, Mary, 140
VAN METER, Roxana Morris, 140, 153-154
VAN METER, Ruth, 205
VAN METER, Sue Ella, 211, 220

WAGGONER, W. T., 117, 185
WALKER, Lois, 223
WALKER, Walter R., 54
WALKER, Warner, 168
WALLACE, Frank, 140
WALLACE, Mrs. Etta, 140, 144
WARD, Beatrice, 215
WARD, John L., 34, 53, 56, 57, 63
WARD, Julian, 150
WARD, L. L., 45, 52, 53, 56

WARD, Lucy A., 53, 56
WARD, Ruth, 140
WARD, W. E., 26, 32
WARREN, A. J., 5
WATKINS, Ella, 62
WATKINS, G. W., 54
WATKINS, H. I., 84, 148
WATKINS, Mrs. H. I., 153-154
WATKINS, Irvin, 211
WATSON, J. T., 215, 222
WATSON, J. W., 58
WATSON, M. R., 58
WEEMS, T. J., 36, 81, 84, 147
WEST, Mary A., 56
WEST, Robert, 161
WEST, William, 5
WHEELER, James R., 7
WHITAKER, Nancy E., 55
WHITE, John F., 85
WHITEHEAD, John R., 111, 113, 152, 186
WHITESIDES, Charlie, 70
WHITESIDES, Will W., 53, 109
WHITLOCK, J. H., 63
WHITTINGTON, W. W., 53
WILBUR, Mrs. D. O., 207
WILKERSON, Annie, 139
WILKERSON, Curtis K., 118, 121, 131
WILLIAMS, Reedy, 83
WILLIAMS, W. E., 54, 61, 75

WILLIAMSON, C. W., 211
WILLIS, W. F., 226-227
WILMURTH, Alexander, 25-27
WILMURTH, Isabel, 56
WILSON, Mrs. Harry, 131
WILSON, Joe Max, 12
WILSON, Truett, 223
WILSON, Mrs. Truett, 232
WILSON, W. L., 54
WITT, Mrs. Booker, 131
WOODWARD, Miss L., 34, 63
WOODY, C. Q., 211
WOODY, Sam, 3, 11, 14
WREN, Joe, 161, 165, 185, 198
WREN, Mrs. Joe (Opal), 198, 204, 206
WREN, Ralph, 201
WRIGHT, Mrs. Barney, 208
WRIGHT, Cart, 105
WRIGHT, Euna, 153
WRIGHT, Midget, 153, 210
WRIGHT, William H., 94
WYLIE, Woodrow, 181
WYMER, H. Y., 18

YALLER, John S., 5
YANT, Ina, 24
YANT, T. M., 224
YARBROUGH, T. B., 117
YOAKLEY, Mrs. Tennie, 34, 59
YOUNG, A. T., 1, 5
YOUNG, Hugh, 5

www.ingramcontent.com/pod-product-compliance
Lightning Source LLC
Chambersburg PA
CBHW060449170426
43199CB00011B/1147